"The inability, or unwillingness, of the US government to address climate change in a meaningful way is a source of puzzlement and frustration for those who see climate change as the central human problem of our time. Nowlin offers students, scholars, and practitioners an insightful and readable framework for understanding our failure to act. His appraisal of contemporary environmental policymaking is both well-grounded and sobering."

— *Megan Mullin, Duke University, USA*

"This is a great book! It offers a framework for understanding policymaking and climate change, integrates theoretical insights, and brings to bear rich empirical data to ground its comprehensive coverage. Readers will leave this book with a structured way of thinking about the political challenges associated with climate change and what the future might hold."

— *Christopher M. Weible, University of Colorado, USA*

"Invoking the language of markets, Nowlin's volume provides a comprehensive framework for understanding environmental policymaking. This work is rare in its comprehensiveness, thoughtfully mapping the interrelated roles of policy actors within varied institutions and across levels of government, while also providing ample empirical evidence showing how agendas are constructed and why polarization is occurring, among a plethora of other findings. One of the most complete pictures of US environmental policy I have seen and a must for the bookshelves of both academics and advocates."

— *Michael Jones, Oregon State University, USA*

ENVIRONMENTAL POLICYMAKING IN AN ERA OF CLIMATE CHANGE

As the world considers how to deal with the impacts of a changing climate, it's vital that we understand the ways in which the United States' policymaking process addresses environmental issues. A mix of existing theory and original analysis, *Environmental Policymaking in an Era of Climate Change* applies recent policy scholarship to questions of environmental governance, with a particular focus on climate change. The book examines how competing political actors influence policies within and across institutions, focusing on both a macro-level, where formal bodies set the agenda, and a meso-level, where issues are contained within policy subsystems.

Divided into two sections, the book incorporates insights from political science and public policy to provide the reader with a better understanding of how environmental policy decisions are made. Part I offers a framework for understanding environmental policymaking, exploring the history of environmental policy, and discussing the importance of values in environmental policy. Part II applies the framework to the issue of climate change, focusing on agenda-setting and the role of formal institutions in the policymaking process, covering topics that include Congress, the Executive and Judicial branches, and how climate change cuts across policy subsystem boundaries. By placing specific climate change case studies in a broader context, *Environmental Policymaking in an Era of Climate Change* will help students enrolled in political science, public administration, public policy, and environmental studies courses – as well as all those interested in the impacts of policy on climate change – to understand what is, and will likely continue to be, one of the most pressing policy issues of our time.

Matthew C. Nowlin is an assistant professor of political science at the College of Charleston in Charleston, SC, USA. He holds a PhD in political science with an emphasis in public policy and public administration from the University of Oklahoma. Matthew's research interests include environmental and energy policy and politics. His work has appeared in *Policy Studies Journal*; *Public Administration*; *Review of Policy Research*; *Risk Analysis*; *Politics, Groups, and Identities*; *Social Science Quarterly*; and *Weather, Climate, and Society*.

POLITICS OF AMERICAN PUBLIC POLICY

General Editor

Matt Grossmann
Director of the Institute for Public Policy and Social Research and
Associate Professor of Political Science,
Michigan State University, USA

The Politics of American Public Policy, edited by Matt Grossmann, provides insightful and integrated approaches to policymaking in particular issue areas. Each book applies scholarly lessons to the politics of a contemporary policy controversy, with attention to currently-debated policy options over ideal formulations. The books guide students to important theories of policymaking and research on American governance while capitalizing on their interests in specific substantive areas. Instead of becoming bogged down in policy details or historical narrative, the books offer lessons on the key actors, ideas, institutions, and trends driving policymaking. For more information about the series, or to submit a book proposal, please contact series editor Matt Grossmann at matt@mattg.org

Recently Published Books

Tax Politics and Policy
by Michael Thom

Environmental Policymaking in an Era of Climate Change
by Matthew Nowlin

ENVIRONMENTAL POLICYMAKING IN AN ERA OF CLIMATE CHANGE

Matthew C. Nowlin

Routledge
Taylor & Francis Group

NEW YORK AND LONDON

First published 2019
by Routledge
52 Vanderbilt Avenue, New York, NY 10017

and by Routledge
2 Park Square, Milton Park, Abingdon, Oxon OX14 4RN

Routledge is an imprint of the Taylor & Francis Group, an informa business

Library of Congress Cataloging-in-Publication Data
A catalog record has been requested for this book

ISBN: 978-1-138-21672-3 (hbk)
ISBN: 978-1-138-21693-8 (pbk)
ISBN: 978-1-315-44172-6 (ebk)

Typeset in Bembo
by Newgen Publishing UK

To Robin, whose love and support make everything possible
To Brandon and Alexis, who give me hope for the future

CONTENTS

LIST OF FIGURES

LIST OF TABLES

ACKNOWLEDGMENTS

First, I would like to thank several friends, colleagues, and collaborators whose thoughtful comments and conversations over the years very much influenced every aspect of this book, including Tad Conner, Kuhika Gupta, Tyler Hughes, Walt Jatkowski, Hank Jenkins-Smith, Mike Jones, Phil Jos, Gibbs Knotts, Glen Krutz, Tom Rabovsky, Jordan Ragusa, Joe Ripberger, Carol Silva, Geoboo Song, and Annette Watson. In addition, I would like to thank the students that have suffered through my public policy and environmental policy courses, whose comments, questions, and insights informed much of my thinking on these issues.

Much of the data used in this book comes from congressional hearings about climate change. I would like to thank several students that assisted in the collection, organizing, and coding of the hearings data, including Catherine Alexander, Dominique Awis, Victoria Davis, and Virginia Whorley. I would also like to thank Catherine Hutchison for her assistance with the index. In addition, an extra thanks to Presley Leopard for her help in coding the hearing topics and Nicole Popp for her work on climate policy at the state level. I also rely quite a bit on data from the *Comparative Agendas Project* and I would like to thank Frank Baumgartner, Bryan Jones, and their many collaborators for creating and maintaining such an amazing resource. Partial funding for this project came from the Center for Public Choice and Market Process, School of Business, College of Charleston. I would like to thank Pete Calcagno with the center for his continued assistance and support. Funding for the national survey data discussed in Chapter 4 came from a project funded by the Gulf Research Program of the National Academies of Sciences, Engineering, and Medicine, and funding for the South Carolina data came from a grant from the South Carolina Sea Grant Consortium. I would like to thank Susan Lovelace from Sea Grant for her guidance, support, and willingness to collaborate.

I would also to thank Matt Grossman for his support of the book proposal and manuscript.

Most importantly, I need to thank my wife Robin for her unending supply of encouragement. Finally, I would like to thank my best buddy Lincoln Nowlin, who was by my side (and feet) for much of the writing of this book. You are now and forever a good boy.

PART I
Foundations

1

INTRODUCTION

In 2017 the United States underwent a number of natural disasters and extreme weather events. At the beginning of 2017, the state of California experienced its wettest winter on record, having experienced its driest just two years earlier. The cycle of drought-to-deluge, where extreme drought is followed by record-breaking precipitation, has increased in California since 1980 (Lin II and John 2017). Later in 2017, California saw its most destructive wildfire season ever, with over 9,000 fires across the state that burned over 1.3 million acres. Several wildfires continued into December for the first time since records begin in 1936. Outside of California, wildfires raged across several states in the Pacific Northwest and western United States, including Washington, Oregon, Idaho, and Montana, exacerbated by dry conditions and extreme heat.

The extreme heat resulted from a heatwave in the western United States in the summer. California was hit particularly hard, with several cities breaking heat records, including San Francisco that reached a high of 106°F. Other parts of the country were affected by extreme heat as well. In June, flights had to be cancelled in Phoenix, AZ due to abnormally high temperatures. Also in June, Las Vegas, NV, Olympia, WA, and Seattle, WA all broke, or tied, record high temperatures. South Florida experienced its hottest July ever, with only one day that month failing to reach 90°F.

The hurricane season of 2017 was marked by three category 4 hurricanes hitting the United States. Brock Long, the administrator of the Federal Emergency Management Agency (FEMA), stated to Congress that, "To say this [2017] hurricane season has been historic is an understatement" (Long 2017). In late August 2017 Hurricane Harvey pounded the states of Texas and Louisiana, leaving record rainfall in Houston, TX, where Harvey unleashed more than 4 ft of rain. This was shortly followed by Hurricane Irma which cut a swath through Florida. Finally, in September 2017, Hurricane Maria devastated Puerto Rico, leaving the vast majority of the island without power for months, and as many as 3,000 to 4,500 or more deaths (Kishore et al. 2018; Milken Institute School of Public Health 2018).

The extreme weather and disaster events of 2017 led many to wonder whether or how much of the seemingly extreme events were a result of climate change. For example, California governor Jerry Brown noted the California wildfires are the "new normal" as a result of climate change and that, "This could be something that happens every year or every few years" (Vives, Etehad, and Cosgrove 2017). More bombastically, Governor Brown also stated that, "The world is not on the road to heaven, it's on the road to hell" as a result of climate change (Skelton 2017). Climate scientists have long noted that climate change is likely to make some extreme weather events more likely; however, until recently scientists were not likely to attribute any single weather event to climate change. Yet the science of attribution is expanding rapidly (see Diffenbaugh et al. 2017).

Climate attribution science examines the degree to which events are pushed outside the bounds of what would be predicted with natural variability alone. Recently, scientists for the first time were able to attribute three specific extreme heat events in 2016 to human-induced climate change, including the record global heat of 2016, heat across Asia, and a marine heatwave off the coast of Alaska (Herring et al. 2018).

Apart from extreme heat events, attribution science is also advancing with regard to extreme precipitation. According to the Environmental Protection Agency (EPA), the number of heavy precipitation events have increased in the United States (US Environmental Protection Agency 2016). As the climate warms, evaporation of water increases and the air is able to hold more water. One recent study noted that the probability and intensity of extreme precipitation events in the US Gulf Coast region have increased since 1900, likely as a result of climate change (van der Wiel et al. 2017). In addition, several recent studies noted that climate change made the extreme precipitation associated with Hurricane Harvey more likely (Emanuel 2017; van Oldenborgh et al. 2017; Risser and Wehner 2017). Apart from increased participation, scientists expect warming ocean temperatures to increase the intensity of hurricanes, and sea-level rise to make hurricane-induced flooding more destructive to coastal communities.

The impacts of human activity on the environment are such that we are likely in a new geographic epoch dubbed the *Anthropocene* (Steffen, Crutzen, and McNeill 2007; Steffen et al. 2018; Waters et al. 2016). Human activity has had a significant impact with regard to ozone depletion, forest loss, land conversion, and biodiversity loss (Dryzek 2016, 937). However, perhaps the most significant impact comes from the increasing levels of greenhouse gases in the atmosphere that are likely to significantly alter the climate over the next century, and we are likely already seeing the effects now; therefore, *we are in an era of climate change.*

In this book, I explore how climate change can be addressed in the United States given the nature of the actors and institutions involved in environmental policymaking and governance. To do this, I develop a framework to examine the environmental policymaking process in the United States. The framework will be discussed in detail in Chapter 2, but the next section provides a brief overview.

Environmental Policymaking and Politics

Environmental policymaking in the United States is the result of a set of interactions between policy actors within and across multiple policymaking venues that are nested within a larger environmental policymaking system. The environmental policymaking system is a *complex system* consisting of the various macro-institutions of government, multiple policy subsystems, and multiple policy actors. It comprises a system, where systems are understood to be a "set of components that contain energy flows between the components and where these energy flows are regulated between components in some manner" (McGuire 2012, 10). The environmental policymaking system is nested within the social, economic, and natural environments, and these environments emit information signals that are continuously bombarding the system, creating energy flows that permeate throughout the system. Therefore, in essence, *the environmental policymaking system is an information-processing system.*

To understand the complexities of information processing and environmental policymaking, I develop a framework to identify the important components of environmental policymaking and the relationships among those components.[1] The components of the framework include information signals as inputs, the policy-making system, and the public policies that are generated as outputs. A simplified version of the environmental policymaking framework is presented in Figure 1.1.

The process of policymaking involves taking some inputs, processing them through the environmental policymaking system and turning them into outputs that then feed back into the system as inputs. Inputs are information signals emitted by the external environment; the system includes all the actors, institutions, and subsystems involved in policymaking; and the outputs are policies that can take multiple forms, such as legislation, executive orders, agency rules, or court decisions. The process of feedback involves the implementation and evaluation of the policy outputs. Finally, the multiple policy outputs associated with environmental issues that have developed over time constitute the *green state.*

Inputs are information flows from the social, economic, and natural environment, and contain signals about potential problems, possible solutions, and political support or opposition. The arrows in the depiction of the framework above represent the movement of information signals through the environmental

Inputs (Information Flows) → Environmental Policymaking System (Actors, Institutions, Subsystems) → Outputs (Public Policy)

FIGURE 1.1 The environmental policymaking framework simplified

policymaking process. As information signals reach the system, they must gain a significant amount of attention from the system, reach a critical mass, or reach a certain threshold to be prioritized and placed on the policymaking agenda. The policymaking agenda includes all the issues that are being considered within the environmental policymaking system. Once on the agenda, it becomes more likely that the issue will be addressed through some sort of policy action.

The environmental policymaking system is comprised of the macro-institutions of policymaking, including the Congress, the executive, and judiciary, as well as policy subsystems, which are configurations of actors and institutions organized around particular policy domains and geographic areas. Much of the development of policy occurs within policy subsystems, and information signals are sent back and forth between the macro-institutions and subsystems. Each of the macro-institutions offers a unique *institutional pathway* for information flows to become policy outputs (Klyza and Sousa 2013). For example, the congressional pathway is legislation and the judicial pathway is court decisions. However, policymaking authority is diffused across multiple institutions, which allows the other institutions to act as pivot points or veto players, such as when the president is able to veto legislation passed by Congress or the courts determine a particular policy action to be unconstitutional.

Policy subsystems also include multiple levels of government such as federal, state, and local. Subsystems are semi-autonomous from the macro-institutions and they connect states to federal environmental policymaking creating a *polycentric* system of policymaking authority. Polycentric "connotes many centers of decision-making which are formally independent of each other" (Ostrom, Tiebout, and Warren 1961, 831). As a result of polycentricity, environmental policy decisions are made across multiple institutions and across multiple levels of government. Polycentricity and institutional diversity are important for the functioning of the environmental policymaking system in the same way that species diversity is important for ecosystem functioning (Norberg et al. 2008).

The diffusion of decision-making authority within the environmental policy-making system creates friction that makes the process of turning information into policy outputs disproportionate, resulting in an over- or under-reaction to information signals (Jones and Baumgartner 2005; Maor, Tosun, and Jordan 2017). Path dependence – the tendency of past choices to constrain future choices – is another factor that creates friction in the environmental policymaking process. As a result, any future approaches to address climate change are likely to be constrained by the ways in which environment policy has developed in the United States.

Inherent in the process of environmental policymaking are feedback loops that occur as policies are implemented and evaluated. Policy implementation is the act of turning policy into action; however, the process of implementation often involves creating policy, such as when an executive agency creates rules to implement legislation. The evaluation of policies to determine whether the policy has met its goal may create new inputs by identifying shortcomings or unintended consequences that may need attention. Policies are constantly being evaluated by actors within and outside the major policymaking institutions and the information generated by these evaluations is fed back into the policymaking system.

The above discussion briefly presented the broad strokes of the framework that will be used and developed throughout the book to better understand environmental policymaking and the potential policymaking pathways available to address climate change in the United States. The next section briefly discusses the political conflicts that exist within the broader environmental policymaking process.

The Politics of Environmental Policymaking

The environmental policymaking framework illustrates the nature and major components of the complex environmental policymaking process. As noted, the process involves the interaction of multiple policy actors, and these interactions are driven by and create a unique set of environmental politics.

At the micro-level of environmental policymaking are policy actors. Policy actors are individuals or groups either inside or outside the government that are engaged in the policymaking process. They are assumed to be seeking to increase their own *utility*, where utility is defined simply as an individual's subjectively defined sense of well-being. In the environmental policymaking process the utility of policy actors is reflected in their policy preferences. Policy preferences are preferences for government action (or inaction) with regard to particular policy issues. In addition, it is assumed that policy actors are rational, in that they choose actions and strategies that they believe will make attaining their policy goals more likely. However, policy actors are only rational in a bounded sense and are therefore subject to biases and heuristics in the processing of information (see Jones 1999; Sunstein 2002).

At the heart of environmental politics is the interaction of *values* and *issue definitions* (Layzer 2012). Values – ideas about what is morally right or wrong – shape environmental policy conflict in important ways. The key value conflicts at play involve the proper relationship between humans and the natural world, which hinges on the question of the degree to which finite natural resources are to be used for the advancement of humankind or whether those resources should be preserved. A second value conflict is based in political ideology and the proper role of government in regulating actions that may cause environmental harm. As Chapter 4 will demonstrate, values are arraigned in a hierarchically structured value-system where *core* values, such as political ideology, form the foundation and constrain environmental values regarding the balance between human activity and the natural world. These values, in turn, work to inform specific policy attitudes regarding possible government actions. In addition, values drive notions of utility and policy preferences. Finally, value orientations guide the ways in which information, including scientific and technical information, is processed and understood (see Kahan, Jenkins-Smith, and Braman 2011).

Environmental policy is geared toward solving environmental problems; therefore the way that the problems are understood, or defined, is important. The way an issue is defined helps to determine whether or not that issue receives the attention of policymakers and the public. Because of the importance of issue definitions, policy actors often develop competing definitions to encourage, or prevent, action on those issues. For example, if there is a strong scientific consensus regarding the anthropogenic causes of climate change, then that implies a need for action on the part of governments. Therefore, creating doubt about the scientific consensus makes policy action on climate change less likely. Another example is to frame environmental issues as a trade-off with economic growth by implying that environmental protection will lead to reduced economic growth. When framed as such a trade-off, environmental policy change becomes less likely. As Pielke Jr. (2011) states, the "iron law of climate policy" is that "when policies focused on economic growth confront policies focused on emissions reductions, it is economic growth that will win out every time" (46).

Values and issue definitions interact in important ways. Indeed, issue definitions themselves are often a function of values, with certain value-systems being more (or less) amiable to certain frames. For example, the environment-economy trade-off frame is well suited to a conservative ideology that is skeptical of government intervention regarding economic activity. The ways in which values can guide the effectiveness of certain frames on particular audiences is related to the broader notion of how values often guide the processing of political and policy information. For example, science can play a key role in defining environmental issues. Science helps to determine the severity of the problem, the nature of the risks, and whether or not action may be required. In addition, the nature of environmental risk assessment is highly technical and these assessments are often performed by scientists and other experts employed by federal agencies. However, the ways in which science in general, and environmental risk specifically, is understood by both policymakers and the public can be colored by their value systems. The conflicts between values, issue definitions, and science define environmental policymaking in a way that is different from other policy issues.

A third factor that shapes environmental policy disputes are questions of *property rights*. Property rights disputes within environmental policy involve the ownership of natural resources and who has the right to do what with resources such as land, water, plants, minerals, and wildlife (Andrews 2013, 24). For many natural resources, property rights are difficult to determine and enforce because of open access and the high cost of exclusion, such as with public goods, which are non-rivalrous and non-excludable, and common-pool goods that are rivalrous, but non-excludable. Conflicts over property rights exist between individuals; state and local governments; and the federal government. For example, disputes over control of land in the western United States between state and local governments and the federal government has been an issue since the late 1970s.

Another important consideration for environmental policymaking is that of *transactions costs*, which are defined as all costs associated with environmental policy choices, including decision and implementation costs as well as the costs associated with the impacts of policy choices.[2] Decision costs include those associated with the collection and processing of information relevant to making a decision. These can include the nature of the problem to be addressed as well as the potential political consequences of addressing the problem in a particular way. Implementation costs include costs associated with putting the policy into action, such as monitoring and enforcement costs. Finally, policy actions may impose some costs to society such as higher taxes or slowed economic growth. Both action and inaction on environmental issues create transactions costs, and which transactions costs are higher is decided through the environmental policymaking process that includes both technical and political considerations.

Finally, environmental policy tends to be *regulatory*, with policy goals that involve prohibiting or eliminating a behavior, such as burning coal to produce electricity, that is understood to have problematic consequences. The development of regulatory policies is typically conflictual, with one set of policy actors seeking to control the behavior of another set of policy actors (Anderson 2015). In addition, regulatory policies distribute (or redistribute) costs and benefits within society, and the ways in which costs and benefits are distributed creates a unique type of politics.

According to Wilson (1982), the distribution of costs and benefits can create up to four types of politics, including *majoritarian politics, interest-group politics, client politics*, and *entrepreneurial politics*. Majoritarian politics involve situations where the costs and benefits are diffused across society such that no group(s) can capture a disproportionate share of the benefits or be burdened with a disproportionate share of the costs. Interest-group politics involve concentrated costs and benefits such that one group(s) benefits at the expense of another group(s), such as regulation that creates a barrier to entry for other firms. Client politics involve concentrated benefits with diffuse costs and often is a result of *rent-seeking* by firms, where firms seek to gain something of value from the policymaking process such as a targeted tax break or subsidy. Finally, entrepreneurial politics have concentrated costs and diffuse benefits, such as policies aimed at reducing air pollution. Entrepreneurial politics create a type of politics where those that are expected to bear the costs are motivated to participate, yet those that receive the diffuse benefits may free-ride on the efforts of others.

The politics surrounding environmental policymaking tends to be steeped in controversy. The degree and nature of conflicts within the domain of environmental policy tends to shift, but some key points of contention have tended to be present throughout. These contentious areas include conflicting values, the way issues are defined, property-rights, transactions costs, and the nature of regulatory policy. All of these contentious aspects tend to be present in most areas of policy;

however, they take on some unique qualities in environmental policy issues and they have all made addressing climate change difficult.

Plan of the Book

The focus of this book is to develop a framework that describes the complex process of environmental policymaking in the United States. The framework is used to guide and organize the book, with each chapter further developing the elements of framework. In addition, I use the framework to examine the capacity for the United States to address climate change, with that capacity being a function of the environmental policymaking process as well as various previous environmental policy decisions that constitute the green state. The book is split into two parts, with the first part of the book providing the foundation for understanding the environmental policymaking process, and the second part using that framework to discuss climate policymaking in the United States.

Part I: Foundations

In Chapter 2, I develop the environmental policymaking framework by discussing the nature of collective-action problems at the heart of environmental issues and how institutions, specifically markets and governments, are developed to address such problems. Next, Chapter 2 outlines in more detail the environmental policymaking framework sketched above, including a discussion of the information signals, the components of the environmental policymaking system, and the policy outputs. Then, using data from the *Comparative Agendas Project*, I empirically demonstrate the usefulness of the framework. Finally, Chapter 2 provides a brief introduction to environmental policy design and the selection of policy instruments to achieve policy goals.

The green state is the web of previous environmental policy decisions that includes legislation, executive agency rules, and court decisions. The previous decisions that constitute the green state provide both opportunities and constraints for the development of climate policy in the United States. Chapter 3 discusses the thickening of the green state that occurred over time and across multiple eras, which are defined by the nature of the environmental policy conflicts and the times of policies that developed within a certain time period. Several eras are identified including the *development era* (1800–1890), the *conservation era* (1890–1962), the *environmentalism era* (1962–1980), the *reform era* (1980–2000), and the current *climate change era* (2000–present). In addition, the discussion of the climate change era includes the scientific basis of climate change as well as international and US actions (and inactions) aimed at addressing climate change.

At the foundation of the environmental policymaking process is the set of values held by the various actors that operate within the process. Chapter 4 discusses the structure of value-systems that includes core values, environmental values, and policy attitudes. Core values are fundamental ideas that span multiple policy areas. These values can include conservative vs. liberal political ideology as well as more foundation cultural values regarding the structure of social relationships embodied by tendencies to prefer *hierarchical, egalitarian, individualists*, or *fatalists* ways-of-life. Core values influence values about the environment, which are values based on the preferred relationship between humans and nature. Policy attitudes are ideas and preferences about specific policy questions, such as the risks posed by climate change. Values are hierarchically structured such that core values influence environmental values and both in turn influence policy attitudes. In addition, Chapter 4 examines how values shape cognition, or how individuals think about and process information related to policy issues. Using survey data, I demonstrate the structure of values systems, how increased sophistication – measured by a series of scientific knowledge questions – can exacerbate ideological polarization, and the nature of value-based polarization with regard to specific climate change solutions.

Part II: The Environmental Policymaking System and Climate Policy

For climate change to be addressed by the environmental policymaking system it must first gain the attention of the system. The process of gaining system attention is known as agenda-setting, and Chapter 5 examines the dynamics behind climate change reaching the agenda. In Chapter 5, using data from congressional hearings between 1975 and 2016, I examine the impact of information in the problem stream and system variables (party control of chamber and previous attention) on attention to climate change by Congress. In addition, I examine the various dimensions of the climate change issues and how policy actors attempt to manipulate those dimensions to frame the issue of climate change.

Chapter 6 examines the macro-institutions of the environmental policymaking system, including Congress, the president and executive branch agencies, and the court, as well as the pathways they provide for environmental policymaking. In addition, Chapter 6 includes the approaches the macro-institutions have taken to address climate change, as well as the structure of diffuse power amongst them that creates critical pivot points and veto players that make policy development complex. Specifically, Chapter 6 examines polarization in Congress on environmental issues, the role of congressional committees in the processing of information, various pieces of the legislation that have been discussed to deal with climate change, and the Climate Solutions Caucus in the House. With regard to the executive branch, Chapter 6 examines presidents and executive orders, rulemaking by executive agencies, the Environmental Protection Agency (EPA), and mechanisms of political control that influence the capacity of the EPA. Finally, Chapter 6 examines the roles of the courts and judicial review, and includes a discussion of several important climate change cases.

Apart from the macro-institutions, the environmental policymaking system also includes policy subsystems that are formed around policy issues and include multiple levels of government. Policy subsystems are networks of sub-units (e.g., congressional committees, bureaus) of the larger macro-institutions. However, some issues, such as climate change, span multiple policy subsystems to form a *policy regime*, which is a network of policy subsystems linked by a common and complex problem. Chapter 7 explores the climate change policy regime of the United States, which includes the various subsystems, topics, and policies dealing with climate change across multiple levels of government. Much of the US climate policy regime is a result of actions by states that are developing climate policies in the absence of federal action. In addition, Chapter 7 discusses important actors with regard to environmental policymaking, including interest groups and scientists as well as the coalitions, which are a network of actors that share some policy beliefs about climate change.

Chapter 8 concludes the book with a discussion of several factors important to the future of climate policy and governance in the United States, including polarization, mobilization, the endangerment finding, the courts, and polycentricity.

Notes

1 I draw on the notion of a framework, as opposed to a theory or model, developed by Elinor Ostrom (see Ostrom 2011, 2007).
2 For a comprehensive overview of the use of the term transactions costs, see Allen (1998).

References

Allen, Douglas W. 1998. "Transaction Costs." *Encyclopedia of Law & Economics*. http://reference.findlaw.com/lawandeconomics/literature-reviews/0740-transaction-costs.html\#Allen,\%20Douglas\%20W.\%20.

Anderson, James E. 2015. *Public Policymaking*. 8th ed. Stamford, CT: Cengage Learning.

Andrews, Richard N.L. 2013. "Environmental Politics and Policy in Historical Perspective." In *The Oxford Handbook of Environmental Policy*, Oxford: Oxford University Press, 23–47.

Diffenbaugh, Noah S., Deepti Singh, Justin S. Mankin, Daniel E. Horton, Daniel L. Swain, Danielle Touma, Allison Charland, Yunjie Liu, Matz Haugen, Michael Tsiang, and Bala Rajaratnam. 2017. "Quantifying the Influence of Global Warming on Unprecedented Extreme Climate Events." *Proceedings of the National Academy of Sciences* 114(19): 4881–4886.

Dryzek, John S. 2016. "Institutions for the Anthropocene: Governance in a Changing Earth System." *British Journal of Political Science* 46(4): 937–956.

Emanuel, Kerry. 2017. "Assessing the Present and Future Probability of Hurricane Harvey's Rainfall." *Proceedings of the National Academy of Sciences* 114(48): 12681–12684.

Herring, Stephanie C., Nikolaos Christidis, James P. Hoell, James P. Kossin, Carl J. Schreck III, and Peter A. Scott. 2018. "Explaining Extreme Events of 2016 from a Climate Perspective." *Bulletin of the American Meteorological Society* 99(1): S1–S157.

Jones, Bryan D. 1999. "Bounded Rationality." *Annual Review of Political Science* 2: 297–321.

Jones, Bryan D., and Frank R. Baumgartner. 2005. *The Politics of Attention: How Government Prioritizes Problems*. Chicago, IL: University of Chicago Press.

Kahan, Dan M., Hank C. Jenkins-Smith, and Donald Braman. 2011. "Cultural Cognition of Scientific Consensus." *Journal of Risk Research* 14(2): 147–174.

Kishore, Nishant, Domingo Marqués, Ayesha Mahmud, Mathew V. Kiang, Irmary Rodriguez, Arlan Fuller, Peggy Ebner, Cecilia Sorensen, Fabio Racy, Jay Lemery, Leslie Maas, Jennifer Leaning, Rafael A. Irizarry, Satchit Balsari, and Caroline O. Buckee. 2018. "Mortality in Puerto Rico After Hurricane Maria." *New England Journal of Medicine* 379: 162–170.

Klyza, Christopher McGrory, and David Sousa. 2013. *American Environmental Policy: Beyond Gridlock*. Cambridge, MA: MIT Press.

Layzer, Judith A. 2012. *The Environmental Case: Translating Values into Policy*. 3rd ed. Washington, DC: CQ Press.

Lin II, Rong-Gong, and Paige St John. 2017. "From Extreme Drought to Record Rain: Why California's Drought-to-Deluge Cycle Is Getting Worse." *Los Angeles Times*. www.latimes.com/local/lanow/la-me-record-rains-20170410-story.html.

Long, Brock. 2017. "Written Testimony of FEMA Administrator for a Senate Committee on Homeland Security and Governmental Affairs Hearing Titled '2017 Hurricane Season: Oversight of the Federal Response'." Department of Homeland Security. www.dhs.gov/news/2017/10/31/written-testimony-fema-administrator-senate-committee-homeland-security-and.

Maor, Moshe, Jale Tosun, and Andrew Jordan. 2017. "Proportionate and Disproportionate Policy Responses to Climate Change: Core Concepts and Empirical Applications." *Journal of Environmental Policy & Planning* 19(6): 599–611.

McGuire, Chad J. 2012. *Environmental Decision-Making in Context: A Toolbox*. Boca Raton, FL: CRC Press.

Milken Institute School of Public Health. 2018. *Ascertainment of the Estimated Excess Mortality from Hurricane María in Puerto Rico*. George Washington University. http://prstudy.publichealth.gwu.edu/.

Norberg, Jon, James Wilson, Brian Walker, and Elinor Ostrom. 2008. "Diversity and Resilience of Social-Ecological Systems." In *Complexity Theory for a Sustainable Future*, eds. Jon Norberg and Graeme S. Cumming. New York, NY: Columbia University Press, 46–79.

Ostrom, Elinor. 2007. "Institutional Rational Choice: An Assessment of the Institutional Analysis and Development Framework." In *Theories of the Policy Process*, ed. Paul A. Sabatier. Boulder, CO: Westview Press, 21–64.

———. 2011. "Background on the Institutional Analysis and Development Framework." *Policy Studies Journal* 39(1): 7–27.

Ostrom, Vincent, Charles M. Tiebout, and Robert Warren. 1961. "The Organization of Government in Metropolitan Areas: A Theoretical Inquiry." *American Political Science Review* 55(4): 831–842.

Pielke Jr., Roger. 2011. *The Climate Fix: What Scientists and Politicians Won't Tell You About Global Warming*. New York, NY: Basic Books.

Risser, Mark D., and Michael F. Wehner. 2017. "Attributable Human-Induced Changes in the Likelihood and Magnitude of the Observed Extreme Precipitation During Hurricane Harvey." *Geophysical Research Letters* 44(24): 12457–12464.

Skelton, George. 2017. "Gov. Jerry Brown Warns Climate Change Has Us 'on the Road to Hell.' California's Wildfires Show He's on to Something." *Los Angeles Times*. www.latimes.com/politics/la-pol-ca-skelton-jerry-brown-wildfires-20171214-story.html (December 29, 2017).

Steffen, Will, Paul J. Crutzen, and John R. McNeill. 2007. "The Anthropocene: Are Humans Now Overwhelming the Great Forces of Nature." *AMBIO: A Journal of the Human Environment* 36(8): 614–621.

Steffen, Will, Johan Rockström, Katherine Richardson, Timothy M. Lenton, Carl Folke, Diana Liverman, Colin P. Summerhayes, Anthony D. Barnosky, Sarah E. Cornell, Michel Crucifix, Jonathan F. Donges, Ingo Fetzer, Steven J. Lade, Marten Scheffer, Ricarda Winkelmann, and Hans Joachim Schellnhuber. 2018. "Trajectories of the Earth System in the Anthropocene." *Proceedings of the National Academy of Sciences*, forthcoming.

Sunstein, Cass R. 2002. "Probability Neglect: Emotions, Worst Cases, and Law." *The Yale Law Journal* 112(1): 61–107.

US Environmental Protection Agency. 2016. "Climate Change Indicators: Heavy Precipitation." *US EPA.* www.epa.gov/climate-indicators/climate-change-indicators-heavy-precipitation.

van der Wiel, Karin, Sarah B. Kapnick, Geert Jan van Oldenborgh, Kirien Whan, Sjoukje Philip, Gabriel A. Vecchi, Roop K. Singh, Julie Arrighi, and Heidi Cullen. 2017. "Rapid Attribution of the August 2016 Flood-Inducing Extreme Precipitation in South Louisiana to Climate Change." *Hydrology and Earth System Sciences* 21(2): 897–921.

van Oldenborgh, Geert Jan, Karin van der Wiel, Antonia Sebastian, Roop Singh, Julie Arrighi, Friederike Otto, Karsten Haustein, Sihan Li, Gabriel Vecchi, and Heidi Cullen. 2017. "Attribution of Extreme Rainfall from Hurricane Harvey, August 2017." *Environmental Research Letters* 12(12).

Vives, Ruben, Melissa Etehad, and Jaclyn Cosgrove. 2017. "Southern California's Fire Devastation Is 'the New Normal,' Gov. Brown Says." *Los Angeles Times.* www.latimes.com/local/lanow/la-me-socal-fires-20171210-story.html (December 29, 2017).

Waters, Colin N., Jan Zalasiewicz, Colin Summerhayes, Anthony D. Barnosky, Clément Poirier, Agnieszka Galuszka, Alejandro Cearreta, Matt Edgeworth, Erle C. Ellis, Michael Ellis, Catherine Jeandel, Reinhold Leinfelder, J.R. McNeill, Daniel deB. Richter, Will Steffen, James Syvitski, Davor Vidas, Michael Wagreich, Mark Williams, An Zhisheng, Jacques Grinevald, Eric Odada, Naomi Oreskes, and Alexander P. Wolfe. 2016. "The Anthropocene Is Functionally and Stratigraphically Distinct from the Holocene." *Science* 351(62–69).

Wilson, James Q. 1982. "The Politics of Regulation." In *The Politics of Regulation*, Basic Books, 357–394.

2

A FRAMEWORK FOR ENVIRONMENTAL POLICYMAKING

Introduction

On December 12, 2015, in Paris, France, 195 countries reached an agreement to reduce emissions of greenhouse gases in an effort to keep the rise of the average global temperature below 2°C in the 21st century. The Paris Agreement resulted from the latest in a series of international negotiations regarding climate change that began in 1992 with the United Nations Framework Convention on Climate Change (UNFCCC) signed at the Earth Summit in Rio de Janeiro. Though many have expressed concerns that it does not do enough to stem the potential adverse impacts of climate change, the Paris Agreement represents the first time that the world's largest greenhouse gas emitters – China, the United States, the European Union, India, and the Russian Federation – have agreed to develop plans to reduce emissions. The Paris Agreement went into effect on November 4, 2016, after being ratified by at least 55 countries that account for at least 55 percent of total global greenhouse gas emissions. Just a few days later, on November 8, 2016, Donald Trump was elected president of the United States, putting the US commitment to the agreement, and its commitment to addressing climate change, in doubt. On June 1, 2017, Trump announced his intention to withdraw the United States from the Paris Agreement.

The agreement reached in Paris in 2015 was a milestone achieved after numerous negotiations since the creation of the UNFCCC in 1992. Two of the major controversies surrounding global efforts to address climate change are: 1) should emission targets for countries to reduce their greenhouse gases be legally binding; and 2) what should be required of the emerging economies of the BRICS (Brazil, Russia, India, China, and South Africa) countries? The previous major agreement, the Kyoto Protocol, which was negotiated in 1997 and ratified in 2005, placed binding commitments on developed countries to reduce overall greenhouse gas emissions by 5.2 percent below 1990 levels, yet placed no binding targets on BRICS countries, most notably China and India. While the United States was a signatory to the Kyoto Protocol, it never officially ratified the agreement. Since it was a treaty, it required ratification by the US Senate. In 1997, the US Senate voted 95–0 on a resolution disapproving any international climate change agreement that did not require emission reductions of emerging countries or could have a potentially negative economic impact on the United States, and therefore the Clinton administration never brought the Kyoto Protocol to the Senate for ratification. Then, in 2001, George W. Bush withdrew the United States from the protocol, citing concerns about the lack of reduction targets for China and India as well as concerns about negative impacts on economic growth for the United States.

In contrast to the Kyoto Protocol, the Paris Agreement did not prescribe binding emission reduction targets; rather, countries developed their own emission reduction goals through *intended nationally determined contributions* (INDCs). All countries, including both China and India, submitted INDCs. Additionally, the Paris Agreement urged developed countries to provide financial support for developing countries to both reduce their emissions as well as adapt to the impacts of climate change. This financial support would come through the Green Climate Fund, which was first discussed as part of the Copenhagen Accord in 2009 and officially established in 2010. The Paris Agreement also included a target of less than a 2°C increase in the Earth's average temperature, with a goal of a less than 1.5°C increase. The agreement was a major milestone because it addressed the sticking points of binding reductions and how the BRICS countries should be handled, which then allowed nearly every country to agree to address climate change. However, how well countries are able to keep their commitments, the impacts of those commitments on reducing climate change, and the fallout from the Trump administration's intended withdrawal remain to be seen.

The issue of climate change is the greatest and most pressing environmental problem that the world faces, or perhaps has ever faced. While some countries and regions face greater threats from climate change, no country is immune from its potential impacts. However, mobilizing collective action to address climate change has been difficult and is illustrative of the myriad challenges that are present in many areas of environmental policy.

Inherent in environmental issues are collective-action problems. Collective-action problems arise when the goals of individuals conflict with those of the group, or when individual and collective interests are misaligned or in conflict. For example, the problem of global climate change is such that, apart from perhaps the largest emitters of greenhouse gases, the actions of any one country are not likely to have a substantial impact on overall greenhouse gases in the atmosphere, yet countries face some costs associated with limiting their emissions. Additionally, greenhouse gases placed in the atmosphere impact the globe, and so the impacts are not confined to just the countries that produce them. Therefore, individual countries have an incentive to free-ride and let other countries bear the costs of greenhouse gas reductions, since the free-riding countries can still benefit from the mitigation efforts of others without having to bear the costs. A key question when dealing with climate change, or any environmental problem, is how can collective-action problems be overcome?

One answer to addressing collective action is through the creation and maintenance of institutions. In brief, institutions are the rules, norms, and procedures that structure interactions, and the interactions result in some collective outcome (Crawford and Ostrom 1995; Hodgson 2006; Jones, Sulkin, and Larsen 2003). Additionally, institutions constrain the behavioral choices of individuals through informal norms as well as formal rules (North 1990). Finally, institutions tend to endure through changes in individuals within the institution as well as changing external circumstances (March and Olsen 2008).

Institutions can take a wide variety of forms, from formal to informal, to address specific collective dilemmas. Markets and governments are the two root institutions through which societal issues, including environmental issues, are addressed in the United States. The next section explains how markets, governments, and the combination of both, address collective dilemmas, particularly with regard to environmental issues.

Markets and Governments

Addressing collective dilemmas is typically thought to fall into the domain of either the state or the market. The United States is a market economy with a political culture of limited government, or government only when necessary. Therefore, the market is often thought to be the baseline for determining the proper allocation and management of society's resources, including natural resources. Governments only become engaged when markets are not allocating some resources in the way that society prefers. The market is also thought to be the benchmark institution against which resource allocation questions are measured. In political rhetoric, markets and governments are often presented as separate; however, in practice, markets and government are inextricably linked. Additionally, the market vs. the government is in many ways a false dichotomy, as several voluntary mediating institutions exist between the individual and the state (see Ostrom 2010).

"The market" is not simply a single institution, rather, there are any number of markets operating simultaneously that all involve a collection of actors buying and selling goods and services. Markets are decentralized institutions that promote voluntary exchange between buyers and sellers (Keohane and Olmstead 2007; Munger 2000). The rules associated with the market include the specific medium of exchange, a way to communicate the price, and a notion of property rights that signals who owns – and can therefore exchange – certain goods.

The central feature of markets is exchange, which means the trading of one good or service for another. The use of exchange provides for gains from trade which are one of the key benefits of a markets. Gains from trade arise through the distribution of talents and preferences in society as well as from individuals pursuing their own self-interest. For example, if there are two households in close proximity to each other, with one, *Household 1*, that produces chickens and the other, *Household 2*, that produces potatoes, both households could gain by trading. *Household 1* would gain starch and *Household 2* would gain protein, both essential for a healthy diet. Both households could gain without imposing additional production costs, since each household is already producing chickens or potatoes. Additionally, both households are pursuing their own interests by producing commodities that are useful for them, as well as potentially valuable for trading.

A second important component of a market is that it is decentralized. Decentralized means that price and quantity are determined by supply and demand, not by a central authority such as the state. Additionally, decentralized markets also tend to be voluntary, meaning that the choice to purchase a good or service at a certain price is in the hands of the buyer and the seller and not mandated by a central authority. This means that there is no third-party arbitrating trades between *Household 1* and *Household 2*, rather the households are coming to their own agreed-upon price – X number of chickens for X number of potatoes – that is mutually beneficial.

When functioning properly, markets provide the most *efficient* distribution of resources. Efficiency can be understood as the maximization of the well-being of society following the utilitarian maxim of the "greatest good for the greatest number." Additionally, efficiency can be defined as maximizing the difference between costs and benefits such that the most benefits are obtained for the least cost. Finally, efficiency can be thought of terms of *Pareto efficiency* or Pareto optimum, where resources are allocated in such a way so that any change in allocation would result in someone being worse off without someone else benefiting. Markets produce efficiency through the aggregation of individuals pursing their own financial interests and engaging in trade.

The law of supply and demand is illustrative of the power and efficiency of markets. The principle behind the law of supply and demand is premised on buyers seeking to obtain a desired good for the least cost, and sellers seeking to sell a good for the largest gain or profit. For the buyer, as the price increases they will demand less of the good, but for the seller, as the price increases they will provide more of the good, all else equal. Therefore, at some price points there is more demand than quantity, and at other price points there is more quantity than demand. A functioning market will reach the equilibrium point where the quantity demanded and the quantity supplied align through exchange and without a centralized authority guiding the process. The price of the good is set at the market clearing equilibrium point where supply and demand converge. The equilibrium point is also considered Pareto efficient because no other distribution of the resource would benefit one without harming another.

For example, *Household 2* decides to sell some of its potatoes to *Household 1*. How much should *Household 2* charge *Household 1* for a pound of potatoes? One way to determine the price of a pound of potatoes is for the two households to negotiate. *Household 1* has a maximum amount that it is willing to pay for a pound of potatoes and *Household 2* has a minimum amount that it is willing to accept for a pound of potatoes. A successful negotiation ends and a transaction ensues when the two parties agree to a price that is less than or equal to the amount *Household 1* is willing to pay and greater than or equal to the amount *Household 2* is willing to accept. The law of supply and demand in the market is the aggregation of this type of transaction. Therefore, demand is equal to willingness to pay and supply is equal to willingness to accept, and the market clearing price is where those points intersect.

Given the ability of markets to distribute resources efficiently, why would government ever be necessary? To address this question, it is useful to imagine a world without governments. Philosophers have termed such an existence the *state of nature*. In the state of nature there are no governing authorities and as a result there are no protections of private property. Thomas Hobbes noted that such an existence would be "solitary, poor, nasty, brutish and short," therefore individuals would enter into a *social contract* and willingly surrender much of their personal liberty to a strong sovereign. Hobbes termed such a sovereign the Leviathan. The *Leviathan* envisioned by Hobbes is typically understood as a strong central government that has a monopoly on the use of force. Others have noted that the state of nature may not be so dismal, yet it is certainly not ideal particularly without protections of private property. John Locke argued that to escape the state of nature, individuals enter into a social contract with a government in order for that government to protect their rights to "life, liberty, and property."

In the state of nature there are no costs to not recognizing private property, therefore property can be stolen without repercussions. This can be illustrated in a simple collective-dilemma game with two players, as shown in Figure 2.1. In the game, both players have the option to *Steal* or ¬*Steal* (not Steal) from the other player. The pay-offs, in terms of expected utility, for each player are shown below.

If both player 1 and player 2 choose not to steal, their pay-offs are 1. If player 1 chooses not to steal, but player 2 chooses to steal, the pay-off for player 1 is –1

Player 2

		¬*Steal*	*Steal*
	¬*Steal*	(1, 1)	(–1, 2)
Player 1	*Steal*	(2, –1)	(0, 0)

FIGURE 2.1 A collective-dilemma game for two players

and for player 2 is 2, and vice versa. If both players choose to steal then their pay-offs are each 0. In this type of one-shot game, it is assumed that each player knows the choices and pay-offs for the other player, and there is no communication or bargaining between the players before they move. Therefore, the *Nash equilibrium* – the point at which neither player can gain from a unilateral change in strategy – is for both players to steal. Regardless of what player 2 does, player 1 will be better off to steal.

A similar example is the "snatch game", described by Ostrom (2005). Let's remember the two households, with one household, *Household 1*, that produces chickens and another household, *Household 2*, that produces potatoes. As discussed above, if both households were to cooperate and exchange goods, they would both be better off. However, since this is the state of nature, there are no costs associated with one household stealing from the other. Therefore, neither household is likely to try to enter into an exchange, for fear of revealing what they own to the other player that could then "snatch" their property.

The state-of-nature game and the snatch game illustrate how equilibrium points in collective-dilemma games tend to be *sub-optimal*, meaning that both players could be made better off if they were to act differently. In the above examples, sub-optimal outcomes resulted, in part, because each player is pursuing their individual interest with less regard to the collective interest. The types of trade-offs associated with individual vs. collective interests are at the heart of collective dilemmas. Beyond the interests of the players, however, lies the fact that there are no costs associated with stealing the other player's property. Imposing costs on the theft of property, such as punishment, is a key role of governments, and is one reason why individuals might enter into a social contract.

Following from Locke, one of the most essential functions of governments is the protection of *property rights*. Property rights are the rights of individuals to own or control property, and these rights include the right to use, to transfer ownership, and exclude the use of the property by others (Anderson and Libecap 2014). The establishment and protection of property rights are essential for the gains from trade to be realized, otherwise property could just be stolen. In both the state-of-nature game and the snatch game, theft carried no costs, but through the enforcement of property rights, governments punish theft, thereby adding costs that are, ideally, above the potential gains from the theft. According to Hanley, Shogren, and White (2013), a property rights regime has the following characteristics,

> **Comprehensive**: all resources are either privately or collectively owned, and all entitlements are defined, well-known, and enforced.
> **Exclusive**: all benefits and costs from use of a resource accrue to the owner(s), and only to the owner(s), either directly or by sale to others. This applies to both private and common-property resources.
> **Transferable**: property rights should be transferable from one owner to another through a voluntary exchange. The owner has an incentive to

conserve the resource beyond the time during which he or she expects to make use of it.

Secure: property rights to resources should be secure from involuntary seizure or encroachment by other people, firms, and governments. Security provides the owner with an incentive to improve and preserve a resource while it is in his or her control, rather than exploit the assets (13).

Governments, through the establishment and enforcement of laws, help ensure a functioning property rights regime, which is a vital pre-condition for a market economy. As will be discussed, property rights are often a feature of environmental policy disputes.

In addition to property rights, governments also address *market failures*. Markets fail when they do not produce the most efficient, and/or a socially desired, outcome. Achieving efficiency requires markets to meet a few assumptions, yet these assumptions are often difficult to meet in practice. As stated by Fullerton and Stavins (1998),

> Private markets are perfectly efficient only if there are no public goods, no externalities, no monopoly buyers or sellers, no increasing returns to scale, no information problems, no transaction costs, no taxes, no common property and no other 'distortions' between the costs paid by buyers and the benefits received by sellers (433)

Fullerton and Stavins (1998) go on to note that these "conditions are obviously very restrictive, and they are usually not all satisfied simultaneously in the real world" (433). Market failures tend to fall into one of several categories, including a) insufficient competition, b) asymmetric information, c) externalities, d) common-pool goods, and e) public goods.

Markets require competition to achieve Pareto efficient outcomes. With perfect competition, neither the buyer nor seller can independently impact the price, therefore the price is determined by the interaction of buyers and sellers. When this assumption is not met, monopolies – a market with a single seller – or monopsonies – a market with a single buyer – can occur, and the single buyer or seller sets the price. Given the nature of some goods, natural monopolies can arise. For example, public utilities can be considered natural monopolies because of the large infrastructure costs needed to develop transmission lines for electricity. These costs act as barriers to entry for other firms, thereby restricting competition.

A perfect market also requires complete information, meaning that both the buyer and the seller know the quality of the good. Information asymmetries arise when one party knows more about the good than the other. Used cars are a leading example. The seller of a used car is going to have information of the car's history (e.g., it was in a flood) that the buyer is not able to access. Therefore, the buyer is disadvantaged and may be willing to pay more than they would if they had complete information. Information asymmetries lead to *adverse selection*, where the party with more information uses it to their advantage. For example, firms are likely to have informational advantage over local communities regarding the environmental impact of their operations and may use that information when selecting a location.

A third type of market failure is *externalities*. Externalities occur when a market transaction fails to capture the total costs or benefits associated with the transaction, or the property-right fails to be exclusive. In a perfectly functioning market, where the assumption of a complete market is met, all of the costs and benefits associated with a transaction are included in the price. As discussed above, the price of a good is determined by the intersection of supply and demand, and in an efficient market this same point equates to the intersection of marginal costs (MC) – the cost of the next additional unit – and marginal benefits (MB), the benefit of the next additional unit. Therefore, in an efficient market $MB = MC$. However, externalities happen when the social cost or benefit differs from the marginal cost or benefit. Most problematic are *negative externalities* that shift *costs* to parties not involved in the transaction. With a negative externality, the social marginal cost is greater than the private marginal cost that is reflected by the price. Therefore, the price is not fully reflective of the total costs associated with the production and consumption of the good.

A host of environmental problems can occur as a result of negative externalities, with pollution being the quintessential example. Pollution involves potentially harmful contaminants that get released into the natural environment and have subsequent impacts which can create additional costs to society, such as negative consequences on human health, affecting individuals not involved in the market transactions. The costs of the impacts are not captured by the market price.

For example, coal is an abundant and, from a private marginal cost standpoint, inexpensive source of energy. According to the US Energy Information Administration, coal accounted for about 30 percent of the nation's electricity in 2016 (US Energy Information Administration 2018). Coal-fired power plants produce electricity by burning coal to heat water, and the steam is used to drive a turbo generator. However, the burning of coal produces several harmful air pollutants including sulfur dioxide (SO_2), nitrogen oxides (NO_x), carbon dioxide (CO_2), and small particulates. These pollutants have the potential to adversely impact the health of individuals regardless of whether or not they are receiving electricity generated from the plant. Indeed, facilities often seem to be located on the state's border, where the pollutants are shifted downwind (Monogan, Konisky, and Woods 2017). The adverse health effects of coal add additional costs to society that are not accounted for in the price of electricity that consumers pay. Given that not all costs are included, the market is likely to produce more than what is efficient, or beyond what the market for coal-fired electricity would produce if it was functioning perfectly.

Market failures may also be a function of the type of good, most notably with *public goods* and *common-pool goods*. Goods can vary by their excludability and whether or not it is a rival good. Excludability refers to the ease with which a person can be excluded from consuming the good, and a rival good is a good that, once consumed by one person, cannot be consumed by anyone else. *Private goods* are goods like shoes, cars, electronic devices that are excludable, with price typically preventing the consumption of private goods, and are rival meaning that a particular pair of shoes purchased by one person cannot be purchased by another. In contrast to private goods, *public goods* are both non-excludable and non-rival, meaning that individuals cannot be prevented from consuming (i.e., enjoying the benefits of the good) and consumption is not zero-sum, therefore more than one individual can consume the good. Public goods, such as national defense, clean air, and species protection, tend to be undersupplied by markets and are therefore often provided by governments. *Club goods* are goods that are excludable and non-rival, such as seeing a play in a theatre, cable television, or household electricity. Natural monopolies often arise around club goods. Finally, *common-pool goods* are goods such as a fishery that are rival but difficult to exclude. A common-pool good tends to be overconsumed.

The potential for overconsumption of common-pool goods can lead to the *tragedy of the commons* (Hardin 1968). In Garrett Hardin's original essay, he uses the example of a pasture that is freely available for herdsmen to use for their cattle. In a classic example of a collective dilemma, it is in the interest of each of the individual herdsmen to add to his herd, since the herdsmen can gain all the benefits of an additional head of cattle and the costs of overgrazing are diffused across all the herdsmen. Under such a scenario, consumption occurs beyond what the pasture can provide until the resource is depleted. Thus, acting in their own interests the herdsmen produce an outcome that is detrimental to all, hence the tragedy. The market failure is that, due to the nature of the good (non-excludability and rivalrous), it tends to be consumed until it's depleted.

The tragedy of the commons can be illustrated using the prisoner's dilemma game, as shown in Figure 2.2. In the prisoner's dilemma, two criminals are apprehended and each is offered the same deal by the police. If one prisoner (player 1) *defects* from his partner (player 2) and confesses, he receives less time in prison then if he *cooperates* with his partner; however, if he cooperates and the partner defects, he would receive more prison time. The pay-offs in this game are presented below.

If neither player confesses, meaning they cooperate with each other, they each receive a pay-off of 1. If one player defects while the other cooperates, the pay-off for the cooperator is 2 and the defector is -1. Finally, if both players defect then their pay-offs are 0. The pay-off to cooperate is higher for both players, yet, similar to the state of nature game, the Nash equilibrium point is for both players to defect. Similarly, in the tragedy of the commons the Nash equilibrium point is for the individual to consume the resource unabated, even though cooperation is in

Player 2

Cooperate Defect

		Cooperate	*Defect*
Player 1	*Cooperate*	(1, 1)	(−1, 2)
	Defect	(2, −1)	(0, 0)

FIGURE 2.2 The prisoner's dilemma game

the collective interest. This helps explain why fisheries tend to be depleted, as well as why it is difficult for countries to agree to lower their greenhouse gas emissions.

Public goods are goods that are non-excludable and non-rival and tend to be undersupplied by the market. Many, if not most, environmental amenities could be considered public goods, such as clean air, clean water, pristine forests, waterways, beaches, and public parks. With each of these goods exclusion of non-payers is costly or impossible, and the non-rival nature of public goods means that consumption is also difficult to contain. Therefore, markets tend to undersupply public goods. Additionally, part of the failure related to public and common-pool goods is the difficulty in defining property rights. Property rights should be secure, and the non-excludable nature of public goods makes that difficult. Absent clear property rights, a market is missing (Anderson and Libecap 2014).

Following Coase (1960), some scholars argue that environmental problems are not market failures but rather result from the lack of clearly defined and enforced property rights (e.g., Anderson 2004). With a property-rights approach, environmental problems arise not because of externalities or the nature of environmental goods, but rather as a result of diverse preferences for environmental goods and natural resources. Therefore, pollution may not necessarily be a market failure, but rather pollution is a result of a missing market because "air" is a public good and as a result property rights are hard to define and enforce. If property rights regarding air and pollution were defined, the issue of pollution could be addressed through bargaining. Diverse preferences for environmental goods imply that some may prefer and thus be willing to pay for clean air, and others may prefer and be willing to pay to pollute; therefore, through bargaining, the party that valued the use of the air most would obtain the property right. The externality approach implicitly assumes that the property rights to many natural resources are shared among all in society, and therefore, society's property rights are infringed by the presence of a negative externality. However, the property-rights approach makes no assumption about who owns the property right, rather it is a question of conflicting preferences that may be solved by the affected parties through bargaining.

A market-failure vs. a property-rights approach to understanding environmental problems can lead to different ideas about how to solve those problems. A market-failure approach implies a need for government intervention, often in the form of regulatory policy, whereas a property-rights approach implies the need to create and maintain a market for the natural resource. Therefore, the property-rights approach would involve less government intervention, likely only to enforce the agreed-upon property right.

Enforcing property rights and addressing market failures are typically considered within the realm of government institutions. Governments, once established, enact and enforce policies to address collective dilemmas, including market failures. However, how is it determined that a market failure, or sub-optimal outcome, has occurred that government should address? Once the need for government intervention is determined, how is the government response decided? Chapter 1 illustrated the general framework of environmental policymaking that will be used to address those questions, and the next section discusses the framework in more detail.

Environmental Policy and Governance

Governments seek to adjust sub-optimal outcomes and market failures through the enactment and implementation of public policy. Public policy can be defined as the outcomes of government processes that are aimed at alleviating a societal problem. Scholars have developed various definitions of public policy and most of those definitions contain the following attributes: a) public policy is made by public (i.e., government) authorities; b) public policy is goal-oriented; c) public policy includes patterns of action taken over time; d) public policy is a product of demand on governments by individuals or groups; and e) public policy is based on values and value conflicts.[1]

The notion of public authorities separates public policy from policies adopted by private entities, and this distinction implies that government authorities are acting in the interest of the general public and not in the interest of a few. In addition, public authority is held accountable through the election of public officials as opposed to market mechanisms.

The goal-oriented nature of public policy means that it is purposeful and aimed at achieving the improvement of some sub-optimal social outcome or market failure. However, policy, particularly legislation, may at times be enacted symbolically, rather than aimed at truly addressing a problem.

Public policy should be thought of as a series of decisions and actions made by multiple policy actors over time, as opposed to a single point in time such as the passage of a piece of legislation by Congress, or a decision by the Supreme Court. Policies develop over time as a result of the decisions and actions of multiple actors across multiple institutions.

Public policy is typically a product of demand, meaning that some entity such as an interest group or an elected official's constituent demanded that a particular problem be addressed by government. Policy development occurs largely through policy actors pressing for change within and across the institutions of government.

Finally, policy is the product of contested value orientations. Values – ideas about what is morally right and wrong – inform what problems government should address and how they should address them. In many policy areas the participants are informed by different values, and the nature of the value-based conflicts often shape the development of policy.

Environmental policy is public policy that deals with the management of natural resources. Kraft (2011) provides a comprehensive definition of environmental policy, where environmental policy

> Refers to government actions that affect or attempt to affect environmental quality or the use of natural resources. It represents society's collective decision to pursue certain environmental goals and objectives and to use particular tools to achieve them. Environmental policy is not found in any single statute or administrative decision. Rather, it is set by a diverse collection of statutes, regulations, and court precedents that govern the nation, and it is affected by the attitudes and behavior of the officials who are responsible for implementing and enforcing the law. Environmental policy includes not only what governments choose to do to protect environmental quality and natural resources but what they decide *not* to do; a decision not to act means that governments allow other forces to shape the environment (13–14).

As discussed above, government actions in the form of public policy are typically the result of some demand placed on government to address a problem. At the core of each problem that someone wants addressed is likely one or more market failures, and the nature of the market failure may dictate the type of policy response. For example, if a market is not achieving efficiency because of monopoly power, the government may intervene following the tenets of the Sherman Anti-Trust Act of 1890, which allows individuals and/or governments to bring court challenges to companies that may have price-setting capabilities. If information asymmetries exist, the government may enact policies that require information disclosure such as with the Toxic Release Inventory (TRI). Externalities, such as pollution, can be addressed through policies that limit the amount of pollutants that a plant may release, or dictate the types of technology that firms must use to reduce emissions of pollutants. For example, the Clean Air Act of 1977 encouraged firms to use chemical "scrubbers" on tall smokestacks to remove sulfur dioxide and nitrogen oxides. To address common-pool resource problems, governments can intervene by limiting the amount of the common-pool good that can be consumed. Catch limits for particular species or within certain fishing areas are an example of government action aimed at elevating the tragedy of the commons. Finally, governments can provide public goods like clean air, clean water, and public parks, to ensure a sufficient supply of those goods exist. Each of the above examples of environmental policy involve strong government intervention; however, as will be discussed throughout the book, there are multiple interventions or policies that governments can introduce to address environmental problems.

Ultimately choices about policy are choices about *governance*. Governance as applied to public policy can be defined as the "regimes of laws, rules, judicial decisions, and administrative practices that constrain, prescribe, and enable the provision of publicly supported goods and services" (Lynn, Heinrich, and Hill 2001, 7). In essence, public governance is the sum of tasks that governments choose to perform across all branches and levels (Bertelli 2012). Public governance, in the aggregate, includes the many decisions by governmental entities over time, including the problems that are addressed, the policies designed to address them, and the way that those policies are implemented.

What could be considered under the umbrella of environment policy and governance touches nearly every aspect of modern society, including public lands and waters; wilderness; wildlife; pollution; ecosystem services; human health and safety; energy use; transportation; urban design and building standards; agriculture and food production; and human population growth (Kraft 2011). Decisions about particular government actions are a result of a complex process of environmental policymaking.

The Environmental Policymaking Process

Policymaking and governance in the environmental realm is a process that involves a series of decisions made by multiple actors within and across multiple institutions over long periods of time. The actors and institutions are situated in the environmental policymaking system that receives inputs in the form of information from social, economic, and natural environments, and translates those inputs into outputs, in the form of public policy. The environmental policy outputs lead to *feedback* processes where information is fed back into the system as inputs. The environmental policymaking system is analogous to an ecosystem, and it receives energy in the form of information flows. Using a box-model – a "form of modeling the energy flows within components of a system" (McGuire 2012, 40) – Figure 2.3 illustrates the environmental policymaking process.[2]

At the center of the environmental policymaking process is the policymaking system that contains *policy actors* and *policymaking institutions* as well as the policy subsystems that are structured by institutions and through which actors interact. Additionally, policy subsystems connect the multiple levels of government in the US federalist system to the macro-institutions of the federal government. The environmental policymaking system functions as an information-processing system, with information signals that flow towards the system. If those signals receive significant attention through the agenda-setting process, they enter the system and flow through the macro-institutions of government and the various policy subsystems, and then come out as policies. Then, information flows through the feedback processes of implementation, where information travels back to the system, and evaluation, where information flows back into inputs. Information

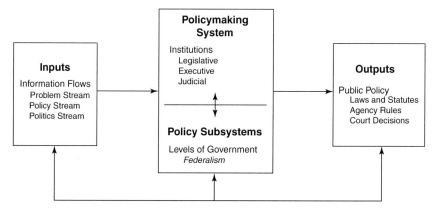

FIGURE 2.3 The environmental policymaking process

flows are both *exogenous* – developed outside the system – and *endogenous*, produced by actors and institutions within the system.

Information flows, either exogenous or endogenous, can be characterized as belonging to one of three streams, including a *problem* stream that contains information regarding various societal conditions, a *policy* stream containing ideas and potential solutions to problems, and a *politics* stream containing information pertinent to political concerns such as public opinion (Kingdon 2003). Information in the problem stream tends to be *entropic* or diverse and comes from multiple and often competing sources, whereas information in the policy stream tends to be *expert* information that is focused on developing courses of action for governments to pursue (Baumgartner and Jones 2015).

A perfectly responsive policymaking system would exist in a constant state of equilibrium, where information changes are matched by proportionate policy changes. However, the environmental policymaking system creates friction that causes the system to either over- or under-respond to changes in information (Jones, Sulkin, and Larsen 2003).

The friction created within the environmental policymaking system keeps the system, or more precisely the various subsystems that constitute the system, from remaining in constant equilibrium, and the lack of a steady-state is one of the features of environmental policymaking that creates complexity. Indeed, the environmental policymaking system can be understood as a complex system where complex systems include: a) interdependent parts that combine to produce system behavior; b) negative and positive feedback loops; c) a tendency toward path-dependent behavior; d) bottom-up emergence; and e) periods of stability interrupted by large changes (Cairney and Geyer 2015, 2). In addition, entities within a complex system interact over a "contact structure or network" (Page 2010, 17). Within the environmental policymaking system, institutions determine the rules, or "contact structure", within which diverse and interdependent policy actors are bound. In addition, institutions provide the structure through which networks develop. Finally, policy actors within the system adapt through learning and feedback, and subsequent policy outputs become more likely to change as a result.

The environmental policymaking system creates friction in responding to information and therefore reacts to changes in information flows in a disproportionate manner, and, as a result, environmental policymaking does not proceed in a linear fashion, where proportional policy adjustments are made in response to changes in information flows. Rather, the environmental policymaking system responds to information in a disjointed way, often by over- or under-reacting to information signals (Jones and Baumgartner 2005). As a result of these dynamics, policy tends to be stable for long periods of time, but then experiences a *punctuated equilibrium* that allows for dramatic policy change. Despite the friction imposed by the environmental policymaking system, the institutions within it help by providing some stability to the process as well as creating specific pathways for information flows to become particular forms of policy.

The Environmental Policymaking System

The environmental policymaking system includes policy actors and the institutions in which they interact. Environmental policy is a result of the interaction of actors and institutions, where policy actors seek to obtain their goals within the constraints and opportunities offered by institutions. Institutions are the regular patterns of behavior that are present in the complex environment of policymaking and they work to provide structure to the complexities of policymaking. The structure is provided by institutions through their capacity as rules and norms that policy actors follow. Further, institutions can be considered equilibrium methods of decision-making that range from stable – existing in roughly the same form for long periods of time – to relatively fragile. Finally, institutions act as the major *pathways* of policymaking (Klyza and Sousa 2013). The form and design of policy is determined, in large part, by the institutional pathway through which the policy develops.

Macro-Institutions

The macro policymaking institutions that are part of the environmental policymaking system are those prescribed by the Constitution, including the Congress, the executive, and the judiciary. The macro-institutions are those that are most often in the media and are the most visible to the public. Apart from being the most visible, the macro policymaking institutions are instrumental in shaping the form that environmental policies can take, with several forms possible that depend on the institutional pathway through which the policy is developed. Forms of public policy include: legislation passed by Congress; rules and regulations promulgated by executive agencies; executive orders issued by presidents; and legal decisions made by courts.

Congress: Congress plays a central role in the environmental policymaking system and is the main conduit through which information flows are processed. To facilitate its work, Congress is organized into committees and subcommittees that are divided by policy jurisdiction and have authority within certain policy domains. Through its committees, Congress is able to process information flows regarding multiple policy issues at the same time. Committees provide information to Congress largely through hearings and by proposing legislation for the chamber to consider. Congressional hearings allow committees to bring in witnesses to testify regarding important policy issues. Hearings are called by the committee that holds the relevant jurisdiction and are used to gather information regarding developing societal problems, hear a variety of opinions about proposed legislation, conduct investigations, and oversee the conduct of executive agencies.

Both the House and the Senate have several standing committees that engage in the development of environmental policy. In the House important committees include: Agriculture; Energy and Commerce; Natural Resources; Space, Science, and Technology; and Transportation and Infrastructure. The Senate committees are: Agriculture, Nutrition, and Forestry; Commerce, Science, and Transportation; Energy and Natural Resources; and Environment and Public Works. The committees in the House and Senate span the broad range of environmental policy issues, including agriculture, energy, natural resources, transportation, and science.

Congressional committees are a vital part of how proposed legislation becomes law. Members of Congress introduce bills for consideration and those bills are assigned to the relevant committee(s) and/or subcommittee(s). Committees consider the legislation and decide whether or not to move the legislation forward to be considered by the entire chamber. The assignment of bills to committees empowers those committees to be the gatekeepers of what Congress considers. Once a bill is approved by a committee it must pass both the House and Senate, in the same form, and be signed by the president to become law.

An additional important organizing feature for Congress are political parties. The fact that Congress is a majoritarian electoral institution helps to empower parties, because parties and their "brand" help connect voters to electoral institutions. Knowing which party an elected official or candidate belongs to can provide a wealth of information to voters about that official's views on a host of political and policy issues. Additionally, political parties, through their leadership structure, help members of Congress coordinate on collective goals. In the House, the Speaker of the House, arguably the most important legislator in the United States, is elected by the House membership and is a member of the majority party. The House leadership also includes the majority leader, the minority leader (selected by the minority party), and various "whips" that work to secure the votes of party members. Leadership in the Senate consists of the president pro tempore, who is typically the longest-serving member of the majority party, as well as the majority and minority leaders, with each being selected by their respective party caucus. Finally, committee chairs are selected by parties and they can shape how information is processed within their committees. The two political parties have become increasingly polarized over environmental issues since the "environmental decade" of the 1970s, and this polarization is reflected in congressional deadlock on many important environmental issues, including climate change.

The Executive: the executive branch consists of the presidency and the various executive branch agencies. The president is the unitary head of the executive branch and as an individual possesses what Teddy Roosevelt termed the *bully pulpit*. Presidential speeches, statements, and even tweets, are reported by the media, and presidents use this as a way to bring attention to issues as well as to persuade and/or mobilize members of Congress and the public in an effort to shape the policymaking agenda. Indeed, some scholars have argued that presidential power is largely found in the president's ability to persuade (Lovett, Bevan, and Baumgartner 2015; Neustadt 1991). However, the ability of presidential speech to shape policymaking has been shown to be limited (Canes-Wrone 2001; Villalobos, Vaughn, and Azari 2012). Finally, presidents have multiple direct levers of authority that go beyond the bully pulpit (Howell 2003).

As prescribed by the US Constitution, the president's policymaking authority comes from the ability to veto legislation. Bills that pass Congress must be signed or vetoed by the president, and if vetoed Congress needs a two-thirds majority in both chambers to override. Often, presidents use the threat of a veto to shape the legislative process by clearly demarcating the pivot point – the point at which the president will accept or veto – of the legislation.

Section II of the Constitution also empowers the president to execute the law. Under the power to execute the law, the president has become the chief executive of what Waldo (2007) called the *administrative state*. The administrative state emerged when the responsibilities of executive branch agencies began to grow over the course of the late 19th and throughout the 20th centuries as the federal government became involved to a greater depth and across a larger number of societal problems. The various agencies in the executive branch as well as the various rules and regulations those agencies have promulgated constitute the administrative state.

Within the executive branch, jurisdiction over environmental policy issues is fragmented across several agencies and departments. The Executive Office of the President includes the Council on Environmental Quality, the Office of Management and Budget (OMB), and the Office of Science and Technology Policy. In addition, there are several cabinet level agencies that deal with environmental issues including the Departments of Agriculture, Commerce, Energy, Interior, and Transportation. Finally, there are several independent agencies, most notably the Environmental Protection Agency (EPA) as well as the Nuclear Regulatory Commission and the Tennessee Valley Authority.

The role of the president as chief executive of the administrative state is the most consequential with regard to environmental policy (Vig 2019). One policy tool of the chief executive are executive orders. Executive orders have traditionally been used to provide instructions for agencies on how policy should be implemented, but some significant executive orders are increasingly seen as ways for the president to make policy and, as such, can be considered an output of the policymaking system.

Apart from executive orders, the president also oversees the rulemaking process of executive agencies. The rules and regulations promulgated by executive agencies are the most prominent pathway for executive branch policymaking. Agencies make rules through a quasi-legislative administrative process that was outlined in the *Administrative Procedure Act* (APA) of 1946. The APA requires that agencies first issue a proposed rule, or a notice of proposed rulemaking, in the Federal Register. Following the proposed rule, agencies open a comment period and accept comments about the proposed rule from stakeholders, including the public. At some point after the comment period ends, agencies issue a final rule. Increasingly, presidents have sought to control agency rulemaking by requiring agencies to submit rules considered to be significant to the OMB for review.

The Courts: the major source of impact of the courts on environmental policymaking is through judicial review. Judicial review, established in *Marbury v. Madison* (1803), is the authority possessed by the courts to determine the constitutionality of laws and the actions of the legislative and executive branches as well as state and local governments. With the power of judicial review, the courts can significantly impact the development of environmental policy and governance. Additionally, court decisions, particularly appellate courts, create precedents that are followed by lower courts.

The court system in the United States is a dual system, where cases begin in either the state court system or the federal court system. Prior to the 1970s environmental issues were considered a state and local concern, and therefore most disputes were settled within the state court system. However, since the dominance of federal environmental legislation that began in the 1970s, more and more environmental cases are decided in federal courts.

Apart from judicial review, the courts can shape environmental policy in a number of other ways including by determining standing to sue, the choice of standards of review, interpretation of the law, and the choice of remedy (O'Leary 2019). Standing is the right to sue and is established by courts on the basis of harm to one party because of the actions of another party. The standard of review refers to the amount of deference given by the court to the decisions of previous courts.

Courts, particularly lower courts, tend to follow the legal precedents established by other courts. Judicial review gives courts a great degree of authority to interpret the law to determine the meaning and intent of the law. Finally, courts are able to determine what remedy to apply. As a result, decisions issued by courts are a form of public policy.

Policy Subsystems and Policy Actors

The macro-level institutions create particular pathways for information to flow and actors to navigate. However, given the number and complexity of issues that are typically being addressed by these institutions, much of policymaking occurs within *policy subsystems*.[3] Policy subsystems are configurations of actors and institutions organized around particular policy domains and are semi-autonomous from the broader policymaking system. The environmental policymaking system is made up of the various constitute policy subsystems.

As noted by Jenkins-Smith et al. (2018), subsystems "are defined by a policy topic, territorial scope, and the actors directly or indirectly influencing policy subsystem affairs" (139). Depending on the nature of the policy issue, there is an infinite number of combinations of actors and institutions engaged in any particular policy subsystem. This is especially true in systems like the United States that contain multiple policymaking venues and decision points. However, the jurisdiction of congressional committees works to structure policy subsystems and thereby organizes the flow of information from multiple policy actors, including from the various executive branch agencies, interest groups, and experts regarding the issues within the committees' domain. Congressional committees are the connective tissue between policy subsystems and the macro-institution of Congress, as well as the main conduit through which information flows in the environmental policymaking system.

Another feature of subsystems is that they are *intergovernmental* and can be defined by a geographic area as well as a policy area (Zafonte and Sabatier 1998). The intergovernmental nature of policy subsystems is a result of *federalism*, where policymaking authority is shared across multiple levels of government including the federal, state, and local level. For example, policies aimed at hydraulic fracturing (fracking) as a way to develop oil and natural gas reserves developed in the state of New York are the result of interactions between actors within a unique subsystem from those policies developed in Colorado. However, both subsystems are nested within the larger US energy policy subsystem. Finally, multiple subsystems and levels of government create a *polycentric* system, where multiple centers of decision-making authority exist.

Policy actors are individuals, groups, or coalitions involved in the policymaking process that seek to see their preferences for policy enacted. The policy preferences of policy actors are their preferred courses of action to address societal problems. Policy preferences are driven by the values and beliefs held by the policy actor

(Sabatier and Jenkins-Smith 1993). Values, discussed in Chapter 4, are normative ideas about right and wrong, and policy beliefs include ideas about how the policy problem is defined, or understood, often in terms of the seriousness, the causes, and the consequences of the problem. Policy beliefs are informed by some combination of values and self-interest, and values and beliefs inform the specific policy preferences of actors.

There are a range of policy actors active in the environmental policymaking process both within and outside of official government positions. Actors within government include members of Congress, administrators and civil servants within executive branch agencies, and state and local government officials, among others. Policy actors outside government include interest groups, scientists, experts, members of the media, and the public.

Policy actors within and outside of government have a portfolio of behaviors or strategies that they can engage to achieve their preferences, and the institutional arrangements of the policymaking process provide constraints as well as opportunities for actors to engage in influencing policy choices. Skillful policy actors are entrepreneurs and are able to navigate the myriad alternative policymaking venues. Indeed, entrepreneurs often scan the terrain and choose the venue they see as most amiable to their policy preferences.

The interaction of policy actors and institutions within the policymaking system is the kernel of the environmental policymaking process. As such, these interactions are part of a dynamic process that occurs within an ever-changing information environment.

Making Environmental Policy

The framework used here posits that the environmental policymaking process involves the flow of information through a policymaking system that includes policy actors and institutions which, through policy subsystems, shape information flows into outputs in the form of policy. With regard to environmental policy, the outputs are geared toward addressing a host of issues related to natural resource management, land use, energy production, and biodiversity, among others.

To empirically demonstrate the framework, I will estimate two models. The first model is an attention model predicting attention to information by the policymaking system, and the second is an output or lawmaking model.[4] The attention model can be stated as,

$$A_t = \alpha + \beta I_{t-1} + \gamma S_t + \epsilon_t$$

In the above model, A = attention, I = the inputs, or information flows, and S = the system variables. The attention model posits that increases in attention to issues are a function of information and factors within the environmental policymaking system.

The output model can be stated as,

$$O_t = \alpha + \delta A_{t-1} + \eta I_{t-1} + \lambda S_t + \epsilon_t$$

In the output model, O = outputs, or public policy and A = attention, I = inputs and S = the system variables. As shown, policy results from attention, information, and system variables.

The attention and outputs models together show that policy results first from issues gaining the attention of the policymaking system (i.e., reaching the policymaking agenda) and second that policy results from attention to information combined with conditions present in the policymaking system. Next, I will estimate both models with regard to environmental issues.

Data to estimate the models comes from the *Comparative Agendas Project*, using data from the major topic *Environment* from the years 1947 to 2014.[5] To estimate the *attention* variable, I use the number of congressional hearings about the environment held each year. The *output* variable is the number of environmental public laws passed by Congress and signed by the president each year. In the framework and in the models, attention and outputs are both functions of information and the processing of that information within the environmental policymaking system. To estimate the *inputs*, I use the total number of *New York Times* stories about the environment lagged one year. This estimation approach assumes that an increase in the number of *New York Times* articles is associated with new or changing information related to environmental issues.[6] Additionally, the lag allows time for Congress to respond to changing information, and the lag also controls for contemporaneous reporting of congressional activity. Next, the *system* variables include mentions of the environment by the president in the State of the Union address each year, which signals the president's interest in environmental issues and his attempts to impact the agenda of Congress. In addition, given the partisan nature of environmental issues, I also include whether the president is a Democrat, and whether the Democratic party has control of both houses of Congress. I expect that a Democratic president and a Democratic Congress will be more likely than a Republican president or Congress to address environmental issues. Finally, I lag congressional hearings one year to predict environmental laws. Table 2.1 shows the OLS model results.

Looking first to the attention model in Table 2.1, as the number of *New York Times* articles about the environment increases in year, Y_t so does the number of congressional hearings about the environment in year Y_{t+1}. However, none of the system variables were significant predictors of attention. For the output model, the number of *New York Times* articles in the previous year were not a significant predictor of laws, which indicates that the information carried by the media may only influence attention but not subsequent output. Looking to the system variables, as expected a Democratic Congress is more likely than a Republican one to pass environmental legislation. However, State of the Union statements and

TABLE 2.1 Environmental Policymaking: Hearings and Laws, 1947–2014

	Attention and output:	
	Hearings	Public laws
New York Times articles$_{t-1}$	2.339***	0.127
	(0.667)	(0.113)
State of the Union statements	0.054	0.052
	(0.648)	(0.094)
Democratic Congress	0.933	2.411*
	(9.638)	(1.409)
Democratic President	-7.342	-1.292
	(9.493)	(1.381)
Hearings$_{t-1}$		0.059***
		(0.019)
Constant	35.863***	2.038
	(12.640)	(1.939)
Observations	67	67
Adjusted R^2	0.154	0.230

Note: *p<0.10; **p<0.05; ***p<0.01

a Democratic president did not seem to have an influence in predicting environmental legislation. Finally, as expected increased attention in the form of congressional hearings is a significant predictor of public laws.

The above analysis demonstrates that broadly speaking, and as shown in Figure 2.3, environmental policymaking tends to follow from increased attention due to changing information coupled with factors within the policymaking system. However, the inherent complexity of the process means that policymaking is not a smooth linear process where policy adjustments are made in proportion to changing information. Rather, policymaking occurs within the environmental policymaking system where actors, institutions, and subsystems work to respond to and shape information flows, creating a disjointed process.

Much of what occurs in the environmental policymaking system involves the interaction of macro-institutions and policy subsystems. For the most part, the macro-institutions can only process information related to one (or at most, a few) issues at a time. However, policy subsystems allow for the processing of information about multiple issue simultaneously. For example, Congress can only vote on one piece of legislation at a time, but congressional committees can hold multiple hearings about several pieces of legislation at once. The parallel processing of information within subsystems coupled with the serial processing of macro-institutions creates a punctuated equilibrium pattern of environmental policymaking (Baumgartner 2006; Baumgartner and Jones 1993; Baumgartner, Jones, and Mortensen 2018). Such a pattern involves long periods of policy stability and incremental policy changes that are periodically interrupted by major policy change. Policy stability is typically a function of subsystem stability. As long as the actors, institutions, and definition of an issue remain constant within the subsystem, any policy change is likely to be incremental. Stable policy subsystems create friction that raises the transactions costs associated with making a policy change (Jones, Sulkin, and Larsen 2003).

Major policy change is often brought about by issues being pushed from their various subsystems onto the agenda of the macro-level policymaking institutions. Information flows are typically handled within subsystems, but under certain conditions issues break out of their subsystem and reach the agenda of the macro-institutions, making policy change more likely. Often this happens as a result of pressure from changing information streams, new policy actors, and new policy venues being exerted on a subsystem or a set of related subsystems.

The pattern of punctuated policy change that results from issues moving from subsystems to macro-institutions has been illustrated using government budgets as the policy output (Breunig and Koski 2006; Jones, Baumgartner, and True 1998; Jones, Zalányi, and Érdi 2014). If environmental policymaking was a smooth linear process involving incremental adjustments in response to changing conditions, then budget changes would be normally distributed. However, government budget changes tend to have distributions with high kurtosis, indicated by several cases in the tails of the distribution. Figure 2.4 illustrates both the percent change of the US federal budget for environmental issues from 1947 to 2014 as well as the percent of the overall federal budget dedicated to environmental issues from 1947 to 2015.[7] A normal distribution is overlaid on the percent change graph to illustrate the deviations from normal.

As shown, budgetary changes clearly exhibit a punctuated equilibrium pattern, with the majority of changes being small, or incremental, yet with several large changes in the tails of the distribution. The distribution of percent changes has a high level of kurtosis with $K = 5.432$, where a normal distribution has a $K = 3$. In terms of the percent of the overall federal budget, the average percent for the years 1947 to 2015 was 1.738. As can be seen, a large increase in federal spending on the environment occurred in the early 1970s, where environmental spending reached nearly 4.5 percent of the total federal budget. However, since the late 1980s, spending on the environment has hovered between 1 and 1.5 percent. The disjointed pattern of budget changes demonstrates that environmental policymaking as a whole tends to follow a pattern of subsystem-driven incremental changes coupled with large changes driven by information changes and attention from the macro-institutions.

As demonstrated in Table 2.1, environmental policymaking occurs as information gains attention from the policymaking system and that information is shaped into the various forms of policy. However, this process produces incremental to no policy change for most issues most of the time, but abrupt large-scale policy changes for a few issues. This process was demonstrated in Figure 2.4 using environmental budget change at the federal level in the United States. Next, I show the pattern of environmental policy outputs for each of the three macro-institutions.

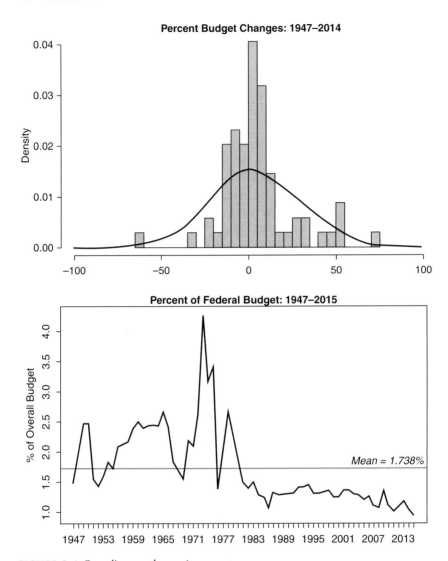

FIGURE 2.4 Spending on the environment

The specific form of policy outputs is the result of the particular institutional pathway from which the policy was generated. Each of the macro-institutions has a unique form of policy that it alone can produce. For example, only Congress can make laws, only the courts can issue judicial decisions, and only presidents can issue executive orders. Figure 2.5 shows the number of environmental policy outputs from each macro-institution from 1947 to 2015.[8] Each dot represents that number of outputs in each year and the lines are LOESS – local regression – curves that illustrate the general pattern of environmental policy over the time period.

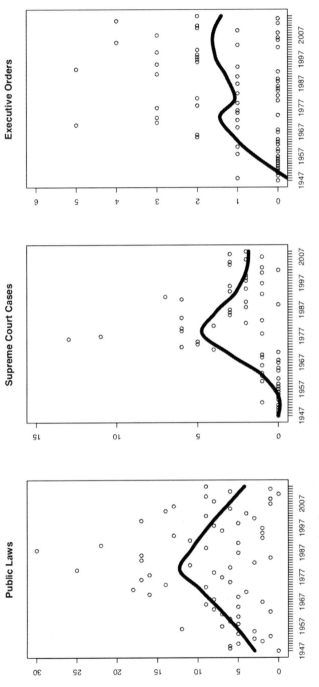

FIGURE 2.5 Environmental policy outputs, 1947–2015

As Figure 2.5 indicates, the most active period of environmental legislation was the 1970s, peaking around 1978. In terms of the Supreme Court, the number of environmental cases decided by the court peaked in the late 1970s and early 1980s. This is a similar pattern as Congress, which points to the time period as being especially important for the development of environmental policy. Finally, the number of executive orders about environmental issues increased under Nixon in the early 1970s before declining and then increasing again in the late 1980s. The pattern of increasing executive orders corresponds to the rise of the president as chief executive of the administrative state.

The above discussion, guided by the framework, explored the overall broad pattern of environmental policymaking in the United States. The next section describes the nature of environmental policy design.

Environmental Policy Design

The environmental policymaking system, through the interaction of actors and institutions within policy subsystems, transforms information flows into public policies. However, the complex nature of the system, coupled with institutional friction, creates a process of long-term policy stability with punctuated policy change. Environmental policy outputs across each of the three macro-institutions were most prominent during the environmentalism era of the 1970s.

The form – legislation, rule, court decision – that policy takes as it passes through the environmental policymaking system is dependent, in part, on its institutional pathway. But, inherent in all the alternative forms of policy is a *policy design*, which refers to the content of public policy (Schneider and Ingram 1997, 2). Embedded within policy designs are the goals of the policy, the causal framework, the policy instruments, the targets of the policy, and the implementation structure. Each of these factors is described below.

Environmental Policy Goals

The goals of policy are simply the outcomes that the policymakers wish for the policy to achieve. At the most basic level, the policy goal is to address the problem that necessitated the policy response. Ideally, policies are designed to solve, or at least lessen, the impacts of a societal problem.

According to Stone (2002), public policy goals can be categorized into four major categories: equity, efficiency, security, and liberty. The meanings of these goals and how they may, or may not, apply in specific contexts is contentious. For example, equity, or equality, can be understood in multiple ways, but in the United States equity as a policy goal generally refers to equal access to opportunities for success, more so than equal outcomes. Within environmental policy, equity goals could be related to concerns about environmental justice, such as the disproportionate exposure to environmental risks and hazards that communities of color and lower socio-economic status tend to face (see Mohai, Pellow, and Roberts 2009). In addition, equity may refer to the negative impacts that policy choices may have on some communities. For example, climate policies that are designed to reduce the use of coal may cause job losses in the coal industry.

Efficiency generally refers to goals that seek to enhance outputs relative to a certain level of inputs. When functioning properly, markets produce the most efficient allocation of society's resources, yet when markets fail policies can serve to improve the efficiency of resource allocations. Apart from being a goal, efficiency is also an evaluative criterion used to measure various policy alternatives. All things equal, it would be better for society if its resources were used more efficiently rather than less efficiently. During the growth of environmental policy in the 1970s, efficiency was not a major goal or concern, rather the focus was on public health and safety. However, as environmental policy developed, emphasis was increasingly placed on efficiency and reaching desired outcomes using market-based mechanisms.

Security generally refers to goals associated with public safety, and for environmental policy this could refer to policies that reduce harmful pollution. Liberty deals with goals that increase freedom and choice for individuals. Often security and liberty are considered as trade-offs. For example, to reduce the impacts of a harmful pollutant, the "liberty" of a firm to dump waste into a river would be limited.

For environmental policy, policy goals are typically broadly defined as some level of environmental protection, harm reduction, or improved management of a natural resource. However, the specific goals of a policy are often a function of how the problem is defined. If the problem is defined as a market failure associated with a negative externality, such as pollution, then the goal of the policy is to reduce or eliminate the negative externality. However, often policy actors don't agree on the issue definition and therefore won't agree on a policy goal. Under these conditions, if a policy is developed it may have multiple, competing, or ambiguous goals. Multiple goals occur as a result of policies addressing multiple problems or one problem in multiple ways. Competing goals are goals stated within a policy that may be incongruent or require trade-offs, such as reducing emissions and reducing energy prices, for example. Finally, ambiguous policy goals leave it to others, such as executive agencies, to fill in the details and create specific goals.

Once a goal is in mind, decision-makers need to select one (or more) alternative instruments to reach the desired goal(s). The choice of policy instruments is based on the causal framework that is adopted by policymakers, where a causal framework connects the choice of a policy alternative to the policy goal.

Causal Framework

Policy goals are defined in terms of the outcome that is desired, and the causal framework embedded within a policy design is the theory that connects the policy to the desired policy outcome. A causal framework within a policy design includes the policy choice, or instrument, the desired outcome, and the causal relationships between policy choice and outcome (Esterling 2004, 48).

The causal framework includes the underlying logic, explicit or implied, of how p, the policy, will *cause Y*, the outcome. The logic of the causal framework is connected to how the issue is defined. For example, if climate change is defined as a pollution problem associated with greenhouse gas emissions, then addressing that problem requires dealing with the pollution externality such as with a carbon tax. One part of the underlying logic of a carbon tax is that an increase in price as a result of the tax will *cause* a decrease in the consumption of carbon-intensive fuels, thereby reducing overall greenhouse gas emissions.

However, there is often a lot of uncertainty and ambiguity associated with a causal framework. The uncertainty between policies and outcomes can be expressed as $x = p + \omega$, where x is some desired outcome, p is a policy designed to achieve that outcome, and ω is a random variable representing the uncertainty of the relationship between x and p (see Krehbiel 1991). Uncertainty, ω, is in part a function of the quality of the data associated with the causal framework, such that more data (information) can reduce the uncertainty. Policymakers often rely on experts both inside and outside government agencies to reduce the uncertainty, ω, between policy choices and outcomes.

The ambiguity of the causal framework is typically a function of the complexity of policy issues as well as the tendency for values to influence how policy issues are understood. By definition, ambiguity allows for multiple interpretations of the same underlying facts, therefore an increase in information may not reduce ambiguity in the same way as it may reduce uncertainty.

The choice of policy, p, involves the choice of policy instruments. Instruments are the means through which policy goals are achieved, so a causal framework connects the policy instruments to the outcome. The selection of instrument choice is both a technical and a political process.

Environmental Policy Instruments

Policy goals are the ends of policy choices, policy instruments are the means, and the causal framework is what logically connects the means to the end. Much of environmental policy is regulatory in nature, therefore the selection of policy instruments is largely the selection of mechanisms of regulation. In other words, consideration of environmental policy instruments addresses what tools can be used to change the behavior of economic sectors, firms, or individuals. Often the behavior in question has led to a market failure.

There are several types of environmental policy instruments and they have been categorized in different ways. One set of categorical distinctions are *command-and-control* versus *market-based* instruments. Command-and-control regulations require firms, by force of law, to reach a particular standard of performance or use a specific type of technology. Market-based instruments use market mechanisms to incentivize firms to change their behavior. Another way of categorizing instruments is as "carrot, sticks, or sermons," where carrots are economic incentives, sticks are command-and-control regulations, and sermons are the provision of information, with all being geared toward the changing of behavior (Bemelmans-Videc, Rist, and Vedung 2003).

To capture the potential range of policy instruments, I draw on the policy instrument matrix developed by The World Bank (1997) that delineates four broad types of environmental policy instruments including *using markets*, *creating markets*, *using environmental regulation*, and *engaging the public* (also see Sterner and Coria 2012). Using markets involves policy instruments such as taxes, subsidies, and user fees. Creating markets includes the establishment of property rights and tradable permits. Environmental regulations are the command-and-control instruments of performance or technology standards. Finally, engaging the public includes stakeholder engagement, collaboration, and information provision.

The choice of policy instrument is embedded in the *regulatory structure*, which itself is embedded within the larger policy design. The regulatory structure includes "1) the command embedded in the regulation, 2) the target of the regulation, 3) the consequences of compliance or non-compliance with the command, and 4) the regulator" (Bennear and Coglianese 2012, 583). The command is what is required of the target – the entities whose behavior the policy seeks to change – to do or not to do, the consequences are what is imposed on the target for compliance or non-compliance, and the regulator is the entity that creates, monitors, and enforces the policy. The overall regulatory structure is compatible with any of the above instruments, and each element of the regulatory structure allows for some flexibility.

The policies that were developed during the 1970s were largely command-and-control type environmental regulations (Fiorino 2006). With command-and-control, the command is a requirement to reach a particular outcome, and control is the monitoring and imposition of sanctions if the goal is not reached. The command may be related to a performance standard such as the Clean Air Act of 1970, which requires that criteria pollutants do not exceed certain levels. Alternatively, the command may require a particular type of technology be used, such as catalytic converters that reduce the toxicity of vehicle emissions.

Command-and-control type regulations are connected to the market-failure understanding of environmental problems. For example, in the case of a negative externality such as pollution, the command-and-control response is to limit the amount of pollution that the plant may emit, or require a particular technology be used to limit emissions. These commands are followed by a strict monitoring and enforcement regime. In the case of a common-pool resource, the quantity of the resource that can be extracted is limited and those limits are enforced. Finally, with a public good, the good is provided directly by the government, such as a national park, or is provided indirectly through regulations, such as clear air.

As environmental policy developed into the 1980s, there was an increasing willingness to employ other types of instruments, particularly market-based instruments that used markets or created markets. One approach to pollution reduction using markets is a tax, often called a Pigouvian tax for economist Arthur Cecil Pigou, that is set at the difference between Private Marginal Cost (PMC) and Social Marginal Cost (SMC) (Pigou 2013). A Pigouvian tax corrects a market failure associated with a negative externality where the SMC > PMC such that the PMC + Tax = SMC. Subsidies are another example of a using-markets instrument which rewards desired behavior such as reducing emissions. Examples of subsidies include grants, low-interest loans, and loan guarantees.

Another set of market-based instruments involves creating markets. The notion of creating markets is based on the work of Ronald Coase (Coase 1960). Coase critiqued the notion of externalities and argued that externalities are the result of poorly defined property rights. For example, if a factory emits fumes that impact a nearby laundry by darkening the clothes left out to dry, the externality approach argues that the factory is causing some harm to the laundry and therefore that potential harm should be ameliorated through regulations or taxes. However, a Coasean approach would argue that it's not the case that the factory is harming the laundry, but rather it's a disagreement over who has the property right to use the air, the factory for emitting fumes or the laundry for drying clothes. For Coase, the costs are reciprocal, with the factory imposing a cost on the laundry and the laundry, if it were successful in restricting the emissions of the factory, would be imposing a cost on the factory. But, with externalities the costs are assumed to flow in one direction, from the factory to the nearby community. As noted by Anderson and Libecap (2014), under a Coasean approach "environmental problems arise from *missing markets* rather than from *market failure*" (55, italics in original). Markets are missing because of ill-defined property rights.

An example of a creating-markets approach to environmental policy is an emissions-trading system, such as a cap-and-trade program. Under a cap-and-trade regime, emissions are capped at a certain level and emission permits or allowances are distributed to firms that can then use, bank, or sell the permits. By setting a cap the policy creates scarcity and makes a non-rivalrous public good into something closer to a rivalrous private good, which creates value. In addition, by distributing emission allowances the policy creates a property-right for emissions, which can therefore encourage bargaining.

A final type of policy instrument is to engage the public. A perfectly functioning market has complete information, where both the buyer and seller are perfectly informed about the product. However, information asymmetries often exist and one policy approach is to require information disclosure. For example, the Toxic Release Inventory (TRI) is a publicly available database that discloses toxic chemical releases as well as management practices by industry and government. Disclosure requirements such as the TRI have had an overall positive, but uneven, impact on the environmental performance of corporations (Kraft, Stephan, and Abel 2011).

The Selection of Environmental Policy Instruments

The choice of which type or types of policy instruments to use is both a technical and political process. Often choices are not of one instrument over another, but of the proper mix of instruments. On the technical side, the choice of instrument is usually evaluated on efficiency grounds, with the most efficient instrument being the most favored.

To determine which policy alternative is most efficient, analysts perform a *benefit-cost analysis* (BCA). BCA is a systematic way to consider and compare the trade-offs associated with different policy instruments. In brief, BCA measures in dollar values the benefits and costs of each policy alternative and recommends the option that maximizes efficiency, where efficiency is understood as the maximization of net benefits. When considering total benefits and costs, the maximization of net benefits is the point at which the difference between the benefits and costs is greatest. On the margins, and just as with supply and demand, efficiency occurs when marginal costs (MC) are equal to marginal benefits (MB), $MC = MB$. Apart from efficiency, policy instruments can also be evaluated on their effectiveness, which is defined as benefits being greater than the costs associated with the policy. Benefit-cost analysis is required for executive agency rules that are estimated to have large economic impacts. In addition, some of the information in the policy stream consists of BCA performed by interest groups, academics, and other experts. However, technical considerations such as BCA are not the only things considered in designing environmental policy.

On the political side, instrument choice is a function of the political considerations involved in coalition-building. Political considerations include the reaction of private-sector groups to the potential policy, the desires of environmental groups, public opinion, the concerns of politicians that represent geographic areas, and the requirement to build a supportive coalition among those disparate actors. Policy design choices usually involve a mix of technical and political considerations. In addition, each instrument has some advantages and disadvantages.

Parts of the calculus involved in environmental policy instrument choice include how the problem is defined, the goal of the policy, and the nature of the causal framework. In addition, Eisner (2007) notes that: "It is useful to view the decision over instrument choice as being shaped by three factors: informational constraints, the priority attached to certainty of results, and compatibility with existing regulatory statutes" (16). As discussed above, uncertainty and ambiguity exist regarding the causal framework and these factors act as leading information constraints. Much as market participants may not have perfect information, decision-makers and regulators do not have perfect information either. For policymakers, uncertainty and ambiguity exist around the degree or severity of the problem, the proper instruments, and the impacts of the policy. The uncertainty and ambiguity associated with the policy include the ability of the policy to address the problem as well as the political impacts of particular policy choices and the unintended consequences of a policy. For example, political impacts can include the mobilization of actors in response to a policy change (see Nowlin 2016), and an unintended consequence of the Clean Air Act "grandfather clause" was that it allowed older, dirtier coal plants to be in service longer, so that firms could avoid the costs associated with the New Source Review provisions of the Clean Air Act. Uncertainty can be reduced with data, while ambiguity is addressed through the political process when the "winners" decide on and develop a particular policy.

As noted, uncertainty exists surrounding the impacts the policy, p, will have on outcome Y. The importance placed on the certainty of a particular outcome can influence instrument choice. In general, policy actors have preferences over outcomes,[9] and when desire for certainty is high, it is more likely that a command-and-control environmental regulation will be chosen (Eisner 2007). By requiring a certain performance standard or a certain technology coupled with strict enforcement, command-and-control regulations can all but guarantee a particular result. However, the transactions costs associated with information processing, monitoring, and enforcement to achieve guaranteed results are high. In addition, firms under such regulation may shirk, delay, and litigate, or firms may stop innovating once they reach the regulated outcome, all of which create additional costs. Critiques of command-and-control regulations are based on the costs and inefficiencies associated with those approaches compared with market-based approaches.

Finally, the development of environmental policy is largely path-dependent, meaning that new environmental policy developments are constrained by previous decisions. Therefore, new environmental policies typically fit within the existing regulatory structure of environmental governance. This is particularly true in highly polarized policy areas such as environmental policy, when it is less likely that there will be broad agreement to attempt new policy options or experiments to address problems through legislation. As will be discussed in Chapter 6, the narrowing of the congressional pathway of environmental policymaking due to polarization has meant a shift to executive branch pathways of policymaking, which are more constrained by past choices.

In part to address concerns about costs, environmental regulation has become increasingly flexible since the legislation of the early 1970s such as the Clean Air and Water Acts. Flexibility can be applied to any part of the regulatory structure including the command, the target, the consequences, and the regulator (Bennear and Coglianese 2012), but flexibility in command is particularly important. A flexible command allows the regulated entity multiple ways to reach the desired goal. For example, a performance standard is more flexible than a technology standard because even though a performance standard requires a certain result, it allows firms to determine the most cost-effective way to obtain that result.

The use of market-based instruments such as using and creating markets also adds flexibility to environmental regulations. Some of the early attempts at market-based reforms begin in the mid-to-late 1970s with forms of trading such as the EPA's offsetting, bubbling, and netting programs. Under the offset program initiated by the EPA in 1976, new facilities can be brought online in non-attainment areas if emission reductions occur in other facilities within that region that would "offset" the emissions of the new facility (Andrews 2006). In addition, under the offset program facilities were able to bank reductions below the required level for future use. Both bubbling and netting treat the emissions output of firms as if they come from a single source (Salzman and Thompson Jr 2013). Bubbling imagines a "bubble" covering an entire facility with multiple emissions sources (e.g., smokestacks) such that firms can reach attainment goals by reducing overall emissions of the facility, rather than meeting reduction requirements for each emissions source.[10] Netting allows firms to avoid permit requirements at a facility for a new or modified source, if the emissions increases from the new source can be compensated for by reducing emissions at that same facility from another source such that there is no net increase in emissions. Each of the approaches were a precursor to the Clean Air Act Amendment of 1990 that introduced a cap-and-trade program for sulfur dioxide emissions.

In addition to selection of instruments, questions exist about at which point in the production chain regulation should occur. For example, a simplified causal chain that shows the path from industrial development, to air pollution, to some negative health outcome could be understood as follows:[11]

(A)Planning → (B)Behavior → (C)Output → (D)Outcome

In the above example, (A) *Planning* involves gathering information, determining site location, and other preliminary decisions; (B) *Behavior* refers to the running of the facility; (C) *Output* includes the emissions from the facility, and (D) *Outcome* is what happens as a result of the behavior and outputs of the facility such as decreased air quality, or increased rates of childhood asthma. As noted, policymakers have preferences over outcomes such as increased air quality and decreased rates of asthma, yet the causal framework within any policy design should have some understanding of the causal chain of production to determine what type of instrument should be used and when in the production chain.

To achieve the desired outcome, or at least make the desired outcome more likely, policymakers typically concentrate on the behavior, or the source of pollution, and output, or the point of impact, of facilities. Some of the policy instrument choices available for the behavior stage include technology standards that require the use of specific technologies or incentives to shift to cleaner energy sources such as coal with lower sulfur content. Adopting a technology standard at point B would reduce flexibility in attaining outcome goals, while a performance standard at point B could introduce increased flexibility by allowing facilities to determine the most cost-effective way to achieve the required emissions limits. A host of instruments exists to alter the output of a facility, point C, including the use of markets such as taxes, or creating markets with emissions trading or cap-and-trade programs, or command-and-control style performance standards. Finally, information disclosure instruments could be useful at point A during the initial planning phases of a facility.

From a technical perspective, instruments that improve efficiency, have low transactions costs, and allow flexibility are generally preferred. However, political considerations and a desire for certainty of outcomes can lead to policy instruments that are less efficient, have higher costs, and less flexibility than other policy alternatives.

Implementation Structure

Policy implementation involves turning a policy into action through the application of its instruments and enforcement of its requirements. However, implementation is not simply following a clear set of directions, rather implementation involves a host of policy actors making decisions that jointly impact other policy actors. In addition, policy implementation also involves the making of policy such as when executive agencies create rules.

The implementation structures that are embedded in a policy design outline the organizations that will be tasked with putting the goals of the policy into action (Hall and O'Toole 2000). The number of organizations can vary from one or a few executive agencies to several policy actors across multiple levels of government as well as non-profits, private sector actors, and other stakeholders. As the number and diversity of actors increases, policy implementation becomes less about government and more about governance. Increasingly, as policy instruments have become more flexible, environmental policy has involved collaboration and horizontal networks as opposed to top-down, command-and-control regulations. These shifting dynamics have led to an increase in *collaborative governance*.

Collaborative governance is defined as,

> A governing arrangement where one or more public agencies directly engage non-state stakeholders in a collective decision-making process that is formal, consensus-oriented, and deliberative and that aims to make or implement public policy or manage public programs or assets.
>
> *Ansell and Gash 2008, 544*

A prominent example of collaboration is *negotiated rulemaking*, or "reg-neg." Negotiated rulemaking arose over concerns about the possible adversarial nature of the rulemaking process, and reg-neg was codified in 1990 by the passage of the Negotiated Rulemaking Act. The act encourages, but does not require, agencies to "bring interested parties together to negotiate the text of a proposed rule before that proposed rule is published in the *Federal Register*" (Klyza and Sousa 2013, 196). However, reg-neg has rarely been used and the evidence for its effectiveness over the traditional rulemaking process is, at best, unclear (Coglianese 1997).

There are several reasons for the growth of collaborative governance in environmental policy including: the limited utility of command-and-control regulations; a better understanding of the connections between ecosystems and social systems as well as the inability of existing policy instruments to address those interdependencies; increasing political conflict over environmental issues; and a trend toward efficiency in policy instruments (Gerlak, Heikkila, and Lubell 2013). Given the continuing, and even growing, prominence of each of the conditions that inspired collaborative approaches in policy designs, they are likely to continue to be a feature of environmental policy.

Conclusion

Environmental issues involve a number of collective-action problems that arise when choices made by one impact others. Collective dilemmas are typically addressed by institutions, and the prominent institutions in the United States are markets and states. Markets are structured through property rights that are established and enforced by governments, and when functioning well they provide society with the most efficient mechanism to distribute its resources. However, markets sometimes fail and the market failures associated with externalities, common-pool goods, and public goods are particularly relevant to environmental issues. When market failures occur, governments address those failures through policy.

This chapter presented a framework of environmental policymaking that will be used and developed throughout the book. The framework places information and information processing at the center of environmental policy choices, as environmental policies are the result of changes in information signals coupled with the interaction of actors and institutions within the environmental policymaking system. In addition, the information processing capabilities of individuals and institutions within the environmental policymaking system creates friction that results in a disjointed process of stability and large change.

The utility of this framework was demonstrated through empirical analysis of environmental policymaking that showed environmental policy to be a result of information change, attention, and system components. In addition, the punctuated nature of environmental policy was demonstrated by budgetary changes with regard to environmental issues. The number of environmental policy outputs from each of the macro-institutions was shown to peak in the late 1970s. Finally, environmental policy designs were examined, including the types of policy instruments available to address environmental policy problems. The coming chapters will apply this framework to explore the historical and potential future development of climate policy in the United States.

Notes

1 See Birkland (2016) for more about how public policy is defined.
2 A common critique of systems models and box-modeling is that important processes are confined to a "black box" and the inner-workings of the box are unknown (see Wellstead, Howlett, and Rayner 2015). However, much of the book is spent exploring the workings of the "black box" of the environmental policymaking system.
3 Various terms have been used to described policy subsystems; see McCool (1998) for an overview.
4 This modeling approach is based on Jones and Baumgartner (2005), 227–230.
5 Available from the *Comparative Agendas Project*: www.comparativeagendas.net/.
6 More specific types of indicators will be used to estimate congressional attention to climate change in Chapter 5.
7 Data for both graphs is from the *Comparative Agendas Project*.
8 Data is from the *Comparative Agendas Project*. For public laws the years are 1947–2014, for Supreme Court Cases the years include 1947–2009, and for Executive Orders the years are 1947–2015.
9 Although some policy actors have a preference over particular instruments (see Béland, Howlett, and Mukherjee 2018).
10 The EPA's bubble policy was the subject of *Chevron U.S.A., Inc. v. Natural Resources Defense Council, Inc*, which established the Chevron doctrine.
11 Adapted from Bennear and Coglianese (2012), 585.

References

Anderson, Terry L. 2004. "Donning Coase-Coloured Glasses: A Property Rights View of Natural Resource Economics." *Australian Journal of Agricultural and Resource Economics* 48(3): 445–462.

Anderson, Terry L., and Gary D. Libecap. 2014. *Environmental Markets: A Property Rights Approach*. Cambridge: Cambridge University Press.

Andrews, Richard N.L. 2006. *Managing the Environment, Managing Ourselves: A History of American Environmental Policy*. 2nd ed. New Haven, CT: Yale University Press.

Ansell, Chris, and Alison Gash. 2008. "Collaborative Governance in Theory and Practice." *Journal of Public Administration Research and Theory* 18(4): 543–571.

Baumgartner, Frank R. 2006. "Punctuated Equilibrium Theory and Environmental Policy." In *Punctuated Equilibrium and the Dynamics of US Environmental Policy*, ed. Robert Repetto. New Haven, CT: Yale University Press, 24–46.

Baumgartner, Frank R., and Bryan D. Jones. 1993. *Agendas and Instability in American Politics*. Chicago, IL: University of Chicago Press.

———. 2015. *The Politics of Information: Problem Definition and the Course of Public Policy in America*. Chicago, IL: University of Chicago Press.

Baumgartner, Frank R., Bryan D. Jones, and Peter B. Mortensen. 2018. "Punctuated Equilibrium Theory: Explaining Stability and Change in Public Policymaking." In *Theories of the Policy Process*, eds. Christopher M. Weible and Paul A. Sabatier. New York, NY: Westview Press, 55–102.

Bemelmans-Videc, Marie-Louise, Ray C. Rist, and Evert Oskar Vedung, eds. 2003. *Carrots, Sticks, and Sermons: Policy Instruments and Their Evaluation*. New Brunswick, NJ: Transaction Publishers.

Bennear, Lori S., and Cary Coglianese. 2012. "Flexible Approaches to Environmental Regulation." In *The Oxford Handbook of US Environmental Policy*, Oxford: Oxford University Press, 582–604.

Bertelli, Anthony Michael. 2012. *The Political Economy of Public Sector Governance*. Cambridge: Cambridge University Press.

Béland, Daniel, Michael Howlett, and Ishani Mukherjee. 2018. "Instrument Constituencies and Public Policy-Making: An Introduction." *Policy and Society* 37(1): 1–13.

Birkland, Thomas A. 2016. *An Introduction to the Policy Process: Theories, Concepts, and Models of Public Policy Making*. 4th ed. New York, NY: Routledge.

Breunig, Christian, and Chris Koski. 2006. "Punctuated Equilibria and Budgets in the American States." *Policy Studies Journal* 34(3): 363–379.

Cairney, Paul, and Robert Geyer. 2015. "Introduction." In *Handbook on Complexity and Public Policy*, eds. Robert Geyer and Paul Cairney. Cheltenham: Edward Elgar Publishing Limited, 1–18.

Canes-Wrone, Brandice. 2001. "The President's Legislative Influence from Public Appeals." *American Journal of Political Science* 45(2): 313–329.

Coase, Ronald H. 1960. "The Problem of Social Cost." *Journal of Law & Economics* 3: 1–44.

Coglianese, Cary. 1997. "Assessing Consensus: The Promise and Performance of Negotiated Rulemaking." *Duke Law Journal* 46(6): 1255–1349.

Crawford, Sue E.S., and Elinor Ostrom. 1995. "A Grammar of Institutions." *The American Political Science Review* 89(3): 582–600.

Eisner, Marc Allen. 2007. *Governing the Environment: The Transformation of Environmental Regulation*. Boulder, CO: Lynne Rienner.

Esterling, Kevin M. 2004. *The Political Economy of Expertise: Information and Efficiency in American National Politics*. Ann Arbor, MI: University of Michigan Press.

Fiorino, Daniel J. 2006. *The New Environmental Regulation*. Cambridge, MA: The MIT Press.

Fullerton, Don, and Robert Stavins. 1998. "How Economists See the Environment." *Nature* 395(6701): 433–434.

Gerlak, Andrea K., Tanya Heikkila, and Mark Lubell. 2013. "The Promise and Performance of Collaborative Governance." In *The Oxford Handbook of US Environmental Policy*, eds. Sheldon Kamieniecki and Michael E. Kraft. Oxford: Oxford University Press, 413–436.

Hall, Thad E., and Laurence J. O'Toole. 2000. "Structures for Policy Implementation: An Analysis of National Legislation, 1965–1966 and 1993–1994." *Administration & Society* 31(6): 667–686.

Hanley, Nick, Jason Shogren, and Ben White. 2013. *Introduction to Environmental Economics*. 2nd ed. Oxford: Oxford University Press.

Hardin, Garrett. 1968. "The Tragedy of the Commons." *Science* 162(3859): 1243–1248.

Hodgson, Geoffrey M. 2006. "What Are Institutions?" *Journal of Economic Issues* 40(1): 1–25.

Howell, William G. 2003. *Power Without Persuasion: The Politics of Direct Presidential Action*. Princeton, NJ: Princeton University Press.

Jenkins-Smith, Hank C., Daniel Nohrstedt, Christopher M. Weible, and Karin Ingold. 2018. "The Advocacy Coalition Framework: An Overview of the Research Program." In *Theories of the Policy Process*, eds. Christopher M. Weible and Paul A. Sabatier. New York, NY: Westview Press, 135–172.

Jones, Bryan D., and Frank R. Baumgartner. 2005. *The Politics of Attention: How Government Prioritizes Problems*. Chicago, IL: University of Chicago Press.

Jones, Bryan D., Frank R. Baumgartner, and James L. True. 1998. "Policy Punctuations: US Budget Authority, 1947–1995." *The Journal of Politics* 60(1): 1–33.

Jones, Bryan D., Tracy Sulkin, and Heather A. Larsen. 2003. "Policy Punctuations in American Political Institutions." *The American Political Science Review* 97(1): 151–169.

Jones, Bryan D., László Zalányi, and Péter Érdi. 2014. "An Integrated Theory of Budgetary Politics and Some Empirical Tests: The US National Budget, 1791–2010." *American Journal of Political Science* 58(3): 561–578.

Keohane, Nathaniel O., and Sheila M. Olmstead. 2007. *Markets and the Environment*. 2nd ed. Washington, DC: Island Press.

Kingdon, John W. 2003. *Agendas, Alternatives, and Public Policies*. 2nd ed. New York, NY: Longman.

Klyza, Christopher McGrory, and David Sousa. 2013. *American Environmental Policy: Beyond Gridlock*. Cambridge, MA: MIT Press.

Kraft, Michael E. 2011. *Environmental Policy and Politics*. 5th ed. Boston, MA: Pearson.

Kraft, Michael E., Mark Stephan, and Troy D. Abel. 2011. *Coming Clean: Information Disclosure and Environmental Performance*. Cambridge, MA: The MIT Press.

Krehbiel, Keith. 1991. *Information and Legislative Organization*. Ann Arbor: The University of Michigan Press.

Lovett, John, Shaun Bevan, and Frank R. Baumgartner. 2015. "Popular Presidents Can Affect Congressional Attention, for a Little While." *Policy Studies Journal* 43(1): 22–43.

Lynn, Laurence E., Carolyn J. Heinrich, and Carolyn J. Hill. 2001. *Improving Governance: A New Logic for Empirical Research*. Washington DC: Georgetown University Press.

March, James G., and Johan P. Olsen. 2008. "Elaborating the 'New Institutionalism'." In *The Oxford Handbook of Political Institutions*, eds. R.A.W. Rhodes, Sarah A. Binder, and Bert A. Rockman. Oxford: Oxford University Press, 3–22.

McCool, Daniel. 1998. "The Subsystem Family of Concepts: A Critique and a Proposal." *Political Research Quarterly* 51(2): 551–570.

McGuire, Chad J. 2012. *Environmental Decision-Making in Context: A Toolbox*. Boca Raton, FL: CRC Press.

Mohai, Paul, David Pellow, and J. Timmons Roberts. 2009. "Environmental Justice." *Annual Review of Environment and Resources* 34(1): 405–430.

Monogan, James E., David M. Konisky, and Neal D. Woods. 2017. "Gone with the Wind: Federalism and the Strategic Location of Air Polluters." *American Journal of Political Science* 61(2): 257–270.

Munger, Michael C. 2000. *Analyzing Policy: Choices, Conflicts, and Practices*. New York, NY: W.W. Norton & Company.

Neustadt, Richard E. 1991. *Presidential Power and the Modern Presidents: The Politics of Leadership from Roosevelt to Reagan*. New York, NY: Free Press.

North, Douglass C. 1990. *Institutions, Institutional Change and Economic Performance*. Cambridge: Cambridge University Press.

Nowlin, Matthew C. 2016. "Policy Change, Policy Feedback, and Interest Mobilization: The Politics of Nuclear Waste Management." *Review of Policy Research* 33(1): 51–70.

O'Leary, Rosemary. 2019. "Environmental Policy in the Courts." In *Environmental Policy: New Directions for the Twenty-First Century*, eds. Norman J. Vig and Michael E. Kraft. Thousand Oaks, CA: CQ Press, 144–167.

Ostrom, Elinor. 2005. *Understanding Institutional Diversity*. Princeton, NJ: Princeton University Press.

———. 2010. "Beyond Markets and States: Polycentric Governance of Complex Economic Systems." *American Economic Review* 100: 641–672.

Page, Scott E. 2010. *Diversity and Complexity*. Princeton, NJ: Princeton University Press.

Pigou, Arthur C. 2013. *The Economics of Welfare*. 2013 edition. New York, NY: Palgrave Macmillan.

Sabatier, Paul A., and Hank C. Jenkins-Smith. 1993. *Policy Change and Learning: An Advocacy Coalition Approach*. Boulder, CO: Westview Press.

Salzman, James, and Barton H. Thompson Jr. 2013. *Environmental Law and Policy*. 4th ed. St. Paul, MN: Foundation Press.

Schneider, Anne, and Helen Ingram. 1997. *Policy Design for Democracy*. Lawrence, KS: University of Kansas Press.

Sterner, Thomas, and Jessica Coria. 2012. *Policy Instruments for Environmental and Natural Resource Management*. 2nd ed. New York, NY: Resources for the Future.

Stone, Deborah. 2002. *Policy Paradox: The Art of Political Decision Making*. 2nd ed. New York, NY: W.W. Norton & Co.

The World Bank. 1997. *Five Years After Rio: Innovations in Environmental Policy*. Washington DC: The World Bank.

US Energy Information Administration. 2018. "Electricity in the United States – Energy Explained, Your Guide to Understanding Energy." www.eia.gov/energyexplained/index.php?page=electricity_in_the_united_states.

Vig, Norman J. 2019. "Presidential Powers and Environmental Policy." In *Environmental Policy: New Directions for the Twenty-First Century*, eds. Norman J. Vig and Michael E. Kraft. Thousand Oaks, CA: CQ Press, 88–116.

Villalobos, José D., Justin S. Vaughn, and Julia R. Azari. 2012. "Politics or Policy? How Rhetoric Matters to Presidential Leadership of Congress." *Presidential Studies Quarterly* 42(3): 549–576.

Waldo, Dwight. 2007. *The Administrative State: A Study of the Political Theory of American Public Administration*. New Brunswick, NJ: Transaction Publishers.

Wellstead, Adam, Michael Howlett, and Jeremy Rayner. 2015. "How Useful Is Complexity Theory to Policy Studies? Lessons from the Climate Change Adaptation Literature." In *Handbook on Complexity and Public Policy*, eds. Robert Geyer and Paul Cairney. Cheltenham: Edward Elgar Publishing Limited, 399–413.

Zafonte, Matthew, and Paul A. Sabatier. 1998. "Shared Beliefs and Imposed Interdependencies as Determinants of Ally Networks in Overlapping Subsystems." *Journal of Theoretical Politics* 10(4): 473–505.

3

THE GREEN STATE AND THE CLIMATE CHANGE ERA

Introduction

Environmental policy in the United States has developed into a rather large and complex *green state*. The green state is a subset of the broader administrative state that is organized around institutions, statutes, regulations, and court decisions regarding environmental issues (Klyza and Sousa 2013). It is the *policy infrastructure* that provides both opportunities and constraints for the future development of environmental policy. The green state has developed over time through a process of layering that occurred through several eras, with the policies and institutions developed in one era building on those of the previous era(s).[1] The development of environmental policy through the various eras exhibits *path dependency*, where policy debates and decisions in the previous era inform those of the current era. Often, minority voices in one era become the dominant voice of the next. Given the nature of path dependency in policy development, the green state has become entrenched and difficult to dismantle in the ways in which some policy actors would prefer. Overall, the pattern of environmental policymaking and governance is one of what Klyza and Sousa (2010) term "green drift," where policy moves generally in the direction preferred by environmentalists. The pattern of green drift has occurred even as conservative activists and elected officials have sought to roll back environmental laws and regulations (Layzer 2012a).

The development of the green state is marked by eras where differences are based, in part, on the relationship between the government and the private market. In particular, each era tends to emphasize a particular type of regulatory regime, where a regulatory regime is defined as a "configuration of policies and institutions which structure the relationship between social interests, the state, and economic actors in multiple sectors of the economy" (Eisner 2000, 1). The most consequential era of environmental policy development was the *environmentalism era*, which lasted from about 1962 to 1980 and saw the development of federal policies aimed at addressing environmental issues.

The first era is the *development era*, which lasted most of the 19th century and was defined by geographical expansion and the use of natural resources for economic growth. Generally, there was very little federal government involvement in environmental and natural resource management during the development era. The *conservation era* saw an increase in government activity, which was often focused on the proper management of natural resources. The *environmentalism era* was the shift that laid the foundation for the bulk of the green state. During this time-period the majority of significant environmental laws were passed. The *reform era* saw a shift in focus from building the green state to attempts to deconstruct it. This era also saw a rise in pessimism about how well governments can manage large and complex societal problems. Finally, the current *climate change era* is defined by the problem of global climate change, which is a result of anthropogenic forcing occurring from the use of carbon dioxide and other greenhouse gases. Indeed, scientists have stated that the planet is in a new geological epoch, the Anthropocene, as a result of the impacts of human activity. Climate change impacts, or is impacted by, all the other various environmental issues. The current climate change era is further defined by political polarization and skepticism. The skepticism of the current era includes not just the skepticism of some regarding the science of climate change but also skepticism about the various policy tools that have been relied on in the past to deal with environmental policy issues.

This chapter explores the evolution of environmental policy in the United States. Chapter 2 outlined the theoretical framework as well as the important aspects of environmental policy designs. The framework illustrates the major components of the environmental policymaking process which includes information signals and the environmental policymaking system. In this chapter I examine the development of environmental policy and politics. The environmental policymaking process coupled with the historical development through successive eras of environmental policy shape the future possibilities of climate policy. Finally, I discuss the science and politics surrounding climate change.

Development Era: 1800–1890

The development era was driven by the ethos of growth. It was marked by a young country's expansion to the West. In 1803 the land size of the United States doubled following the Louisiana Purchase, and by 1849 it spanned the coasts after the acquisition of California following the Mexican-American War of 1846–1848. Westward expansion was seen as "Manifest Destiny" with God ordaining the country's growth (Benson and Craig 2017). Another component of Manifest Destiny was the taming of the "wild areas," including the native plants and wildlife as well as bringing western civilization to the indigenous population. The view that humans had domination over nature was prevalent during this period. This entitled us to extract and exploit natural resources for development, with little to no oversight or consideration of the consequences.

Overall, this period was one of economic liberalization, with very little government involvement or regulation. Indeed, what actions the federal government took encouraged continued expansion. The General Survey Act of 1824 provided authority to the federal government to develop transportation routes through roads and canals for military and commercial purposes. This legislation followed from the Supreme Court decision *Gibbons v. Ogden*, also in 1824, which held that the commerce clause gave the federal government power to regulate navigation among that states. Together, these provided the foundation for government involved in transportation and infrastructure development.

Additionally, public land began to be made readily available for development. The Homestead Act of 1862 granted settlers in the West 160 acres of land, largely for farming. It required that settlers farmed the land for five years and made improvements. By 1900 approximately 80 million acres of land had been made available under the act. Along these same lines, mining practices in the West encouraged the extraction of minerals. During and after the California Gold Rush in 1849, the informal practice was that prospectors were allowed to stake mining claims on public lands. Several federal statutes codified these practices, most notably the General Mining Act of 1872 that gave rights to prospectors to stake claims to extract gold, silver, cinnabar, copper, and other valuable deposits. Finally, practices were also put in place to encourage development of timber resources such as the Free Timber Act of 1878 which "allowed residents of western states to cut timber freely on public lands for farming, mining, or other 'domestic purposes'" (Hillstrom 2010, 91).

While the dominant view of the era was one of development and use of natural resources, a movement begin to emerge that sought to recognize that a harmonious relationship should exist between humanity and nature. Most notably, George Perkins Marsh wrote in *Man and Nature* (1864) that, "Man everywhere is a disturbing agent. Wherever he plants his foot, the harmonies of nature are turned to discords." Other prominent preservationist thinkers included Ralph Waldo Emerson, Henry David Thoreau, and John Muir, who went on to found the Sierra Club in 1892. All of these thinkers argued for the intrinsic value of nature. Additionally, others began to worry about the sustainability of development practices as well as the deleterious impact they were having on the environment. These concerns developed into the conservation movement, and lead to the creation by Congress of Yellowstone National Park in 1872. In addition, the Forest Reserve Act of 1891 allowed the president to create forest reserves from public land, permanently withdrawing it from development.

During this era the United States expanded its territory across the continent and became a leading industrial nation. However, the lax regulation that existed during the era provided a tenuous foundation for the emergence of the green state. Indeed, the inherent tension between development and careful management that occurred during this period has shaped the tensions within environmental politics ever since.

Conservation Era: 1890–1962

The Conservation Era saw the rise of concern for the proper management of natural resources. It coincided with the Progressive Era which lasted from about 1890 to 1920. The Progressive Era was marked by changing views of the relationship between the state and the economy, as well as a series of anti-corruption political reforms. In general, the Progressive Era is when the government first sought to address market failures across multiple areas of life, including public lands and natural resources, through conservation practices. *Conservation* is defined as efforts to "limit excesses and encourage both businesses and individuals to use the nation's vast natural resources more carefully through government regulation" (Kline 2011, 61).

The leading voices of the conservation movement were President Teddy Roosevelt and the first head of the Forest Service, Gifford Pinchot. In contrast to the preservationist ideas of John Muir that sought to leave nature alone, conservation sought to manage the use of natural resources, such as forests, to make them sustainable. In his first address to Congress in December of 1901 Theodore Roosevelt stated that:

> Wise forest protection does not mean the withdrawal of forest resources, whether of wood, water, or grass, from contributing their full share to the welfare of the people, but, on the contrary, gives the assurance of larger and more certain supplies. The fundamental idea of forestry is the perpetuation of forests by use. Forest protection is not an end of itself; it is a means to increase and sustain the resources of our country and the industries which depend on them.
>
> *Hillstrom 2010, 178*

As noted by Caulfield (1989), conservation held to three major tenets, with the first being "*Conservation is not the locking up of resources; it is their development and wise use*" (20). This first tenet is very much in line with the notion of conservation standing in opposition to preservation. Conservation sought not to "lock up" natural resources, but rather to develop them in ways that lead to economic growth without overexploitation, whereas preservationists sought to keep nature pristine and untouched.

The second tenet of conservation is "*Conservation is the greatest good, for the greatest number, for the longest time*" (Caulfield 1989, 20–21). For many conservationists, the development and use of natural resources can help to ensure the utilitarian maxim of the "greatest good for the greatest number." However, that maxim is attained through careful public management of resources, not necessarily through a *laissez-faire* approach to the wants of private interests. As Pinchot wrote in his

1910 book *The Fight for Conservation*, "The natural resources must be developed and preserved for the benefit of the many, not just the few." Pinchot goes on to note that, "Conservation means the greatest good to the greatest number for the longest time" (excerpted in Hillstrom 2010, 212).

Finally, the third tenet of conservation is "*The federal public lands belong to all the people*" (Caulfield 1989, 21).[2] The implication of this statement is that the property rights of public lands belong to all and are to be managed by the federal government in the name of the people. This understanding has led to tensions between the federal government and several states in the western United States, as the majority of land management by the federal government is in the western states and Alaska. Currently, 46.4 percent of the land in 11 western states – Arizona, California, Colorado, Idaho, Montana, Nevada, New Mexico, Oregon, Utah, Washington, and Wyoming – is managed by the federal government, largely the Bureau of Land Management (BLM) and the Forest Service (FS) (Vincent, Hanson, and Argueta 2017).

Underlying conservation efforts, as well as the larger progressive era reforms, was a developing reliance on science and expertise to solve public problems. The political reforms of the time sought to eliminate the patronage-and-spoils systems that existed, where employment in the federal government was given to party members and political allies, and replace them with a federal government that employed neutral experts that managed natural resources according to the best available science. As noted by Hays (1959), "Conservation, above all, was a scientific movement, and its role in history arises from the implications of science and technology in the modern society" (2). Under this view, elected officials would develop policies containing goals, and the executive branch agencies would use their expertise to achieve the desired outcome.

Several important pieces of legislation were passed during this time-period including the Forest Service Act (1891), the Lacey Act (1900), the Reclamation Act (1902), the Antiquities Act (1906), the Weeks Act (1911), and the Mineral Leasing Act (1920). Each of these laws established ways for the federal government to become active in the scientific management of land and natural resources.

As the economy grew during the 1920s, environmental issues became less salient and the Progressive Era ethos of an active federal government faded. However, the Great Depression and the election of Franklin Roosevelt lead to a resurgence of demand for government action. As part of the New Deal response to the Great Depression, several public works programs were initiated such as the Grand Coulee Dam in Washington State. Additionally, the Dust Bowl of the 1930s – a result of a severe drought and land mis-management – brought government responses such as the Taylor Grazing Act (1934), which limited livestock grazing on public lands, and the Soil Conservation and Domestic Allotment Act (1936) that incentivizes farmers to limit production and shift to less soil-depleting crops.

The period following World War II saw unprecedented economic growth in the United States. However, the growing economy began to put pressure on natural resources through overuse, pollution, and waste. The results of which led to the environmentalism era.

Environmentalism Era: 1962–1980

The environmentalism era is a period of time in the United States in which concern about the environment and policies to address environmental issues reached an apex. Many of the policies created in the environmentalism era were geared toward managing the potential threats to human health as a result of some of the growing by-products of economic growth, such as pollution, as well as potential over-confidence in science and technology stemming from the conservation era and into the post-war period. The concern about pollution was sparked by several focusing events including the publication of *Silent Spring* in 1962.

While no single event is responsible for the rise of public attention of environmental issues that began in the early 1960s, the publication of *Silent Spring* by Rachel Carson in 1962 is certainly a watershed moment. Carson, an ecologist and researcher in the Fish and Wildlife Service, was one of the first to give voice to concerns over the use of DDT and other pesticides, and the potential negative impacts that use may have on wildlife, humans, and the ecosystem as a whole. One of the underlying components of Carson's argument was a concern about over-reliance on science and technology in post-World War II society, without regard to the potential harmful effects. As Carson argued,

> I contend, furthermore, that we have allowed these chemicals to be used with little or no advance investigation of their effect on soil, water, wildlife, and man himself. Future generations are unlikely to condone our lack of prudent concern for the integrity of the natural world that supports all life.
>
> *Carson 1962, 12*

Following the publication of *Silent Spring,* a social movement that in some ways mirrored the civil-rights movement and the anti-Vietnam War movement occurring at the time began to grow around concern for the environment. The nascent environmental movement was spurred on by several highly visible ecological disasters including: visible smog in several major cities; the Santa Barbara, California oil spill in 1969; the Cuyahoga River fire in Ohio also in 1969; and the Love Canal incident that occurred in the late 1970s, where citizens of the Love Canal neighborhood in Niagara Falls, NY became ill after exposure to toxic waste that had been dumped in the area throughout the late 1940s and early 1950s. Apart from those disasters, the publication of the *Earthrise* photograph in 1968, taken by the crew of Apollo 8 while orbiting the moon, was the first color photograph of the planet and it worked to galvanize the growing levels of concern for the environment.

The events of the 1960s paved the way for the *environmental decade* of the 1970s. The first *Earth Day*, modeled after the teach-ins developed by those protesting the

Vietnam War, occurred on April 22, 1970. The Earth Day teach-ins were designed to provide information to advocates about environmental issues. Senator Gaylord Nelson of Wisconsin, a long-time advocate and policy entrepreneur for environmental issues, is credited with developing Earth Day and envisioned it as a way to move environmental issues onto the national policymaking agenda. As noted by Webber (2008), "Nelson raised the funds for the first Earth Day, hired a director to begin organizing the event, and wrote letters to all 50 governors and the mayors of major cities asking them to issue Earth Day proclamations" (318). An estimated 20 million Americans participated in Earth Day events across the country, and Earth Day has been recognized on April 22 for each subsequent year.

During the period of the early 1970s, enhancing environmental protections was a goal of many elected officials from both political parties, even conservative Senator Barry Goldwater (R–AZ) (Drake 2010). In his 1970 State of the Union address, President Nixon stated that:

> Restoring nature to its natural state is a cause beyond party and beyond factions. It has become a common cause of all the people in this country. It is the cause of particular concern to young Americans because they more than we will reap the grim consequences of our failure to act on the programs which are needed now if we are to prevent disaster later – clean air, clean water, open spaces. These should once again be the birthright of every American. If we act now they can.
>
> *quoted in Layzer 2012b, 36*

Nixon and Congress followed those words with action that included the creation of the Environmental Protection Agency in 1970. In July 1970, Nixon submitted to Congress Reorganization Plan No. 3, which sought to centralize executive authority for environmental issues within one agency as opposed to having that authority dispersed across several different agencies. The EPA was officially established on December 4, 1970.

Apart from the establishment of the EPA, several major pieces of legislation were passed between 1962 and 1980 that were aimed at addressing environmental issues such as air pollution, water pollution, land use, hazardous waste, and biodiversity. The majority of legislation that emerged in the environmentalism era was based on the idea that emerged from the conservation era that environmental problems could be addressed through expertise and uniform regulations administered by executive branch agencies, which are separate from the electoral institutions (Fiorino 2006). In addition, most of the legislation from this period featured command-and-control type policy instruments. Table 3.1 illustrates the major environmental laws enacted during the environmentalism era.

One of the early major pieces of environmental legislation was the National Environmental Protection Act (NEPA) of 1969. NEPA created the Council on Environmental Quality, within the Executive Office of the President, to advise the

TABLE 3.1 Major Environmental Laws, 1962–1980

Law	Year
Clean Air Act	1963
Land and Water Conservation Fund	1964
Wilderness Act	1964
Solid Waste Disposal Act	1965
Water Quality Act	1965
Clean Water Restoration Act	1966
Air Quality Act	1967
National Trail Systems Act	1968
Wild and Scenic Rivers Act	1968
National Environmental Policy Act	1969
Clean Air Act Amendments	1970
Resources Recovery Act	1970
Water Quality Improvement Act	1970
Coastal Zone Management Act	1972
Federal Environmental Pesticide Control Act	1972
Federal Water Pollution Control Act Amendments	1972
Marine Mammal Protection Act	1972
Marine Protection, Research, and Sanctuaries Act	1972
Endangered Species Act	1973
Land Use Policy Act	1974
Safe Drinking Water Act	1974
Strip Mining Act	1974
Federal Land Policy and Management Act	1976
Fisheries Conservation and Management Act	1976
National Forest Management Act	1976
Resource Conservation and Recovery Act	1976
Toxic Substances Control Act	1976
Clean Air Act Amendments	1977
Clean Water Act	1977
Federal Water Pollution Control Act Amendments	1977
Surface Mining Control and Reclamation Act	1977
Environmental Pesticide Control Act Amendments	1978
National Parks and Recreation Act	1978
Public Utility Regulatory Policies Act	1978
Alaska Lands Act	1980
Comprehensive Environmental Response, Compensation, and Liability Act	1980

Laws and years taken from Lester (1989, 2), Klyza and Sousa (2013, 33), and Vig and Kraft (2019, 403–411)

president, coordinate with agencies, and develop initiatives aimed at addressing environmental issues. In addition, NEPA also requires agencies to produce *environmental assessments* and *environmental impact statements* to examine the potential impacts on the environment of federal actions.

Much of the concern surrounding environmental issues dealt with air quality and pollution. This is due, in part, to the fact some air pollution (e.g., smog) is clearly visible and is therefore likely to raise public concern. The original Clean Air Act (CAA), passed in 1963, created the first federal program, housed in the then US Public Health Service, to conduct research on effective monitoring and reduction of air pollution. However, the CAA of 1963 was deemed to be inadequate and was amended in 1970.

The Clean Air Act Amendment of 1970 required the federal government as well as state governments to regulate emissions from stationary (industry) and mobile (vehicle) sources. The CAA established a set of *National Ambient Air Quality Standards* (NAAQS) for six *criteria air pollutants* including ozone, carbon monoxide, sulfur dioxide, particulate matter, lead (which was added in 1977), and nitrogen dioxide. These standards are set by the EPA, "at a level that must 'protect public health' with an 'adequate measure of safety'" (Salzman and Thompson Jr 2013, 115). The courts have allowed the EPA to determine what constituents an "adequate measure of safety."

The CAA was later amended in both 1977 and 1990. The 1977 amendment was largely intended to strengthen the structure of the 1970 CAA. For example, the amendment required the EPA to review the NAAQS every five years. The 1990 amendment established a market-based cap-and-trade system for sulfur dioxide emissions to reduce acid rain. Under the cap-and trade-system, the total annual amount of sulfur dioxide emissions was capped, and plants were issued allowances which could be used or traded. Overall, there has been a marked decline of major air pollutants, which indicates that the regulatory policies of the environmentalism era were largely successful in reducing air pollution (Kraft 2011; Sunstein 2002; US Environmental Protection Agency 2011).

The Cuyahoga River fire of 1969 brought the issue of water contamination to the attention of the public and policymakers in a dramatic way. Although that river had caught fire several times previously, the fire of 1969 occurred at a time of rising concern for the environment, and it helped to increase support for federal legislation to address water pollution.

Water pollution can come from *point sources* that release pollution directly into a waterway. However, there are also *indirect sources* that don't release pollutants directly into the waterway but rather through the sewage system. Finally, *nonpoint source* pollution occurs as a result of rain or snow that washes contaminants such as pesticides, motor oil, or mine tailings into a waterway. The Federal Water Pollution Control Act, also known as the Clean Water Act of 1972 (CWA), was established to address each of these potential sets of pollutants. The CWA set the ambitious goal of eliminating and preventing the discharge of all pollutants from the nation's waterways. Despite the nearly impossible goals of the CWA, it passed Congress by wide margins in both the House and the Senate. The law was vetoed by President Nixon; however, his veto was overridden and the CWA became law.

Despite the goal of eliminating all pollutants, the CWA mostly regulated point-source pollution, while requiring states to develop plans to reduce nonpoint-source pollution. Unlike with air pollution, the impacts of policies on water quality is not as certain.

Most of the policies developed in the environmentalism era were based on a top-down, command-and-control type of regulation. Command-and-control regulation typically contains little to no flexibility and includes a performance standard – requiring the attainment of a specific goal – and/or a technology standard, which requires that a particular type of equipment be used to achieve the desired goals. For example, the CAA development of NAAQS contained uniform standards across the country, despite the fact that the sources and consequences of pollution often vary by region. In addition, the CAA of 1977 encouraged the use of technology, "scrubbers," to reduce emissions of SO_2 and NO_x, as opposed to building taller smokestacks to disperse emissions higher in the atmosphere and farther from the local area.

The environmentalism era saw a prolific growth in the number as well as the goals of legislation aimed at addressing pollution and safeguarding natural resources. This golden-era period laid the groundwork for the development of the green state, which is the intricate web of legislation, rules and regulations, and court decisions that constitutes the current environmental policy regime. However, even at the time there were undercurrents of opposition to the growing green state, even as much of the legislation drew broad bipartisan support.

One of the early signs of opposition came from the business community which was concerned about the costs associated with the new regulations being put in place. Indeed, in some instances private interests were successful in delaying implementation of the Clean Air Act, such as when the automobile industry was able to push back deadlines for meeting new emissions controls.

A second strand of opposition was the *Sagebrush Rebellion*, which grew in the late 1970s in several western states as a result of the dissatisfaction of cattle ranchers with land management policies and grazing restrictions. In large part, the Sagebrush Rebellion was in response to the Federal Land Policy and Management Act of 1976, which tightened federal control over land in the western states. The Sagebrush Rebellion advocated for federal land in the West to be given over to the states to manage.

The voices of opposition became dominant following the election of Ronald Reagan in 1980. Reagan ran on a platform of deregulation, and he also explicitly supported the Sagebrush Rebellion stating that, "I happen to be one who cheers on and supports the 'Sagebrush Rebellion'" (Bump 2016). With the energy crisis of the 1970s and the perceived overreach of the environmental movement, Reagan's message of deregulation found support among private interests and the public. Once in office, Reagan made political appointments to Interior and the EPA that shared his goals of regulatory rollback. Reagan was ultimately not completely successful in dismantling the green state, yet several reforms were initiated during his presidency that continue to shape how environmental policy choices are made. In addition, the reform era saw the beginnings of partisan polarization regarding environmental issues.

Reform Era: 1980–2000

According to Mazmanian and Kraft (1999), the environmental movement contains three separate *environmental epochs*, with each epoch containing a distinct understanding of and approach to environmental problems. The first environmental epoch was defined as "Regulating for environmental protection" and is dated from 1970 to 1990. The first environmental epoch largely overlaps with the environmentalism era presented here, which involved an increased federal government presence in environmental issues, largely through command-and-control regulation.

The second epoch was termed, "Efficiency-based regulatory reform and flexibility" and lasted from 1980 into the 1990s (Mazmanian and Kraft 1999). As noted, Reagan came to the presidency in 1981 with a desire to reform and rollback many federal regulations. To accomplish this, Reagan appointed sympathetic agency heads, centralized rulemaking authority within the Executive Office of the President by requiring the Office of Management and Budget to review significant regulations, and by requiring Regulatory Impact Analysis that included benefit-cost analysis be performed on proposed regulations that would have significant economic impacts. Executive Order 12291, issued by President Reagan in 1981, stated that, "Regulatory action shall not be undertaken unless the potential benefits to society for the regulation outweigh the potential costs to society" and that "Regulatory objectives shall be chosen to maximize the net benefits to society" (Reagan 1981).

In 1981, Reagan appointed Anne Gorsuch, the mother of later Supreme Court justice Neil Gorsuch, as EPA administrator. Like Reagan, Gorsuch was a strong conservative who sought to curtail the activities of the agency she was heading. As noted by Hillstrom (2010), "During Gorsuch's twenty-two months at the EPA, enforcement referrals to the Justice Department were cut in half, the agency's budget was cut by more than 20 percent, and the morale of rank-and-file staff plummeted" (478). In addition, she hired as advisors individuals from many of the industries that the EPA is charged with regulating. Even though she shared the goals of President Reagan, Gorsuch was forced to resign as EPA director in March 1983 following a series of scandals involving the mismanagement of money dedicated to Superfund.

Reagan appointed another conservative, James Watt, to head the Department of the Interior. Like Gorsuch at EPA, Watt had a history of conservative activism and came to the Interior Department as a devotee of the Sagebrush Rebellion, and was committed to encouraging development on public lands. During his tenure, Watt leased over a billion tons of coal on federal land, at what was termed in a 1983 House report "fire sale prices" (Reuters 1983). However, Watt was fired by the Reagan administration in 1983 after making controversial statements about members of a coal-advisory panel.[3]

Perhaps as a result of the controversies that surrounded two high-profile Reagan appointees, or because of the nature of mobilization and counter-mobilization in politics, the early Reagan-era environmental reforms started to produce a backlash of their own. For example, public concern and support for government spending on the environment begin to increase; environmental interest groups saw increases in members and financial support; and a number of local groups developed that were concerned about environmental hazards in their own communities.

Despite Reagan's commitment to rolling back environmental regulations, several important pieces of environmental legislation were passed that reinforced or even strengthened the green state during the Reagan presidency. These included the Resource Conservation and Recovery Act Amendments of 1984, the Safe Drinking Water Act of 1986, the Superfund Amendments and Reauthorization Act of 1986, and the Clean Water Act Amendments of 1987. In addition, Reagan supported the Montreal Protocol on Substances that Deplete the Ozone Layer, which is an international treaty that committed the United States to reducing the use of chlorofluorocarbons in refrigerators, air-conditioners, and hairspray. The Montreal Protocol has largely been successful in protecting the ozone layer – a layer of ozone in the stratosphere that absorbs solar radiation – and is seen as a model of international cooperation to address an environmental issue. When signing the treaty in 1988, Reagan issued a statement that concluded,

> The Montreal protocol is a model of cooperation. It is a product of the recognition and international consensus that ozone depletion is a global problem, both in terms of its causes and its effects. The protocol is the result of an extraordinary process of scientific study, negotiations among representatives of the business and environmental communities, and international diplomacy. It is a monumental achievement.
>
> *Reagan 1988*

Several lasting impacts on environmental policymaking resulted from the Reagan presidency and the broader reform era. The first involves a shift away from an exclusive focus on command-and-control regulations to address environmental problems and towards market-based approaches. Market-based regulations allow more flexibility in the achievement of environmental policy goals by attempting to influence or create markets as opposed to top-down, performance and/or technology standards.

As discussed in Chapter 2, the drift towards market-based approaches such as EPA's offsets policy began in the 1970s, although they received a boost with the election of Reagan. But it was not just conservatives that saw the benefits of moving away from a strict reliance on command-and-control regulation. Writing in *The Wall Street Journal* in 1986, Fred Krupp, the new executive director of the environmental interest group *Environmental Defense Fund* (EDF), stated that a "third stage of environmental activism is emerging" (Krupp 1986). Krupp noted that the first stage began with Theodore Roosevelt and conservation, and the second began with Rachel Carson and *Silent Spring*. The third stage that Krupp saw emerging is

> one that is not satisfied with the precast role of opponent to environmental abuses. Its practitioners recognize that, behind the waste dumps and dams and power plants and pesticides that threaten major environmental harm, there are nearly always legitimate social needs – and that long-term solutions lie in finding alternative ways to meet those underlying needs.
>
> *Krupp 1986*

Under Krupp's leadership, the EDF was an early proponent of cap-and-trade and other market-based approaches to acid rain and climate change (Pooley 2010). The third stage that Krupp saw emerging largely came to fruition in the ways that the Reagan, H.W. Bush, Clinton, W. Bush, and Obama administrations approached environmental problems. Each administration favored, to varying degrees, the use of policy instruments other than command-and-control regulations to address environmental problems.

Another environmental policy legacy from this time-period is the growth of the administrative presidency, particularly with regard to overseeing the rulemaking process of the various executive agencies. Following Reagan, each subsequent president, including Democrats Clinton and Obama, have required the Office of Information and Regulatory Affairs (OIRA) within the Office of Management and Budget (OMB) to review certain regulations before they are proposed and finalized. Part of this review includes benefit-cost analysis and instructions to only promulgate rules where benefits exceeds costs.

George H.W. Bush served as Reagan's vice president, and was elected to succeed him as president in 1988. During the presidential campaign, Bush noted that he would be an "environmental president" (Vig 2019, 94). The largest domestic environmental accomplishment of the H.W. Bush presidency was the Clean Air Act Amendments of 1990. Bush supported and signed the CAA of 1990, which was aimed at addressing the problem of acid rain. Acid rain – precipitation in the atmosphere that has become acidic from mixing with SO_2 and NO_x – can negatively impact forests, soil, and waterways. The CAA of 1990 adopted a market-based, cap-and-trade program to reduce emissions of SO_2 and NO_x, largely from coal-fired power plants. A cap-and-trade program sets a limit, a cap, on overall emissions and issues tradable emission permits to utility companies. Companies that fall under the cap may sell or bank their permits, and companies over the cap can buy emission permits from other utilities. The program is largely seen as successful in reducing overall emissions of both SO_2 and NO_x (Keohane 2009;

Layzer 2012b; Stavins 1998). Despite its seeming success, the CAA of 1990 is the last major piece of environmental legislation passed in the United States.

The election of Clinton and Gore in 1992 brought hope to environmentalists of a resurgence in attention to environmental issues. Gore, as a senator from Tennessee, had long been a policy entrepreneur on environmental issues, and had written a best-selling book, published in June 1992, about the environment titled *Earth in the Balance: Ecology and the Human Spirit*. One of the first initiatives of the Clinton administration was a BTU (British thermal unit) tax. The BTU tax would have placed a tax on energy sources based on their heat content. A British thermal unit is the amount of heat needed to raise the temperature of a pound of water by 1°F. However, the BTU tax proved to be unpopular among the public as well as members of Congress from both parties. Ultimately, it was dropped in favor of an increase in the gas tax that was part of the Omnibus Budget Reconciliation Act of 1993.

President Clinton was certainly more concerned about environmental issues than Reagan or H.W. Bush, yet at the same time he was also interested in government reforms that could increase efficiency and move beyond the command-and-control regulations of the environmentalism era. In 1993, Clinton launched the National Performance Review (NPR) and placed Vice President Gore in charge. In announcing NPR Clinton stated,

> Our goal is to make the entire federal government both less expensive and more efficient, and to change the culture of our national bureaucracy away from complacency and entitlement toward initiative and empowerment. We intend to redesign, to reinvent, to reinvigorate the entire national government.
>
> *Gore 1993, 1*

In line with the goal of reinventing government, Clinton issued Executive Order 12866, which built on Reagan's EO 12291, and called for benefit-cost analysis when considering significant rules. In addition, EO 12866 called for the use of flexible performance standards, or "performance objectives" rather than "specifying the behavior or manner of compliance" (Clinton 1993).

The 1994 mid-term elections gave the Republicans a majority in both chambers of Congress, which was the first time since World War II that Republicans held the majority in the House of Representatives. The Republicans elected to Congress in 1994 were, broadly speaking, more conservative than previous congressional Republicans, particularly those elected in the House. As a result, the period of the early 1990s marked a shift in polarization on a host of issues, with Republicans pushing the skepticism-of-government rhetoric of Reagan even further. However, at least some of that skepticism was shared by President Clinton, who stated in his 1996 State of the Union address that, "The era of big government is over." But the early 1990s period crystallized partisan polarization across a host of policy issues including environmental issues, and the polarization of partisan elites on the environment began to extend to the public during this period (McCright, Xiao, and Dunlap 2014).

The issue of climate change began to rise on the policy agenda in the United States at the end of the environmentalism era and into the reform era, reaching an early crescendo in 1988, which was at that time the warmest year on record. By the late 1990s, and with the partisan debate over the Kyoto Protocol, climate change became polarized among party elites as well as the public (Krosnick, Holbrook, and Visser 2000). In addition, from this point forward climate change became the overriding environmental issue. The next section examines both the science and politics of climate change.

The Climate Change Era

The US president receives a report from a science advisory board that states:

> Through his worldwide industrial civilization, Man is unwittingly conducting a vast geophysical experiment. Within a few generations he is burning the fossil fuels that slowly accumulated in the earth over the past 500 million years … By the year 2000 the increase in CO_2 will be close to 25%. This may be sufficient to produce measurable and perhaps marked changes in climate, and will almost certainly cause significant changes in the temperature and other properties of the stratosphere … The climatic changes that may be produced by the increased CO_2 content could be deleterious from the point of view of human beings.

The year was 1965 and the president that received the report was Lyndon Johnson (The Environmental Pollution Panel 1965, 126–127). The lead author of the report was Roger Revelle, who Al Gore would later credit as the person that introduced him to the greenhouse effect and climate change when Gore was Revelle's student at Harvard. Since the time of the report, the growth rate of CO_2 has nearly quadrupled (Blunden, Arndt, and Hartfield 2018). As the 1965 report indicates, the potential negative impacts of climate change have been known by elected officials for over 50 years; however, the scientific basis of climate change has been understood for much longer.

The Science of Climate Change

The scientific underpinning of climate change is the *greenhouse effect*. The sun radiates energy to the Earth and much of that energy is reflected back into space. However, through the greenhouse effect, several greenhouse gases in the atmosphere trap some of the sun's energy, allowing the Earth to warm. The greenhouse effect was first posited by physicist Joseph Fourier in the 1820s, and was demonstrated empirically by John Tyndall in 1859 (see Tyndall 1861). In 1896, Svante Arrhenius found that change in CO_2 levels in the atmosphere would impact the overall temperature of the Earth (Arrhenius 1896).

To better understand climate change, it is important to define a few terms that are often conflated in political rhetoric, including climate, climate change, and global warming. According to the Intergovernmental Panel on Climate Change (IPCC) *climate* is defined as:

> the average weather, or more rigorously, as the statistical description in terms of the mean and variability of relevant quantities over a period of time ranging from months to thousands or millions of years. The classical period for averaging these variables is 30 years, as defined by the World Meteorological Organization. The relevant quantities are most often surface variables such as temperature, precipitation, and wind.
>
> *Intergovernmental Panel on Climate Change 2014*

Climate is defined as the average weather over a period of time, typically 30 years, although climate change and weather are often conflated by the elected officials and the public. Indeed, local weather conditions can impact how the public thinks about climate change (see Egan and Mullin 2012; Borick and Rabe 2014; Lo and Jim 2015). Elected officials such as California Democratic governor Jerry Brown and Senator James Inhofe (R–OK) – who (in)famously brought a snowball to the Senate floor to show that climate change isn't happening – point to specific weather events as evidence for (or against) climate change. However, even as attribution science advances, it is important to note that climate and weather are not the same and short-term fluctuations of localized weather conditions are not necessarily indicative of climate change.

According to the US Environmental Protection Agency, *climate change* refers to "any substantial change in measures of climate (such as temperature or precipitation) lasting for an extended period (decades or longer)" (US Environmental Protection Agency 2016, 3). The IPCC defines climate change as "a change in the state of the climate that can be identified (e.g., by using statistical tests) by changes in the mean and/or the variability of its properties, and that persists for an extended period, typically decades or longer" (Intergovernmental Panel on Climate Change 2014). Therefore, climate change can be understood as changes in the average weather that last for an extended period of time.

The terms "climate change" and "global warming" are often used as synonyms, although they do have distinct meanings. *Global warming* is the "average increase in the temperature of the atmosphere near the Earth's surface" (US Environmental Protection Agency 2016, 3). Scientists have noted that the average temperature of the Earth has increased about 0.8° Celsius (1.4°F) since 1900 (National Academy of Sciences and the Royal Society 2014). Figure 3.1 shows the annual global land and sea temperature anomalies from 1880 to 2017, in Celsius, relative to the

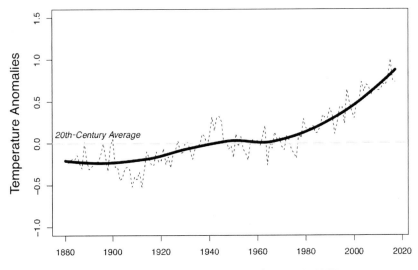

FIGURE 3.1 Global land and sea temperature anomalies, 1880–2017

20th-century average of temperature anomalies.[4] As shown, the record of observed temperature anomalies indicates an increasingly warmer planet.

Figure 3.1 starkly illustrates evidence for global warming, which as noted refers to the observed increases in the average temperature of the Earth. Climate change refers to changes in multiple measures of climate, not just temperature. Yet much of the focus of scientists is on increased temperatures because that is the principal driver of many other changes (Dessler and Parson 2010).

As noted, the scientific understanding of climate change is based on the understanding of the greenhouse effect, where heat-trapping gases in the atmosphere radiate some of the sun's energy back to the planet. The greenhouse effect involves *climate forcing*, which "refers to a change in the Earth's energy balance, leading to either a warming or cooling effect over time" (US Environmental Protection Agency 2016, 7). Positive climate forcing increases the temperature of the Earth, whereas negative forcing decreases it. The bulk of Earth's atmosphere, about 96–99 percent, does not contain any greenhouse gases but rather contains oxygen, nitrogen, and argon (Dessler and Parson 2010). The remaining parts of the atmosphere are made up of the greenhouse gases including water vapor (H_2O), carbon dioxide (CO_2), methane (CH_4), nitrous oxide (N_2O), and several fluorinated gases such as hydrofluorocarbons, perfluorocarbons, and sulfur hexafluoride.

Of all the greenhouse gases, water vapor accounts for roughly two-thirds of the greenhouse effect. Water vapor, together with oxygen, nitrogen, and argon, constitute roughly 99.95 percent of the atmosphere. However, the remaining greenhouse gases play a vital role in regulating the Earth's temperature and atmospheric concentrations of each have increased, with CO_2 being the most notable, as a result of human activity.

In the 20th century, scientists developed a more sophisticated understanding of the greenhouse effect and the potential for human-caused temperature changes. Papers by G.S. Callendar argued that CO_2 emissions from fossil fuels will likely increase average temperatures (Callendar 1938, 1949). In 1956 Gilbert Plass published *The Carbon Dioxide Theory of Climatic Change*, which posited that the Earth's surface temperature increases in response to increases in atmospheric CO_2 (Plass 1956). However, Roger Revelle and his colleague Hans Suess found that the Earth's oceans absorbed much of the excess heat produced by fossil fuel use (Revelle and Suess 1957). In the late 1950s, Charles Keeling, with the Scripps Institution of Oceanography, began taking detailed measurements of the atmospheric concentrations of CO_2 at the Mauna Loa Observatory on the island of Hawaii. In a paper published in 1960 Keeling noted that the observations showed that, with regard to CO_2 in the atmosphere, "the degree of variability is smaller and the variations are more systematic than previously believed" (Keeling 1960, 200).

CO_2 is naturally occurring, but the large observed increase in atmospheric CO_2 has occurred as humans industrialized and begun increasingly using carbon from fossilized plant and animal material to produce energy. Deforestation and the burning of fossil fuels that include oil, natural gas, and coal, have led CO_2 levels to exceed an average of 400 parts-per-million (ppm) – meaning 400 molecules of CO_2 per 1 million molecules of dry air – a level not seen in at least 800,000 years (Intergovernmental Panel on Climate Change 2013). Figure 3.2 shows the concentration of CO_2 in the atmosphere during the last 800,000 years, where negative values indicate the years before the common era.

The historical data used in Figure 3.2 comes from ice-core data, which is a common proxy used to measure historic atmospheric conditions (see Mann, Bradley, and Hughes 1998). Ice cores trap pockets of air which scientists are able to use to estimate historical temperatures and CO_2 levels. The more recent data comes from multiple air monitoring sites placed around the world.[5]

The warming of the Earth as a result of human-produced CO_2 emissions is evidenced by several indicators. Each of the empirically measured indicators discussed below is moving in the direction expected if global warming was occurring.

Average global temperature: as discussed above, there is substantial evidence that the average temperature of the Earth has increased. This evidence is gained through instrument measures of land and sea-surface temperatures that have been collected since the late 1880s. The global average temperature increased 1.2°F (0.7°C) from 1986 to 2016 relative to 1901 through 1961. In addition, 16 of the 17 hottest years on record occurred between 2001 and 2016 (US Global Change Research Program 2017). 2017 was the second (according to NASA), or third (according to

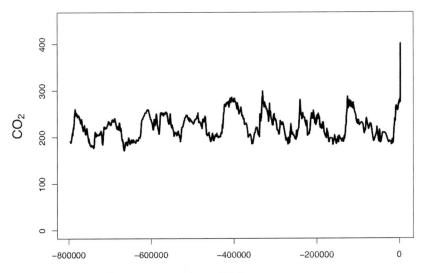

FIGURE 3.2 Atmospheric concentrations of CO_2

NOAA) hottest year since the mid-to-late 1800s, behind only 2016 and 2015 (Blunden, Arndt, and Hartfield 2018).

Sea level: the Global Mean Sea Level (GMSL) has risen about 7–8 inches since 1900, which is a faster rate of increase than any century in the past 2,800 years (US Global Change Research Program 2017). In addition, nearly half of that increase, about 3 inches, has occurred since 1993 (Chen et al. 2017). Sea-level rise occurs as a result of melting land ice and thermal expansion, where warmer oceans occupy more space. From the mid-1990s to the early 2010s, there was a six-fold increase in the contribution of melting land ice to sea-level rise, largely from the Greenland and Antarctic ice sheets (Bamber et al. 2018).

Ocean heat content: much of the warming that has occurred, an estimated 90 percent, has been absorbed by the ocean (Intergovernmental Panel on Climate Change 2013). The ocean surface temperature has increased by about 1.3°F (0.7°C) during the 20th century (US Global Change Research Program 2017), with an estimated increase of 0.302°F since 1969 (Levitus et al. 2009).

Sea ice: overall, the amount of sea ice has been decreasing, although not in a uniform manner. In the Arctic, since 1979 the sea extent has decreased at an annual average rate of 3.5 percent to 4.1 percent per decade (Intergovernmental Panel on Climate Change 2013; US Global Change Research Program 2017). In the summer of 2018, some of the oldest ice in the Arctic began to break-up for the first time on record (Watts 2018). Since 1979, sea ice has increased in some parts of Antarctica by about

1.7 percent per decade, although in 2017 winter-time maximum sea ice extent reached its second-lowest recorded amount ("Antarctic Sea Ice Shrinks for Second-Straight Year" 2018).

Glacier record: glaciers have been in retreat in multiple areas around the world, including the Alps, Andes, Himalayas, Rockies, Alaska, and Africa, as a result of human-induced climate change (Roe, Baker, and Herla 2017).

Scientists agree that the observed changes in climate are a direct result of human activity. As noted by the US Environmental Protection Agency (2016), "Natural factors have caused the climate to change during previous periods of the Earth's history, but human activities are the primary cause of the changes that are being observed now" (3). It is estimated that the *likely*[6] anthropogenic contribution to the observed temperature increases is between 93 and 123 percent (US Global Change Research Program 2017). The estimates extend beyond 100 percent because the Earth's temperature would likely be slightly cooler absent human influence.

Notions of the scientific consensus regarding climate change are politically controversial, although the evidence clearly points to the fact that climate scientists agree about the anthropogenic causes of climate change (see Oreskes 2004; Anderegg et al. 2010; Bolsen, Druckman, and Cook 2015; Cook et al. 2013; Doran and Zimmerman 2009; Farnsworth and Lichter 2012; Lichter, Farnsworth, and Rolfe-Redding 2015; Rosenberg et al. 2010; Verheggen et al. 2014). A recent study by Cook et al. (2016) examined several studies that illustrate the agreement of scientists regarding climate change. Using several measures, including surveys of scientists and examinations of the peer-reviewed climate science literature, Cook et al. (2016) found that 90 to 100 percent of climate scientists agree that human-caused climate change is occurring. In addition, Cook et al. (2016) found that the scientists who are skeptical regarding anthropogenic climate change tend not to be climate scientists but have expertise in other areas.

There are several pieces of evidence that indicate that climate change is a result of anthropogenic forcing rather than natural processes. As noted, current levels of CO_2 are averaging above 400ppm, the highest in 800,000 years as indicated by ice-core data (US Global Change Research Program 2017). In addition, the levels of CO_2 have risen at a faster rate in the last 200 years, when the industrial revolution began, than the previous 800,000. Also, analysis of carbon isotopes in the atmosphere indicates that the post-industrial age increase of CO_2 comes from the burning of fossil fuels, rather than natural forces. One indication is the declining ratio of the ^{14}C isotope in the atmosphere. ^{14}C has a short half-life and is not present in fossil fuel sources, therefore a lower ratio of ^{14}C to other carbon isotopes is evidence that the increase in atmospheric CO_2 is from fossil fuels (Levin and Hesshaimer 2000). In addition, plants have a lower ratio of ^{13}C to ^{12}C than exists in the atmosphere because plants take up more ^{12}C in photosynthesis than the heavier ^{13}C isotope. In the last 200 years the $^{13}C/^{12}C$ ratio in the atmosphere has been falling, and the increase in ^{12}C, indicates that the increased atmospheric CO_2 comes from the burning of fossilized CO_2 from plants (Ghosh and Brand 2003).

The anthropogenic impacts (I) on the environment are thought to be a result of population (P), affluence (A), and technology (T) such that $I = P \star A \star T$. This formulation is known as the Kaya Identity and/or the IPAT model (Kaya and Yokobori 1998; Rosa et al. 2015). The IPAT model is multiplicative, meaning that the impact of one component depends on the other components. Using the IPAT model to estimate CO_2 emissions, Dietz and Rosa (1997) found that increasing population impacts emissions, yet economic growth (A) is non-linear in its effect, leveling off at about $10,000 per capita.

Historically, the United States, the most affluent country in the world, has been the largest contributor of CO_2 and cumulatively has contributed more than any other country to the increase of CO_2 in the atmosphere. However, as the population and affluence of China grew in the last decade, China began to lead the world in overall CO_2 emissions. In 2017, China accounted for nearly 27.6 percent of total global emissions, with the United States emitting about 15.2 percent, followed by the European Union at 10.6 percent, India at 7 percent, the Russian Federation at 4.6 percent, and Japan at 3.5 percent (BP 2018).

In the United States in 2016, the largest proportion of greenhouse gas emissions came from CO_2 at 82 percent. Methane is second at 10 percent, followed by nitrous oxide at 5 percent, and fluorinated gases at 3 percent. The transportation sector produces the largest percentage of greenhouse gases (GHG) in the United States at 28.7 percent, followed by the electricity sector at 28.6 percent. In 2016 GHG emissions from the transportation sector passed emissions from the electric power sector for the first time, and transportation emissions are on track to be the largest US source in 2017 as well (Rhodium Group 2018). US emissions in 2016 from industry were 21.7 percent, agriculture was 9.5 percent, commercial real estate was 6.4 percent, and residential housing was 5.1 percent. Overall, transportation emissions rose as all other sources fell from 2015 to 2016 (see US Environmental Protection Agency 2018).

Scientists are clear that the average temperature of the Earth is increasing and that the increase is due to human activity. In addition, the science is clear that there will be impacts as a result of climate change. As discussed in Chapter 1, 2017 saw several extreme weather events, including hurricanes, floods, and wildfires, and many of those events were likely made worse by climate change. According to Romm (2016, 73–74), some of the potential impacts of a changing climate include,

- Very high temperature rise, especially over land
- Worsening Dust Bowl conditions over the US Southwest, Southern Europe, and many other regions around the globe that are heavily populated and/or heavily farmed

- Sea-level rise of up to 1 ft by 2050, and 4–6 ft (or more) by 2100, rising as much as 12 inches or more each decade thereafter
- Massive species loss on land and sea
- Much more extreme weather
- Food insecurity – the increasing difficulty of feeding 7 billion, then 8 billion, and then 9 billion people in a world with an increasingly inhospitable climate
- Myriad direct and indirect health impacts

The severity of the impacts depends on how much the average temperature of the Earth increases. The Paris Agreement is set to limit the increase to 2°C, with a goal of 1.5°C. According to the baseline scenario presented by the Intergovernmental Panel on Climate Change (2014) – the scenario where no changes are made – the average temperature of the Earth is expected to increase between 3.7°C and 4.8°C over pre-industrial levels by 2100. A 2014 report by the World Bank stated that, "Under current policies there is about a 40 percent chance of exceeding 4°C by 2100 and a 10 percent chance of exceeding 5°C" (World Bank Group 2014, xviii). The report also notes that,

> If the planet continues warming to 4°C, climatic conditions, heat and other weather extremes considered highly unusual or unprecedented today would become the new climate normal – a world of increased risks and instability. The consequences for development would be severe as crop yields decline, water resources change, diseases move into new ranges, and sea levels rise. The task of promoting human development, of ending poverty, increasing global prosperity, and reducing global inequality will be very challenging in a 2°C world, but in a 4°C world there is serious doubt whether this can be achieved at all.
>
> *World Bank Group 2014, xvii*

In addition, the impacts of climate change are projected to have large economic consequences (see Stern 2007; Burke, Hsiang, and Miguel 2015; Dell, Jones, and Olken 2012; Moore and Diaz 2015). The longer we wait to act, the more serve the economic consequences are likely to be.

While there is virtually no uncertainty among climate scientists that climate change is occurring as a result of human activities, there are uncertainties about how much the average temperature will increase, as well as what the severity of the adverse impacts will be. One of the sources of uncertainty is the *feedbacks* in the climate system that may exacerbate the impacts of climate change. Feedbacks include the melting of ice, which allows more heat to be absorbed by land and the oceans (ice would reflect some sunlight back out into space), increased ocean evaporation which puts more water vapor into the atmosphere, and the melting of permafrost resulting in the release of trapped carbon and methane (National Academy of Sciences and the Royal Society 2014). Changes in these feedbacks could amplify the level of greenhouse gases in the atmosphere. In addition, there are four "tipping point scenarios" of concern to scientists including, "The collapse of large ice sheets, large scale changes in ocean circulation, feedback processes by which warming triggers more warming, and enhanced warming over the long run" (Nordhaus 2013, 56). One recent study found that breaching such tipping points may result in "hothouse Earth," where the average temperature of the Earth would exceed 4°C to 5°C degrees warmer than the pre-industrial era (Steffen et al. 2018).

Another source of uncertainty regarding future warming involves how governments, industry, and individuals respond in the coming years. As noted, the baseline models predict warming of 3.7°C to 4.8°C, although mitigation actions to reduce fossil fuel use can avoid the higher-end estimated increase. Scholars have developed models to estimate potential emissions scenarios based, roughly, on the features of the IPAT model, including population changes, economic growth, and technology change.

One set of models, the Special Report on Emissions Scenarios (SRES), was developed in the 1990s and issued by the IPCC in 2000 (Nakicenovic et al. 2000). The SRES models included four "storylines" termed A1, A2, B1, and B2.

- A1 storyline and scenario family: a future world of very rapid economic growth, global population that peaks in mid-century and declines thereafter, and rapid introduction of new and more efficient technologies.
- A2 storyline and scenario family: a very heterogeneous world with continuously increasing global population and regionally oriented economic growth that is more fragmented and slower than in other storylines.
- B1 storyline and scenario family: a convergent world with the same global population as in the A1 storyline but with rapid changes in economic structures toward a service and information economy, with reductions in material intensity, and the introduction of clean and resource-efficient technologies.
- B2 storyline and scenario family: a world in which the emphasis is on local solutions to economic, social, and environmental sustainability, with continuously increasing population (lower than A2) and intermediate economic development (Intergovernmental Panel on Climate Change 2000).

For its fifth assessment report issued in 2014, the IPCC replaced the SRES with the Representative Concentration Pathways (RCPs). The RCPs combine four pathways that were developed by different research teams. The pathways are named based on the level of forcing – global energy imbalance measured in watts per square meter (W/m²) – RCP 8.5, RCP 6, RCP 4.5 and RCP 2.6 (Wayne 2013). The estimated temperature increases by 2100 range from 1.5°C with RCP 2.6 to 4.9°C with RCP 8.5.

The data for the RCPs is available to download from a centralized database.[7] While the RCPs include socioeconomic data in their projections, since the pathways were developed separately using various socioeconomic data sources, the database does not include socio-economic data. Additionally, a complementary set of models was developed, termed the Shared Socioeconomic Pathways (SSPs), that can be used in conjunction with the RCPs to develop emissions scenarios (Riahi et al. 2017).

The SSPs take social-economic factors such as population, urbanization, GDP, and education as well as various mitigation and adaptation actions into account to project potential emissions scenarios. Then, five narratives were developed that describe, "major socioeconomic, demographic, technological, lifestyle, policy, institutional and other trends" and are based on the challenges associated with developing and implementing mitigation and adaptation policies (Riahi et al. 2017, 157). The five narratives are,

- SSP 1: Sustainability – Taking the Green Road (low challenges to mitigation and adaptation)
- SSP 2: Middle of the Road (medium challenges to mitigation and adaptation)
- SSP 3: Regional Rivalry – A Rocky Road (high challenges to mitigation and adaptation)
- SSP 4: Inequality – A Road Divided (low challenges to mitigation, high challenges to adaptation)
- SSP 5: Fossil-fueled Development – Taking the Highway (high challenges to mitigation, low challenges to adaptation)

The SSP 1 narrative assumes choices that are focused on increased sustainability, better management of common-pool resources, reductions in inequality, and less resource and energy consumption. SSP 2 is roughly a continuation of the current trajectory with continuing inequality, slow progress towards sustainability goals, moderate population growth that levels off mid-century, and gradual reductions in resource and energy use. SSP 3 assumes "resurgent nationalism," security concerns, regional conflicts, declining investments in technology and education, slow economic development, increasing inequality, and declining population growth in developed countries and increasing population growth in developing economies. SSP 4 assumes increasing global inequality and a fragmentation between countries that are internationally connected and develop knowledge and capital, and countries that are "labor-intensive" and "low-tech," as well as countries that invest and develop in new energy technologies and those that invest in fossil fuels. Finally, SSP 5 assumes that countries develop markets, experience rapid technological growth, and that global economic growth increases but is coupled with an increase in fossil fuel use and a faith in technological solutions to environmental problems.

Using SSP baselines, assuming no mitigation policies, emission estimates range from 5.0 to 8.7 W/m^2, above both RCP 2.6 and RCP 4.5, indicating a temperature increase of 3°C to 4.9°C. Currently we are on track to see an estimated increase in the average temperature of the Earth of 3.1°C to 3.7°C by 2100

(Tollefson 2018). The eventual pathway that we take will be a function of the choices that international, national, and sub-national governing bodies, as well as private corporations, businesses, and individuals, make.

International Climate Policy

The international response to climate change has developed into a loosely configured international climate change regime.[8] The international climate regime has been termed a "regime complex," where regime complexes are "marked by connections between the specific and relatively narrow regimes but the absence of an overall architecture or hierarchy that structures the whole" (Keohane and Victor 2011, 8).

The climate change regime complex began to develop following the initial emergence of climate change as an issue of global concern, which occurred as a result of the work of a group of international scientists that was studying the atmosphere. The Global Atmospheric Research Program (GARP) was established by the International Council of Scientific Unions (ICSU) and the World Meteorological Organization (WMO) in 1967 to study the behavior of the atmosphere in order to be able to better predict weather patterns.[9] In 1974, GARP organized a conference for scientists to discuss the issue of climate change, which lead to the World Climate Conference (WCC) in Geneva in 1979, the first international climate conference. Bert Bolin, the chair of GARP's organizing committee from 1968–1971 stated, "The bulk of the [WCC] presentations concerned the physical basis for understanding the characteristics of the climate and its changes in the past and possible human-induced changes in the future" (Bolin 2007, 31). During the conference, the scientists reached a consensus that there was a, "serious concern that the continued expansion of man's activities on earth may cause significant extended regional and even global changes of climate" (World Meteorological Organization 1979, 1–2). Also in 1979, the National Research Council issued a report, *Carbon Dioxide and Climate: A Scientific Assessment*, that reached similar conclusions (National Research Council 1979).

A major turning-point occurred in 1985 at an international conference sponsored by the United Nations Environment Programme (UNEP), the WMO, and the ICSU held in Villach, Austria. One of the topics at the conference was the realization that methane and other greenhouse gases that were emitted by agriculture and other industries could have nearly as much impact on warming as CO_2. As stated by Bolin, "Suddenly the climate change issue became much more urgent" (Weart 2018). A conference statement was issued which stated, "As a result of the increasing concentrations of greenhouse gases, it now believed that in the first half of the next century, a rise of global mean temperature could occur which is greater than any in man's history" (UNEP/WMO/ICSU 1985, 1).

In 1987 the WMO congress and UNEP governing council agreed that an intergovernmental assessment panel on climate change should be created (Bolin

2007). During this same time-period, the depletion of the ozone layer was a major concern. The ozone layer brought to the fore an environmental problem that existed on a global scale that, therefore, required a global response. In addition, the successful negotiation of the Montreal Protocol provided a framework to use for other global environmental problems. There was hope that a similar process would be successful in addressing climate change (Dryzek, Norgaard, and Schlosberg 2013).

Based on the recommendations of WMO and UNEP, the Intergovernmental Panel on Climate Change (IPCC) was established by the United Nations General Assembly in 1988. The role of the IPCC was to provide independent scientific knowledge and advice regarding climate change by coordinating the work of thousands of scientists around the world. The IPCC produces assessment reports every five to seven years that synthesize the current scientific consensus on climate change and these reports also provide a "summary for policymakers" that explains the science in a non-technical manner. Assessment reports have been issued in 1990, 1996, 2001, 2007, and 2013. The first assessment report from 1990 stated that observed warming was likely caused by human activity, and the IPCC has only grown more confident in that conclusion. In addition, the first assessment report helped inform the negotiating process of the United Nations Framework Convention on Climate Change (UNFCCC) that was adopted at the Earth Summit in Rio de Janeiro, Brazil, in 1992.

The UNFCCC provides the framework through which international climate agreements, such as the Kyoto Protocol and the Paris Agreement, were negotiated. It encourages, but does not require, countries to reduce their greenhouse gas emissions. In addition, the UNFCCC categorizes countries as Annex I countries that are industrialized or in transition to a market economy, Annex II countries that include only industrialized countries, and non-Annex I countries that are considered as developing countries. Since 1995 the countries within the UNFCCC have met at yearly Conference of the Parties (COP) meetings to negotiate and attempt to coordinate responses to climate change.

At the third COP in Japan in 1997, the Kyoto Protocol was formally adopted as an addition to the UNFCCC, and it entered into force in 2005. The Kyoto Protocol set binding greenhouse gas emissions reduction targets on Annex I countries of 5.2 percent from 1990 levels, but issued no binding reductions for developing countries. Table 3.2 shows the percent change in GHG emissions for several countries from 1990 to 2014.[10]

As shown, overall emissions from China and India spiked by 309 percent and 180 percent respectively since 1990. For the United States, there was a 12 percent increase, and for the EU there was a 28 percent decrease from 1990 levels. Overall global emissions increased 44 percent from 1990 to 2014. The emission reduction goals of the Kyoto Protocol have not been met, although one analysis suggests that the reductions in emissions were greater than they would have been without the Kyoto Protocol (Aichele and Felbermayr 2013).

TABLE 3.2 Percent Change in Greenhouse Gas Emissions, 1990–2014

Country	Percent change
China	+309.41
India	+180.31
Canada	+35.19
Japan	+20.55
United States	+11.98
European Union (28)	-26.77
Russian Federation	-37.09
Global	**+44.12**

As noted in Chapter 2, the two major controversies surrounding the UNFCCC process, particularly for the United States, were the questions of binding emissions and requirements for developing countries. From the US perspective – as reflected in the Byrd-Hagel Resolution that passed the Senate 95–0 in 1997 – the concern was that the United States would be required to reduce energy consumption, while developing countries, such as China and India, that were beginning to emit nearly as much as the United States would not. From the perspective of the developing countries, the concern was that they would be unable to reach the same standard of living as developed countries because of the earlier behavior of those very countries. The answer in Kyoto was to require emission reductions from developed countries but not from developing countries.

The Paris Agreement, reached in December 2015, addressed those concerns by having every country, including developing countries, determine their own level of emission reductions. The agreement reached in Paris was made possible by an earlier bilateral agreement between China and the United States that was reached in 2014, where the United States agreed to reduce emissions by 26 to 28 percent of 2005 levels by 2025 and China agreed to reach "peak carbon emissions" by 2030 (Landler 2014). China attained its first CO_2 emissions reduction goal – a reduction of 40 to 45 percent of 2005 levels by 2020 – three years early. In 2017 China had reduced its CO_2 *emissions per unit of GDP* by 46 percent from 2005 levels (UNFCCC 2018). Global greenhouse gas emissions seemed to be leveling between 2014–2016, although 2017 saw an uptick of emissions of 1.5 percent from 2016 levels. Even as China reached its goal of emission reductions per unit of GDP early, China's net emissions increased, as did those in India, as their economies grew in 2017.

The Paris Agreement aims to limit temperature increases to 2°C, with a goal of 1.5°C by 2100. However, even if every country met their current pledged reductions, the estimated temperature increase would be between 2.6°C and 3.2°C (Tollefson 2018). To address inadequacies in the initial set of pledges, the Paris Agreement included a pledge-and-review system, where the pledges are examined in the light of overall global emissions every five years. This process allows for adjustments to be made to the pledged reductions, and diplomatic pressure to be placed on countries to reduce emissions further (Falkner 2016).

United States Climate Politics

The issue of climate change first rose on the domestic policymaking agenda of the environmental policymaking system in the reform era, yet the United States was an active participant in the development of the international climate regime. In 1988, the Reagan administration was largely supportive of the creation of the IPCC, though there was disagreement in the administration regarding the seriousness of climate change. Additionally, George H.W. Bush signed the UNFCCC in June 1992 and it was ratified by the Senate. The UNFCCC sought to reduce the amount of greenhouse gases in the atmosphere to address climate change, but it called for no binding reduction requirements. Indeed, H.W. Bush only agreed to sign the treaty once mandatory emission targets were changed to voluntary targets. The domestic debate over the Kyoto Protocol cemented the partisan polarization of climate change, it was never officially ratified by the United States, and the United States withdrew in 2001.

During the 2000 presidential campaign, candidate George W. Bush gave a speech on energy in Saginaw, Michigan on September 29. During the speech he stated:

> With the help of Congress, environmental groups and industry, we will require all power plants to meet clean air standards in order to reduce emissions of sulfur dioxide, nitrogen oxide, mercury and carbon dioxide within a reasonable period of time. And we will provide market-based incentives, such as emissions trading, to help industry achieve the required reductions.[11]

The statement was a clear indication that candidate George W. Bush supported a requirement for power plants to reduce CO_2 emissions under the Clean Air Act. As president, W. Bush appointed former New Jersey governor Christine Todd Whitman as EPA administrator, and in a February 2001 interview on CNN's *Crossfire* she stated:

> George Bush was very clear during the course of the campaign that he believed in a multi-pollutant strategy, and that includes CO_2, and I have spoken to that. He has also been very clear that the science is good on global warming. It does exist. There is a real problem that we as a world face from global warming and to the extent that introducing CO_2 to the discussion is going to have an impact on global warming, that's an important step to take.[12]

Following the CNN interview, several Republican senators sent a letter to President W. Bush asking his position on both the Kyoto Protocol and efforts to regulate greenhouse gases under the Clean Air Act. In his response, President W. Bush stated that he did not support the ratification of the Kyoto Protocol and reversed his earlier campaign position stating, "I do not believe, however, that the government should impose on power plants mandatory emissions reductions for carbon dioxide, which is not a 'pollutant' under the Clean Air Act." He continued by casting doubt on the science of climate change by noting the, "incomplete state of scientific knowledge of the causes of, and solutions to, global climate change" (Bush 2001).

In line with his campaign speech, in 2002 President W. Bush put forward the *Clear Skies Initiative*, which proposed a cap-and-trade program – modeled after the Clean Air Act Amendment of 1990 which his father signed as president – for sulfur dioxide, nitrogen oxide, and mercury to reduce emissions of those pollutants. Yet the reversal on climate change was to remain throughout his presidency. In 2001 President W. Bush officially withdrew the United States from the Kyoto Protocol, and the administration did not issue a finding regarding the harm of CO_2 as ordered by the Supreme Court in 2007 in the *Massachusetts v. Environmental Protection Agency* ruling. In addition, the W. Bush administration never produced a National Climate Assessment as required under the Global Change Research Act of 1990, although several interim assessments were produced.

The focus of the W. Bush presidency was energy development, more so than environmental protection. President W. Bush put Vice President Dick Cheney in charge of an energy task force in 2001 that called for, "major increases in future energy supplies, including domestic oil, gas, nuclear, and 'clean coal' development, and for streamlining environmental regulations to accelerate new energy production" (Vig 2019, 98). Many of these proposals became part of the Energy Policy Act of 2005.

There were also concerns that political appointees in the W. Bush administration were altering science reports about climate change. Rick Piltz, an official with the US Global Change Research Program which produces the National Climate Assessment, resigned in 2005 after ten years. He stated that:

> It happened really starting in the first year of the new administration. At the same time that the president was pulling out of the Kyoto Protocol negotiations, the White House science office was telling us to start deleting all references to the National Assessment of Climate Change Impacts, a major study that we had just completed.
>
> And then it got worse. Starting in 2002, '03, '04, the White House Council on Environmental Quality [CEQ], which is a political office represented by their chief of staff, Phil Cooney, started exercising a kind of political policing function in directing the program not to even make any reference to the existence of the National Assessment, marking up reports to Congress to play down the global warming problem and so forth.[13]

The presidency of W. Bush expanded the reform era criticisms of the approaches of the environmentalism era at a time when climate change was becoming an important and pressing issue. Generally, there was a loss of confidence in the command-and-control tools of the environmentalism era, and a broader continued loss of faith in the government to solve large problems, particularly following the conduct of the war in Iraq, the failed response to Hurricane Katrina, and the Great Recession that began toward the end of the W. Bush presidency.

There was also a concern that the environmental movement, which had helped to usher in the environmentalism era, had since morphed into another "special interest" seeking only technical policy fixes. As Shellenberger and Nordhaus (2005) argued:

> The marriage between vision, values, and policy has proved elusive for environmentalists. Most environmental leaders, even the most vision-oriented, are struggling to articulate proposals that have coherence. This is a crisis because environmentalism will never be able to muster the strength it needs to deal with the global warming problem as long as it is seen as a "special interest." And it will continue to be seen as a special interest as long as it narrowly identifies the problem as "environmental" and the solutions as technical.

In addition, during the reform era – particularly the Reagan and W. Bush presidencies – the goal of environmental groups became the maintenance of previous victories as opposed to an expansion of environmental efforts. Environmental groups and their allies in Congress were fighting to maintain the green state against efforts at retrenchment, and thus may have been ill-equipped to begin to address climate change.

The election of Barack Obama as president, coupled with the ongoing efforts of many in Congress to pass climate legislation, seemed to be a point at which serious efforts to address climate change by the federal government were possible. As a candidate, Obama had supported a cap-and-trade program for greenhouse gases and had promised to make science central in his administration. After having won the Democratic nomination in June 2008, in a moment of rhetorical excess Obama stated that, "we will be able to look back and tell our children that this was the moment … when the rise of the oceans began to slow and our planet began to heal" (Pitney 2008).

President Obama was clear in his intent to address climate change. In addition, he seemed to embody both the broader vision called for by Shellenberger and Nordhaus (2005) and others such as Van Jones – an activist who sought to combine environmental and social justice issues that Obama appointed as an environmental advisor – and a technocratic approach to governing choices. Indeed, Obama seemed to have incorporated the lessons of the reform era by supporting market-based approaches to climate change, benefit-cost analysis in decision-making, support for performance standards, and the streamlining of federal regulations. During Obama's first term, Harvard law professor Cass Sunstein served as administrator of the Office of Information and Regulatory Affairs (OIRA), and he notes that during that time government regulations were streamlined and simplified by, "including the use of plain language, reductions in red tape, readable summaries of complex rules, and the elimination of costly, unjustified requirements" (Sunstein 2013, 2).

As will be discussed throughout the book, from 2003 to 2016 multiple efforts were made to address climate change using the tools of the green state and within the confines of the environmental policymaking process outlined in Chapter 2. However, the election of Donald Trump in 2016, coupled with intensifying polarization, has brought new tests to the resiliency of the green state and new challenges to addressing climate change.

Conclusion

Despite the challenges presented by policy actors attempting to dismantle the green state, it has thus far remained relatively robust. A large part of this robustness is due to the status-quo bias of the policymaking process in the United States. Radical departures from previous policy choices are rare, given the tendency of path dependence as well as the multiple veto players and pivot points that are present in the policymaking system. In addition, a broad, diverse, and dense network of interest groups aimed at protecting the gains of the environmentalism era have largely been effective. However, new challenges to the green state are being raised and the ability of the green state, even if it remains as it is, to address climate change is an open question.

Given the overwhelming evidence of anthropogenic climate change and its potential negative impacts coupled with the estimates of increased temperatures absent any action, it is clear that the world needs to respond to climate change with some sense of urgency to prevent the worst-case scenarios. In addition, while mitigation actions could slow the process of climate change even if no more greenhouse gases were placed in the atmosphere, we would still have to deal with the changes wrought by what has already been emitted. Therefore, we will likely need to adapt to some changes such as higher sea levels, ocean acidification, and increased temperatures.

The issue of climate change is "the mother of externalities" (Tol 2009). Climate change is also full of collective action problems, making the development and coordination of efforts difficult. In the United States, climate change arose at the same time as challenges to previous policy approaches left policymakers with increased uncertainty regarding how regulatory actions should be constructed.

Notes

1 For the demarcation of the various eras, I draw from Hillstrom (2010); Klyza and Sousa (2013); Lester (1989); Vig and Kraft (2019); and Kline (2011).

2 Caulfield (1989) notes a fourth, "*Comprehensive, multiple-purpose river basin planning and development should be utilized with respect to the nation's water resources*" (21) that is not discussed here.

3 Specifically, Secretary Watts stated that the panel was above reproach because it included, "a black … a woman, two Jews, and a cripple" (Little 2004).

4 Data from NOAA National Centers for Environmental Information, obtained here: www.ncdc.noaa.gov/cag/.

5 The data used to create Figure 3.2 was obtained here: www.epa.gov/climate-indicators/climate-change-indicators-atmospheric-concentrations-greenhouse-gases.

6 "Likely" refers to a likelihood of 66 to 100 percent based on language developed by the IPCC.

7 Available here: www.iiasa.ac.at/web-apps/tnt/RcpDb/dsd?Action=htmlpage&page=about

8 The domestic climate change regime will be explored in Chapter 7.

9 In 1980 GARP was changed to the World Climate Research Programme (WCRP).

10 Data from the World Resources Institute: http://cait.wri.org/

11 See here: http://web.archive.org/web/20010111035000/http://www.georgebush.com/News/speeches/092900_energy.html

12 See here: http://transcripts.cnn.com/TRANSCRIPTS/0102/26/cf.00.html

13 See here: www.pbs.org/wgbh/pages/frontline/hotpolitics/interviews/piltz.html

References

Aichele, Rahel, and Gabriel Felbermayr. 2013. "The Effect of the Kyoto Protocol on Carbon Emissions." *Journal of Policy Analysis and Management* 32(4): 731–757.

Anderegg, William R.L., James W. Prall, Jacob Harold, and Stephen Schneider. 2010. "Expert Credibility in Climate Change." *Proceedings of the National Academy of Sciences* 107(27): 12107–12109.

"Antarctic Sea Ice Shrinks for Second-Straight Year." 2018. phys.org. https://phys.org/news/2018-03-antarctic-sea-ice-second-straight-year.html (August 26, 2018).

Arrhenius, Svante. 1896. "On the Influence of Carbonic Acid in the Air Upon the Temperature of the Ground." *Philosophical Magazine and Journal of Science* 41(251): 237–276.

Bamber, Jonathan L., Richard M. Westaway, Ben Marzeion, and Bert Wouters. 2018. "The Land Ice Contribution to Sea Level During the Satellite Era." *Environmental Research Letters* 13(6): 063008.

Benson, Melinda Harm, and Robin Kundis Craig. 2017. *The End of Sustainability: Resilience and the Future of Environmental Governance in the Anthropocene*. Lawrence, KS: University Press of Kansas.

Blunden, Jessica, Derek S. Arndt, and Gail Hartfield, eds. 2018. "State of the Climate in 2017." *Special Supplement to the Bulletin of the American Meteorological Society* 99(8).

Bolin, Bert. 2007. *A History of the Science and Politics of Climate Change: The Role of the Intergovernmental Panel on Climate Change*. Cambridge: Cambridge University Press.

Bolsen, Toby, James N. Druckman, and Fay Lomax Cook. 2015. "Citizens', Scientists', and Policy Advisors' Beliefs About Global Warming." *The ANNALS of the American Academy of Political and Social Science* 658(1): 271–295.

Borick, Christopher P., and Barry G. Rabe. 2014. "Weather or Not? Examining the Impact of Meteorological Conditions on Public Opinion Regarding Global Warming." *Weather, Climate, and Society* 6(3): 413–424.

BP. 2018. BP Statistical Review of World Energy. www.bp.com/en/global/corporate/energy-economics/statistical-review-of-world-energy.html

Bump, Philip. 2016. "That Time Ronald Reagan Joined a 'Rebellion' but Still Couldn't Change Federal Land Laws." *The Washington Post.* www.washingtonpost.com/news/the-fix/wp/2016/01/04/even-sagebrush-rebel-ronald-reagan-couldnt-change-federal-land-use-in-the-west/.

Burke, Marshall, Solomon M. Hsiang, and Edward Miguel. 2015. "Global Non-Linear Effect of Temperature on Economic Production." *Nature* 527(7577): 235–239.

Bush, George W. 2001. "Letter to Members of the Senate on the Kyoto Protocol on Climate Change." www.presidency.ucsb.edu/ws/?pid=45811.

Callendar, G.S. 1938. "The Artificial Production of Carbon Dioxide and Its Influence on Temperature." *Quarterly Journal of the Royal Meteorological Society* 64(275): 223–240.

———. 1949. "Can Carbon Dioxide Influence Climate?" *Weather* 4(10): 310–314.

Carson, Rachel. 1962. *Silent Spring.* Boston, MA: Houghton Mifflin Company.

Caulfield, Henry P. 1989. "The Conservation and Environmental Movements: An Historical Analysis." In *Environmental Politics and Policy: Theories and Evidence*, ed. James P. Lester. Durham, NC: Duke University Press, 13–56.

Chen, Xianyao, Xuebin Zhang, John A. Church, Christopher S. Watson, Matt A. King, Didier Monselesan, Benoit Legresy, and Christopher Harig. 2017. "The Increasing Rate of Global Mean Sea-Level Rise During 1993–2014." *Nature Climate Change* 7(7): 492–495.

Clinton, William J. 1993. "Executive Order 12866: Regulatory Planning and Review." www.presidency.ucsb.edu/ws/?pid=61560.

Cook, John, Dana Nuccitelli, Sarah A. Green, Mark Richardson, Bärbel Winkler, Rob Painting, Robert Way, Peter Jacobs, and Andrew Skuce. 2013. "Quantifying the Consensus on Anthropogenic Global Warming in the Scientific Literature." *Environmental Research Letters* 8(2).

Cook, John, Naomi Oreskes, Peter T. Doran, William R. L. Anderegg, Bart Verheggen, Ed W. Maibach, J. Stuart Carlton, Stephan Lewandowsky, Andrew G. Skuce, Sarah A. Green, Dana Nuccitelli, Peter Jacobs, Mark Richardson, Bärbel Winkler, Rob Painting, and Ken Rice. 2016. "Consensus on Consensus: A Synthesis of Consensus Estimates on Human-Caused Global Warming." *Environmental Research Letters* 11(4).

Dell, Melissa, Benjamin F. Jones, and Benjamin A. Olken. 2012. "Temperature Shocks and Economic Growth: Evidence from the Last Half Century." *American Economic Journal: Macroeconomics* 4(3): 66–95.

Dessler, Andrew, and Edward A. Parson. 2010. *The Science and Politics of Global Climate Change: A Guide to the Debate.* 2nd ed. Cambridge: Cambridge University Press.

Dietz, Thomas, and Eugene A. Rosa. 1997. "Effects of Population and Affluence on CO2 Emissions." *Proceedings of the National Academy of Sciences* 94(1): 175–179.

Doran, Peter T., and Maggie Kendall Zimmerman. 2009. "Examining the Scientific Consensus on Climate Change." *Eos, Transactions American Geophysical Union* 90(3): 22–23.

Drake, Brian Allen. 2010. "The Skeptical Environmentalist: Senator Barry Goldwater and the Environmental Management State." *Environmental History* 15(4): 587–611.

Dryzek, John S., Richard B. Norgaard, and David Schlosberg. 2013. *Climate-Challenged Society.* Oxford: Oxford University Press.

Egan, Patrick J., and Megan Mullin. 2012. "Turning Personal Experience into Political Attitudes: The Effect of Local Weather on Americans' Perceptions About Global Warming." *The Journal of Politics* 74(03): 796–809.

Eisner, Marc Allen. 2000. *Regulatory Politics in Transition*. 2nd ed. Baltimore, MD: Johns Hopkins University Press.

Falkner, Robert. 2016. "The Paris Agreement and the New Logic of International Climate Politics." *International Affairs* 92(5): 1107–1125.

Farnsworth, Stephen J., and S. Robert Lichter. 2012. "The Structure of Scientific Opinion on Climate Change." *International Journal of Public Opinion Research* 24(1): 93–103.

Fiorino, Daniel J. 2006. *The New Environmental Regulation*. Cambridge, MA: The MIT Press.

Ghosh, Prosenjit, and Willi A. Brand. 2003. "Stable Isotope Ratio Mass Spectrometry in Global Climate Change Research." *International Journal of Mass Spectrometry* 228(1): 1–33.

Gore, Al. 1993. *From Red Tape to Results: Creating a Government That Works Better & Costs Less: Report of the National Performance Review*. National Performance Review.

Hays, Samuel P. 1959. *Conservation and the Gospel of Efficiency: The Progressive Conservation Movement, 1890–1920*. Cambridge, MA: Harvard University Press.

Hillstrom, Kevin. 2010. *US Environmental Policy and Politics: A Documentary History*. Washington DC: CQ Press.

Intergovernmental Panel on Climate Change. 2000. *Special Report on Emissions Scenarios*. Cambridge: Cambridge University Press. www.grida.no/climate/ipcc/emission/index.htm.

———. 2013. "Summary for Policymakers." In *Climate Change 2013: The Physical Science Basis. Contribution of Working Group I to the Fifth Assessment Report of the Intergovernmental Panel on Climate Change*, www.ipcc.ch/pdf/assessment-report/ar5/wg1/WG1AR5_SPM_FINAL.pdf (October 8, 2017).

———. 2014. *Climate Change 2014: Synthesis Report. Contribution of Working Groups I, II and III to the Fifth Assessment Report of the Intergovernmental Panel on Climate Change*. Geneva, Switzerland: Intergovernmental Panel on Climate Change. www.ipcc.ch/report/ar5/syr/.

Kaya, Yoichi, and Keiichi Yokobori, eds. 1998. *Environment, Energy, and Economy: Strategies for Sustainability*. New York, NY: United Nations University.

Keeling, Charles D. 1960. "The Concentration and Isotopic Abundances of Carbon Dioxide in the Atmosphere." *Tellus* 12(2): 200–203.

Keohane, Nathaniel O. 2009. "Cap and Trade, Rehabilitated: Using Tradable Permits to Control US Greenhouse Gases." *Review of Environmental Economics and Policy* 3(1): 42–62.

Keohane, Robert O., and David G. Victor. 2011. "The Regime Complex for Climate Change." *Perspectives on Politics* 9(1): 7–23.

Kline, Benjamin. 2011. *First Along the River: A Brief History of the US Environmental Movement*. 4th ed. Lanham, MD: Rowman & Littlefield.

Klyza, Christopher McGrory, and David Sousa. 2010. "Beyond Gridlock: Green Drift in American Environmental Policymaking." *Political Science Quarterly* 125(3): 443–463.

———. 2013. *American Environmental Policy: Beyond Gridlock*. Cambridge, MA: MIT Press.

Kraft, Michael E. 2011. *Environmental Policy and Politics*. 5th ed. Boston, MA: Pearson.

Krosnick, Jon A., Allyson L. Holbrook, and Penny S. Visser. 2000. "The Impact of the Fall 1997 Debate About Global Warming on American Public Opinion." *Public Understanding of Science* 9(3): 239–260.

Krupp, Frederic D. 1986. "New Environmentalism Factors in Economic Needs." *The Wall Street Journal*. www.wsj.com/articles/SB117269353475022375.

Landler, Mark. 2014. "US and China Reach Climate Accord After Months of Talks." *The New York Times*. www.nytimes.com/2014/11/12/world/asia/china-us-xi-obama-apec.html.

Layzer, Judith A. 2012a. *Open for Business: Conservatives' Opposition to Environmental Regulation*. Cambridge, MA: The MIT Press.

———. 2012b. *The Environmental Case: Translating Values into Policy*. 3rd ed. Washington, DC: CQ Press.

Lester, James P. 1989. *Environmental Politics and Policy: Theories and Evidence*. Durham, NC: Duke University Press.

Levin, Ingeborg, and Vago Hesshaimer. 2000. "A Unique Tracer of Global Carbon Cycle Dynamics." *Radiocarbon* 42(1): 69–80.

Levitus, Syd, John I. Antonov, Timothy P. Boyer, Ricardo A. Locarnini, Hernan E. Garcia, and Alexey V. Mishonov. 2009. "Global Ocean Heat Content 1955–2008 in Light of Recently Revealed Instrumentation Problems." *Geophysical Research Letters* 36(7): L07608.

Lichter, Robert S., Stephen J. Farnsworth, and Justin Rolfe-Redding. 2015. "Scientific Opinion on Climate Change Across Two Decades." *Journal of Climatology & Weather Forecasting* 3(3).

Little, Amanda. 2004. "A Look Back at Reagan's Environmental Record." *Grist*. https://grist.org/article/griscom-reagan/.

Lo, Alex Y., and C. Y. Jim. 2015. "Come Rain or Shine? Public Expectation on Local Weather Change and Differential Effects on Climate Change Attitude." *Public Understanding of Science* 24(8): 928–942.

Mann, Michael E., Raymond S. Bradley, and Malcolm K. Hughes. 1998. "Global-Scale Temperature Patterns and Climate Forcing over the Past Six Centuries." *Nature* 392(6678): 779–787.

Mazmanian, Daniel A., and Michael E. Kraft. 1999. "The Three Epochs of the Environmental Movement." In *Toward Sustainable Communities: Transition and Transformations in Environmental Policy*, eds. Daniel A. Mazmanian and Michael E. Kraft. Cambridge, MA: MIT Press, 3–42.

McCright, Aaron M., Chenyang Xiao, and Riley E. Dunlap. 2014. "Political Polarization on Support for Government Spending on Environmental Protection in the USA, 1974–2012." *Social Science Research* 48: 251–260.

Moore, Frances C., and Delavane B. Diaz. 2015. "Temperature Impacts on Economic Growth Warrant Stringent Mitigation Policy." *Nature Climate Change* 5(2): 127–131.

Nakicenovic, Nebojsa, Joseph Alcamo, A. Grubler, K. Riahi, R. A. Roehrl, H.-H. Rogner, and N. Victor. 2000. *Special Report on Emissions Scenarios (SRES), a Special Report of Working Group III of the Intergovernmental Panel on Climate Change*. Cambridge: Cambridge University Press.

National Academy of Sciences, and The Royal Society. 2014. Climate Change: Evidence and Causes. https://royalsociety.org/topics-policy/projects/climate-change-evidence-causes/?utm_source=social_media\&utm_medium=hootsuite\&utm_campaign=standard.

National Research Council. 1979. *Carbon Dioxide and Climate: A Scientific Assessment*. Washington, DC: National Academies of Sciences. https://doi.org/10.17226/12181.

Nordhaus, William D. 2013. *The Climate Casino: Risk, Uncertainty, and Economics for a Warming World*. New Haven, CT: Yale University Press.

Oreskes, Naomi. 2004. "The Scientific Consensus on Climate Change." *Science* 306(5702): 1686.

Pitney, Nico. 2008. "Obama's Nomination Victory Speech in St. Paul." *Huffington Post*.

Plass, Gilbert N. 1956. "The Carbon Dioxide Theory of Climatic Change." *Tellus* 8(2): 140–154.

Pooley, Eric. 2010. *The Climate War: True Believers, Power Brokers, and the Fight to Save the Earth*. New York, NY: Hachette Books.

Reagan, Ronald. 1981. "Executive Order 12291." National Archives. www.archives.gov/federal-register/codification/executive-order/12291.html.

———. 1988. "Statement on Signing the Montreal Protocol on Ozone-Depleting Substances." www.presidency.ucsb.edu/ws/?pid=35639.

Reuters. 1983. "Watt Is Criticized on US Coal Leases." *The New York Times*. www.nytimes.com/1983/04/26/us/watt-is-criticized-on-us-coal-leases.html (June 11, 2018).

Revelle, Roger, and Hans E. Suess. 1957. "Carbon Dioxide Exchange Between Atmosphere and Ocean and the Question of an Increase of Atmospheric CO2 During the Past Decades." *Tellus* 9(1): 18–27.

Rhodium Group. 2018. "Final US Emissions Numbers for 2017." https://rhg.com/research/final-us-emissions-numbers-for-2017/.

Riahi, Keywan, Detlef P. van Vuuren, Elmar Kriegler, Jae Edmonds, Brian C. O'Neill, Shinichiro Fujimori, Nico Bauer, Katherine Calvin, Rob Dellink, Oliver Fricko, Wolfgang Lutz, Alexander Popp, Jesus Crespo Cuaresma, Samir Kc, Marian Leimbach, Leiwen Jiang, Tom Kram, Shilpa Rao, Johannes Emmerling, Kristie Ebi, Tomoko Hasegawa, Petr Havlik, Florian Humpenöder, Lara Aleluia Da Silva, Steve Smith, Elke Stehfest, Valentina Bosetti, Jiyong Eom, David Gernaat, Toshihiko Masui, Joeri Rogelj, Jessica Strefler, Laurent Drouet, Volker Krey, Gunnar Luderer, Mathijs Harmsen, Kiyoshi Takahashi, Lavinia Baumstark, Jonathan C. Doelman, Mikiko Kainuma, Zbigniew Klimont, Giacomo Marangoni, Hermann Lotze-Campen, Michael Obersteiner, Andrzej Tabeau, and Massimo Tavoni. 2017. "The Shared Socioeconomic Pathways and Their Energy, Land Use, and Greenhouse Gas Emissions Implications: An Overview." *Global Environmental Change* 42: 153–168.

Roe, Gerard H., Marcia B. Baker, and Florian Herla. 2017. "Centennial Glacier Retreat as Categorical Evidence of Regional Climate Change." *Nature Geoscience* 10(2): 95.

Romm, Joseph. 2016. *Climate Change: What Everyone Needs to Know*. Oxford: Oxford University Press.

Rosa, Eugene A., Thomas K. Rudel, Richard York, Andrew K. Jorgenson, and Thomas Dietz. 2015. "The Human (Anthropogenic) Driving Forces of Global Climate Change." In *Climate Change and Society: Sociological Perspectives*, eds. Riley E. Dunlap and Robert J. Brulle. Oxford: Oxford University Press, 32–60.

Rosenberg, Stacy, Arnold Vedlitz, Deborah F. Cowman, and Sammy Zahran. 2010. "Climate Change: A Profile of US Climate Scientists' Perspectives." *Climatic Change* 101(3–4): 311–329.

Salzman, James, and Barton H. Thompson Jr. 2013. *Environmental Law and Policy*. 4th ed. St. Paul, MN: Foundation Press.

Shellenberger, Michael, and Ted Nordhaus. 2005. *The Death of Environmentalism: Global Warming Politics in a Post-Environmental World*. www.thebreakthrough.org/images/Death_of_Environmentalism.pdf.

Stavins, Robert N. 1998. "What Can We Learn from the Grand Policy Experiment? Lessons from SO2 Allowance Trading." *The Journal of Economic Perspectives* 12(3): 69–88.

Steffen, Will, Johan Rockström, Katherine Richardson, Timothy M. Lenton, Carl Folke, Diana Liverman, Colin P. Summerhayes, Anthony D. Barnosky, Sarah E. Cornell, Michel Crucifix, Jonathan F. Donges, Ingo Fetzer, Steven J. Lade, Marten Scheffer, Ricarda Winkelmann, and Hans Joachim Schellnhuber. 2018. "Trajectories of the Earth System in the Anthropocene." *Proceedings of the National Academy of Sciences*, forthcoming.

Stern, Nicholas. 2007. *The Economics of Climate Change: The Stern Review.* Cambridge: Cambridge University Press.

Sunstein, Cass R. 2002. *Risk and Reason: Safety, Law, and the Environment.* Cambridge: Cambridge University Press.

———. 2013. *Simpler: The Future of Government.* New York, NY: Simon & Schuster.

The Environmental Pollution Panel. 1965. *Restoring the Quality of Our Environment.* The White House: President's Science Advisory Committee.

Tol, Richard S.J. 2009. "The Economic Effects of Climate Change." *Journal of Economic Perspectives* 23(2): 29–51.

Tollefson, Jeff. 2018. "Can the World Kick Its Fossil-Fuel Addiction Fast Enough?" *Nature.* www.nature.com/articles/d41586-018-04931-6.

Tyndall, John. 1861. "On the Absorption and Radiation of Heat by Gases and Vapours, and on the Physical Connexion of Radiation, Absorption, and Conduction." *Philosophical Magazine and Journal of Science* 22(146): 169–194.

UNEP/WMO/ICSU. 1985. *An Assessment of the Role of Carbon Dioxide and of Other Greenhouse Gases in Climate Variations and Assorted Impacts.* Wellington, NZ.

UNFCCC. 2018. China Meets 2020 Carbon Target Three Years Ahead of Schedule. https://unfccc.int/news/china-meets-2020-carbon-target-three-years-ahead-of-schedule.

US Environmental Protection Agency. 2011. The Benefits and Costs of the Clean Air Act from 1990 to 2020. www.epa.gov/sites/production/files/2015-07/documents/fullreport_rev_a.pdf (March 7, 2018).

———. 2016. Climate Change Indicators in the United States, 2016. www.epa.gov/climate-indicators (August 1, 2017).

———. 2018. Inventory of US Greenhouse Gas Emissions and Sinks: 1990–2016. www.epa.gov/sites/production/files/2018-01/documents/2018_complete_report.pdf.

US Global Change Research Program. 2017. "Climate Science Special Report: Fourth National Climate Assessment, Volume I." In eds. D.J. Wuebbles, D.W. Fahey, K.A. Hibbard, D.J. Dokken, B.C. Stewart, and T.K. Maycock. https://science2017.globalchange.gov (December 8, 2017).

Verheggen, Bart, Bart Strengers, John Cook, Rob van Dorland, Kees Vringer, Jeroen Peters, Hans Visser, and Leo Meyer. 2014. "Scientists' Views About Attribution of Global Warming." *Environmental Science & Technology* 48(16): 8963–8971.

Vig, Norman J. 2019. "Presidential Powers and Environmental Policy." In *Environmental Policy: New Directions for the Twenty-First Century*, eds. Norman J. Vig and Michael E. Kraft. Thousand Oaks, CA: CQ Press, 88–116.

Vig, Norman J., and Michael E. Kraft. 2019. *Environmental Policy: New Directions for the Twenty-First Century.* 10th ed. Thousand Oaks, CA: CQ Press.

Vincent, Carol Hardy, Laura A. Hanson, and Carla A. Argueta. 2017. *Federal Land Ownership: Overview and Data.* Congressional Research Service.

Watts, Jonathan. 2018. "Arctic's Strongest Sea Ice Breaks up for First Time on Record." *The Guardian.* www.theguardian.com/world/2018/aug/21/arctics-strongest-sea-ice-breaks-up-for-first-time-on-record (August 26, 2018).

Wayne, G.P. 2013. *The Beginner's Guide to Representative Concentration Pathways.* Skeptical Science. www.skepticalscience.com/rcp.php.

Weart, Spencer R. 2018. *The Discovery of Global Warming: Revised and Expanded Edition.* Online Edition. Cambridge, MA: Harvard University Press. https://history.aip.org/climate/index.htm.

Webber, David J. 2008. "Earth Day and Its Precursors: Continuity and Change in the Evolution of Midtwentieth-Century US Environmental Policy." *Review of Policy Research* 25(4): 313–332.

World Bank Group. 2014. *Turn Down the Heat: Confronting the New Climate Normal*. World Bank.

World Meteorological Organization. 1979. *Declaration of the World Climate Conference*. United Nations.

4

VALUE SYSTEMS AND ENVIRONMENTAL POLICY

Introduction

Why do disagreements exist about climate change? The vast majority of climate scientists agree about the basics of climate change, including that the average temperature of the Earth is warming due to human activity and, as a result, there will likely be long-term negative consequences. However, some elected officials and many in the public view the science surrounding climate change as far from settled and/or view the risk as negligible. The reason for the disparities in views about climate change are not necessarily because one side of the debate rejects or denies science or the scientific method; indeed, many of those skeptical of climate science try to claim that the science is on their side rather than the other. Hence, climate change debates are not about science *per se*, rather they are shaped by worldviews and values embedded in particular political and cultural identities (Hoffman 2015).

Disagreements over environment policy issues broadly, and climate change specifically, are often based in differences in values. Values determine an individual's ideas about right and wrong, and are typically resistant to change. According to Schwartz (1992, 4), "Values (1) are concepts or beliefs, (2) pertain to desirable end states or behaviors, (3) transcend specific situations, (4) guide selection or evaluation of behavior and events, and (5) are ordered by relative importance." Values shape and constrain beliefs, where beliefs are things that are thought to be true. Finally, values form the basis for attitudes, which are evaluations, positive or negative, about specific issues (Dietz, Fitzgerald, and Shwom 2005, 346).

Values are organized in a hierarchical system where general, broadly applicable, values constrain more specific policy attitudes (Jenkins-Smith et al. 2018; Peffley and Hurwitz 1985; Sabatier and Jenkins-Smith 1993). Value systems form a causal chain from abstract values to policy domain-specific values, and finally to policy issue-specific attitudes. The most broadly applicable values are termed core values, and include such values as political ideologies, altruism, traditionalism, individualism, and egalitarianism. Core values help define domain-specific values, such as those that deal with the ethics associated with the management of natural resources. Finally, core and environmental values constrain attitudes about issues like land management, energy production, and climate change.

One of the most notable roles that values play in environmental disputes is the ways in which they shape our cognition. By shaping cognition, values determine how we think about environmental policy issues and how we process information pertinent to political and policy debates. Typically, policy attitudes are motivated by a desire for congruence with values, rather than a desire for accuracy. As a result, we tend to only accept information that comports with our values. Values provide clarity in the face of complexity, and reasoning is often a post-hoc value-based justification for our initial beliefs (Haidt 2001).

The cognitive functions responsible for information processing can be understood through a two-systems model of cognitive processing. System 1 "operates automatically and quickly, with little or no effort and no sense of voluntary control," whereas, system 2 processing "allocates attention to the effortful mental activities that demand it, including complex computations" (Kahneman 2013, 20–21). Both systems can operate to determine policy attitudes, with system 1 processing deriving heuristic-based attitudes and system 2 deriving carefully reasoned, evidence-based attitudes. As noted, reasoning is often employed after some initial judgment has been made likely through system 1 processing. Therefore, system 2 reasoning often provides justification for the conclusions reached through processing by system 1.

This chapter explores the nature of value systems and their importance in shaping environmental policy disputes by examining how the public translates values into policy attitudes. First, this chapter delineates the hierarchical structure of value systems. Then, core values and environmental values are explained. Next, the cognition function of values is discussed. Then, public opinion data is used to demonstrate the influence of core values and environmental values on the perceived risks of climate change. Finally, I examine support for various policy approaches to address climate change.

Value System

Values and beliefs can be understood to be organized within a system that is hierarchically structured from broadly applicable values-based beliefs to attitudes about specific issues. Values at one level of the hierarchy influence, or constrain, values at the next level. At the broadest level, and therefore the most far-reaching in terms of influence, are *core values*. Following core values are domain-specific values, such as environmental values that concern the relationship between humans and the

FIGURE 4.1 Hierarchically structured value system

natural world. Finally, policy attitudes are evaluations about particular policy issues that can include preferences about what policy issues government should address and how they should address them. Figure 4.1 illustrates the value system structure.

The hierarchical structure of values implies a consistency across each level. For example, if left-leaning political liberalism is an individual's core value, then she is likely to be supportive of government regulations that restrict pollution. In addition, values not only influence specific policy attitudes, but may also shape pro-environmental behavior among members of the public (see Stern 2000; Stern, Dietz, and Kalof 1993). Finally, values can play a role in the formation of coalitions of policy actors, where actors coordinate activities based on shared beliefs at the domain-specific level (Sabatier and Jenkins-Smith 1993). The next section examines core values.

Core Values

Core values are foundational values that span multiple policy domains and involve,

> very general normative and ontological assumptions about human nature, the relative priority of fundamental values such as liberty and equality, the relative priority of the welfare of different groups, the proper role of government vs. markets in general, and about who should participate in governmental decision-making.
>
> *Sabatier and Weible 2007*

With regard to policy debates, the most publicly visible and openly discussed core values are political ideology and partisanship. Media coverage of politics and statements from elected officials often make use of political ideology – conservative vs. liberal – to infer a wide range of policy attitudes. Political ideology is thought to exist on a single dimension from liberal (left) to conservative (right), and ideological disagreements tend to be about the size, scope, and nature of government. Disputes about the size of government are related to taxes, spending, and the overall size of the federal budget. Scope refers to disagreements over what belongs in the public vs. the private sphere, and what types of behavior should or shouldn't be regulated by government. Finally, disputes about the nature of government center on whether or not government is viewed as a vehicle for collective decision-making or as a non-representative entity that imposes rules.

Political parties are coalitions of differing regional, ideological, and interest group factions, and they play a key role in enabling coordination among various actors by helping to facilitate collective action among those that share some core values. Additionally, partisanship acts as an informational shortcut for a public that is largely not consistently ideological (Kinder and Kalmoe 2017). In the last several decades, the parties at the elite level have sorted more along ideological lines, with liberals more consistently aligning with the Democratic party and conservatives aligning with the Republican party. As parties and ideologies became aligned, polarization tended to increase at the elite level, making some issues, such as climate change, much more contentious. The polarization regarding climate change at the elite level has influenced partisan polarization among the public, particularly following the debate over the Kyoto Protocol in 1997 that had Democratic President Clinton positioned on one side and congressional Republicans on the other (Brulle, Carmichael, and Jenkins 2012; Krosnick, Holbrook, and Visser 2000).

Debates about the size, scope, and nature of government can be seen within environmental policy disputes that are fought across ideological and partisan divisions. For example, a larger government has more capacity to monitor environmental conditions and find problems that may require government action, thereby increasing the role of government. The process of increased monitoring leading to increased government action has been termed the paradox-of-search (Baumgartner and Jones 2015). Typically, liberals and Democrats are more accepting of a larger government to address environmental issues than are conservatives and Republicans.

Environmental policy disputes also involve questions of the scope of government, particularly with regard to questions of market failures and the regulation of business practices that might have negative environmental consequences. Should governments put a regulatory regime in place to address common-pool resources, as liberals and Democrats may support, or should governments simply demarcate property rights and then allow market forces to address common-pool resources, a policy likely favored by conservatives and Republicans?

Questions regarding the representative nature of government are also present in environmental policy issues. For example, disputes over land management and ownership in the western United States, which led to the Sagebrush Rebellion, illustrate the tension between a federal government that is seen as far removed and unrepresentative of local interests versus local governments that are understood to be closer to the people and therefore more representative. The representative nature of government is particularly salient with regard to the relationship between elected officials and bureaucrats working within executive branch agencies. The bureaucrats that develop regulatory policy are often seen, typically by conservatives and Republicans, as usurping policymaking authority that is within the purview of elected officials. As environmental policy developed from the environmentalism era these differing views of government have led to increased partisan gridlock.

The construction of the green state that took place during the environmentalism era, particularly the environmental decade of the 1970s, was largely bipartisan, with both Republicans and Democrats supporting environmental legislation.

However, since that time the two major political parties have increasingly diverged on environmental policy issues, and this is reflected by both elected officials and the public (Calvert 1989; Dunlap, Xiao, and McCright 2001; Kim and Urpelainen 2017; McCright and Dunlap 2013; Shipan and Lowry 2001).

The basis of political party divisions is largely driven by views about the size, scope, and nature of government. As discussed in Chapter 3, these cleavages started to become closely connected to environmental policy disputes toward the end of the environmentalism era and culminating with the election of Ronald Reagan. Beginning in the early 1980s, Republicans became associated with the view that government regulation in general, and environmental regulation in particular, leads to slower economic growth. The command-and-control instruments of the environmentalism era were of particular concern, and opposition to such approaches was likely a driving force in opposition to environmental regulation in general. This type of "solution aversion" is likely at play with regard to climate change, as some of the policy options suggested involved the same type of policy instruments used to address previous environmental problems (Campbell and Kay 2014).

In Congress, increasing differences in environmental votes across the two political parties from 1969 to 1999 were a result of fewer conservative southern Democrats, an increase in environmental interest group membership, decreased salience of environmental issues, economic conditions, turnover in Congress, and increases in overall ideological (left–right) divergence (Shipan and Lowry 2001). These results point to the importance of ideological cleavages and other fractures within and across the coalitions of the two major parties, as well as external conditions represented in the problem information stream, such as economic growth, and the politics information stream, including interest group representation and public opinion.

Following elected officials, the public has become divided along ideological and partisan lines regarding environmental issues. In general, the policy attitudes of the public align along a single dimension of ideology only for those that are engaged and knowledgeable about political issues. However, political parties act as important cues for the mass public and, as elites have become more polarized, that has sent strong signals to the public thereby allowing the public to sort themselves along partisan lines (see Levendusky 2010). This can be seen in the increasing polarization among the public between self-identified liberals and Democrats compared with conservatives and Republicans regarding spending on the environment. Figure 4.2 uses data from the General Social Survey from 1973 to 2016 to illustrate partisan differences on the question of government spending on the environment.

Figure 4.2 shows the mean of environmental spending, where 1 indicates "too little" and 0 indicates "too much" or "about right" for self-identified liberals, Democrats, conservatives, and Republicans.[1] As can be seen, ideological and partisan differences were present for most years, although the differences between the parties seem to have grown since the early 1990s. While partisan polarization on

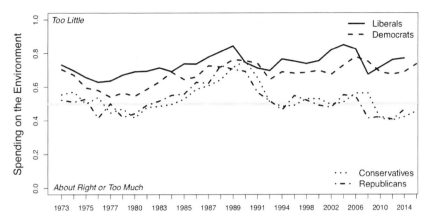

FIGURE 4.2 Public opinion on environmental spending by ideology and party, 1973–2016

the environment started in the late 1970s and early 1980s among elites, among the public it has been increasing since about 1993, coinciding with when the Republicans won control of the House of Representatives. Finally, it should be noted that, although public opinion is polarized, it is really only since 2008 that a majority of conservatives and Republicans stopped thinking that the government spent too little on environmental protection.

Apart from political values, other types of core values have been identified. For example, Values-Beliefs-Norms (VBN) theory posits that pro-environmental attitudes and behaviors follow from core values to environmental beliefs, then to norms, and finally to behavior. Various iterations and applications of VBN have applied different sets of values, but some of those that are consistently applied include altruistic, biospheric, egoistic (self-interest), traditionalism, and openness to change (Dietz, Kalof, and Stern 2002; Henry and Dietz 2012; Stern 2000; Stern et al. 1999). Applications of VBN theory have consistently found that core values are predictors of environmental attitudes and behaviors, although a consistent set of measures of core values that has a strong theoretical grounding as well as valid measurement is preferable. One such theory is *cultural theory*, which was initially developed by anthropologist Mary Douglas, with important contributions by political scientist Aaron Wildavsky (Douglas and Wildavsky 1982; Wildavsky 1987).

Cultural theory provides a general structure for value orientations, based on dimensions of sociality that can encompass a range of other core values like political ideology and partisanship as well as biospheric altruism and traditionalism. This allows cultural theory to act as a single underlining theory of core values (Ripberger et al. 2014). Acting as a measure of core values, cultural theory has been found to be a strong predictor of public opinion regarding several scientific and technical issues, including the risks and benefits associated with vaccines (Song 2014); the risks associated with nuclear waste (Jenkins-Smith 2001); and the public's views on nuclear weapons and the threat of terrorism (Ripberger, Jenkins-Smith, and Herron 2011). Additionally, cultural theory has been demonstrated to be an important predictor of environmental attitudes (Ellis and Thompson 1997; Steg and Sievers 2000) and views about climate change (Goebbert et al. 2012; Jones 2011; Pendergraft 1998). Finally, cultural theory posits several *myths of nature* that are associated with each cultural type (Thompson, Ellis, and Wildavsky 1990). The next section examines cultural theory, the ways-of-life it posits, and the associated myths of nature.

Cultural Theory

Cultural theory posits that core values stem from orientations based in *social relations* – patterns of interpersonal relationships – that structure *cultural biases*, where values are shared among individuals. Culture bias and social relations combine to form viable "ways-of-life" or cultural types. Individuals derive domain-specific values and policy attitudes that follow from, and therefore support, their preferred cultural type (Thompson, Ellis, and Wildavsky 1990).

The groupings that determine the various cultural types exist along two dimensions: a grid dimension and a group dimension. The grid dimension concerns the degree to which individuals are constrained by rules, consigned to particular roles, and are able to negotiate their position. As noted by Douglas (2003), "In a high-grid environment, everything is classified and individual choice is heavily restricted" (1352). The group dimension refers to how important it is for individuals to be integrated within groups. In high-group contexts, individual needs become subservient to the well-being of the group. Combining the grid and group dimensions produces four cultural types, or viable ways-of-life, including hierarchy, egalitarianism, individualism, and fatalism.

Cultural types provide a basis for core values by anchoring individuals to how social relationships *should* be structured. Adherents to the various cultural types form views about specific policy issues based on consistency with their notions of idealized social relationships and the bias that those relationships represent. With regard to environmental issues, the values inherent in each of the four cultural types are associated with four respective myths of nature. The four myths of nature are based on the perceived stability of the ecosystem, which then provide guidance for how humans should interact with the natural world. Figure 4.3 illustrates the four cultural types and their corresponding myth of nature. Below, each cultural type and myth of nature is summarized, and survey questions used to measure each cultural type are included.

Hierarchical: the hierarchical cultural type is high on both the grid and group dimension, therefore hierarchs value group cohesion and solidarity coupled with clearly defined roles and delineated authority within the group. For hierarchs, clear lines of authority within bounded groups create the most harmonious societal

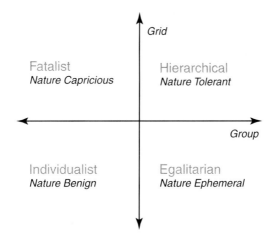

FIGURE 4.3 Cultural theory and myths of nature

arraignment. With regard to nature, hierarchs view nature as tolerant. The nature-tolerant myth implies that nature provides resources for human development, but the extraction of those resources should be carefully managed by experts and the benefits distributed according to the social orderings of the hierarchy. Agreement with the following statements indicates a tendency towards hierarchy.

- *The best way to get ahead in life is to work hard to do what you are told to do*
- *Society is in trouble because people do not obey those in authority*
- *Society would be much better off if we imposed strict and swift punishment on those who break the rules*

Egalitarian: egalitarians are low on the grid dimension and high on the group dimension and, as a result, egalitarians prefer group cohesion and equality among group members. Being low on the grid dimension means that egalitarians reject social stratification among members of the group. For egalitarians nature is seen as ephemeral, or transient, and therefore vulnerable to human activity. Since we can't be sure of the permanence of nature, it should not be disturbed. The following statements represent the egalitarian worldview.

- *What society needs is a fairness revolution to make the distribution of goods more equal*
- *Society works best if power is shared equally*
- *It is our responsibility to reduce differences in income between the rich and the poor*

Individualist: individualists are low on both the grid and group dimension; therefore, they prefer societies where individuals are free to compete and negotiate with each other without the constraints of group cohesion or authority. For an individualist, nearly all aspects of society should resemble a market, so that merit, determination, and hard work are properly rewarded. Individualists see nature as benign and forgiving. Since nature is robust to the impacts of humans, we should exploit its resources in support of entrepreneurial activity. Individualists are more likely to agree with the following statements.

- *Even if some people are at a disadvantage, it is best for society to let people succeed or fail on their own*
- *Even the disadvantaged should have to make their own way in the world*
- *We are all better off when we compete as individuals*

Fatalist: the fatalist cultural type, also termed isolates (Douglas 2003), are low on the group dimension, meaning that they typically value little, to no, group attachments. However, fatalists are also high on the grid dimension, therefore they are likely to feel as though their choices are constrained by the social stratification that is externally imposed and beyond their control. Fatalists typically exist within groups that are marginalized by the larger society, and as a result may withdraw or be prohibited from participation in collective action. The fatalist's view of nature is that nature is capricious and therefore unable to be controlled, or perhaps even fully understood, by humans. Fatalists tend to agree with the following statements.

- *The most important things that take place in life happen by chance*
- *No matter how hard we try, the course of our lives is largely determined by forces beyond our control*
- *For the most part, succeeding in life is a matter of chance*

Large, diverse societies produce a cultural plurality where competition among the different cultural types exists (Schwartz 1991). With regard to environmental issues, "environmentalism has become enmeshed in a culture war between individualists and egalitarians" (Ellis and Thompson 1997, 183). The culture war competition is driven not just by the core values exemplified by cultural theory but also by the environmental values associated with the myths of nature. The next section examines environmental values.

Environmental Values

In addition to core values, environmental policy disputes are also based on differences in environmental values, which concern the "appropriate relationship between humans and the natural world" (Layzer 2012, 2). Environmental values are connected to the various myths of nature that are derived from the four cultural types. However, environmental values can also be represented as existing along a single dimension that roughly divides into two factions. On one side of the divide are *environmentalists* that view nature as having intrinsic worth and in need of protection from human activity. Environmentalists are most likely to accept the nature-ephemeral myth associated with egalitarianism, although some environmentalists may accept the nature-tolerant myth of the hierarchs, where natural resources can be used if that use is well managed.

At the other end of the continuum are what Layzer (2012) terms *cornucopians*, and they view nature as an abundant source of resources for human development. Cornucopians are likely to be individualistic and view nature as benign, although some may also see the importance of hierarchy and careful management of natural resources. Since environmental values are largely about the relationship between humans and nature, specifically the impacts on nature that humans may have, the fatalist myth of nature-capricious is not considered an environmental value. Rather, the nature-capricious myth is a result of the lack of agency that is generally felt by fatalists.

While it is useful to think of environmental values as operating along a single dimension, there are several types of environmentalists and environmental values that vary by emphasis. Early environmental values included *preservationists*, such as John Muir, which grew during the development era and emphasized the need for nature to be preserved and protected from human interference. In the preservationist's view, any human interference with nature is likely to be harmful to nature's delicate balance. In addition, preservationists argued that humans can benefit from spending time in nature. Indeed, some research has shown improved health benefits resulting from experience with nature (Bratman et al. 2015; Maller et al. 2006). Strands of the preservationist's ethos are present within many environmentalists' groups and individuals arguing for increased environmental protection. Preservationists are closely associated with the nature-ephemeral myth of the egalitarians.

In addition to preservationists, *conservationists* were also considered to be early environmentalists. Conservationists formed the foundation for the conservation era and they are concerned with the protection of nature, but also recognize that nature can provide resources for human use. Conservationists, like hierarchs, believe that natural resources can, and should, be properly managed to ensure their continued availability. In current debates conservation is often considered a middle ground, or establishment position, between cornucopians and environmentalists, as actors on both sides of environmental policy debates use the rhetoric of conservation. This use of conservation rhetoric may indicate that both cornucopians and environmentalists accept some degree of development, coupled with some preservation. Disagreements arise around the degree of development and the degree of conservation, as well as the trade-offs associated with development vs. conservation.

Since the middle of the 20th century, environmentalists have emphasized *ecology*. Ecology understands natural and social systems to be linked and interdependent, and therefore any harm done to the natural environment is likely to harm humans. Concern about the health impacts of pollution as well as concern about biodiversity loss are often linked with ecology. The focus of ecology for environmentalists was spurred by the publication of *Silent Spring* by Rachel Carson. In addition, going further, *deep ecology* views the right relationship between humans and nature as egalitarian, where humans are merely a part of the larger ecosystem, which should be protected without the consideration of harm to humans (Naess 1973).

Finally, and most recently, environmentalists have focused on *sustainability* (Mazmanian and Kraft 1999). According to the Environmental Protection Agency, sustainability "Creates and maintains the conditions under which humans and nature can exist in productive harmony, that permit fulfilling the social, economic and other requirements of present and future generations" (US Environmental Protection Agency 2014).

On the other side of the environmental values divide are the cornucopians. The focus of cornucopians is the betterment of human societies through economic growth, technological innovation, and individual liberty. Nature, for the cornucopians, is there to provide resources and has little added value on its own. The cornucopian view matches that of the individualists, where nature is viewed as benign and robust to human activities. For much of US history the cornucopian ethos has been the *Dominant Social Paradigm* (DSP) for understanding the relationship between humans and nature (Dunlap and Liere 1984). The DSP includes, "acceptance of laissez-faire capitalism, individualism, growth, and progress, and a faith in science and technology" (Smith 2012, 8).

The Dominant Social Paradigm view is present in those arguing for less environmental regulation. For example, in January 2017, during his first press conference, then White House press secretary Sean Spicer responded to a question about the Keystone XL and Dakota pipelines by stating that,

> The energy sector and our natural resources are an area where I think the president is very, very keen on making sure that we maximize our use of natural resources to America's benefit. It's good for economic growth, it's good for jobs, and it's good for American energy.
>
> *Quoted in Blake 2017*

Along similar lines, in July 2017, then EPA administrator Scott Pruitt stated that, "God has blessed us with natural resources. Let's use them to feed the world. Let's use them to power the world. Let's use them to protect the world" (Guillen and Holden 2017). The focus of both statements on economic growth, jobs, and domestic energy production is a clear statement of the Dominant Social Paradigm, as well as the nature-benign view of the natural world.

As noted, the diverse views of cornucopians and environmentalists can be seen as two points on a unidimensional scale of environmental values. Unidimensional environmental values have been successfully measured by the *New Ecological Paradigm* (NEP) scale. The NEP scale is a widely used measure of environmental values that measures "beliefs about humanity's ability to upset the balance of nature, the existence of limits to growth for human societies, and humanity's right to rule over the rest of nature" (Dunlap et al. 2000, 427).

The NEP scale is measured through a series of questions that reflects both the cornucopian and the environmentalist view. Questions designed to measure cornucopian values use a Likert scale to measure agreement with statements such as:

* *Humans will eventually learn enough about how nature works to be able to control it*
* *The so-called "ecological crisis" facing humankind has been greatly exaggerated*
* *The Earth has plenty of natural resources if we just learn how to develop them*

The environmentalist questions include:

* *The balance of nature is very delicate and easily upset*
* *Humans live on a planet with very limited room and resources*
* *Humans are seriously abusing the environment*

The NEP scale is typically structured so that a higher value on the scale is associated with increasing environmentalism.

Given the hierarchical structure of value systems, the values associated with cultural theory are likely to predict the environmental values measured by the NEP scale. Specifically, egalitarianism is likely to be positively associated with environmentalism, given the close association of environmentalism with the nature-ephemeral myth. In addition, individualism is likely to be negatively associated with environmentalism, given the nature-benign myth of individualists. The nature-tolerant myth of the hierarchs is likely most closely associated with conservation, which is a type of middle ground, therefore hierarchs are likely to be divided between cornucopians and environmentalists. Fatalists view nature as capricious and as a result are not likely to be environmentalists. Finally, in terms of political values, conservatives and Republicans are not likely to be environmentalists.

For purposes of examining the relationship between core and environmental values, I draw on original public opinion survey data from a national survey fielded in October of 2017.[2] In the survey, the NEP scale was measured using the six questions listed above, and those questions were averaged on a 1 to 7 scale, where respondents closer to 1 are associated with cornucopian values and those closer to 7 are associated with environmentalism. Each of the cultural types were measured using the set of three statements listed above for each of the four cultural types. Respondents were asked their agreement with each statement on a 1–7 scale, where 1 indicates strongly disagree and 7 indicates strongly agree. The responses to the three statements associated with each cultural type were averaged into a single 1–7 scale, where higher scores, up to 7, indicate increasing agreement with that cultural type.

Political ideology was measured by asking respondents to place themselves on a 1–7 scale of ideology, where one is strong liberal, 4 is middle of the road, and 7

TABLE 4.1 Core Values and Environmental Values

	Dependent variable
	NEP scale
Hierarchy	-0.013
	(0.029)
Egalitarianism	0.169***
	(0.025)
Individualism	-0.140***
	(0.029)
Fatalism	-0.091***
	(0.027)
Ideology (more conservative)	-0.165***
	(0.025)
Partisanship (more Republican)	-0.045**
	(0.022)
Observations	819
Adjusted R^2	0.302

Note: Controlling for age, gender, ethnicity, education, and income
Note: *p<0.10; **p<0.05; ***p<0.01

is strong conservative. Partisanship is measured by combining party identification with the strength of that identification, which produces a 1–7 scale, with 1 being strong Democrat, 4 independent, and 7 being strong Republican.[3] The results are shown in Table 4.1.

As expected, hierarchy is not predictive of environmental values as measured by the NEP scale. Also as expected, increasing egalitarianism is positively associated with environmentalism, and increasing individualism is negatively associated with environmentalism. Finally, fatalism, increasing conservatism, and Republican party attachment are also negatively associated with environmentalism.

Core and environmental values work to shape the way that environmental policy issues are understood and defined in policy debates. As the above analysis shows, core values such as political ideology and the cultural types derived from cultural theory influence environmental values. The next section describes the cognitive mechanisms through which values operate to shape policy attitudes. In addition, it explores the connection between core values, environmental values – as measured by the NEP scale – and attitudes associated with climate change.

Values and Cognition

Values nested in value-systems play a key role in determining specific policy attitudes in part by guiding the way that individuals reason about particular issues.

A large body of research has examined the heuristics and other cognitive processing short-cuts that individuals use when considering complex policy issues. Value-based reasoning involves individuals using system 1 processing to quickly access policy-relevant information based on the implications of that information in light of their values or partisan attachments. For example, a conservative is likely to reject information about the risks of climate change if the implication of accepting that information is a need for government regulation of economic activity.

Political debates surrounding climate change often pivot on the acceptance or rejection of the scientific consensus, or even a broader rejection of science in general. One argument goes that if those that were skeptical of climate change knew that there was a strong scientific consensus, then they would view climate change as risky and support policies to address a changing climate. Indeed, some scholars have termed a recognition of the scientific consensus as a "gateway belief" that leads to an increased likelihood to accept that climate change is happening, man-made, and poses some risks (van der Linden et al. 2015; van der Linden, Leiserowitz, and Maibach 2017; but see Kahan 2017). However, other scholars have found that, regarding the nature of value-based cognition and climate change, a) individuals are likely to use cognitive filters, b) these filters reflect our cultural identity, and c) cultural identity overrides scientific reasoning (Hoffman 2015, 3–4). Therefore, specific policy attitudes are often formed from a desire to affirm values rather than from a desire to learn from the best-available information.

The use of value-affirming cognitive filters implies that knowledge is not sufficient to change minds about contentious issues like climate change. In fact, increased sophistication can exacerbate polarization on issues that are politically contentious. For example, Hamilton (2011) found that educational attainment tended to increase polarization on climate change, such that Republicans with more education were *less* likely to think that global warming posed a serious threat than less-educated Republicans, whereas, as education increased among Democrats, they were *more* likely to see warming as a threat. Additional work has found that education, science education, and science literacy can increase ideological polarization on issues such as stem cell research, the big bang, evolution, and climate change (Drummond and Fischhoff 2017).

To illustrate the potential for science knowledge to increase polarization on views about climate change along ideological lines, I use public opinion data collected from Pew Research Center in 2009 and 2014. In 2009 Pew asked respondents a serious of five questions about their scientific knowledge, such as "*What have scientists recently discovered on Mars*" and "*Which over-the-counter drug do doctors recommend that people take to help prevent heart attacks.*" In 2014 Pew asked seven traditional science literacy questions, such as "*Is the following statement true or false? Lasers work by focusing sound waves*", "*Does nanotechnology deal with things that are extremely small*", and "*Which is an example of a chemical reaction?*" In both 2009 and 2014, Pew asked respondents whether or not they considered global warming

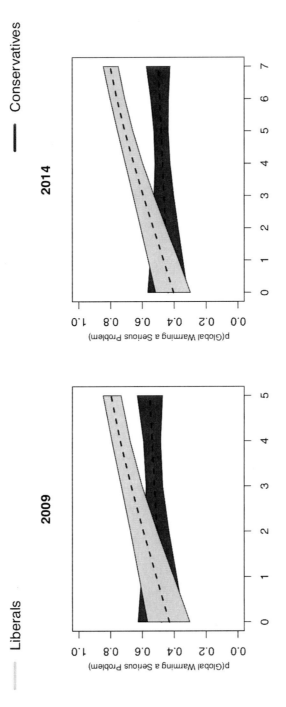

FIGURE 4.4 Ideology, science knowledge, and climate change views

to be a serious problem. Figure 4.4 illustrates the results of the interactive relationship between ideology and science knowledge on the probability of believing that global warming is a serious problem, controlling for partisanship (Democrat or Republican), age, gender, race, education, and income for both 2009 and 2014.

As shown, in both years and with different measures of science knowledge, liberals tend to be more likely to consider global warming a problem as science knowledge increases, whereas increasing science knowledge tends to have no impact on the views of conservatives.

Increased value polarization coupled with increased sophistication is likely a result of the two-system model of cognitive processing, where system 2 reasoning is used to justify the initial values-based intuitions of system 1. Individuals that are more educated or more science-literate may be better-motivated reasoners and better able to employ system 2 to justify their attitudes. In addition, more sophisticated members of the public are also likely to be better attuned to the debates among political and policy elites and can then adjust their views to match the elites with which they agree. The polarized elite debate surrounding climate change is more likely to filter down to those in the public that are more sophisticated than the general, overall public. Finally, sophistication may mean that individuals are better able to find information that supports their viewpoints.

Similar to political values, Kahan et al. (2012) found that polarization across cultural types regarding climate change risk tended to increase with increasing science literacy and numeracy. The work by Kahan and his colleagues has expanded the values associated with cultural theory and associated those values with several cognitive mechanisms that can explain how values and cognition work together to shape policy attitudes. The next section discusses *cultural cognition* as well as *environmental cognition* and several of the mechanisms through which they operate.

Cultural and Environmental Cognition

The work on cultural cognition developed by drawing on the values derived from cultural theory coupled with social psychology research on cognitive processes. According to cultural cognition, cognition is used to align specific policy attitudes with the various sets of values, rooted in the cultures derived from cultural theory, that individuals hold. Specifically, cultural cognition holds that, "individuals, as a result of a complex of psychological mechanisms, tend to form perceptions of societal risks that cohere with values characteristic of groups with which they identify" (Kahan et al. 2012, 732).

Cultural cognition is rooted in cultural theory, although it conceptualizes the cultural ways-of-life in a different way. As opposed to deriving the four cultural types from the grid and group dimensions, cultural cognition sees the grid dimension as a continuum from hierarchy to egalitarianism and the group dimension as a continuum that ranges from individualism to communitarianism. Like cultural theory, cultural cognition is measured through agreement with several statements representing each type. The hierarchy(H)-egalitarianism(E) scale statements are,

- *(H) We have gone too far in pushing equal rights in this country*
- *(H) It seems like blacks, women, gays and other minorities don't want equal rights; they want special rights just for them*
- *(H) Society as a whole has become way too soft and feminine*
- *(E) Our society would be better off if the distribution of wealth was more equal*
- *(E) We need to dramatically reduce the inequalities between the rich and the poor, whites and people of color, and men and women*
- *(E) Discrimination against minorities is still a very serious problem*

The individualist(I)–communitarian(C) statements include

- *(I) The government interferes far too much in our everyday lives*
- *(I) It's not the government's business to try to protect people from hurting themselves*
- *(I) The government should stop telling people how to live their lives*
- *(C) Sometimes the government needs to make laws that keep people from hurting themselves*
- *(C) The government should do more to advance society's goals, even if that means limiting the freedom and choices of others*
- *(C) Government should put limits on the choices individuals can make so they don't get in the way of what's good for society*

While the grid and group measures have the potential to determine four cultural cognition types, the majority of studies orientate individuals as tending towards being hierarch-individualists or egalitarian-communitarians. Hierarch-individualists and egalitarian-communitarians vary in their perceptions of risk across a range of policy issues including the HPV vaccine (Kahan et al. 2010) and nanotechnology (Kahan et al. 2009). With regard to climate change, hierarch-individualists tend to view climate change as posing less of a risk than egalitarian-communitarians (Kahan et al. 2012). Finally, views about who counts as a scientific expert have been demonstrated to be associated with agreement on policy beliefs derived from cultural cognition, as opposed to an expert's background and credentials (Kahan, Jenkins-Smith, and Braman 2011).

Environmental cognition refers to the "way individuals structure their thinking about environmental issues and associated political actions" (Henry and Dietz 2012, 238). It works in a similar way as cultural cognition by drawing on environmental values – values associated with the preferred interactions between humans and nature – to guide an individual's consideration of environmental issues. Given the hierarchical nature of value-systems, cultural values and cognition influence environmental values and cognition. Similar to the value structures of cultural theory and environmentalism, hierarch-individualists are likely to view nature as tolerant and robust to human intervention, whereas, egalitarian-communitarians are likely to view nature as fragile, ephemeral, and needing of protection. Finally, these sets of values are likely to constrain policy attitudes.

The next section discusses the mechanisms employed by cultural and environmental cognition, followed by an illustration of value-based cognition and climate change risk perceptions.

Mechanisms of Cultural and Environmental Cognition

When individuals draw on deeply held values to make sense of environmental policy disputes they do so through a series of psychological mechanisms, of which they may or may not be aware. Kahan (2012) notes five important mechanisms through which cultural cognition, as well as environmental cognition, operate, including cultural identity-protective cognition, culturally biased assimilation of information, cultural availability, cultural credibility, and cultural-identity affirmation.

Cultural identity-protective cognition: cultural identity results from an individual orienting themselves according to their preferred structure of social relationships, which then creates an identity based in the subsequent cultural biases. Cognition in the service of identity-protection ensures that policy attitudes do not threaten an individual's preferred way-of-life. For example, an individualist's identity is based in the belief that individuals in a society should be free to compete and negotiate with others without external interference. Environmental regulation that limits the ability of an entrepreneur to extract resources or develop technology is seen as a threat to the way-of-life preferred by individualists, therefore those with the individualist cultural orientation are not likely to support such policies.

Culturally biased assimilation of information: the mechanism of biased assimilation of information works to ensure that individuals process information about political and policy issues is a way that confirms, rather than refutes, their values. This means that information that supports prior values-based beliefs is weighted more heavily than information that challenges those beliefs. Biased information processing can lead to polarization on issues, as those aligned with a particular cultural orientation acquire information that supports their views and refutes the views of others.

Cultural availability: the availability heuristic posits that individuals are biased in their understanding of probabilities by overestimating the likelihood of events that they can readily bring to mind (Tversky and Kahneman 1973). Cultural availability is the mechanism that guides the selection of salient experiences. For example, egalitarians are more likely to perceive increases in temperatures, droughts, and floods in their local areas than are individualists, even when controlling for actual weather deviations (Goebbert et al. 2012). This is likely because instances of weather events that are perceived to be impacted by climate change are more available to egalitarians than to individualists.

Cultural credibility: notions of credibility are connected to biased-information processing. When shifting through information individuals are likely to place more trust in information that they receive from sources they find credible. The cultural credibility mechanism ensures that credible sources of information are those that align with an individual's prior beliefs and values. For an egalitarian-communitarian, a scientist who argues that climate change is a result of the sun cycle is not likely to be thought of as credible. Indeed, the way individuals perceive the expertise of a scientist can be a function of the scientist's stated positions on contentious issues rather than the credentials of the purported expert. Using an experiment embedded in a survey, Kahan, Jenkins-Smith, and Braman (2011) varied the positions of experts on three contentious issues – climate change, nuclear waste disposal, and gun control – while keeping the credentials (Ivy League education, prestigious academic position) of the experts consistent. Kahan, Jenkins-Smith, and Braman (2011) found that respondents were more likely to rate individuals as experts when the expert's stated positions on the issues matched the positions of the respondent's cultural type. This finding indicates that the credibility of the information and the expertise of the source are determined, in part, through value-based cognition.

Cultural-identity affirmation: the identity affirmation mechanism posits that individuals develop policy attitudes that affirm their cultural identity and biases. For example, the harmful impacts of climate change affirm the suspicions of unencumbered capitalism held by egalitarian-communitarians. One possible implication of identity affirmation is that climate change policy should be a "clumsy solution" that has the potential to appeal to multiple cultural types (Verweij et al. 2006). A clumsy solution for climate change would involve combinations of government oversight, technological development, market forces, and dispersed realms of authority between federal, state, and local government. Such solutions may have the potential to build coalitions of policy actors and receive majority public support. Indeed, Kahan et al. (2015) found that offering geoengineering as a solution to climate change reduced polarization between cultural types. In addition, the deployment of nuclear energy as a low-carbon energy source receives support from individualists (Jones 2011).

Climate Change Risk

To demonstrate the nature of values and policy attitudes, in this section I use unique survey data to predict environmentalism and perceived climate change risk using measures of cultural cognition. The survey data is drawn from residents in South Carolina's eight coastal counties, including Beaufort, Berkeley, Charleston, Colleton, Dorchester, Georgetown, Horry, and Jasper, and is used to demonstrate the influence of cultural and environmental cognition on climate change risk perceptions. The survey was administered online and collected in two waves. The first wave was administered from March 25 to April 8, 2015 to a sample of residents in each county obtained from Survey Sampling International. The second wave was given to a sample from EMC Research and was administered from August 18 to August 29, 2015.

Similar to the measurement of the cultural types discussed above, respondents were asked their agreement on the series of cultural cognition statements on a 1 (strongly disagree) to 7 (strongly agree) scale. For purposes of analysis, dummy variables were created for each cultural type including hierarchs, egalitarians, individualists, and communitarians.[4] Then, dummy variables were created for hierarch-individualists and egalitarian-communitarian. In addition, respondents were asked the New Ecological Paradigm questions discussed above as a measure of environmental values. Next, respondents were asked their perceptions of the risk posed by climate change with 0 indicating no risk and 10 indicating extreme risk. The mean for the climate change risk question was 7.574, indicating a high level of perceived risk from climate change. Finally, respondents were asked a variety of demographic questions that are used as control variables in the following models.

Given the hierarchical nature of value systems, it is expected that cultural cognition will influence environmental cognition and both will influence perceptions of climate change risk. To examine this assertion, I used OLS regression to predict environmentalism, based on the NEP scale, using cultural cognition measures as well as a regression analysis on climate change risk using cultural cognition measures and environmentalism. The results are shown in Table 4.2.

As can be seen, egalitarian-communitarian is associated with an increase in environmentalism as well as an increase in perceived risk from climate change. On the other hand, increasing hierarch-individualism is associated with a decrease in environmentalism as well as a decrease in climate change risk perceptions. Finally, an increase in environmentalism is associated with increased perceptions of climate change risk.

TABLE 4.2 Cultural and Environmental Cognition and Climate Change Risk

	Dependent variable	
	NEP scale	Climate risk
Egalitarian-communitarian	0.271**	0.428*
	(0.112)	(0.234)
Hierarch-individualist	-0.432***	-1.206***
	(0.107)	(0.225)
NEP scale		1.168***
		(0.091)
Observations	532	532
Adjusted R²	0.198	0.410

Note: Controlling for ideology, age, gender, ethnicity, education, and income
Note: *p<0.10; **p<0.05; ***p<0.01

These results illustrate the hierarchical nature of value systems and the impacts of value-based cognition on attitudes about climate change. The next section examines support for several policy approaches to address climate change.

Support for Climate Change Policy Options

The ultimate goal of overcoming the divisions in public opinion concerning climate change is to break the political gridlock associated with the development of policies to mitigate climate change. However, the debate over solutions to climate change was likely a major cause of value-based polarization. Solution-based polarization, termed "solution aversion" (Campbell and Kay 2014), occurs when solutions to problems rather than the problems themselves form the basis for political divisions. Therefore, conservatives and Republicans may not necessarily reject climate science *per se*, but rather reject policies that would involve government regulation to address climate change. Therefore, one way to break the gridlock over climate change might be to focus on policy solutions that could receive majority support.

In general, studies that have examined specific policy options have found support for policy proposals to be driven by the same value distinctions as other climate change opinions (Leiserowitz 2006; Stoutenborough, Bromley-Trujillo, and Vedlitz 2014). However, a large amount of variation exists in support of particular policy options. For example, emission reductions and renewable energy are typically supported by majorities of respondents regardless of value orientations. Yet differences in policy support exist across cultural types. For example, Jones (2011) found that individualists were supportive of nuclear energy as a way to address climate change, and Kahan et al. (2015) found that presenting information about geoengineering as a solution to climate change worked to shift the views of hierarch-individualists about the risks posed by climate change. The difference in views of climate change risk associated with the presentation of a policy solution acceptable to hierarch-individualists provides evidence for solution-aversion as a driver of polarization on climate change.

Using the coastal South Carolina survey data, I examine support for various policies designed to address climate change. Respondents were given the following prompt prior to the policy options questions:

> Various policy solutions have been proposed as ways for the federal government in the United States to deal with climate change. Using a one to seven-point scale where one is *strongly oppose* and seven is *strongly support*, please indicate your support for each of the following policy proposals.

Table 4.3 presents the questions, the mean level of support, and the standard deviations for each of the policy options. In addition, an aggregate measure that averages support for all of the policy options is also presented.

TABLE 4.3 Mean Support for Climate Change Policy Options

Policy option	Mean	sd
Encourage research and development of renewable energy sources like solar or wind power	5.793	1.420
Encourage development of "geoengineering" technology such as filters that remove excess carbon dioxide from the air and high-altitude orbiting reflectors to reduce solar heating	5.165	1.508
Environmental Protection Agency regulations that limit the amount of carbon dioxide and other greenhouse gases that power plants can emit	4.940	1.820
Accept internationally established limits on US production of carbon dioxide and other greenhouse gases thought to cause climate change	4.544	1.818
A cap-and-trade program that sets an overall cap on emissions through allowances that can be bought, sold, or saved for future use	4.267	1.818
Expand the use of nuclear energy	4.258	1.700
A carbon tax that imposes a charge on coal, oil, and natural gas in proportion to the carbon they contain	4.114	1.937
Aggregate policy support	**4.726**	**1.165**

Note that the policy preferences in Table 4.3 are presented in descending order. As shown in other studies (Krosnick and MacInnis 2013; Stoutenborough, Liu, and Vedlitz 2014), renewable energy is a popular option to address climate change with a mean of 5.793 on the 1–7 scale. Geoengineering has the next highest mean with 5.165. A potential carbon tax has the lowest mean at 4.114, which is at about the midpoint of the scale.

To illustrate the differences in support for the various policy options across cultural cognition types, I ran OLS models for each policy option and then ran 1,000 simulations of those models. The results of the simulations are shown in Figure 4.5.

The simulations clearly illustrate the differences in support for policies between the cultural types, particularly concerning EPA regulations, international agreements, cap-and-trade, and the carbon tax. Each of those four policy options is polarized along cultural orientation lines. Renewable energy, geoengineering, and nuclear energy appear much less polarized, with renewable energy and geoengineering favored above the midpoint of the scale by both cultural orientations. Finally, nuclear energy is roughly near the midpoint for both cultural groups.

Conclusion

This chapter examined the role that value systems play in shaping environmental policy attitudes and discourse. Value differences are one of the major bases for

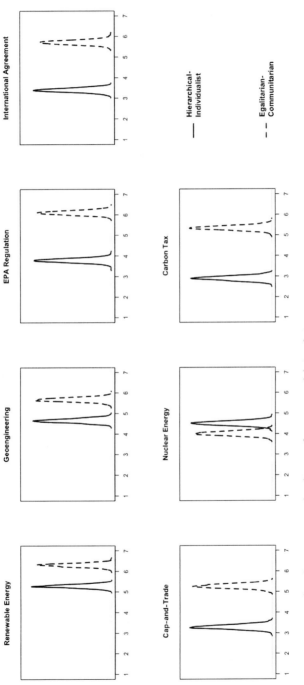

FIGURE 4.5 Cultural cognition and policy preferences model simulations

environmental disputes. Values are hierarchically structured such that broad in scope core values regarding the role of government in society or the preferred structures of social relationships constrain environmental values regarding the relationship between humans and nature. Then, both core and environmental values work to shape attitudes about specific environmental policy issues such as climate change.

Several cognitive mechanisms are employed to translate values into specific attitudes. The two-systems model of cognition posits that on one level, system 1, individuals make quick, intuitive judgments, while more deliberate cognition occurs on another level, system 2. Values inform system 1 intuition and are then reinforced by system 2 reasoning. The method of system 1 and system 2 cognition is aided by a set of mechanisms that seeks to protect and affirm value-based identities as well as motivate information processing.

Political ideology and partisanship tend to be the most clearly expressed core values in public and political debates about environmental policy issues. Partisan and ideological divisions regarding environmental issues have grown over time for both elected officials and the public. Even though many in the public, particularly those that aren't politically engaged, may not clearly align on a single left-right dimension, political parties provide the public with a "team" with which to align to make sense of complex policy issues. As shown in Figure 4.2, divides among the public between self-identified liberals and Democrats and conservatives and Republicans exist regarding support for government spending on the environment, and this division seems to have grown since the early 1990s. Political parties are coalitions of individuals that hold various core values, and parties aide individuals in the public with orientating their values with regard to policy debates.

Salient core values extend beyond political ideology and partisanship. Most notably, cultural theory argues that individuals derive their values from their preferred structure of social relationships. Potential social orderings vary on a grid dimension, which reflects the degree of social regulation, and a group dimension that reflects the preferred degree of social cohesion. These dimensions combine to create four ways of life – hierarchy, egalitarianism, individualism, and fatalism – as well as four associated myths of nature – tolerant, ephemeral, benign, and capricious – that become the foundation for value-based cognition. Combining the value orientations of cultural theory and insights from social psychology, cultural cognition posits that the pivotal culturally derived values are hierarch-individualists and egalitarian-communitarians.

At the domain-specific level of values are environmental values based in questions of the appropriate relationship between humans and nature. While cultural theory provides four myths of nature, environmental values can be reflected in one dimension with cornucopians, who view nature as providing abundant resources, on one end and environmentalists, who view nature as fragile, on the other. Like the four myths of nature, environmental values are constrained by the core values represented by an individual's cultural identity. Core and environmental values constrain attitudes on issues like climate change, through a series of cognitive mechanisms.

Breaking the political impasse over climate change will involve more than education efforts regarding the scientific consensus, it must also involve the development of policy solutions that are amenable to multiple values. The chapter finished with an empirical demonstration of the influence of cultural cognition and environmental values on the perceived risk of climate change as well as the role of cultural cognition in influencing support for various policy options.

Notes

1 The party measures include independents that lean towards that party.
2 Survey respondents came from Survey Sampling International, which provides a Census-balanced pool of respondents.
3 I also controlled for demographics including age, gender, ethnicity, education, and income; however, those results are not presented.
4 For the hierarchy-egalitarianism scale, higher scores indicated an increasing egalitarian orientation, so scores from 1 to 3 on that scale were coded as hierarchs and scores from 5 to 7 were coded as egalitarian. The same process was performed for the individualism-communitarianism scale, with higher values indicating communitarianism. However, given a low number of communitarians in this sample, the coding for communitarians was relaxed to include scores of 4 to 7.

References

Baumgartner, Frank R., and Bryan D. Jones. 2015. *The Politics of Information: Problem Definition and the Course of Public Policy in America.* Chicago, IL: University of Chicago Press.

Blake, Aaron. 2017. "Sean Spicer's Defense of Himself and Explanation of Donald Trump's Sensitivity, Annotated." *The Washington Post.* www.washingtonpost.com/news/the-fix/wp/2017/01/23/sean-spicers-defense-of-himself-and-explanation-of-donald-trumps-sensitivity-annotated/?noredirect=on\&utm_term=.4cea9dc188b5\&utm_term=.000c624482de.

Bratman, Gregory N., Gretchen C. Daily, Benjamin J. Levy, and James J. Gross. 2015. "The Benefits of Nature Experience: Improved Affect and Cognition." *Landscape and Urban Planning* 138: 41–50.

Brulle, Robert J., Jason Carmichael, and J. Craig Jenkins. 2012. "Shifting Public Opinion on Climate Change: An Empirical Assessment of Factors Influencing Concern over Climate Change in the US, 2002–2010." *Climatic Change* 114(2): 169–188.

Calvert, Jerry W. 1989. "Party Politics and Environmental Policy." In *Environmental Politics and Policy: Theories and Evidence*, ed. James P. Lester. Durham, NC: Duke University Press.

Campbell, Troy H., and Aaron C. Kay. 2014. "Solution Aversion: On the Relation Between Ideology and Motivated Disbelief." *Journal of Personality and Social Psychology* 107(5): 809–824.

Dietz, Thomas, Amy Fitzgerald, and Rachael Shwom. 2005. "Environmental Values." *Annual Review of Environment and Resources* 30(1): 335–372.

Dietz, Thomas, Linda Kalof, and Paul C. Stern. 2002. "Gender, Values, and Environmentalism." *Social Science Quarterly* 83(1): 353–364.

Douglas, Mary. 2003. "Being Fair to Hierarchists." *University of Pennsylvania Law Review* 151(4): 1349–1370.

Douglas, Mary, and Aaron Wildavsky. 1982. *Risk and Culture: An Essay on the Selection of Technological and Environmental Dangers*. Berkeley, CA: University of California Press.

Drummond, Caitlin, and Baruch Fischhoff. 2017. "Individuals with Greater Science Literacy and Education Have More Polarized Beliefs on Controversial Science Topics." *Proceedings of The National Academy of Sciences of the United States of America* 114(36): 9587–9592.

Dunlap, R.E., C. Xiao, and A.M. McCright. 2001. "Politics and Environment in America: Partisan and Ideological Cleavages in Public Support for Environmentalism." *Environmental Politics* 10(4): 23–48.

Dunlap, Riley E., and Kent D. Van Liere. 1984. "Commitment to the Dominant Social Paradigm and Concern for Environmental Quality." *Social Science Quarterly* 65(4): 1013–1028.

Dunlap, Riley E., Kent D. Van Liere, Angela G. Mertig, and Robert Emmet Jones. 2000. "New Trends in Measuring Environmental Attitudes: Measuring Endorsement of the New Ecological Paradigm: A Revised NEP Scale." *Journal of Social Issues* 56(3): 425–442.

Ellis, Richard J., and Fred Thompson. 1997. "Seeing Green: Cultural Biases and Environmental Preferences." In *Culture Matters: Essays in Honor of Aaron Wildavsky*, eds. Richard J. Ellis and Michael Thompson. Boulder, CO: Westview Press.

Goebbert, Kevin, Hank C. Jenkins-Smith, Kim Klockow, Matthew C. Nowlin, and Carol L. Silva. 2012. "Weather, Climate and Worldviews: The Sources and Consequences of Public Perceptions of Changes in Local Weather Patterns." *Weather, Climate, and Society* 4(2): 132–144.

Guillen, Alex, and Emily Holden. 2017. "What EPA Chief Scott Pruitt Promised and What He's Done." *POLITICO*. www.politico.com/interactives/2017/scott-pruitt-promises/.

Haidt, Jonathan. 2001. "The Emotional Dog and Its Rational Tail: A Social Intuitionist Approach to Moral Judgment." *Psychological Review* 108(4): 814–834.

Hamilton, Lawrence C. 2011. "Education, Politics and Opinions About Climate Change Evidence for Interaction Effects." *Climatic Change* 104(2): 231–242.

Henry, Adam Douglas, and Thomas Dietz. 2012. "Understanding Environmental Cognition." *Organization & Environment* 25(3): 238–258.

Hoffman, Andrew J. 2015. *How Culture Shapes the Climate Change Debate*. Stanford, CA: Stanford Briefs.

Jenkins-Smith, Hank C. 2001. "Modeling Stigma: An Empirical Analysis of Nuclear Waste Images." In *Risk, Media and Stigma: Understanding Public Challenges to Modern Science and Technology*, eds. James Flynn, Paul Slovic, and Howard Kunreuther. London: Earthscan Press.

Jenkins-Smith, Hank C., Daniel Nohrstedt, Christopher M. Weible, and Karin Ingold. 2018. "The Advocacy Coalition Framework: An Overview of the Research Program." In *Theories of the Policy Process*, eds. Christopher M. Weible and Paul A. Sabatier. New York, NY: Westview Press, 135–172.

Jones, Michael D. 2011. "Leading the Way to Compromise? Cultural Theory and Climate Change Opinion." *PS: Political Science & Politics* 44(04): 720–725.

Kahan, Dan M. 2012. "Cultural Cognition as a Conception of the Cultural Theory of Risk." In *Handbook of Risk Theory: Epistemology, Decision Theory, Ethics, and Social Implications of Risk*, eds. Sabine Roeser, Rafaela Hillerbrand, Per Sandin, and Martin Peterson. Springer, 725–759.

———. 2017. "The 'Gateway Belief' Illusion: Reanalyzing the Results of a Scientific-Consensus Messaging Study." *Journal of Science Communication* 16(5): 1–20.

Kahan, Dan M., Donald Braman, Geoffrey L. Cohen, John Gastil, and Paul Slovic. 2010. "Who Fears the HPV Vaccine, Who Doesn't, and Why? An Experimental Study of the Mechanisms of Cultural Cognition." *Law and Human Behavior* 34(6): 501–516.

Kahan, Dan M., Donald Braman, Paul Slovic, John Gastil, and Geoffrey Cohen. 2009. "Cultural Cognition of the Risks and Benefits of Nanotechnology." *Nature Nanotechnology* 4(2): 87–90.

Kahan, Dan M., Hank C. Jenkins-Smith, and Donald Braman. 2011. "Cultural Cognition of Scientific Consensus." *Journal of Risk Research* 14(2): 147–174.

Kahan, Dan M., Hank Jenkins-Smith, Tor Tarantola, Carol L. Silva, and Donald Braman. 2015. "Geoengineering and Climate Change Polarization Testing a Two-Channel Model of Science Communication." *The ANNALS of the American Academy of Political and Social Science* 658(1): 192–222.

Kahan, Dan M., Ellen Peters, Maggie Wittlin, Paul Slovic, Lisa Larrimore Ouellette, Donald Braman, and Gregory Mandel. 2012. "The Polarizing Impact of Science Literacy and Numeracy on Perceived Climate Change Risks." *Nature Climate Change* 2(10): 732–735.

Kahneman, Daniel. 2013. *Thinking, Fast and Slow.* New York, NY: Farrar, Straus and Giroux.

Kim, Sung Eun, and Johannes Urpelainen. 2017. "The Polarization of American Environmental Policy: A Regression Discontinuity Analysis of Senate and House Votes, 1971–2013." *Review of Policy Research* 34(4): 456–484.

Kinder, Donald R., and Nathan P. Kalmoe. 2017. *Neither Liberal nor Conservative: Ideological Innocence in the American Public.* Chicago, IL: University of Chicago Press.

Krosnick, Jon A., Allyson L. Holbrook, and Penny S. Visser. 2000. "The Impact of the Fall 1997 Debate About Global Warming on American Public Opinion." *Public Understanding of Science* 9(3): 239–260.

Krosnick, Jon A., and Bo MacInnis. 2013. "Does the American Public Support Legislation to Reduce Greenhouse Gas Emissions?" *Daedalus* 142(1): 26–39.

Layzer, Judith A. 2012. *The Environmental Case: Translating Values into Policy.* 3rd ed. Washington, DC: CQ Press.

Leiserowitz, Anthony. 2006. "Climate Change Risk Perception and Policy Preferences: The Role of Affect, Imagery, and Values." *Climatic Change* 77(1): 45–72.

Levendusky, Matthew S. 2010. "Clearer Cues, More Consistent Voters: A Benefit of Elite Polarization." *Political Behavior* 32(1): 111–131.

Maller, Cecily, Mardie Townsend, Anita Pryor, Peter Brown, and Lawrence St Leger. 2006. "Healthy Nature Healthy People: 'Contact with Nature' as an Upstream Health Promotion Intervention for Populations." *Health Promotion International* 21(1): 45–54.

Mazmanian, Daniel A., and Michael E. Kraft. 1999. "The Three Epochs of the Environmental Movement." In *Toward Sustainable Communities: Transition and Transformations in Environmental Policy*, eds. Daniel A. Mazmanian and Michael E. Kraft. Cambridge, MA: MIT Press, 3–42.

McCright, Aaron M., and Riley E. Dunlap. 2013. "Bringing Ideology in: The Conservative White Male Effect on Worry About Environmental Problems in the USA." *Journal of Risk Research* 16(2): 211–226.

Naess, Arne. 1973. "The Shallow and the Deep, Long-Range Ecology Movement. A Summary." *Inquiry* 16(1): 95–100.

Peffley, Mark A., and Jon Hurwitz. 1985. "A Hierarchical Model of Attitude Constraint." *American Journal of Political Science* 29(4): 871–890.

Pendergraft, Curtis A. 1998. "Human Dimensions of Climate Change: Cultural Theory and Collective Action." *Climatic Change* 39(4): 643–666.

Ripberger, Joseph T., Kuhika Gupta, Carol L. Silva, and Hank C. Jenkins-Smith. 2014. "Cultural Theory and the Measurement of Deep Core Beliefs Within the Advocacy Coalition Framework." *Policy Studies Journal* 42(4): 509–527.

Ripberger, Joseph T., Hank C. Jenkins-Smith, and Kerry G. Herron. 2011. "How Cultural Orientations Create Shifting National Security Coalitions on Nuclear Weapons and Terrorist Threats in the American Public." *PS: Political Science & Politics* 44(04): 715–719.

Sabatier, Paul A., and Hank C. Jenkins-Smith. 1993. *Policy Change and Learning: An Advocacy Coalition Approach.* Boulder, CO: Westview Press.

Sabatier, Paul A., and Christopher M. Weible. 2007. "The Advocacy Coalition Framework: Innovations and Clarifications." In *Theories of the Policy Process*, ed. Paul A. Sabatier. Boulder, CO: Westview Press, 189–222.

Schwartz, Barry. 1991. "A Pluralistic Model of Culture." *Contemporary Sociology* 20(5): 764–766.

Schwartz, Shalom H. 1992. "Universals in the Content and Structure of Values: Theoretical Advances and Empirical Tests in 20 Countries." In *Advances in Experimental Social Psychology*, ed. Mark P. Zanna. New York, NY: Academic Press, 1–65.

Shipan, Charles R., and William R. Lowry. 2001. "Environmental Policy and Party Divergence in Congress." *Political Research Quarterly* 54(2): 245–263.

Smith, Zachary A. 2012. *The Environmental Policy Paradox.* 6th ed. Boston, MA: Pearson.

Song, Geoboo. 2014. "Understanding Public Perceptions of Benefits and Risks of Childhood Vaccinations in the United States." *Risk Analysis* 34(3): 541–555.

Steg, Linda, and Inge Sievers. 2000. "Cultural Theory and Individual Perceptions of Environmental Risks." *Environment and Behavior* 32(2): 250–269.

Stern, Paul C. 2000. "New Environmental Theories: Toward a Coherent Theory of Environmentally Significant Behavior." *Journal of Social Issues* 56(3): 407–424.

Stern, Paul C., Thomas Dietz, Troy D. Abel, Gregory A. Guagnano, and Linda Kalof. 1999. "A Value-Belief-Norm Theory of Support for Social Movements: The Case of Environmentalism." *Human Ecology Review* 6(2): 81–97.

Stern, Paul C., Thomas Dietz, and Linda Kalof. 1993. "Value Orientations, Gender, and Environmental Concern." *Environment and Behavior* 25(5): 322–348.

Stoutenborough, James W., Rebecca Bromley-Trujillo, and Arnold Vedlitz. 2014. "Public Support for Climate Change Policy: Consistency in the Influence of Values and Attitudes over Time and Across Specific Policy Alternatives." *Review of Policy Research* 31(6): 555–583.

Stoutenborough, James W., Xinsheng Liu, and Arnold Vedlitz. 2014. "Trends in Public Attitudes Toward Climate Change: The Influence of the Economy and Climategate on Risk, Information, and Public Policy." *Risk, Hazards & Crisis in Public Policy* 5(1): 22–37.

Thompson, Michael, Richard Ellis, and Aaron Wildavsky. 1990. *Cultural Theory.* Boulder, CO: Westview Press.

Tversky, Amos, and Daniel Kahneman. 1973. "Availability: A Heuristic for Judging Frequency and Probability." *Cognitive Psychology* 5(2): 207–232.

US Environmental Protection Agency, OA. 2014. "Learn About Sustainability." *US EPA.* www.epa.gov/sustainability/learn-about-sustainability.

van der Linden, Sander, Anthony Leiserowitz, and Edward Maibach. 2017. "Gateway Illusion or Cultural Cognition Confusion?" *Journal of Science Communication* 16(5): A04.

van der Linden, Sander L., Anthony A. Leiserowitz, Geoffrey D. Feinberg, and Edward W. Maibach. 2015. "The Scientific Consensus on Climate Change as a Gateway Belief: Experimental Evidence." *PLoS ONE* 10(2).

Verweij, Marco, Mary Douglas, Richard Ellis, Christoph Engel, Frank Hendriks, Susanne Lohmann, Steven Ney, Steve Rayner, and Michael Thompson. 2006. "Clumsy Solutions for A Complex World: The Case of Climate Change." *Public Administration* 84(4): 817–843.

Wildavsky, Aaron. 1987. "Choosing Preferences by Constructing Institutions: A Cultural Theory of Preference Formation." *The American Political Science Review* 81(1): 4–21.

PART II

The Environmental Policymaking System and Climate Policy

5

AGENDA-SETTING AND ISSUE DEFINITIONS IN CLIMATE CHANGE POLICYMAKING

Introduction

In June 1988, in the midst of a severe drought and heatwave in the United States, Dr James Hansen, then director of NASA's Goddard Institute for Space Studies, testified before Congress. Dr Hansen opened his testimony by stating:

> I would like to draw three main conclusions. Number one, the earth is warmer in 1988 than at any time in the history of instrumental measurements. Number two, the global warming is now large enough that we can ascribe with a high degree of confidence a cause and effect relationship to the greenhouse effect. And number three, our computer climate simulations indicate that the greenhouse effect is already large enough to begin to effect the probability of extreme events such as summer heat waves.
>
> *US Congress/Senate 1987*

Dr Hansen's testimony drew the attention of Congress and the media to the issue of climate change. The testimony that he delivered in June of 1988 was not new; in fact he had delivered similar testimony several times before. However, perhaps due to the weather conditions in the summer of 1988, his testimony and the issue of climate change garnered intense media, congressional, and public attention in the United States for the first time.

Why do some issues and problems receive the attention of policymakers while others do not? What makes it more (or less) likely that environmental issues will reach the policy agenda? The policy agenda refers to the issues currently being addressed by the policymaking system, and agenda-setting is the process through which policy issues reach the agenda. The environmental policymaking system is constantly receiving *inputs* – information signals – regarding problems that might need to be addressed. However, the policy agenda is finite, and as a result not all problems that may need to be addressed can receive attention. Reaching the agenda is more likely to occur as a result of changes in inputs that make a problem more difficult to ignore.

Being on the policy agenda means that an issue is a high priority and is being actively considered by the environmental policymaking system, which is a necessary condition for a problem to be addressed. Given the limited capacity and importance of the policy agenda, policy actors compete to push their issues on the agenda or, conversely, to keep opponents' issues off the agenda. Being on the agenda, however, does not guarantee action on the issue. As will be shown, Congress has held hundreds of hearings regarding climate change, yet no legislation aimed at curbing greenhouse gases has ever passed both chambers.

This chapter considers the agenda of the environmental policymaking system as a whole, although the broader policy agenda can be divided into the *institutional* agenda and the *decision* agenda. The institutional agenda contains the policy issues that are being actively considered within a particular institution. Agenda-setting at the institutional level involves the choice of which problems gain (or lose) the attention of the institution. Certain actors, by nature of their position within institutions, can act as agenda-setters. For example, party leaders in Congress can determine what bills reach the floor to be voted on, and committee chairs can decide which issues are discussed in hearings. In addition, presidents can send powerful signals throughout the executive branch about issues that they think should be addressed, and presidents can seek to mobilize support in the public and in Congress to consider legislation. Institutional agenda-setters can exercise *positive* agenda power by determining what issues are considered, as well as *negative* agenda power by keeping issues off the agenda.

The decision agenda is where choices are made from among various policy alternatives (Cobb and Elder 1983). For example, congressional hearings about a particular issue constitute that issue being on the institutional agenda, whereas the decision agenda would involve voting on a particular bill. Attention to issues tends to "bottleneck" or "winnow" such that not all problems reach the institutional agenda and even fewer reach the decision agenda (Jones and Baumgartner 2005b; Krutz 2005).

Issues on the institutional agenda are typically processed within the relevant policy subsystems. In particular, congressional committees with jurisdiction over particular policy domains are the institutional anchors of policy subsystems through which information is processed. Congressional committees then move issues to the decision agenda of Congress, such as when a committee recommends and refers a piece of legislation to the entire chamber. Policy actors wishing to make policy change seek to move their issues from the institutional agenda, where parallel processing of multiple issues at once occurs within subsystems, to the decision agenda, where serial processing occurs by the macro political institutions and decisions are made.[1]

The environmental policymaking system is constantly receiving information signals about the multitude of issues in the problem space. The information carried in those signals can be categorized into one of three streams of information, including the problem stream, the policy stream, and the politics stream. According to the *Multiple Streams Approach*, problems become more likely to reach the agenda, and policy change becomes more likely, when the various streams of information are coupled such that a problem is recognized, potential policy solutions are available, and the public and elected officials are intent on addressing the problem (Herweg, Zahariadis, and Zohlnhofer 2018; Kingdon 2003). Some policy actors, termed *policy entrepreneurs*, work to couple the streams to place issues on the agenda. For example, in 1970, by helping to establish the first Earth Day, Senator Gaylord Nelson worked as a policy entrepreneur to get environmental problems on the agenda by recognizing that problems existed, solutions in the form of regulations were available, and the public was sufficiently concerned about environmental issues.

Once a problem is on the agenda, competition shifts to how that problem should be defined and what, if any, solutions should be considered and adopted. Deciding which problems reach the agenda is termed *first-order* agenda-setting, and determining how a problem is defined is termed *second-order* agenda-setting (Weaver 2007). Both first-order and second-order agenda-setting can be thought of as multidimensional spaces, with the first-order agenda being a multidimensional *problem space*, where the dimensions are the various problems that could potentially reach the agenda, and the second-order agenda is the *issue space*, where the dimensions are the various attributes of the problem.

Policy actors seek to manipulate dimensions in the problem space to make it more likely that an issue is addressed by the environmental policymaking system, and policy actors also seek to manipulate the dimensions of the issue space to define the issue in a particular way to make their preferred solution more likely. Specifically, policy actors often attempt to frame issues by highlighting one dimension of the issue over others, add new dimensions to the issue, or alter the evaluation of one (or more) dimension. By framing, or defining, issues, policy actors seek to *persuade* others of the importance of the issue or the effectiveness of their solution and/or to *mobilize* actors to become engaged on the issue. Most environmental policy issues are ambiguous, complex, and contain multiple dimensions, therefore environmental policy issues could potentially be defined in multiple ways.

This chapter explores agenda-setting and climate change by making use of data from congressional hearings about climate change. First, I examine how changes in information inputs, combined with institutional variables, can make attention to climate change more likely. Then, I examine the issue space of climate change by analyzing the topics that the congressional hearings addressed. Finally, I explore attempts to frame climate change through the testimony provided by policy actors at several congressional hearings.

Inputs and Agenda-Setting

The environmental policymaking system takes the inputs it receives from the broader social, political, and natural environments, and translates those into policy outputs. The inputs are information flows that, "contain signals about 'real-world' policy problems, problem definitions, and potential pathways of government action" (Workman, Jones, and Jochim 2009, 76). The policymaking system, largely through its various subsystems, processes the information signals, where information processing refers to "collecting, assembling, interpreting, and prioritizing signals from the environment" (Jones and Baumgartner 2005b, 7). The processing of information involves the shaping of information flows by the policymaking system into public policies. As noted in Chapter 2 and shown below, the form of that output is based on the institutional context from which it originates, as well as the relative position of other institutions on that issue.

Inputs(Information Signals) → Policymaking System(Information Processing)
  → Outputs(Policy)

Policymaking institutions are awash with information signals and cannot adequately attend to all of them, so signals need to be prioritized, or placed on the agenda, through a process of agenda-setting. Issues reach the agenda of the environmental policymaking system when the system pays attention to and processes the information signals related to that issue. However, the vast amount of information signals and the friction inherent in policymaking institutions make the disproportionate processing of information – the tendency of the system to either under- or over-react to information – all but inevitable (Jones and Baumgartner 2005a; Maor, Tosun, and Jordan 2017).

The inputs to the policymaking system can be characterized as belonging to one of three separate streams of information that operate independently. These streams include the problem stream, the policy stream, and the politics stream, and information flows largely carry information signals about problems, policy solutions, or the political situation related to particular issues.

Problem Stream: the information signals contained in the problem stream consists of information about "various conditions that policymakers and citizens want addressed" (Zahariadis 2014, 32). Information in the problem streams tend to be *entropic*, where multiple sources are providing signals about multiple potential problems (Baumgartner and Jones 2015). Information about conditions can be provided by indicators, focusing events, and feedback.

Multiple indicators are tracked by various executive branch bureaucracies, such as environmental conditions monitored by the Environmental Protection Agency, and a change in one or more of these indicators can signify that a potential problem is emerging. However, indicators monitor *conditions* and an important distinction exists between conditions and *problems*. A condition is something that exists in the world that becomes a problem when it is viewed as something that governments can and should address (Guber and Bosso 2013; Stone 1989). Not all conditions become problems. As Herweg, Zahariadis, and Zohlnhofer (2018) states, "indicators only inform about conditions until an actor defines them as problems" (21). Changing indicators can be used by policy actors in attempting to place an issue on the policymaking agenda by convincing others that these changes are indicative of a problem.

Apart from indicators, *focusing events* can bring attention to a particular problem (Birkland 1997). A focusing event is a singular event that generates attention from the public and the media. Indicators are monitored over long periods of time, whereas focusing events are sudden. Focusing events can reinforce long-standing indicators or allow for a problem to be presented in a new way. Examples of focusing events include natural or man-made disasters, such as the BP oil spill in 2010 or Hurricane Katrina in 2005. Additionally, other events such as an international conference or the release of a new scientific finding or report that generates significant media attention can also be considered focusing events. Focusing events that highlight problematic conditions make it more likely that policymakers will pay attention to and attempt to address those conditions.

The third component of the problem stream is *feedback*, which is information about a problem that has been previously addressed. The environmental policymaking process is dynamic which means that information flows back to the system following the development of policies. This information is largely evaluative regarding past policy choices and is provided by multiple sources including executive agencies, interest groups, the media, and the public. Feedback that brings attention to a failing in previous policy or an unintended consequence of a policy can help push issues onto the agenda.

Policy Stream: Information in the policy stream consists of the ideas, or solutions, that policy actors wish to see enacted. The solutions within the policy stream include those developed by experts and interest groups within a policy subsystem. Policy solutions can be developed independently of problems and policy actors may attempt to attach a favored idea or policy solution to a highly salient problem. For example, Boscarino (2009) found that the Wilderness Society and the Sierra Club advocated for sustainable forestry practices by attaching that solution to multiple salient problems including threats to wildlife, damage to recreational areas, water quality, economic losses, and climate change.

Politics Stream: The politics stream contains "three elements: the national mood, [interest] group campaigns, and administrative or legislative turnover" (Zahariadis 2014, 34). Generally, the politics stream provides information about what government actions would be deemed acceptable in a representative system. The national mood is the aggregate opinion of the public, which can vary from liberal, favoring a more active government, to conservative, favoring a less active government (Stimson 1999). The global mood of the public is dynamic and often responsive to the actions of government, meaning that support for active government declines as the government becomes more active (Erikson, Mackuen, and Stimson 2002; Wlezien 1995). Therefore, public opinion can act as a catalyst or a constraint on policy responses to problems.

Interest groups provide political information largely by lobbying elected officials. In the context of agenda-setting, interest groups may lobby policymakers about issues that the group wants placed on the agenda, as well as issues that the group may wish to keep off the agenda. In addition, interest groups can work to mobilize public support or opposition to issues in attempts to pressure elected officials to address (or not address) certain issues.

Finally, elections act as information about what the public prefers. The two political parties in the United States are polarized on environmental issues, which means that electing one party over the other could be a signal about the relative importance in which the public holds environmental issues.

Issues become more likely to emerge on the agenda when the three information streams are coupled, typically by strategic policy actors, so an issue is seen as a problem, a solution is readily available, and there is sufficient political support. However, an opportunity, termed an *agenda window*, must also be present for the coupling of information streams to allow an issue to reach the agenda (Herweg, Zahariadis, and Zohlnhofer 2018). An agenda window, more commonly referred to as a "policy window" (Kingdon 2003), may be predictable, such as an annual budget or renewal of legislation, or unpredictable, such as an unforeseen focusing event. In addition, agenda windows can be created through changes in the problem or policy information streams. For example, a focusing event in the problem stream may open a window to address that issue, or an election of a president and Congress of a different party from the last can open an agenda window in the political stream.

The processing of the streams of information signals is accomplished by the environmental policymaking system, although the system is not able to adequately process and respond to all information signals. To better assess the flow of information signals, inputs are typically processed by semi-autonomous subsystems that are organized around specific policy issues. Subsystems allow the policymaking system to parallel process and to process information related to multiple policy issues at once. Depending on the nature of the subsystem, some policy actors within a subsystem try to contain the flow of information to keep the policy status quo in place, while other policy actors attempt to shape information flows to push for policy change. For most of the time subsystems exist in an equilibrium state, although changes in the information streams that open an agenda window can be used by policy actors to disrupt a subsystem's equilibrium and push an issue on to the agenda of the macro-institutions. As Baumgartner, Jones, and Mortensen (2018) state:

> Sometimes parallel processing within distinct policy communities breaks down, and issues must be handled serially. In the United States, the

macro-political institutions of Congress and the public presidency engage in governmental serial processing, whereby high-profile issues are considered, contested, and decided one – or at most a few – at a time. An issue moves higher on the political agenda usually because new participants have become interested in the debate. (59)

The processing of information in subsystems tends to break down when a changing issue definition is combined with new policy actors becoming involved across new policymaking venues. In line with the operation of a complex system, subsystem stability is maintained, and altered, by feedback dynamics. Positive feedback is self-reinforcing and pushes subsystems out of equilibrium by creating a cascade of new actors and venues in response to shifts in information inputs (Baumgartner and Jones 2002). Policy actors can drive this process by seeking to frame issues to mobilize other policy actors or by shifting to other policy venues. Often actors employ multiple strategies simultaneously. For example, an environmental interest group may attempt to lobby members of Congress, mobilize their activists to stage demonstrations, seek to gain public support, make comments during an agency's rulemaking process, and engage in litigation all at the same time in an effort to alter one, or more, policy subsystems. The intrusion of new actors and new venues can weaken the equilibrium state of policy subsystems making it more likely that conflict, and policymaking, shifts from the subsystem to the macro-institutions.

Negative feedback creates friction that tamps down potential disruptions and maintains the subsystem's equilibrium through incremental policy adjustments as a result of information flows, which helps to keep information signals about problems from overwhelming the subsystem. Additionally, negative feedback results from the counter-mobilization of actors invested in the policy status quo.

One of the earliest examinations of the agenda-setting process argued that problems go through a five-stage issue-attention cycle (Downs 1972). The issue agenda cycle can help illuminate how issues move from policy subsystems to macro-institutions. The first stage of the cycle is the *pre-problem* stage, where problematic conditions exist but have yet to receive much attention. During the pre-problem stage the environmental policymaking system is receiving information about the issue as inputs, but the processing of information is contained within a stable policy subsystem.

The next stage is the *alarmed discovery and euphoric enthusiasm* stage, where a problem has been discovered and public confidence is high that it can be addressed. During this stage new actors are likely to be mobilized to disrupt the existing policy subsystem, starting the process of positive feedback. Alarmed discovery often occurs after a major high-profile event. For example, as discussed in Chapter 3, environmental issues reached the agenda in the 1960s and 1970s, in part as a result of focusing events such as the publication of Rachel Carson's book *Silent Spring*, the Santa Barbara oil spill, and the Cuyahoga River fire. These events helped spark the environmental movement and helped gain the attention of the broader public and elected officials, making the policy accomplishments of the environmentalism era more likely.

The third stage, *realizing the cost*, involves a gradual coming to terms with the costs associated with fully addressing the problem. As the realization of the costs comes into focus, enthusiasm begins to wane. The curbing of enthusiasm leads to the fourth stage, the *gradual decline of intense public interest*. Finally, the fifth stage is the *post-problem* stage. Downs (1972) notes that the post-problem stage is "a twilight realm of lesser attention or spasmodic recurrences of interest" (40). As issues move from discovery to cost realization, the processing of those issues starts to return to policy subsystems that have regained stability.

In the next section, I examine how changes in information signals in the problem stream affect congressional committee attention to climate change.

Climate Change on the Policymaking Agenda

The issue of climate change is becoming increasingly urgent, yet the degree of attention being paid to it by the environmental policymaking system is not matching the urgency. As discussed, the amount of information that the system processes, coupled with the friction generated by institutions and stable policy subsystems, means that information is processed in a disproportionate manner. In the context of climate change, this has produced a dynamic of attention without a proportionate policy response.

Congressional hearings are often used as a measure of system attention, as congressional committees connect policy subsystems to the macro-institutions of policymaking.[2] Figure 5.1 illustrates the number of congressional hearings about climate change from 1975 to 2016.[3] Overall, 439 hearings about climate change took place.

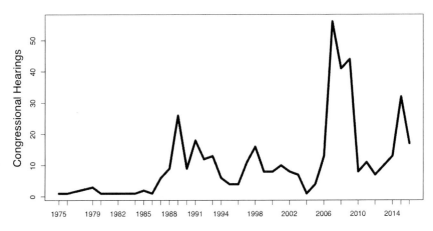

FIGURE 5.1 Congressional attention to climate change, 1975–2016

As can be seen, attention to climate change increased in the late 1980s, when it first gained prominent national and international attention. Another increase occurred in 1997–1998 when the Kyoto Protocol was being considered. The largest spike in attention was from 2007–2009. During this time-period the Democrats had retaken majorities in Congress in the 2006 election and established the *Energy Independence and Global Warming* committee in the House, which provided Democrats in the House with an opportunity to draw attention to the issue of climate change (Lewallen 2018). In addition, the *American Clean Energy and Security Act* (a.k.a. Waxman-Markey) was considered and passed the House in 2009. Finally, an increase is seen in 2014–2015 when the *Paris Agreement* and the Obama administration's *Clean Power Plan* were being developed. Next, I examine potential drivers of congressional attention to climate change.

Problem Stream and Congressional Attention to Climate Change

One of the potential drivers of attention to climate change are the various signals that exist in the problem information stream (Pralle 2009). As signals about problems indicate increasing urgency, the policymaking system becomes more likely to pay attention to the issue. The problem stream provides information about indicators, focusing events, and feedbacks. Liu, Lindquist, and Vedlitz (2011) examined the relationship between changes in the problem stream and attention to climate change from the media and Congress from 1969–2005. They found that focusing events and the net number of scientific publications predicted increased attention to climate change in both the media and Congress, and net increases in atmospheric CO_2 levels predicted increased attention in Congress. Below, I re-examine their findings regarding congressional committee attention with data that ranges from 1980–2016.

Figure 5.2 shows the multiple indicators of climate change used by Liu, Lindquist, and Vedlitz (2011), but ranging from 1980–2016. These indicators include the number of *New York Times* articles about climate change, the Climate Extreme Index (CEI), and the level of CO_2 in the atmosphere. In addition, the number of peer-reviewed scientific publications about climate change, used as a measure of information feedback, is also shown. The number of *New York Times* articles comes from a *LexisNexis* search. The CEI combines measures of monthly maximum and minimum temperatures; daily precipitation; the monthly Palmer Drought Severity Index (PDSI); and the wind velocity of tropical storms and hurricanes that make landfall. The CO_2 level, known as the Keeling Curve, comes from measurements taken at the Mauna Loa Observatory. Finally, the number of scientific publications came from a search of the Web of Science database.[4]

As Figure 5.2 indicates, the severity of the climate change indicators seems to be increasing, thereby signaling an increasing need for policymakers to attend to climate change. The attention model from Chapter 2 noted that attention at time t is a function of information and system level variables: $A_t = \alpha + \beta I_{t-1} + \gamma S_t + \epsilon_t$,

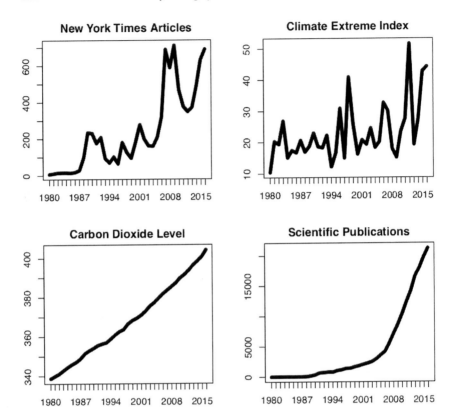

FIGURE 5.2 Climate change problem indicators, 1980–2016

where A is attention in time-period $_t$ and I represents the various inputs at time$_{t-1}$, and S is the system variables at time $_t$. Therefore, as the various climate change indicators increase, I expect attention to climate change in Congress to also increase.

To estimate the agenda model, attention, A_t, is measured as the number of congressional hearings about climate change for each year from 1980 to 2016 shown in Figure 5.1. Additionally, the I_t inputs include those shown in Figure 5.2 for each year as well as several focusing events.

Many of the focusing events were taken from Liu, Lindquist, and Vedlitz (2011, 411), and the events that I added are in italics. The following focusing events were included: the Montreal Protocol in 1987; the Toronto Conference on the Changing Atmosphere and the creation of the Intergovernmental Panel on Climate Change (IPCC) in 1988; the IPCC First Assessment Report and the World Climate Conference in Geneva in 1990; the creation of the United Nations Framework Convention on Climate Change (UNFCCC) in 1992; the IPCC Second Assessment Report and the First Conference of Parties of the UNFCCC in 1995; the Second Conference of Parties of the UNFCCC in 1996; the Third Conference of Parties of the UNFCCC and the Kyoto Protocol in 1997; *the first National Climate Assessment in 2000*; the IPCC Third Assessment Report on Climate Change in 2001; *the release of the film* An Inconvenient Truth *in 2006; the IPCC Fourth Assessment Report in 2007; the 15th Conference of the Parties to the UNFCCC which developed the Copenhagen Accord* and *the second National Climate Assessment in 2009; the IPCC Fourth Assessment Report on Climate Change in 2013; the third National Climate Assessment in 2014;* and *the 21st Conference of the Parties of the UNFCCC that developed the Paris Agreement in 2015.* The focusing events are measured as a total count of events in each year.

The S_t system variables include Democratic control of the congressional chamber holding the hearing, with 1 if Democrats had control and 0 otherwise, as well as the number of hearings held in the previous year to control for the path-dependent nature of issue attention. In addition, following Liu, Lindquist, and Vedlitz (2011) each of the indicator measures and focusing events are lagged one year. Table 5.1 shows the results of the OLS models.

As can be seen, neither problem indicators nor focusing events were predictive of congressional attention to climate change. A Democratic majority in the chamber of Congress holding the hearing was the only significant predictor. The

TABLE 5.1 Congressional Attention to Climate Change, 1980–2016

	Dependent variable
	Hearings
New York Times articles$_{t-1}$	0.030
	(0.028)
Net CO_2 level$_{t-1}$	3.743
	(3.777)
Climate Extreme Index$_{t-1}$	0.236
	(0.211)
Focusing events$_{t-1}$	3.847
	(2.338)
Net scientific publications$_{t-1}$	−0.001
	(0.005)
Democratic Congress	11.085**
	(4.435)
Hearings$_{t-1}$	−0.077
	(0.309)
Constant	−10.536
	(7.171)
Observations	36
Adjusted R^2	0.457

Note: *$p<0.10$; **$p<0.05$; ***$p<0.01$

change in the predictive capacity of the problem indicators from the analysis of Liu, Lindquist, and Vedlitz (2011) is illustrative of the increasingly political nature of climate change. Polarization of climate change increased from 2005, when their data collection ended, to 2016. Additionally, partisan control of Congress changed to the Democrats following the 2006 elections and, as shown in Figure 5.1, this change was associated with an increase in congressional hearings about climate change.

In a similar fashion, little policy change happened as a result of the BP oil spill in 2010, as opposed to the impact of the Santa Barbara oil spill in 1969, likely because of increased polarization on environmental issues (Eisner 2017). As noted, the policymaking system is not always effective in responding in a proportionate manner to the inputs it receives, and partisan polarization on issues may dampen the responsiveness of the policymaking system to information signals in the problem stream. Next, I discuss the other information flows, the policy, and politics streams, associated with climate change.

The Climate Change Policy Stream

For problems to be addressed through policy actions it is important that policy solutions are available. Information in the policy stream is focused on potential solutions in the form of policy instruments that could be implemented to address problems. In addition, information in the policy stream also provides evaluative feedback about the effectiveness of current policies. Policy stream information is considered to be *expert* information, where experts provide information regarding ways to connect solutions to problems (Baumgartner and Jones 2015).

Climate change is of significant complexity, so although policy solutions have been proposed, they are often discussed across multiple policy subsystems. The disjointed nature of climate change policy makes developing an overarching policy aimed at dealing directly with climate change difficult. Generally speaking, there are two broad categories of policy approaches with regard to climate change, *mitigation* and *adaptation*.

Mitigation policies are put in place to try to reduce the amount of greenhouse gases in the atmosphere. As discussed in Chapter 3, greenhouse gas emissions in the United States come from the transportation sector (28.7 percent), the electricity sector (28.6 percent), industry (21.7 percent), agriculture (9.5 percent), commercial real estate (6.4 percent), and residential housing (5.1 percent). Each of these sectors is represented by separate policy subsystems, making policy coordination difficult. Much of the attention of mitigation policies has been on reducing CO_2, which is responsible for 82 percent of greenhouse gas emissions in the United States.

Several policy solutions to reduce greenhouse gases have been proposed, and these solutions are by and large regulatory policies that seek to alter the behavior of individuals and firms. However, there are various mechanisms that governments can use to change behavior, such as command-and-control instruments, using markets, and creating markets. Command-and-control instruments prescribe goals and may also require certain behavior to meet those goals. Using markets includes tax incentive instruments that either add costs to reduce unwanted behavior or provide rebates to encourage desired behavior. Creating markets includes instruments such as emissions trading.

One of the most prominent mitigation policies is a cap-and-trade system where a cap on overall emissions is set and firms are issued emission allowances under the cap. If they emit less than they are allowed they can trade those allowances with others. A cap-and-trade system was developed for sulfur dioxide emissions, SO_2, under the Clean Air Act Amendment of 1990 that has proved to be largely successful at reducing SO_2 levels in the atmosphere. The 1990 CAA has provided the blueprint for a cap-and-trade system to address greenhouse gas emissions, yet despite several bills in Congress to develop a national cap-and-trade system for GHG, none has been successful. However, several states in the mid-Atlantic and northeast United States have developed the *Regional Greenhouse Gas Initiative (RGGI)* that created a cap-and-trade system for the nine states that are involved. Additionally, the state of California has developed its own cap-and-trade system to address GHG.

Apart from policy, technological advances, such as renewable energy production and storage, geoengineering, and carbon capture and storage, may also be important pieces of mitigation. These types of approaches are likely to come from the private sector as a result of market forces. Indeed, much of the reduction in greenhouse gas emissions in the United States is a result of cheaper natural gas replacing coal as a source of electricity, as well as falling prices of renewable sources. However, government policies in terms of tax incentives for producers and consumers to use developing technologies such as hybrid cars and solar energy, as well as government funding of basic scientific research, are vital components to technological advancement and adoption. Indeed, the American Recovery and Reinvestment Act of 2009 provided incentives and funding that helped to spur the growth of renewable energy (Grunwald 2012).

Given the amount of greenhouses gases that have already been placed in the atmosphere, it is unlikely that even intense mitigation efforts at this point will prevent all possible impacts. Therefore, communities will likely need to put some policies in place to deal with the impacts of climate change. Adaptation involves adjusting to the impacts of climate change and can include building sea walls, infrastructure investments, water management, and inland retreat. The regional and local impacts of climate change are variable; therefore, many adaptation approaches are likely to be decided largely at the state and local level.

The Climate Change Politics Stream

The politics surrounding environmental policy generally, and climate change specifically, is driven by partisan polarization. Information in the politics stream includes signals sent by public opinion, interest mobilization, and elections, and this information provides both opportunities and constraints for policy actors.

Public opinion is particularly important, as noted by William Ruckelshaus, the first administrator of the Environmental Protection Agency: "Public opinion remains absolutely essential for anything to be done on behalf of the environment" (US Environmental Protection Agency 1993). Indeed, the policymaking system as a whole is supported by a foundation of public opinion (Jones and Jenkins-Smith 2009). Policy actors seeking policy change often try to mobilize the public to place pressure on existing subsystem arraignments, and often policy actors try to frame their preferred policy solution as supported by the public. Public opinion includes the national mood that represents general public support for a more, or less, active government. The public mood acts as a thermostat, with public preferences for government action decreasing as government activity increases, and vice versa, with preferences for action increasing as government activity decreases in particular policy areas (Wlezien 1995). This is one way in which information signals in the politics stream serve as feedback.

As shown in Chapter 4, public opinion regarding environmental issues is divided along ideological, partisan, and cultural lines. Despite these divisions, overall, majorities of the public across both parties are supportive of environmental protection in the abstract. However, environmental issues are rarely the most salient issue for the public. Figure 5.3 shows the public mood for government action on the environment, which theoretically ranges from 0, indicating no public desire for action on the environment, to 100 which would indicate unanimous support in the public for government action on the environment. The public mood measure is developed by combining multiple questions about government actions into a single scale. In addition, Figure 5.3 shows the percent of the public that considers the environment to be the most important problem, which could also range from 0 to 100.[5]

As shown in Figure 5.3, the environmental mood of the public is largely responsive to government action, with decreases throughout the 1970s during the height of the environmentalism era and increases during the early 1980s when environmental action was receding. In addition, the environmental mood measures ranges from about 65 to 85 on the 0 to 100 scale, indicating consistently strong support for environmental action. However, Figure 5.3 also shows the percent of the public that considers the environment the most important problem (MIP). As can be seen, the MIP indicator, much like the mood indicator, decreased throughout the 1970s as environmental issues were being addressed, and increased during the 1980s when they weren't. However, during the peaks only about 4–4.5 percent of the public indicated that the environment was the most important problem. This illustrates that, overall, the public is supportive of actions by the government to address environmental issues, but the importance of the environment in comparison to other issues is low. This seeming paradox of public support for environmental action in the abstract, yet little concern for the environment relative to

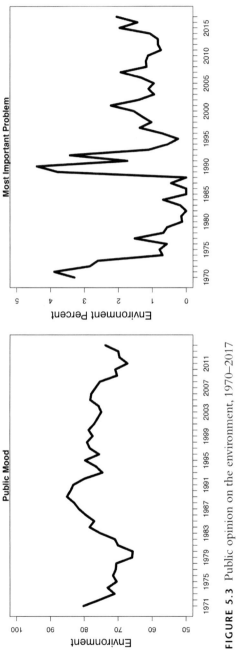

FIGURE 5.3 Public opinion on the environment, 1970–2017

other problems, makes gaining sufficient traction to address environmental issues like climate change on the basis of public support and concern difficult.

Similar to public opinion about the environment more broadly, public opinion about climate change tends to be politically polarized, yet majorities of Americans in most polls express some level of concern about climate change. A recent analysis showed that 73 percent of registered voters in the United States think climate change (global warming) is happening, 59 percent think it's a result of human activity, and 63 percent are worried about climate change (Leiserowitz et al. 2018). However, as with the environment more broadly, climate change is seldom seen as the most important issue, with Leiserowitz et al. (2018) finding that climate change ranked fifteenth across all voters as an important issue when deciding how to vote.

The ideological, partisan, and cultural orientations of the public shape their view of climate change, yet public opinion regarding climate change is perhaps best described by segmenting the public into categories of differing views (Maibach et al. 2011). *Global Warming's Six Americas* posits that the US public can be divided across six segments, including the alarmed, the concerned, the cautious, the disengaged, the doubtful, and the dismissive (Leiserowitz, Maibach, and Roser-Renouf 2009).

The alarmed segment of the public is sure that climate change is a serious issue, they are extremely worried, and they are likely to be taking action. The concerned segment is aware of climate change and its seriousness, but they are not likely to be taking any action, personal or political, to address climate change. The cautious think climate change is an issue, but are less certain about it overall and do not view action on climate change as particularly urgent. The disengaged don't know much or haven't thought much about climate change. The doubtful are not sure that climate change is happening and if it is it may be from natural, rather than anthropogenic, forces. Finally, the dismissive are engaged in climate change but are convinced it isn't happening and that it doesn't need to be addressed in any way. The most recent analysis found that the alarmed constitute 21 percent of the public, the concerned – the largest segment – is 30 percent, the cautious is 21 percent, disengaged is 7 percent, doubtful is 12 percent, and dismissive is 9 percent (Leiserowitz et al. 2018). Overall, these findings indicate that a slim majority, 51 percent, of the public is either alarmed or concerned about climate change.

Apart from public opinion, the politics information stream also includes the activity of interest groups. Interest groups pursue both insider and outsider strategies in attempts to influence policy decisions. Insider strategies involve being part of policy subsystems and engaging directly with other policy actors by providing problem or policy information. Outsider strategies include mobilizing the public and supporting candidates in elections, which creates political information signals. Some environmental interest groups work to mobilize the public and coordinate grassroots efforts regarding climate change. For example, the recent *Keep it in the*

Ground movement is made up of 400 organizations urging governments around the world to adopt policies to stop using fossil fuel-based energy sources.[6]

Elections are the final major piece of the politics stream. As has been shown, neither environmental issues broadly or climate change specifically are seen as the most important issue; therefore, there are not many voters likely to vote on climate change alone. However, election results can have a significant impact on the likelihood of climate change reaching the agenda. For example, following the 2008 election action on climate change seemed likely, and following the 2016 election federal action on climate seems impossible. Even if it's not likely that voters are voting based solely on environmental or climate issues, given the polarization associated with climate change voters are likely to know where the parties stand on those issues. Therefore, the election of a Republican president and Congress in 2016 is a signal that action on climate is not a high priority for the public, even as a majority is concerned about climate change.

The environmental policymaking system is constantly receiving information signals about issues in the problem space and those issues compete for space on the finite agenda of policymakers. As discussed, changes in information signals, coupled with institutional factors can make it more (or less) likely that an issue reaches the policymaking agenda. However, the environmental policymaking system does not simply react to changes in information, rather policy actors attempt to shape information signals to achieve their policy goals. The next section discusses the importance of policy actors and their attempts to define, or frame, issues in a particular way.

Contested Definitions of Climate Change

In July 2003, Senator James Inhofe (R–OK) speaking on the Senate floor stated the following: "Wake up, America. With all the hysteria, all the fear, all the phony science, could it be that man-made global warming is the greatest hoax ever perpetrated on the American people? I believe it is."[7] Seeking again to raise doubt about climate change, in February 2015 Senator Inhofe brought a snowball to the Senate floor in an attempt to demonstrate that the unusually cold winter of 2014–2015 was indicative of the fact that global warming isn't happening. The efforts of Senator Inhofe to cast doubt on the scientific consensus regarding climate change is an attempt to frame the issue. Attempts to frame or define policy issues are a common strategy of policy actors because the way an issue is defined can make it more (or less) likely that the issue will reach the policymaking agenda and, once on the agenda, framing can impact how (or whether) the issue is addressed.

Policy actors attempt to frame information signals to give them meaning and context in attempts to make it more likely that their issue reaches the agenda and that their favored solution is adopted. Broadly speaking, framing strategies involves attempting to *add a dimension to the issue*, what Riker (1986) termed heresthetics, or *alter how a current dimension is evaluated*. A heresthetic framing approach with regard to climate change involves trying to attach a dimension to the issue, such as national security, in an attempt to raise concern about climate change among those concerned about national security issues.

A host of potential strategies exists for policy actors to try to change how the dimensions of issues are evaluated. For example, the problem stream contains entropic information about conditions, such as the fact that the amount of CO_2 in the atmosphere has exceeded 400 parts-per-million (ppm). However, context is needed to know if going beyond 400 ppm of CO_2 in the atmosphere is truly a problem. Distinctions are often made between conditions and problems, and turning a condition into a problem through framing is often necessary for that issue to receive attention from policymakers. Conditions are things that exist in society that may be problematic, but about which there is little that government policy can do to address, whereas problems are things which government should be attempting to solve. Often conditions become problems as a result of how the condition is framed. One particularly potent frame is based on *causality*, where a condition is more likely to be seen as a problem when it is framed so that a) the condition exists as a result of human actions as opposed to natural forces, and b) the issue can be solved by government action (Stone 1989). The causal assignment of blame for undesirable conditions to human activity makes it more likely that the condition will be seen as something that can be solved by human activity. For example, a plant that emits potentially harmful pollutants is a human-caused problem that could be solved through government intervention, whereas tornadoes are a natural phenomenon that cannot be prevented by human actions.

Apart from causality, several other contextual factors can potentially be used for evaluative framing by strategic policy actors. Often, the scope, tractability, and severity of the problem are important considerations. The scope of the problem refers to how big a problem it is and how many people may be affected. The tractability of the problem includes how difficult the problem may be to fix, or how amiable the problem is to government intervention. The severity of the problem involves the seriousness of the problem and the amount of risk it poses. Additional factors include the nature of the population that could be impacted by both the problem and the policy solution. Are those affected by the problem seen as "deserving" of assistance or not? (Ingram, Schneider, and deLeon 2007; Rochefort and Cobb 1993). The nature of the solution is also an important factor when defining a problem. Is the solution offered acceptable to policymakers and/or the public? As discussed in Chapter 4, solution-aversion may explain why conservatives and individualists are skeptical of climate change. Finally, policy actors may employ counter-frames to compete with the frames of other actors (Aklin and Urpelainen 2013). In the process of counter-framing, policy actors engage on the same dimensions but seek to have them evaluated in a different way. Counter-framing can be as effective, if not more so, than framing (Jerit 2008).

With regard to climate change, many of the factors just discussed have long been a part of attempts to frame the issue. One of the most politically contentious dimensions of climate change is the degree of scientific consensus surrounding the issue. A scientific consensus exists regarding the cause, scope, and severity of climate change, however there have been concerted efforts to raise doubts about this consensus by private utility interests and conservative groups (Brulle 2014, 2018; McCright and Dunlap 2000; Oreskes and Conway 2010; Supran and Oreskes 2017). In a memo developed in the mid-to-late 1990s, during the debate over the Kyoto Protocol and well past when climate science was settled, Republican political strategist Frank Luntz wrote:

> The scientific debate remains open. Voters believe there's no consensus about global warming within the scientific community. Should the public come to believe that the scientific issues are settled, their views about global warming will change accordingly. Therefore, you need to continue to make the lack of scientific certainty a primary issue in the debate and defer to scientists and other experts in the field.[8]

Another framing tactic often used with regard to environmental issues is to make the solution seem undesirable. Solutions to climate change, and other environmental issues, are often framed as a trade-off between environmental protection and economic development. This frame is aimed at those that may be concerned about government intervention in the economy as well as those that see nature as a resource to be used for human development.

Whichever framing strategy is employed, the aim is to change how an issue is understood by other policy actors so that they are either persuaded or mobilized to engage on the issue. Increased engagement by policy actors can put pressure on existing subsystem arraignments through positive feedback, or counter pressure from other actors to reinforce the status quo. Using framing to persuade involves convincing policy actors to change their position on an issue. Persuasion is often difficult, particularly with salient and polarized issues like climate change, but it is possible. For example, former Oklahoma Congressman Jim Bridenstine was appointed by Trump in April 2018 to head NASA. As a member of Congress in 2013, Bridenstine stated that, "Global temperature changes, when they exist, correlate with sun output and ocean cycles" (Koren 2018), which is not a statement that is supported by scientific evidence. However, a few months into his tenure at NASA, Bridenstine aligned himself with the scientific consensus on climate. Explaining his change in thinking, Bridenstine stated that he,

> listened to a lot of testimony. I heard a lot of experts, and I read a lot. I came to the conclusion myself that carbon dioxide is a greenhouse gas and that we've put a lot of it into the atmosphere and therefore we have contributed to the global warming that we've seen. And we've done it in really significant ways.

Quoted in Davenport 2018

While Bridenstine's change is not indicative of framing effects, it is indicative of the fact that a change in position is possible, though rare.

Apart from persuasion, framing used for mobilization involves engaging those that already agree to become involved. Often mobilization is aimed at *latent* interests that share preferences but are not currently engaged within a particular subsystem. For example, the *Keep it in the Ground* movement has been effective in engaging multiple policy actors and activists that are concerned about climate change on issues like the proposed Keystone XL pipeline. Another example is the recent arguments made by Senator Sheldon Whitehouse (D–RI), a policy entrepreneur on climate change, that, "There's an entire generation of young voters eager to be motivated on [climate change]" (Giller 2018).

Attention to environmental policy issues operates on two levels. On one level is the problem agenda, where issues exist in a multidimensional problem space, and the next level is the multidimensional issue space that contains the various attributes of the issue (Jones and Baumgartner 2005b). Once on the agenda, attention turns to how the issue should be defined and, following from how the issue is defined, what, if any, policy solutions can be adopted. Issue definitions consist of the aggregation of issue dimensions, weighted by their salience, or importance (Nowlin 2016). The next section examines the various dimensions of climate change examined in congressional hearings from 1975 to 2016, as well as attempts by policy actors in those hearings to frame the issue of climate change.

Dimensions of Climate Change

The complex nature of climate change provides opportunities for policy actors to attempt to (re)define the issue to gain strategic advantage by persuading or mobilizing other policy actors. As noted, framing involves attempts to add a new dimension to the issue or alter how a current dimension is evaluated. In this section, I examine the dimensions of climate change discussed in congressional hearings.

Policy issues are defined within a multidimensional issue space that includes the various attributes of the issue. The issue space consists of information in the three streams that are pertinent to that issue. However, formulating policies to address a problem often involves separating the issue space into its own *problem space* and *solution space* (Baumgartner and Jones 2015; Newell and Simon 1972; Workman and Shafran 2015). The problem space includes the dimensions associated with the problem information stream, and it tends to have multiple dimensions being offered by multiple policy actors, particularly with contentious policy issues like climate change. The solution space involves information elements in the policy stream, and tends to be offered by experts.

To determine the dimensions of climate change, the congressional hearings were examined and coded by the topics and subtopics that were discussed at the hearings. Topics were determined by examining the hearing summaries, which were accessed through the *ProQuest Congressional* database. Hearings were coded for topics and subtopics by using the summaries of each panel of witnesses that appeared at each hearing.[9]

First, I examine the topics that represent the different attributes, or dimensions, of the problem space with regard to climate change. They include *energy*, *land use*, *transportation*, *science*, *international*, and *impacts*. The broad nature of the topics allows for subtopics, which are aspects of the topics that are more specific. For example, discussion of energy includes all types of energy sources such as fossil fuels, nuclear, and renewable sources. Most hearings discussed multiple topics, and the hearings were coded as discussing a topic, 1, or not, 0. Once coded, I calculated the proportion of hearings that discussed each topic by year, and the proportions range from 0, indicating no mention of that topic in that year, to 1, indicating that was the only topic discussed in the hearings for that year. Figure 5.4 illustrates the proportion of hearings that discussed each topic in each year, which shows how attention to topics has evolved over time.

As can be seen, energy is the most prominent dimension, although attention to energy dropped in the late 1980s before rising again in the early 2000s. The science, international, and impacts dimensions were also prominent and variable. The science dimension was particularly prominent when climate change was first on the agenda, although it has subsequently declined in importance. The international dimension reached an apex lasting from the late 1980s to the 1990s when several international climate agreements were discussed. The discussion of the impacts dimension has been relatively steady from 1975 to 2016, ranging between 20 percent to 50 percent of hearings per year discussing the impacts of climate change. Finally, the land use and transportation dimensions were discussed the least, with land use being relatively steady and transportation increasing in the late 2000s and early 2010s as transportation began to take a larger role in US emissions. Next, I examine each dimension in more detail.

Energy: the energy dimension deals with energy use as both a cause of climate change as well as renewable energy as a possible mitigation approach. Overall, the energy dimension was discussed in 47 percent of all hearings, making it the most discussed topic.

Fossil fuels such as coal, oil, and natural gas are the clear dominant energy topic with 63 percent of energy discussions referring to those sources. This is followed by renewable sources including solar, wind, and hydro power at 24 percent. Finally, nuclear was the least mentioned energy source at 5 percent.[10]

Land Use: land use involves discussions of agriculture and forestation in the context of climate change, and was discussed in 13 percent of hearings. For the land use topic, agriculture was discussed more than forestation issues at 55 percent vs. 47 percent. Land use is an important component of climate change as agriculture-based emissions are one of the leading sources of emissions in the United States, and forests can act as carbon sinks, removing carbon from the atmosphere.

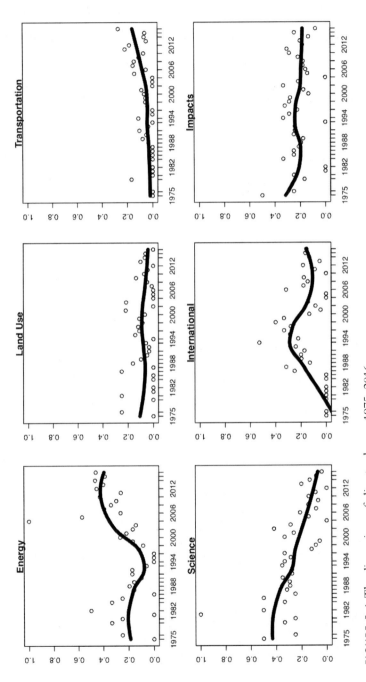

FIGURE 5.4 The dimensions of climate change, 1975–2016

Transportation: the transportation dimension involves all forms of transportation and was present in 16 percent of hearings. One of the most discussed aspects of transportation was automobile emissions, which accounted for 61 percent of hearings regarding transportation. The increase in attention to the transportation dimension in recent years in likely a result of the fact that transportation emissions have been growing as emissions from other sources have been declining. In addition, the fuel economy standards proposed by the Obama administration, which sought a 54.5 mpg standard for cars and light trucks by 2025, also drew congressional attention.

Science: the science dimension deals with hearings that discuss the scientific and/or technical aspects of climate change. This includes testimony provided by scientists and other experts about the scientific basis of climate change. The testimony from Dr James Hansen excerpted at the beginning of this chapter is an example of scientific testimony. Overall, science was discussed at 33 percent of hearings.

International: the international topic involves hearings that heard testimony from representatives from other countries as well as those that discussed global climate change agreements, such as the Kyoto Protocol or the Paris Agreement. Overall, the international dimension was present in 34 percent of all hearings and the discussion of international treaties or agreements was present in 39 percent of hearings that dealt with the international dimension. The most discussed international agreements were the Kyoto Protocol and the Paris Agreement.

Impacts: the impacts dimension includes all discussions of the potential impacts, both positive and negative, of climate change. Overall, 38 percent of hearings discussed the potential impacts, with the economic impacts of climate change being the most discussed at 60 percent, and these impacts include those of climate change itself as well as the impacts of policies meant to mitigate climate change. The economic impacts were followed by potential health impacts at 23 percent. Weather impacts such as storms, drought, flooding, and higher temperatures as a result of climate change were next, discussed at 17 percent of the hearings that addressed impacts. Impacts on oceans and sea level were discussed at 11 percent and 7 percent of hearings, respectively. Finally, potential national security impacts were the least discussed at 5 percent.

Next, I discuss the dimensions of climate change associated with solutions or actions that can be taken to address climate change. Discussions of potential policy solutions also take place in congressional hearings. Committees act as gatekeepers for legislation, and often hear from witnesses about the potential impacts of proposed legislation. Hearings were coded as discussing legislation if a specific bill was mentioned in the hearing summary. Overall, 28 percent of climate change hearings considered one or more pieces of legislation, whereas a higher percentage, 46 percent, did not. This may reflect a larger shift in Congress from legislating to oversight over the last few decades (Lewallen, Theriault, and Jones 2016).

Congressional committees may also consider proposed solutions separate from the consideration of legislation. Overall, 33 percent of hearings considered some type of policy proposal. Policy proposals involve information in the policy stream and includes discussions of potential policies aimed at mitigating or adapting to climate change. The most discussed policy proposal was cap-and-trade with 33 percent of hearings that addressed a policy proposal discussing cap-and-trade. The second most discussed policy was some type of executive agency regulation at 5 percent, and the least discussed policy was a carbon tax discussed at 4 percent of hearings.

Defining policy issues involves the highlighting of dimensions, such as those discussed above, as well as the use of rhetoric to frame how those dimensions are understood. The next section examines attempts by various policy actors to frame the different dimensions of climate change across several congressional hearings.

Framing Climate Change

As defined by Chong and Druckman (2007), "Framing refers to the process by which people develop a particular conceptualization of an issue or reorient their thinking about an issue" (105). Policy actors attempt to frame issues – (re)orient how an issue is understood – by adding (or subtracting) dimensions of policy issues from consideration as well as shape how the dimensions are understood by giving those dimensions a particular meaning or context. In this section, I use excerpts from congressional hearings to examine framing attempts drawn from debates about the scientific consensus, the Kyoto Protocol, the *American Clean Energy and Security Act* introduced in 2009, and the EPA's Clean Power Plan.

Debating the Scientific Consensus

One of prominent dimensions early in the development of climate change as an issue was science, with a number of scientists expressing concern about the increasing amount of greenhouse gasses in the atmosphere. In addition, the anthropogenic causes of climate change were recognized early on in the development of the climate change issue. For example, in a hearing held in April 1980 by the Energy and Natural Resource committee in the Senate (US Congress/Senate 1980), Dr George Woodwell – a prominent scientist and cofounder of the Environmental Defense Fund who at the time was the director of the Marine Biological Laboratory, but in 1985 founded the Woods Hole Research Center – stated:

> The total amount of carbon dioxide in the atmosphere is now about 334 parts per million by volume. The rate of increase is about one and a half parts per million annually. The data that substantiate this change over the past

20 years are overwhelming, and there is little question as to the reality of the change or its current rate. ... The major contribution to the CO_2 problem over the next decades will be the combustion of fossil fuels. If we are to alleviate the atmospheric CO_2 problem, it will be by means of reduction in the use of fossil fuels worldwide, intensive conservation in the use of fossil fuel energy, and by intensive management of the rate at which we deforest the rest of the Earth and reforest sections of the Earth that are now deforested.

The testimony of Dr Woodwell, as well as other scientists on the panel, was truly the first to establish the issue of climate change as an important concern, based on science. In 2016 George Woodwell was quoted as saying, "We knew in the '70s what the problem was," ... "We knew there was a problem with sea level rise, all disruptions of climate. And the disruptions of climate are fundamental in that they undermine all the life on the Earth" (Mooney 2016).

Establishing the causation of climate change as anthropogenic makes it more likely that climate change will be seen as a problem requiring government intervention. As noted above, the nature of the scientific consensus surrounding climate change is one of the most politically contentious aspects of the issue, largely as a result of efforts on the part of conservative and industry activists. This effort is likely intended to undermine the notion of human causation, thereby undermining the notion that government intervention is necessary.

As shown in Figure 5.1, the number of congressional hearings about climate change increased in the late 1980s. Many of the hearings at that time involved scientists and other experts discussing what was then known about climate change and the greenhouse effect. The hearings included a two-part hearing entitled *Greenhouse Effect and Global Climate Change* that was held by the Energy and Natural Resource committee in the Senate (US Congress/Senate 1987). The first part was held in November of 1987 and the second in June of 1988.

The hearings in 1987 involved several climate scientists, including Dr John Firor, who was then the director of the National Center for Atmospheric Research. In his testimony Dr Firor stated:

> I think it is fair to summarize the current feeling in the scientific community, that there is a strong consensus that if we continue to emit greenhouse gases into the atmosphere, that the climate will warm to levels that may take us well outside any historical experience that we have had.

Dr Firor went on to say:

> Let me summarize that by saying that anytime you predict something dramatic people will challenge you, they will mistrust you, and you yourself may wish that the results were not true. Keep in mind, that these calculations have been subjected to fairly rigorous treatment.

Indeed, efforts to undermine the science behind climate change were presented during the same November 1987 hearing. Dr George Hidy from the Electric Power Research Institute, funded by the utility industry for research and development, stated at the hearing that:

> I would like to just note that the consensus on climate change and heating is not really quite as strong as one might assume, I think, from your witnesses so far. And I would like to point out, just editorially, a couple of observations I think it is important in this particular phenomenon to consider, as is the possibility for increasing temperature. I think, to a degree, the temperature record length makes a lot of difference in how you interpret what will happen in the future. For example, if you looked at Dr. Hanson's testimony yesterday, if you took the period between 1940 and 1980, over 40 years, you would find during the period when there was an acceleration, an enormous acceleration in anthropogenic carbon dioxide generation that went into the atmosphere, that the temperature in the world actually went down.

The testimony of Dr Hidy included several rhetorical devices that are still used to try to undermine the scientific consensus surrounding climate change, including choosing a short time-frame, 1940 to 1980 in this case, to obscure the larger trend. A similar tactic has been used more recently when some have argued that a global warming "pause" or "hiatus" began in 1998, and the rate of increase in the Earth's temperature has slowed since. However, subsequent analysis has shown that the pause did not occur (Hausfather et al. 2017; Karl et al. 2015).

Debating the Kyoto Protocol

The international dimension of climate change included hearings about various international agreements as well as hearings that involved approaches that other countries are taking to address climate change. Climate change is truly a global problem and the United States has been involved with international climate diplomacy since the creation of the IPCC in 1988 and the UNFCCC in 1992. The Kyoto Protocol was negotiated under the UNFCCC and adopted in December 1997, although it was never ratified by the United States, which subsequently withdrew from the agreement in 2001. Much of the controversy surrounding the Kyoto Protocol involved the fact that binding emission reductions were required of developed countries, but not of developing countries such as China that are large, and growing, emitters of greenhouse gases.

Beginning in February 1998, the Science Committee in the House (now the Space, Science, and Technology Committee) held a series of four hearings entitled *Road from Kyoto*, which examined the implications of the Kyoto Protocol for the United States (US Congress/House 1998). Witnesses at the hearings included individuals from several executive branch agencies such as the EPA, DOE, Commerce, State, and the Council on Environmental Quality. In addition, witnesses were called from several interest groups and trade associations, including the Environmental Defense Fund, the National Mining Association, and the AFL-CIO.

As noted, framing at times involves efforts to add dimensions to issues and/ or change how existing dimensions are evaluated to shape how issues are understood. When opening the first hearing, Congressman James Sensenbrenner, a Republican from Wisconsin and then chairman of the committee, framed the consideration of Kyoto in terms of three questions, "first, is the science sound; second, will the treaty work, and third, is the treaty fair?" In response to his first question, Sensenbrenner stated that:

> First, is the science sound? No. Professor Bert Bolin, Chairman emeritus of the Intergovernmental Panel on Climate Change – the group of scientists that assesses and reviews the worldwide climate research – told the Kyoto negotiators that the science of climate change has considerable uncertainties and that the climate system is only partly predictable. His repeated emphasis on the scientific uncertainties raised valid concerns about the maturity of the science underpinning the Kyoto Protocol. Even basic questions about the temperature record remain unanswered, and scientists are still grappling with the discrepancy between ground-based and satellite temperature records. In short, what we heard at Kyoto, and have heard subsequently, is that the Kyoto Protocol is based on immature and uncertain science.

In answer to his second question, Sensenbrenner stated:

> Second, will the treaty work? The answer to that is "no" as well. Because developing countries have not been required to assume binding emission reductions, the agreement will merely shift emissions from industrialized countries to developing countries. The end result will be that the United States will lose jobs and the environment will suffer because many of the countries exempted from the agreement also have lower air and water pollution standards.

Finally, with regard to his third question:

> Finally, is the treaty fair? And the answer to that is "no" as well. The Kyoto Protocol only binds the United States and other developed countries to binding greenhouse gas reduction targets, while large polluters such as China, India, Mexico, Indonesia, and Brazil rejected any further role in reducing greenhouse gas emissions. By placing the burden of emissions limits solely

on the United States and the other developed countries, Americans will now be at a competitive disadvantage against foreign competition. Higher energy costs and cumbersome regulations will encourage American industries, agriculture, and jobs to move to those countries where the Protocol imposes no obligations and costs.

Sensenbrenner sought to raise doubt about the causation, scope, and severity of climate change by raising the notion of scientific uncertainty associated with each of those aspects. The implication of this framing is that, if climate change is not human-caused or not that severe, then action would not be necessary or effective. In making his argument, Sensenbrenner seemed to be following the Luntz memo, by raising doubts about the science and invoking a prominent scientist, Dr Bert Bolin. Dr Bolin was the first chairman of the IPCC, and he was instrumental in bringing the issue of climate change to the attention of international political leaders. Additionally, Dr Bolin felt at the time of the Kyoto Protocol that enough was known about the climate system that governments needed to begin to act to reduce the amount of greenhouse gases in the atmosphere (see Bolin 2007; Bolin et al. 1986).

With his second and third questions, Sensenbrenner sought to raise doubt about the solution itself, the Kyoto Protocol, by noting that developing countries are exempted, which, he argues, would lead to continued environmental degradation since those countries do not have the same environmental standards as other countries. Finally, Sensenbrenner used the oft-repeated frame associated with environmental policy solutions that the Kyoto Protocol would lead to job loss in the United States from higher energy costs and regulations.

Speaking in favor of the Kyoto Protocol, Kathleen McGinty, chair of the Council on Environmental Quality within the Executive Office of the President, directly challenged the framing of environmental protection as a trade-off with economic growth by providing a counter-frame.

> Working with the Congress, we have developed a new vision of environmental protection that says the environment and the economy work together. The choice between jobs and the environment is a false one. That is not a vision that was shared by the rest of the world before Kyoto. But in Kyoto, the power of our ideas, the truth of those ideas won the day. The result is that at the heart of the Kyoto Protocol are those mechanisms which will make true that the environment and the economy work together.

McGinty continued by mentioning the flexibility within the protocol that would allow the United States to meet its emissions targets over a longer time-period. In her testimony, McGinty directly challenged the contention that job losses would result from ratifying Kyoto, by providing a counter-frame that the "environment and the economy work together."

Another opponent of the Kyoto Protocol, Candice Holmes from the National Mining Association, accepted climate change as a problem, but criticized the protocol as a solution. She stated:

> Our members agree that potential human-induced climate change is a concern that does need to be addressed. The issue is not action versus inaction, but responsible action. Under that lens, we do not believe the Kyoto Protocol represents a responsible form of action. We believe that it is fatally flawed and really can't be fixed in its current form. Ratifying it would intrude on US sovereignty, cause substantial economic damage and loss of jobs, and yet in the end the primary objective of the Protocol, stabilization of greenhouse gas concentrations, would not be realized.

In her testimony, Holmes seems to be trying to add the dimension of US sovereignty to the debate, while also reiterating the economic impacts as well as the ineffectiveness of the Kyoto Protocol in addressing climate change.

A final example of framing with regard to the Kyoto Protocol is from Michael Marvin of the Business Council for Sustainable Energy. The Business Council for Sustainable Energy is a trade association that represents the natural gas and renewable energy industry. Therefore, the industries that Marvin represented were more likely than then those of the National Mining Association to gain from the protocol. In his testimony, Marvin touched on the science behind climate change by stating that, "The Business Council for Sustainable Energy believes that we have sufficient information about the science of global climate change to merit a response by policymakers." In addition, Marvin argues that others in the private sector are also concerned about climate change.

> I also want to tell this Committee that there actually is more agreement within the business community than there might first appear. For example, let me read you this quote from just last October: "We recognize that there has been an increase in CO_2 It is cause for concern, and we feel very strongly that there needs to be a significant effort to improve the technology that will reduce CO_2 emissions." That statement was made by Jack Smith, Chairman of the Board for General Motors.

In his testimony, Marvin was signaling to conservatives skeptical about climate change that sources they likely trust – industry leaders – accept the science behind climate change, in an attempt to alter the evaluation of the science dimension. However, Marvin gave only tepid support to the Kyoto Protocol by stating:

> I want to say that the Council as a whole believes that the agreement reached in Kyoto could be a first step. I say "could be" because, as has been made clear this morning, there remain enough questions about the treaty's

provisions that it is prudent to withhold a final verdict until some of those more critical holes are filled.

Finally, Marvin indicated the preferred solutions of his organization.

> Together, renewable energy, energy efficiency, and natural gas can form an energy triad that, combined with a market-based emissions trading program and sequestration, will enable this country to meet reasonable international emissions reduction targets. As has been said before, we concur with the concept that the most efficient method to reduce CO_2 emissions is through market-based mechanisms that move away from traditional command-and-control regulation.

The debate over the Kyoto Protocol illustrates many of the framing tactics involved in the larger debate over climate change, including the science, the economic costs, and the nature of the proposed solutions.

Debating the American Clean Energy and Security Act

During the 2000s, congressional action on climate change was focused on several pieces of legislation to create a cap-and-trade system for greenhouse gases. As shown in Figure 5.1, congressional attention to climate change reached its highest point from 2007 to 2009, following the 2006 elections when Democrats won control of both chambers of Congress. The prospect for action on climate increased during the 2007 to 2009 period, with several signals in the politics stream indicating a growing concern about climate change and a growing acceptance that it needed to be addressed. For example, the film *An Inconvenient Truth* appeared in 2006, agreement about climate change being a problem existed between both major party presidential nominees in the 2008 election, and, also in 2008, former Speaker of the House Newt Gingrich appeared with then Speaker Nancy Pelosi on a couch in front of the Capitol in a commercial about the importance of acting on climate change sponsored by a group headed by Al Gore.

The vehicle for a cap-and-trade program that went the farthest was the American Clean Energy and Security Act of 2009 (ACES) that developed in the US House and was sponsored by Representative Henry Waxman (D–CA) and Representative Ed Markey (D–MA). In April of 2009, the Energy and Commerce Subcommittee on Energy and Environment, chaired by Representative Markey, held a hearing that drew over 60 witnesses across a four-day period (US Congress/House 2009). The witnesses were diverse and included current and former members of Congress, including Newt Gingrich, former Vice President Al Gore, executive branch agencies such as DOE and EPA, environmental interest groups, conservative and progressive leaning think tanks, academic experts, state and local government officials, unions, and representatives from the mining, manufacturing, and utility sectors.

Emissions trading, such as the proposed cap-and-trade approach of the ACES, is a market-based approach to address greenhouse gas emissions. The bill was supported by the Obama administration, and in 2008 Obama had campaigned on a cap-and-trade approach to address climate change. However, the bill was being considered during the "Great Recession," and concerns about jobs and the impacts of increased energy prices were high.

Given the concern over the economy, in her testimony EPA Administrator Lisa Jackson framed the ACES in terms of the positive impact it could have on jobs and the economy.

> The American Clean Energy and Security Act would introduce a clean energy requirement for American electric utilities and new energy efficiency programs for American buildings. Those initiatives aim to create good American jobs that cannot be shipped overseas. The legislation would launch programs to promote electric vehicles and deploy technologies for capturing, pipelining, and geologically storing carbon dioxide produced at coal-fueled power plants. Those incentives aim to help American companies make up for lost time in the advanced energy industries that will be to the 2010s what Internet software was to the 1990s.

Administrator Jackson argued that the ACES could help move the country toward being a world leader in the production of green energy. However, during the question-and-answer portion of the hearing, Congressman Steve Scalise (R-LA) pushed back on the notion of the bill creating jobs.

> Mr SCALISE: Thank you, Mr Chairman. Administrator Jackson, in your opening statement you talked about the jobs that would be created, green jobs that would be created, under a cap and trade bill. Can you quantify how many jobs you estimate would be created under this legislation?
>
> Ms JACKSON: I believe what I said, sir, is that this is a jobs bill and that the discussion in its entirety is aimed to jumpstart our moving to the green economy.
>
> Mr SCALISE: And I think you quoted President Obama saying that it was his opinion that this bill would create millions of jobs. I think you used the term millions. Is there anything that you can base your determination on how many jobs would be created?
>
> Ms JACKSON: EPA has not done a model or any kind of modeling on jobs creation numbers.
>
> Mr SCALISE: Because you did do the analysis, and there are definitely a number of questions I have with the assumptions that are made in your analysis. I wasn't sure since you used the term a jobs bill in your opening statement, I just wanted to know if you had anything to quantify or back that up.

Ms JACKSON: Well, I back it up on somewhat common sense which is that if we are trying to move to a clean energy economy, and we heard Secretary Chu talk about the fact that the innovations that we come up with in this country are being used by other countries and manufacturing is moving there. The rhetorical question is what is the plan to keep them here and how do we convince the private sector that we mean it, that we are going to be using the technologies.

The above back-and-forth illustrates how policy actors engage in competitive framing regarding the common frame about the economic impacts of climate policy solutions. Administrator Jackson was attempting to attach the cap-and-trade policy solution to job losses during the Great Recession, which was the most salient concern at the time. Representative Scalise during the question-and-answer period was challenging the basis for the job creation assertion.

Along similar lines, Dr David Kreutzer from the conservative Heritage Foundation argued, based on analysis that Heritage had performed in 2008 on a similar cap-and-trade proposal, that if the ACES were to become law,

> Employment drops overall, but the energy intensive manufacturing sector is especially hard-hit. By 2030, manufacturing employment loses nearly three million jobs because of cap-and-trade's energy restrictions. A map included in the written testimony shows that this impact will be uneven, as manufacturing is relatively more important to the economies of some states than it is to others. Though some of those who lose or never get manufacturing jobs will find employment in the service sector, overall unemployment rises by over 800,000 in some years, due to the effects of cap and trade.

By emphasizing such analysis, opponents of the bill were able to raise concerns about job losses while appearing credible, even as doubts were raised by economists and other experts regarding the methods used and conclusions reached by the Heritage Foundation (see Pooley 2010). In addition to job losses, concerns were raised about the economic costs associated with cap-and-trade. For example, Congressman George Radanovich (R–CA) stated that:

> I, for the life of me, can't figure out how you think that you can do something like this without dramatically increasing the national debt and deficit by subsidizing a false economy and by raising the price to consumers on energy. I think when the public finds out the true cost of this thing, you are going to see a smack-down that the World Wrestling Federation would be proud to see by the public towards this plan, which is unreasonable. I think research, developing efficiencies in energy, and smoothing this transition to another source of fuel, I think, is a great idea. But this cap-and-trade notion, once the public finds out what their price is in the home at the fuel pump,

they are not going to buy this. This will stop. This will not go anywhere when you see the true cost of this thing come down.

However, there are also costs associated with *not* acting on climate change. Dr Frank Ackerman, an economist from Tufts University in Massachusetts, addressed this aspect of the cost dimension by noting:

> Other witnesses have addressed the costs of climate policy. My testimony addresses the other side of the coin, the costs of inaction. Dr Keohane mentioned this briefly in his remarks in the last panel. When it comes to climate change today, there is no longer any choice of avoiding all costs. The status quo is no longer an option. That is, the costs of climate change are not a discretionary purchase, like choosing whether to buy a new car this year or wait another year. It is more like a homeowner deciding whether it is time to repair the ever-widening cracks in the foundation of a house. The longer you wait, the more expensive it will be. Wait long enough, and it may become impossible to save the house.

The above discussion illustrates attempts to change the evaluation of the cost dimension, with Representative Radanovich (R–CA) highlighting the costs of the action – the promised policy – and Dr Ackerman highlighting the costs of inaction, by noting that the negative economic impacts of climate change will only increase the longer we wait to act.

In addition to economic costs, during the hearing Congressman John Shimkus (R–IL) in a rhetorical flourish raised concerns about the costs to democracy of the ACES by stating: "This is the largest assault on democracy and freedom in this country that I have ever experienced. I have lived through some tough times in Congress, impeachment, two wars, terrorist attacks. I fear this more than all of the above activities that have happened."

Debating the Clean Power Plan

The ACES narrowly passed the House, yet it didn't pass the Senate to become law. On a parallel track with the ACES, the EPA was moving ahead with plans to regulate greenhouse gases under the Clean Air Act. The 2007 Supreme Court decision *Massachusetts v. EPA* found that the EPA must regulate greenhouse gases if it found that such gases posed a risk to human health. In 2009 the EPA issued its *endangerment finding*, which determined that CO_2 and other greenhouse gases met the definition of an air pollutant under the Clean Air Act.

In June of 2014 the EPA issued a proposed rule, what would become known as the Clean Power Plan (CPP), that sought to limit the amount of greenhouse gases emitted from existing power plants. The finalized CPP rule was issued in October 2015 and required states to meet emissions targets, but offered flexibility in how those targets could be met. In February 2016, the Supreme Court, in an unprecedented move, issued a stay on implementation of the CPP to allow challenges to the plan to be heard in the lower courts. The Trump administration issued a proposed rule to repeal the CPP in October 2017 and issued its own replacement rule, the American Clean Energy (ACE) rule in August 2018.

In February 2015 the Environment and Public Works committee in the Senate held a hearing to examine the proposed Clean Power Plan (US Congress/Senate 2015). The sole witness was Janet McCabe, the assistant administrator for the Office of Air and Radiation, the office that drafted the Clean Power Plan in the EPA. During the hearing, Senator Inhofe (R–OK) the chair of the committee, once again, challenged the science of climate change.

> First, we will hear over and over again what science says and all that. We are going to have a hearing and we are going to have scientists at a hearing. I think when you don't have science on your side, if you keep saying science is settled, science is settled, science is settled, there is this assumption that is the case.

In the above statement Senator Inhofe is attempting to frame the issue of climate change by shifting how the causation, and perhaps the severity, of climate change is uncertain, by noting the science is not settled. If the causation of climate change as anthropogenic is uncertain, then there is less justification for government intervention. Along these same lines, Senator Wicker (R–MS) challenged the endangerment finding that CO_2 is a pollutant.

> I think you will agree, Ms McCabe, that when my colleagues on the other side of the aisle talk about carbon pollution, it is a new term that has been coined over the last several years. They are not talking about smog or carbon particles in the air, they are talking about CO_2, carbon dioxide.
>
> It sounds so sinister, pollution, dirty and slimy, carbon pollution, but actually they are talking about carbon dioxide. Carbon dioxide doesn't cause lung disease in children or asthma. Carbon dioxide hasn't been shown to cause children to miss school.
>
> I just want the public and the people listening to this, both in the hearing room and perhaps on television, to understand when we use the term dirty carbon pollution, we are talking about nothing other than carbon dioxide.

Also in his statement, Senator Inhofe attempted to add a new dimension to the debate over the Clean Power Plan as a solution – that it is not representative of the will of the people because the people's representatives have not acted on climate change.

> When you stop and realize what we are doing today, we are talking about doing, through regulation, what we have not been able to do through

legislation. In other words, those of us who are accountable to the people – talking about members of the House and the Senate – we have resoundingly rejected the very thing we are talking about today on CO_2 on five different occasions in the last 13 years.

In her opening statement, McCabe highlighted the threat posed by climate change and the need to act, as well as the fact that those conclusions are supported by science.

Climate change is one of the greatest challenges of our time. It already threatens human health and welfare and economic wellbeing, and if left unchecked, it will have devastating impacts on the United States and the planet. The science is clear, the risks are clear and the high costs of climate inaction are clear. We must act.

McCabe goes on to note the health benefits associated with the Clean Power Plan, clearly relying on benefit-cost analysis performed by the EPA.

When fully implemented, the Clean Power Plan is expected to help deliver 730 million tons of reduction in CO_2 emissions, a substantial reduction of harmful pollution. Moreover, it will also lead to thousands of fewer heart attacks and tens of thousands fewer asthma attacks and other health benefits as well.

These reductions will deliver tens of billions of dollars in public health and climate benefits that far outweigh the estimated annual costs of the plan. The soot and smog reductions that will be achieved along with reductions in carbon pollution alone will yield $7 in health benefits for every dollar we invest in meeting the standards.

Another frame that is common in climate change debates is associated with collective-action problems, where opponents of climate change action argue that action on the part of United States will not effectively address climate change if other countries don't act as well. The following exchange between Senator Inhofe, Administrator McCabe, and Senator Merkley (D–OR) illustrates this dynamic.

Senator INHOFE: … The recent analysis finds that China emits 800 million tons of CO_2 in 1 month. According to EPA's proposal, the maximum amount of CO_2 reduction under the Clean Power Plan is around 550 million tons in 1 year.

A question I would have for you, Ms McCabe, is how will the Clean Power Plan impact global CO_2 emissions when China is producing more CO_2 in 1 month than the Clean Power Plan could potentially reduce in 1 year, even if it is implemented?

Ms MCCABE: The Clean Power Plan will certainly result in less CO_2 emissions as well as our clean car rules and other measures we are looking at. There will be less domestic CO_2 from the US as a result of the Clean Power Plan.

This is why it is important for the United States not only to be working domestically but to be working internationally. We recognize this is a global problem and that other countries are emitting CO_2. That is why we have been very aggressive and involved with China.

… Senator MERKLEY: … What happens if each nation, among the nations of the world – India, China and the US are the major carbon dioxide polluters – if each of those nations says, let's not act until the other two nations act and then we will come along later. What happens to the planet in that situation?

Ms MCCABE: This is the dilemma, the tragedy of the commons, Senator. We all have to act. If everybody says we are not going to act because we don't think anybody else will act, then CO_2 emissions will continue to increase, temperatures will continue to rise, and the oceans will get more acidic.

We will have more droughts, we will have more heatwaves, and we will have more suffering around the globe and in this country as a result of the impacts on the climate.

Senator MERKLEY: Is there some possibility that by the US taking this issue seriously and engaging in dialog with all the nations of the world but also with India and China, that we can accelerate action among all three nations?

Ms MCCABE: We absolutely believe so. We believe it is essential for the United States to be asserting and showing leadership.

McCabe made explicit reference to the tragedy of the commons, in which the above discussion is centered. In addition, McCabe addressed the international dimension by illustrating the leadership role that the United States can play by implementing the Clean Power Plan.

Conclusion

The environmental policymaking system is constantly receiving inputs in the form of information signals, and these signals can be categorized as belonging to one of three information streams, including a problem stream, a policy stream, and a politics stream. Changes in the problem stream related to an issue make it more likely that the issue will receive the attention of the system. Once on the agenda, information signals regarding the various dimensions of the topic start to be shaped by policy actors within the policy subsystems that process the information in attempts to frame the issue in particular way.

To become policy output, problem and policy information signals need to be merged when information in the politics streams makes it conducive. Policy actors in favor of the proposed policy change seek to frame issues by adding dimensions or changing the way a particular dimension is evaluated.

With regard to climate change, frames attempted were often about the scientific basis of causation and the acceptability of a particular solution, such as the Kyoto Protocol, the American Clean Energy and Security Act, and the Clean Power Plan.

This chapter illustrated that, given the polarized nature of climate change, strong information signals in the problem stream are no longer enough for the issue to receive attention. In addition, even after climate change is on the agenda, the framing of information signals is often divisive enough to make a policy choice seem untenable.

Notes

1 Chapter 6 includes further discussions of the institutional and decision agendas of the macro-institutions.
2 As will be discussed in Chapter 7, climate change as an issue cuts across multiple policy subsystems.
3 Data comes from a search of the *ProQuest Congressional Database* using the search terms "climate change," "global warming," "greenhouse gas," and "greenhouse effect."
4 To find the *NYT* articles as well as the scientific publications, I used the same search terms that were used to find the congressional hearings including "climate change," "global warming," "greenhouse gas," and "greenhouse effect." The Climate Extreme Index comes from NOAA's website (www.ncdc.noaa.gov/extremes/cei/data-used) and the CO_2 level data is available here: https://scripps.ucsd.edu/programs/keelingcurve/.
5 Data for both graphs comes from the *Comparative Agendas Project*. The environmental mood data was constructed through a series of survey questions, and the most important problem data comes from the Gallup organization.
6 See here: http://keepitintheground.org/
7 Full transcript of the speech available here: www.gpo.gov/fdsys/pkg/CREC-2003-07-28/html/CREC-2003-07-28-pt1-PgS10012.htm
8 See here: https://www.pbs.org/wgbh/pages/frontline/hotpolitics/interviews/luntz.html
9 A codebook of topics was developed before the hearings were coded, and the codebook was adjusted a few times once coding began. There were two coders, and only a few discrepancies in the coding of topics and subtopics developed. The coders discussed these discrepancies until a consensus was reached.
10 Totals will not add up to 100 because some energy hearings, 7 percent, did not discuss one of these types.

References

Aklin, Michaël, and Johannes Urpelainen. 2013. "Debating Clean Energy: Frames, Counter Frames, and Audiences." *Global Environmental Change* 23(5): 1225–1232.

Baumgartner, Frank R., and Bryan D. Jones. 2002. *Policy Dynamics*. Chicago, IL: University of Chicago Press.

———. 2015. *The Politics of Information: Problem Definition and the Course of Public Policy in America*. Chicago, IL: University of Chicago Press.

Baumgartner, Frank R., Bryan D. Jones, and Peter B. Mortensen. 2018. "Punctuated Equilibrium Theory: Explaining Stability and Change in Public Policymaking." In *Theories of the Policy Process*, eds. Christopher M. Weible and Paul A. Sabatier. New York, NY: Westview Press, 55–102.

Birkland, Thomas A. 1997. *After Disaster: Agenda Setting, Public Policy, and Focusing Events.* Washington DC: Georgetown University Press.

Bolin, Bert. 2007. *A History of the Science and Politics of Climate Change: The Role of the Intergovernmental Panel on Climate Change.* Cambridge: Cambridge University Press.

Bolin, Bert, Bo R. Döös, Jill Jäger, and Richard A. Warrick, eds. 1986. *The Greenhouse Effect, Climatic Change, and Ecosystems.* Chichester, UK: Wiley.

Boscarino, Jessica E. 2009. "Surfing for Problems: Advocacy Group Strategy in US Forestry Policy." *Policy Studies Journal* 37(3): 415–434.

Brulle, Robert J. 2014. "Institutionalizing Delay: Foundation Funding and the Creation of US Climate Change Counter-Movement Organizations." *Climatic Change* 122(4): 681–694.

———. 2018. "The Climate Lobby: A Sectoral Analysis of Lobbying Spending on Climate Change in the USA, 2000 to 2016." *Climatic Change*, forthcoming.

Chong, Dennis, and James N. Druckman. 2007. "Framing Theory." *Annual Review of Political Science* 10(1): 103–126.

Cobb, Roger W., and Charles D. Elder. 1983. *Participation in American Politics: The Dynamics of Agenda-Building.* 2nd ed. Baltimore, MD: Johns Hopkins University Press.

Davenport, Christian. 2018. "NASA's New Chief Explores a Fresh Path." *The Washington Post*: A13.

Downs, Anthony. 1972. "Up and Down With Ecology: The Issue Attention Cycle." *The Public Interest* 28(1): 38–50.

Eisner, Marc Allen. 2017. *Regulatory Politics in an Age of Polarization and Drift: Beyond Deregulation.* New York, NY: Routledge.

Erikson, Robert S., Michael B. Mackuen, and James A. Stimson. 2002. *The Macro Polity.* Cambridge: Cambridge University Press.

Giller, Chip. 2018. "Senator: Climate Is a Winning Issue, and Dems Are Missing Out." *Grist.* https://grist.org/article/senator-climate-is-a-winning-issue-and-dems-are-missing-out/.

Grunwald, Michael. 2012. *The New New Deal: The Hidden Story of Change in the Obama Era.* New York, NY: Simon & Schuster.

Guber, Deborah Lynn, and Christopher J. Bosso. 2013. "Issue Framing, Agenda Setting, and Environmental Discourse." In *The Oxford Handbook of US Environmental Policy*, eds. Sheldon Kamieniecki and Michael E. Kraft. Oxford: Oxford University Press, 437–460.

Hausfather, Zeke, Kevin Cowtan, David C. Clarke, Peter Jacobs, Mark Richardson, and Robert Rohde. 2017. "Assessing Recent Warming Using Instrumentally Homogeneous Sea Surface Temperature Records." *Science Advances* 3(1).

Herweg, Nicole, Nikolaos Zahariadis, and Reimut Zohlnhofer. 2018. "The Multiple Streams Framework: Foundations, Refinements, and Empirical Applications." In *Theories of the Policy Process*, eds. Christopher M. Weible and Paul A. Sabatier. New York, NY: Westview Press, 17–54.

Ingram, Helen, Anne Schneider, and Peter deLeon. 2007. "Social Construction and Policy Design." In *Theories of the Policy Process*, ed. Paul A. Sabatier. Boulder, CO: Westview Press, 93–126.

Jerit, Jennifer. 2008. "Issue Framing and Engagement: Rhetorical Strategy in Public Policy Debates." *Political Behavior* 30(1): 1–24.

Jones, Bryan D., and Frank R. Baumgartner. 2005a. "A Model of Choice for Public Policy." *Journal of Public Administration Research and Theory* 15(3): 325–351.

———. 2005b. *The Politics of Attention: How Government Prioritizes Problems*. Chicago, IL: University of Chicago Press.

Jones, Michael D., and Hank C. Jenkins-Smith. 2009. "Trans-Subsystem Dynamics: Policy Topography, Mass Opinion, and Policy Change." *Policy Studies Journal* 37(1): 37–58.

Karl, Thomas R., Anthony Arguez, Boyin Huang, Jay H. Lawrimore, James R. McMahon, Matthew J. Menne, Thomas C. Peterson, Russell S. Vose, and Huai-Min Zhang. 2015. "Possible Artifacts of Data Biases in the Recent Global Surface Warming Hiatus." *Science* 348(6242): 1469–1472.

Kingdon, John W. 2003. *Agendas, Alternatives, and Public Policies*. 2nd ed. New York, NY: Longman.

Koren, Marina. 2018. "Trump's NASA Chief: 'I Fully Believe and Know the Climate Is Changing'." *The Atlantic*. www.theatlantic.com/science/archive/2018/05/trump-nasa-climate-change-bridenstine/560642/.

Krutz, Glen S. 2005. "Issues and Institutions: "Winnowing" in the US Congress." *American Journal of Political Science* 49(2): 313–326.

Leiserowitz, Anthony, Edward Maibach, and Connie Roser-Renouf. 2009. *Global Warming's Six Americas 2009: An Audience Segmentation Analysis*. Yale Project on Climate Change.

Leiserowitz, Anthony, Edward Maibach, Connie Roser-Renouf, Seth Rosenthal, Matthew Cutler, and John Kotcher. 2018. *Politics and Global Warming*. Yale University; George Mason University: Yale Project on Climate Change Communication.

Lewallen, Jonathan. 2018. "Congressional Attention and Opportunity Structures: The Select Energy Independence and Global Warming Committee." *Review of Policy Research* 35(1): 153–169.

Lewallen, Jonathan, Sean M. Theriault, and Bryan D. Jones. 2016. "Congressional Dysfunction: An Information Processing Perspective." *Regulation & Governance* 10(2): 179–190.

Liu, Xinsheng, Eric Lindquist, and Arnold Vedlitz. 2011. "Explaining Media and Congressional Attention to Global Climate Change, 1969–2005: An Empirical Test of Agenda-Setting Theory." *Political Research Quarterly* 64(2): 405–419.

Maibach, Edward W., Anthony Leiserowitz, Connie Roser-Renouf, and C.K. Mertz. 2011. "Identifying Like-Minded Audiences for Global Warming Public Engagement Campaigns: An Audience Segmentation Analysis and Tool Development." *PLoS ONE* 6(3): e17571.

Maor, Moshe, Jale Tosun, and Andrew Jordan. 2017. "Proportionate and Disproportionate Policy Responses to Climate Change: Core Concepts and Empirical Applications." *Journal of Environmental Policy & Planning* 19(6): 599–611.

McCright, Aaron M., and Riley E. Dunlap. 2000. "Challenging Global Warming as a Social Problem: An Analysis of the Conservative Movement's Counter-Claims." *Social Problems* 47(4): 499–522.

Mooney, Chris. 2016. "30 Years Ago Scientists Warned Congress on Global Warming. What They Said Sounds Eerily Familiar." *The Washington Post*. www.washingtonpost.com/news/energy-environment/wp/2016/06/11/30-years-ago-scientists-warned-congress-on-global-warming-what-they-said-sounds-eerily-familiar/.

Newell, Allen, and Herbert Simon. 1972. *Human Problem Solving*. Prentice Hall.

Nowlin, Matthew C. 2016. "Modeling Issue Definitions Using Quantitative Text Analysis." *Policy Studies Journal* 44(3): 309–331.

Oreskes, Naomi, and Erik M. Conway. 2010. *Merchants of Doubt: How a Handful of Scientists Obscured the Truth on Issues from Tobacco Smoke to Global Warming.* New York, NY: Bloomsbury Press.

Pooley, Eric. 2010. *The Climate War: True Believers, Power Brokers, and the Fight to Save the Earth.* New York, NY: Hachette Books.

Pralle, Sarah B. 2009. "Agenda-Setting and Climate Change." *Environmental Politics* 18(5): 781–799.

Riker, William H. 1986. *The Art of Political Manipulation.* New Haven, CT: Yale University Press.

Rochefort, David A, and Roger W Cobb. 1993. "Problem Definition, Agenda Access, and Policy Choice." *Policy Studies Journal* 21(1): 56–71.

Stimson, James A. 1999. *Public Opinion in America: Moods, Cycles, and Swings.* 2nd ed. Boulder, CO: Westview Press.

Stone, Deborah A. 1989. "Causal Stories and the Formation of Policy Agendas." *Political Science Quarterly* 104(2): 281–300.

Supran, Geoffrey, and Naomi Oreskes. 2017. "Assessing ExxonMobil's Climate Change Communications (19772014)." *Environmental Research Letters* 12(8): 1–18.

US Congress/House. 1998. *Road from Kyoto, Part I: Where Are We, Where Are We Going, and How Do We Get There?: Hearing Before the Committee on Science. 105th Congress, 2nd session, February 4, 1988.*

———. 2009. *The American Clean Energy Security Act of 2009: Hearing Before the Subcommittee on Energy and Environment of the Committee on Energy and Commerce. 111th Congress, 1st session, April 21, 22, 23, 24, 2009.*

US Congress/Senate. 1980. *Effects of Carbon Dioxide Buildup in the Atmosphere: Hearing Before the Committee on Energy and Natural Resources. 96th Congress, 2nd session, April 3, 1980.*

———. 1987. *Greenhouse Effect and Global Climate Change: Hearings Before the Committee on Energy and Natural Resources. 100th Congress., 1st session… November 9 and 10, 1987.*

———. 2015. *Oversight Hearing: Examining EPA's Proposed Carbon Dioxide Emissions Rules from New, Modified, and Existing Power Plants: Hearing Before the Committee on Environment and Public Works. 114th Congress, 1st session, February 11, 2015.*

US Environmental Protection Agency. 1993. "William D. Ruckelshaus: Oral History Interview." https://archive.epa.gov/epa/aboutepa/william-d-ruckelshaus-oral-history-interview.html (July 4, 2018).

Weaver, David H. 2007. "Thoughts on Agenda Setting, Framing, and Priming." *Journal of Communication* 57(1): 142–147.

Wlezien, Christopher. 1995. "The Public as Thermostat: Dynamics of Preferences for Spending." *American Journal of Political Science* 39(4): 981–1000.

Workman, Samuel, Bryan D. Jones, and Ashley E. Jochim. 2009. "Information Processing and Policy Dynamics." *Policy Studies Journal* 37(1): 75–92.

Workman, Samuel, and JoBeth S. Shafran. 2015. "Communications Frameworks and the Supply of Information in Policy Subsystems." In *Policy Paradigms in Theory and Practice, Studies in the Political Economy of Public Policy*, eds. John Hogan and Michael Howlett. Palgrave Macmillan UK, 239–267.

Zahariadis, Nikolaos. 2014. "The Multiple Streams Framework: Structure, Limitations, Prospects." In *Theories of the Policy Process*, eds. Paul A. Sabatier and Christopher Weible. Boulder, CO: Westview Press, 25–58.

6

PATHWAYS AND PIVOTS

Macro-Institutions and Climate Change Policy

Introduction

Prior to a Cabinet meeting in January 2014, President Obama stated the following:

> One of the things that I will be emphasizing in this meeting is the fact that
> we are not just going to be waiting for legislation in order to make sure that
> we are providing Americans the kind of help that they need. I've got a pen,
> and I've got a phone. And I can use that pen to sign executive orders and
> take executive actions and administrative actions that move the ball forward
> in helping to make sure our kids are getting the best education possible,
> making sure that our businesses are getting the kind of support and help
> they need to grow and advance, to make sure that people are getting the
> skills that they need to get those jobs that our businesses are creating. One
> of the things that I'm going to be talking to my Cabinet about is how do
> we use all the tools available to us, not just legislation, in order to advance a
> mission that I think unifies all Americans.[1]

Obama was expressing his frustration at what he perceived to be the inability or
unwillingness of Congress to move legislation forward on a host of issues. Because
of congressional gridlock on many issues, including environmental and climate
policy, Obama was stating his intention to use the policymaking pathways available to him to move policy forward.

The macro-institutions of the environmental policymaking system – Congress,
the executive, and the courts – create pathways for information signals to be
processed and turned into a unique form of policy. The institutional pathways
and forms of policy include legislation passed by Congress and signed by the

president, executive orders, agency rules, and court decisions, among others. These institutions shape the processing of information for policymaking, in large part, by determining the rules under which policy actors operate. The rules can be structured and formal, or they can be unstructured, informal norms; either way, they shape the nature of the pathway available to policy actors. Together, the rules and pathways provide stability to the complexities of environmental policymaking as well as constraints and opportunities that policy actors must successfully navigate to achieve their policy goals. Each institution has its own script – a set or sets of processes and procedures – that, "names the *actors*, their respective *behavioral repertoires* (or *strategies*), the *sequence* in which actors choose from them, the *information* they possess when they make their selections, and the *outcome* resulting from the combination of actor choices" (Shepsle 2008, 24, italics in the original).

Each institution contains its own script that shapes its policymaking pathway, yet the macro-institutions do share a similar structure, namely, the division of labor based on jurisdictions that encourages specialization (Shepsle 2010). The jurisdictional specialization of institutions works to reduce the transactions costs associated with information-processing. Jurisdictions create subunits within larger institutions, such as congressional committees in Congress or bureaus within administrative agencies, that create a division of labor, which allows the institutions to parallel process information about multiple issues simultaneously. In addition, this structure ensures specialization with regard to the issues under that subunit's jurisdiction.

As President Obama's quote illustrates, often when strategic policy actors are unable to alter the policy status quo within one policymaking institution or venue, they shift to another. Multiple policymaking venues create opportunity structures for actors to use when attempting to initiate policy change (Gupta 2014; Lewallen 2018; Sheingate 2006). However, the macro-institutions were designed by Madison and the other authors of the Constitution to diffuse power through a structure in which each institution acts as a check on the others. This structure, where ambition checks ambition and separate institutions share power, is there to ensure that policy decisions result from deliberation among actors across institutions, such that no one institution or policy actor can exert total control over decision-making. Because of the diffuse nature of policymaking authority each of the pathways can be checked by one, or both, of the other macro-institutions. Therefore, the environmental policymaking system contains multiple pivot points and veto players that can make durable policy change more difficult to achieve.

Legislation, the policymaking pathway of Congress, tends to be the central focus of policy actors seeking to make lasting change to the status quo, because legislation tends to be the most difficult form of policy to undo (but see Ragusa and Birkhead 2015). For example, the environmental legislation that arose during the environmentalism era has been largely resilient in the face of challenges (Sousa and Klyza 2017). The legislative process, prescribed by the US Constitution, requires agreement by several pivotal institutional actors including majorities of

50 percent +1 in both chambers of Congress, and the president. However, as partisan gridlock has increased legislation has needed a filibuster-proof majority of 60 in the Senate. As defined by Tsebelis (2002), veto players are, "individual or collective actors whose agreement is necessary for a change of the status quo" (19). Therefore, successful legislation must navigate the institutional pivot and veto points of the median voter in the House, the filibuster pivot in the Senate, and the veto pivot of the president (Krehbiel 1998).

The number of veto players, and the ideological distance between them, create the space for a set of policy alternatives that could replace the status quo. Several veto points that are ideologically distant from each other, such as exists with many environmental policy issues including climate change, creates a small *winset*, or a small space in which a set of successful policy alternatives are possible (Tsebelis 2002). The inability of legislation to navigate the various pivot points results in gridlock, and a small winset implies a large gridlock interval. Kraft (2019) defines gridlock as the "inability to resolve conflicts in a policymaking body such as Congress, which results in government inaction in the face of important public problems" (123). As shown in Chapter 5, several indicators are showing that climate change is becoming an increasingly important public problem, but because of the polarized nature of environmental policy, which creates distance among the veto players as well as the multiple pivot points that must align, significant legislation to address climate change has not been achieved.

The legislative actions of Congress and the president are subject to judicial review by the courts. The power of judicial review allows the courts to act as a veto player by determining the constitutionality of the actions of the other two macro-institutions. Court decisions are the pathway through which the courts make policy, with the Supreme Court being the final arbiter of legal disputes.

Apart from the pivot points and veto players, policymaking institutions are connected by chains of delegation, where one institutional actor delegates some policymaking authority to another (Moe 1984). The most fundamental delegation of authority occurs from the people to their elected representatives within the electoral institutions of the Congress and the presidency. Next in the chain is the delegation from electoral institutions to the administrative agencies within the executive branch. Once legislation is enacted, authority is delegated to administrative agencies to implement the legislation, often through the promulgating of rules and regulations. Through the creation of rules, administrative agencies within the executive branch are also making policy. Even as the president is an important pivot point in the legislative process, the rulemaking process of executive branch agencies is the most prominent pathway of executive branch environmental policymaking.

The various macro-institutions of the environmental policymaking system create their own pathways of policymaking, and they exist in a shared policymaking space where the preferences of the institutional actors need to align and the delegation of policymaking authority occurs. This chapter explores the unique pathways of the legislative, executive, and judicial institutions, and how those pathways have been used with regard to climate policy. In addition, this chapter explores the impacts of "separate branches sharing power" and delegation on the potential for climate policy to develop.

Congress

On March 13, 2018, Senator Sheldon Whitehouse (D–RI) gave his 200th speech about climate change on the Senate floor. He stated:

> As I give my 200th "Time to Wake Up" speech, the most obvious fact standing plainly before me is not the measured sea-level rise at Naval Station Newport; it is not the 400 parts per million carbon dioxide barrier we have broken through in the atmosphere; it is not the new flooding maps that coastal communities like Rhode Island's must face; it is not the West aflame; it is not even the uniform consensus about climate change across universities, national laboratories, scientific societies, and even across our military and intelligence services, which warn us, as Senator Reed indicated, that climate change is fueling economic and social disruption around the world. No. The fact that stands out for me, here at No. 200, is the persistent failure of Congress to even take up the issue of climate change. One party will not even talk about it. One party in the executive branch is even gagging America's scientists and civil servants and striking the term "climate change" off of government websites. In the real world, in actual reality, we are long past any question as to the reality of climate change. The fact of that forces us to confront the questions: What stymies Congress from legislating or from even having hearings about climate change? What impels certain executive agencies to forbid even the words?

Since April 2012, Senator Whitehouse has given a "Time to Wake Up" speech about climate change every week that the Senate has been in session. In his speeches, Senator Whitehouse has consistently called for Congress to act on the threat of a changing climate. The lack of congressional action prompted his question, "What stymies Congress from legislating or from even having hearings about climate change?"

As shown in Chapter 5, Congress has held several hundred hearings about climate change from 1975 to 2016, yet with the exception of the American Clean Energy and Security Act (ACES) passing the House in 2009, no climate legislation has been successful in either chamber. In an effort to address Senator Whitehouse's question, this section examines the polarized nature of the parties in Congress over environmental issues, the structure of Congress and its committees, climate change legislation that Congress has considered, and finally the Climate Solutions Caucus in the House.

Congress was established in Article I of the US Constitution, which lists the enumerated, or specifically listed, powers of Congress. These powers include the ability to lay and collect taxes, regulate commerce, and make laws for the "necessary and proper" execution of powers. The framers of the Constitution intended Congress to be the most powerful branch, which is evidenced by Madison arguing in Federalist No. 51 that, "In republican government, the legislative authority necessarily predominates." However, recently concerns have been raised about the ability of Congress to function because of the increasing polarization between the two parties.

As a branch of government, Congress serves as a representative body and a policymaking body. Congress as a representative body is an electoral institution, whereby candidates seek to become members of Congress by winning the most votes in their districts in the House, or their state in the Senate. Therefore, the actions of members of Congress are driven, in no small part, by a desire to be re-elected (Mayhew 2004). Political parties help facilitate the connection between voters and elected officials by designing a process through which candidates are selected. Historically candidates were chosen through deal-making by party leaders, but in the last several decades candidates are selected by voters through primary elections. In addition, parties also provide important cues for voters on where the candidate stands on multiple issues.

While the founders designed a system of "separate branches sharing power", Congress is the pivotal, or "keystone" institution in policy development (Fiorina 1989). The centrality of Congress in policymaking is shown in its power to introduce legislation, provide budget appropriations, confirm executive and court appointments, and oversee the actions of the executive branch agencies. Among its many powers, the largest policymaking function of Congress is the drafting and passing of legislation. Because of the veto power, Congress must work in consultation with the president on legislation, but legislating is largely in the hands of Congress. Policy in the form of legislation is foundational because it grants authority to executive branches' agencies to implement and enforce legislative goals, and determining legislative intent is often a critical part of judicial decision-making.

In making legislation Congress has increasingly been moving away from *regular order*. Regular order refers to the standard, or "textbook," process of crafting and passing legislation. In brief, the standard process of legislative development begins with a bill being introduced by a member of Congress, which is then assigned to the proper committee to be considered and possibly "marked-up" or amended. The bill is then voted on by the committee and sent to the full body for consideration. If the bill passes the full chamber it is then sent to the other chamber to be considered. If the bill passes in the same form in both chambers, it is sent to the president for his signature or veto. As opposed to the regular order process, bills are increasingly being developed by party leaders, then sent to the committees, and finally to the floor (Curry 2015).

Despite its central role in the policymaking system, Congress has, in recent years, been seen as a "broken branch," as evidenced by the collapse of regular order in both the legislative and budget process and in the seeming inability of Congress to address pressing problems (Mann and Ornstein 2008, 2016). The difficulties within Congress as a problem-solving body are driven, in part, by the ever-increasing polarization of the two parties. While differences *between* the parties are hampering Congress's ability to address problems, political parties do help reduce the transactions costs associated with coordinating the actions of members *within* parties. Party leaders work to facilitate coordination of their own members to create and maintain intra-party coalitions in the pursuit of the party's policy goals.

The two major political parties are increasingly polarized on multiple issues, particularly the environment. For example, Kim and Urpelainen (2017) found that if a state or district moved from a Republican member of Congress to a Democratic member, the probability of pro-environmental voting increased by 40 percent. The two parties have become increasingly divided on environmental issues over the last two decades. For each year since the early 1970s, the League of Conservation Voters (LCV) has tracked how members of Congress vote on important environmental bills. The LCV provides a score, from 0 to 100 with 0 indicating all anti-environmental votes and 100 indicating all pro-environmental votes, for each member based on how they voted on each of the dozen or so bills the LCV tracks each year. Figure 6.1 illustrates the growing divide across the parties using the average LCV scores for each party in both chambers from 1972 to 2017.

As can be seen, polarization has always been present, even during the golden era of environmental legislation in the early 1970s. However, the divide has seemingly grown each year as Democrats more and more cast votes that are rated as pro-environmental and Republicans cast votes rated as anti-environmental by the LCV.

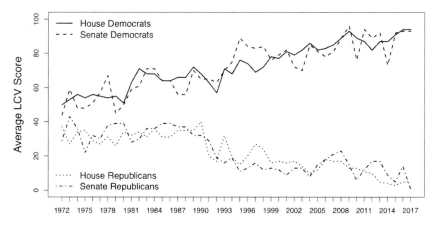

FIGURE 6.1 Congressional polarization on environmental issues, 1972–2017

Several factors likely contribute to increased congressional polarization on environmental issues, including the values of those within the two parties, interest group influence, and the complexity of environmental problems (Kraft 2019). As discussed in Chapter 4, the parties see the role of government in starkly different terms, particularly with regard to government regulation of economic activity. Republicans became increasingly skeptical about environmental legislation and regulation as the environmentalism era waned, and this skepticism was accelerated by the election of Reagan as president. Republican skepticism is grounded in a general doubt about the effectiveness of government to address problems, as Reagan famously said: "Government isn't the solution, government is the problem." There are additional concerns about the top-down, command-and-control mechanisms used as a means of regulation, and the costs imposed on businesses and consumers as a result of those regulations. Following Reagan, the Republican party seems to have become increasingly hostile to environmental regulation, with Republican congressional majorities elected in 1994, President George W. Bush, and President Trump each surpassing the last in their strident rhetoric and actions regarding environmental regulation.

Another important factor in congressional polarization on environmental issues is the alignment of interest groups with the two parties. In general, environmental interest groups have aligned with Democrats and tend to support Democratic candidates for office, whereas business and industry groups, particularly utility interests, tend to align with the Republican party. This alignment of interest groups can impact members of Congress. For example, Shipan and Lowry (2001) found that as the membership of the Sierra Club rose, so did partisan polarization on environmental voting in the Senate. Along similar lines, Kim and Urpelainen (2017) found that an increase in one-sided Political Action Committee (PAC) donations from oil and gas interests to Republican members of Congress also increased polarization on environmental issues. While it is not likely that interest group support is enough on its own to shift the preferences of elected officials – interest groups tend to support those that already agree with them – interest group support likely constrains the type of legislation that a member of Congress could support, which can make deal-making and vote-trading on contentious issues more difficult.

With regard to climate change, conservative advocates and interest groups have successfully mounted a well-funded climate-change counter-movement that has sought to undermine the scientific consensus and has likely worked as a restraint on Republican members of Congress in addressing climate change (Brulle 2018; Layzer 2012; McCright and Dunlap 2003). For example, Congressman Bob Inglis (R–SC), who had acknowledged the seriousness of climate change and in December 2008 penned a *New York Times* op-ed with conservative economist Arthur Laffer calling for a carbon tax (Inglis and Laffer 2008), was defeated in the 2010 primary election by a more conservative Tea Party candidate Trey Gowdy. According to *OpenSecrets.org* Trey Gowdy's largest career campaign contributor is

Koch Industries (see The Center for Responsive Politics 2018), which is one of the major funders behind the climate-change counter-movement (Brulle 2014).

A third factor that may exacerbate polarization is the inherent complexity of environmental issues. Environmental issues are scientifically and technically complex involving the need for a high level of knowledge regarding such things as the potential human health effects of a given level of a pollutant and the potential impacts of rising CO_2 levels on ocean acidification. To assist with the development of information about complex issues, Congress created the Congressional Research Service (CRS) in 1914 and the Congressional Budget Office (CBO) in 1974 to provide it with sophisticated analysis of issues as well as estimates of the potential impacts of legislation. In addition, from 1972 to 1995, Congress had the Office of Technology Assessment (OTA), which was focused on science and technology issues including the environment. However, the 104th Congress led by the Republicans elected in 1994 disbanded the OTA (Bimber 1996).

In addition to the scientific complexity, there is also political complexity associated with environmental issues. The political complexity includes the previously discussed differing ideological and environmental values of the two major parties in Congress, but also the regional nature of congressional elections coupled with regional variation in environmental problems and concerns. For example, when running as a Democrat in 2010, senatorial candidate Joe Manchin from West Virginia shot a hole through the House's ACES bill in a campaign ad in an expression of his opposition to cap-and-trade climate policy. Then candidate Machin's opposition to the ACES bill was based not in partisanship, but in the fact that the bill may have adversely impacted his future constituents, as West Virginia is a coal-producing state. In 2016, West Virginia produced 11 percent of total US coal, second only to Wyoming (US Energy Information Administration 2018).

Apart from the regional complexities, political complexities are also enhanced by the difficulty for elected officials to be able to claim political credit for successfully addressing climate change. The time-scale of climate change is such that the benefits of mitigation actions that are done now may not be seen for years, or even decades. Members of Congress rarely operate on time-scales beyond the next election. Additionally, the collective dilemma nature of climate change is such that even if the United States immediately stopped producing greenhouse gases, other countries would likely continue, which could dilute US efforts (Rabe 2010).

Given that political credit-claiming is difficult on as issue like climate change, it is difficult to receive constituent support. In addition, and as noted in Chapter 5, environmental issues in general, and climate change specifically, tend to garner public support in the abstract, yet those issues are not particularly salient to the public. Public opinion on climate change can impact the actions of members of Congress. For example, votes on four separate pieces of cap-and-trade legislation were found to be influenced by public concern about climate change (Vandeweerdt, Kerremans, and Cohn 2016). Overall, congressional responsiveness to constituent concerns makes building support for climate policies that may have costs in the short-term, but benefits in the long-term, difficult.

Finally, political complexity is also enhanced by the nature of regulatory policy to address climate change, which creates diffuse benefits and concentrated costs. These types of policies create an entrepreneurial politics, where those few that are to be negativity impacted are more likely to engage on the issue than the more numerous that would benefit. For example, Kim, Urpelainen, and Yang (2016) found that coal companies tended to lobby collectively against ACES, whereas renewable energy companies tended to lobby individually. Since coal companies were expected to bear the brunt of the costs associated with the cap-and-trade bill, they were successful in overcoming collective-action problems to negotiate as a group.

Polarization and the associated gridlock on environmental issues has increased in recent years, making action on climate change in Congress difficult. What action has taken place in Congress has been centered around the committee system, which plays a key role in processing information. As noted, each of the macro-institutions is structured through a jurisdictional-based division of labor that encourages specialization, and Congress does this through its committee system.

Committees and Information-Processing

Congress, through its committees and subcommittees, acts as the focal point of policy development. The committee system in Congress allows for the parallel processing of information signals about multiple issues and the development of expertise regarding the issues within a committee's jurisdiction. Committees are also the anchors that tether policy subsystems to the macro-institution of Congress. As noted by Workman, Jones, and Jochim (2009), "at the center of [the] information-generating system are the congressional committee system and the set of policy subsystems built around the committee system" (84).

Members of Congress tend to have preferences over outcomes, rather than specific preferences over policies. For example, members would prefer a less polluted natural environment, but members aren't able to choose particular outcomes; they must instead choose policies that will hopefully make the desired outcome more likely. Congress relies on its committees to process the relevant information and develop the requisite expertise to inform the full chamber about the potential impacts of legislative alternatives.

In order to incentivize expertise, Congress delegates some policymaking authority to its various committees on the policy issues that are within the committee's jurisdiction. The jurisdiction of a committee is based on policy domains (e.g., agriculture, defense, energy, labor) and these jurisdictions are mirrored across both the House and the Senate (Deering and Smith 1997). However, the jurisdictional structure in Congress is dynamic and may feature competition between committees attempting to exert influence over particular issues (Baumgartner,

Jones, and MacLeod 2000; Sheingate 2006; Talbert, Jones, and Baumgartner 1995). These dynamics lead committees to try to both protect their existing jurisdictional turf and expand their jurisdiction to other policy domains (King 1997). In addition, some committees have a broader jurisdictional span, meaning that they can claim jurisdiction across multiple policy issues. Broader jurisdictions are associated with committee fragmentation, where multiple issues are considered by the committee. As a result, committees with broad jurisdictions must deal with multiple sets of policy actors. For example, the Energy and Commerce committee in the House and the Environment and Public Works committee in the Senate have broad jurisdictions and are highly fragmented (Deering and Smith 1997, 89–90).

The various types of authority that are granted to congressional committees include gatekeeping, proposal, inter-chamber bargaining power, and oversight authority (Shepsle 2010, 384). Gatekeeping authority is a *negative* agenda-setting power as it allows committees to keep legislation from advancing, whereas proposal authority is a *positive* agenda-setting power that committees can exercise to move legislation forward. Gatekeeping and proposal power are authorities associated with the development of policy and policy designs, whereas inter-chamber bargaining and oversight occur following the passage of a bill. However, party leaders are increasingly claiming both negative and positive agenda-setting powers over committees with regard to bills (Cox and McCubbins 1993, 2005; Curry 2015).

Inter-chamber bargaining arises because of the Constitutional requirement that bills pass both chambers of Congress in the same form. However, bills often differ as they make their way through the House and Senate, so conference committees are often formed where members of both chambers, largely from the respective committees with jurisdiction, meet to reconcile differences in the bills. Oversight authority grants committees autonomy to monitor the actions of the executive branch that fall within the committee's jurisdiction. These authorities combine to make congressional committees the focal point of information-processing within the policymaking system.

The problem of climate change crosses jurisdictional boundaries and could conceivably fall under the purview of multiple committees. To address climate change Congress could consider issues related to energy, land use, transportation, or foreign relations, among others. As shown in Chapter 5, Congress has held 439 hearings dealing with climate change from 1975 to 2016, and those hearings considered multiple dimensions of climate change. Table 6.1 shows the House and Senate committees that held those hearings on climate change.

As shown, the Energy and Commerce committee in the House and the Environment and Public Works committee in the Senate held the most climate change-related hearings. As noted above, the Energy and Commerce and Environment and Public Works committees have large jurisdictional spans and are highly fragmented across multiple issues. Additionally, those committees are

TABLE 6.1 Climate Change Hearings by Committee, 1975–2016

Committee	Chamber	Number	Percent
Agriculture	House	5	1.12
Energy and Commerce	House	74	16.55
Energy Independence and Global Warming	House	34	7.61
Foreign Affairs	House	13	2.91
Natural Resources	House	16	3.58
Oversight and Government Reform	House	18	4.03
Science, Space, and Technology	House	64	14.32
Small Business	House	7	1.57
Transportation and Infrastructure	House	4	<1
Ways and Means	House	5	1.12
Agriculture, Nutrition, and Forestry	Senate	10	2.24
Commerce, Science, and Transportation	Senate	41	9.17
Energy and Natural Resources	Senate	45	10.07
Environment and Public Works	Senate	71	15.88
Finance	Senate	8	1.79
Foreign Relations	Senate	12	2.68
Homeland Security and Governmental Affairs	Senate	8	1.79

central to energy and environmental issues. It is therefore not surprising they those committees would be the most active on climate change. The Science, Space, and Technology committee in the House and the Energy and Natural Resources committee in the Senate held the next highest percentage of hearings. Overall, those four committees held nearly 57 percent of all hearings about climate change. The configuration of committees most active in climate change illustrates that it is largely seen as an energy and environmental issue as well as a science issue. However, the fact that committees that address agriculture, transportation, and foreign affairs issues also held hearings point to the complexity of climate change.

Committees are central to Congress's ability to process information, although congressional reforms initiated in the 104th Congress have centralized some policymaking authority away from committees and toward party leadership. Most notably, the Gingrich Congress reduced congressional committee staff, reduced the number of committees, and term-limited committee chairs. The selection of committee chairs is determined by the majority party and they tend to be selected on the basis of seniority. However, by slashing staff and term-limiting committee chairs, Congress has shifted authority away from committees and created more centralized power for the majority party (Stewart 2001). This trend has continued since the 104th Congress and, as a result, committee chairs have become beholden to party leadership.

The centralization of authority towards party leaders, combined with increasing polarization, has hampered the ability of Congress to act as a problem-solving body.

These dynamics have also impacted the ways in which congressional committees process information. In the House, party leaders (including committee chairs) have used their power to guide the flow of information that rank-and-file members of the committee receive (Curry 2015). In addition, the types of information on which committees focus has seemed to change since the 1970s. Increasingly, committees focus on information that would have a partisan advantage rather than a problem-solving advantage. Lewallen, Theriault, and Jones (2016), examined the purpose of hearings held by committees (address a problem, implementation, or solution) as well as the stance of the hearing (positional or exploratory) and found that, from 1971–1972 to 2007–2009, the percentage of hearings that addressed a potential policy solution decreased from 71 percent in 1971–1972 to 30 percent in 2007–2008, whereas, the percent of hearings that took a stance on an issue (positional) increased from 19 percent to 30 percent. This indicates that committees may be increasingly focusing on information signals in the politics streams, as opposed to the problem and policy streams.

The seeming shift from information-processing for problem-solving to information-processing for partisan gain has only served to exacerbate value-based divisions on environmental issues. Partisan divisions, coupled with compromised information-processing, make it far less likely that Congress will attempt to address climate change. This is compounded by the fact that the nature of agenda-setting dynamics in Congress makes it difficult for issues to move from the institutional agenda in Congress to the decision agenda. The next section examines the decision agenda of Congress with regard to climate change.

Climate Change Legislation

Despite holding hearings and considering several approaches to address climate change, Congress has failed to pass any legislation that could potentially address climate change. As noted by Rabe (2010), the absence of Congress in federal climate-change policymaking is "conspicuous" (260). But, as has been shown, climate change has reached the institutional agenda of Congress on a fairly regular basis. In addition, Congress has voted on multiple bills to address climate change, though none has successfully passed both chambers. The lack of successful climate change legislation is indicative of the winnowing process in Congress.

Policy issues are winnowed down such that there are multiple issues being processed in parallel on the institutional agenda, although very few make it to the decision agenda. Winnowing refers to "the process by which the House and Senate determine which small proportion of bills will receive committee attention among thousands introduced" (Krutz 2005, 314). Receiving committee attention is a necessary step in moving bills forward and, given the fragmented nature of environmental policy and the subsequent expectation that environmental legislation will be referred to multiple committees, it is possible that this fragmentation will make it more difficult for environmental legislation to advance. However,

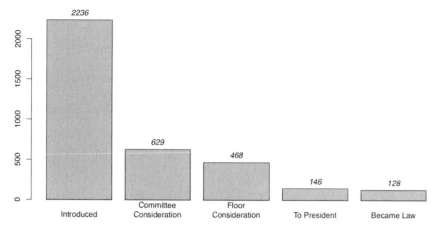

FIGURE 6.2 Climate change winnowing, 1977–2016

Krutz and Jorgensen (2008) found that environmental legislation that is referred to multiple committees is *more* likely to receive committee attention than bills that are not referred to multiple committees. However, bills that are referred to multiple committees are no more likely than other bills to pass out of the committee.

Figure 6.2 shows the winnowing process for bills introduced that include the terms climate change, global warming, greenhouse gas, or greenhouse effect from 1977 to 2016.[2] As Figure 6.2 clearly illustrates, only a small fraction of legislation that is introduced makes it successfully through the winnowing process to become law.

As shown, from 1977 to 2016, 2,236 bills were introduced, 629 received committee consideration, 486 were consider on the floor of either chamber, 146 were sent to the president, and 128, or 5.72 percent of those introduced, became law. The vast majority of the bills that made it thought each stage of the process were appropriations and budget authorizations.

Apart from appropriations bills, a few bills meant to enhance research capabilities become law, including the National Climate Program Act of 1978 (NCPA) and the Global Change Research Act of 1990 (GCRA). The NCPA established funding for climate research, as well as six Regional Climate Centers to develop and provide various types of climate data to the public. After signing the NCPA, President Carter issued a memorandum to executive agency heads stating that, "I am pleased to commit the Nation to this Program of improving our understanding of climatic changes, both natural and man-induced" (Carter 1978).

The GCRA called for the creation of the US Global Change Research Program (USGCRP) to coordinate research of global environmental changes and their potential impacts across various federal agencies. Overall, 13 agencies participate in the USGCRP, including the Department of Agriculture, the Department of Energy, the National Oceanic and Atmospheric Administration (NOAA)

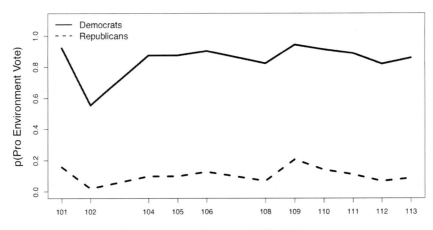

FIGURE 6.3 Climate change votes in Congress, 1989–2014

within the Department of Commerce, the National Science Foundation, and the Environmental Protection Agency. The mandate of the USGCRP is to "develop and coordinate a comprehensive and integrated United States research program which will assist the Nation and the world to understand, assess, predict, and respond to human-induced and natural processes of global change" (US Global Change Research Program n.d.). The USGCRP is responsible for the National Climate Assessment, which provides information about the impacts of climate change to the United States. To date, four National Climate Assessments have been produced, in 2000, 2009, 2014, and 2018.

The analysis of environmental voting in Congress by Kim and Urpelainen (2017) found that, from 1989 to 2014, which included the 101st Congress to the 113th Congress, 58 bills about climate change were considered. Overall, climate change legislation was the most polarized of all environmental issues considered. Using data from Kim and Urpelainen (2017),[3] Figure 6.3 illustrates the predicted probability of voting yes on a climate change bill by party affiliation, controlling for congressional session. The votes include the cap-and-trade bills discussed below, as well as other votes such as an amendment to prohibit use of the social cost of carbon.

As shown in Figure 6.3, Democratic members of Congress were far more likely than Republican members to vote for bills aimed at addressing climate change across each session of Congress. In the next section, I discuss five attempts to pass bipartisan cap-and-trade legislation in Congress from 2003 to 2009.

Cap-and-Trade in Congress

Climate Stewardship Acts: from 2003 to 2007, Senators John McCain (R–AZ) and Joseph Lieberman (D/I–CT) introduced a series of three bills in the Senate that aimed to create a cap-and-trade system for greenhouse gas emissions. The first was the Climate Stewardship Act of 2003 (CSA). The CSA would have limited green-house gas production, beginning in 2010, from the utility, industrial, commercial, and transportation sectors to 2000 levels for the first six years, then to 1990 levels in the following years. The bill would have covered roughly 70 percent of GHG emissions in the United States (Pizer and Kopp 2003). Emission allowances were to be allotted by sector and then to specific firms that could use or trade their allowances. The bill attracted eight cosponsors, including one other Republican, Olympia Snowe (R–ME), but it was ultimately defeated in the Senate by a vote of 55 to 43 on October 30, 2003.

Next, in 2005 McCain and Lieberman introduced the Climate Stewardship and Innovation Act (CSI). The CSI was similar to the CSA of 2003, but it called for the creation of a public/private Climate Change Credit Corporation to oversee the distribution of emission allowances, or "climate credits." The bill had two cosponsors, Senator Snowe and then Senator Barack Obama (D–IL). It was defeated in the Senate with a 60 to 38 vote in June 2005. Finally, McCain and Lieberman introduced the CSI of 2007. It was similar to the previous versions and was able to attract ten cosponsors, including Susan Collins (R–ME) and Norm Coleman of Minnesota (R–MN). However, it was never brought to a vote in the Senate.

America's Climate Security Act of 2007: following the failures of the Climate Stewardship Acts, Lieberman, Senator John Warner (R–VA), and Senator Barbara Boxer (D–CA) introduced the America's Climate Security Act of 2007 (ACS), and it was reported out of the Senate's Environment and Public Works committee in December 2007. The centerpiece of the ACS was a cap-and-trade program for the five greenhouse gases that are covered under the Kyoto Protocol, including carbon dioxide, methane, nitrous oxide, sulfur hexafluoride, and perfluorocarbons, and a separate cap-and-trade program for hydrofluorocarbons. Like the previous Climate Stewardship Acts, the caps would set an annual limit on the amount of the above-listed greenhouse gases from the utility, industrial, commercial, and transportation sectors. In addition, under the ACS the EPA would distribute the allowances to sectors and firms, with some being distributed to the Climate Change Credit Corporation, pre-viously proposed in the CSI. The Climate Change Credit Corporation would auction the allowances they were allocated to fund the development of energy technologies, worker education and training, and energy assistance for low-income households (Congressional Budget Office 2008).

The ACS was brought to the floor in June 2008 and introduced by Senator Boxer (D–CA). Introducing the bill, Senator Boxer stated:

> Mr President, this is a historic day, not only for our country, but I think the world is watching us. It is because we have a pressing issue called global warming, climate change; you could call it either one. Scientists have told

us that in fact we have a very small window right now within which to respond. But it is a historic day because for the first time we have what I call tripartisan legislation out of the Environment and Public Works Committee. It is the Boxer-Lieberman-Warner bill. It is a Democrat, it is an Independent, and it is a Republican. We have come together to say to our colleagues and to the American people: Finally, we are going to deal with this critical challenge.[4]

Despite the seeming optimism of Senator Boxer and the "tripartisan" nature of the bill, it ultimately did not pass the Senate. Senator McConnell, pulling a procedural move to stall the vote, required the clerks to read aloud the entire bill over an eight-hour period. Following the reading, the Senate voted 48 to 36 to invoke cloture, which was far short of the filibuster pivot of 60 votes needed to end debate.

While the ACS did not pass the Senate, or even get an up-or-down vote, there was optimism that similar approaches would ultimately be successful. Following the defeat of the ACS, Frances Beinecke, then president of the Natural Resources Defense Council, stated that, "We have taken comprehensive global warming legislation farther than it has ever gone before", and "A national limit on global warming pollution is inevitable" (Pooley 2008).

Optimism was high during the 2008 election that the federal government was on the verge of addressing climate change. Both major party candidates supported climate policy, as did a coalition of industry leaders, as did even the strange "couch-fellows" pair of Newt Gingrich and Nancy Pelosi, who appeared together in a commercial urging climate-change action. The optimism only increased following the election of Barack Obama and large Democratic congressional majorities.

American Clean Energy and Security Act of 2009: the American Clean Energy and Security Act of 2009 (ACES) originated in the House and was developed by Henry Waxman (D–CA), chairman of the Energy and Commerce committee, and Edward Markey (D–MA), chairman of the Energy and Commerce's subcommittee on Energy and Environment and chairman of the Select Committee on Energy Independence and Global Warming. As shown in Table 6.1, those committees are central to the processing of information related to climate change. Like the previous legislative attempts in the Senate, the ACES was built around a cap-and-trade program for greenhouse gases. The ACES covered seven GHGs, the same six as the ACSA, as well as nitrogen trifluoride, but HFCs were to be covered under a separate cap. The GHG emission reduction caps were set at the following levels,

2012: 3% below 2005 emission levels (~12% above 1990 emission levels)
2020: 17% below 2005 (~4% below 1990)
2030: 42% below 2005 (~33% below 1990)
2050: 83% below 2005 (~80% below 1990) (Larsen, Kelly, and Heilmayr 2009, 3; Pew Center on Global Climate Change 2009)

Under the ACES, roughly 75 percent of the emissions allowances were to be distributed freely, with the remaining allowances being auctioned. Then, in 2026, the mix of freely distributed allowances vs. those that were auctioned would begin to shift, and by 2050 60 percent of allowances would have been given freely vs. 40 percent that would have been auctioned. The logic behind freely distributing the bulk of the emissions allowances was to shield consumers from large and sudden increases in energy prices (Pooley 2010). The revenue raised from the auction of allowances would have been used to offset higher energy costs to producers and consumers, as well as invested in research and development regarding renewable energy, energy efficiency, and carbon capture and storage, and used to assist displaced workers, among other uses. An analysis by the Congressional Budget Office found that the ACES would have been deficit-neutral over the first decade (Congressional Budget Office 2009).

The complex politics of climate change involves not just polarization between the parties, but differences within each party that are often based on regional concerns. With these concerns in mind, Waxman and Markey worked with Democrats from fossil-fuel-intensive districts when crafting the ACES. In addition, Waxman and Markey also worked to build support with other important stakeholders, including business and environmental groups. The process of crafting the ACES is indicative of the shift from a committee-driven process towards a more centralized party-driven process of creating legislation.[5]

The ACES was officially introduced in May 2009, and during the mark-up process in the Energy and Commerce committee, Republicans offered nearly 400 amendments, likely in an effort to stall the bill. However, the bill passed the committee by a 33–25 vote, with four Democrats on the committee voting in opposition, and one Republican voting in favor. The bill was brought to the floor of the House and passed with a thin seven-vote margin of 219 to 212. Overall, 44 Democrats opposed the bill and eight Republicans supported it.

The approach of Waxman and Markey worked, as the ACES was successful in securing passage in the House, but the effort was doomed in the Senate. Efforts to craft companion legislation in the Senate were being undertaken by Senators John Kerry (D–MA), Lindsey Graham (R–SC), and Joseph Lieberman (I–CT); however, it was clear that it could not reach 60 votes to break a filibuster, so no companion legislation was brought to a vote in the Senate in the 111th Congress.

The inability of Congress to pass legislation to address climate change was, in part, a function of political complexities and the institutional rules of Congress. The political complexes led to several provisions being added to the ACES to attract support, which ballooned the bill beyond 1,400 pages. Most notably, the provision of emissions allowances was seen as "giveaways" to various industries to gain support for, or at least dull opposition to, the bill. However, the distribution of allowances became a frame that opponents attached to the ACES. As Myron Ebell from the Competitive Enterprise Institution stated: "We did a good job of showing that a bunch of big companies – Goldman Sachs, the oil companies, the big utilities – would get windfall profits because they'd been given free ration coupons" (Broder 2010). Reflecting on the ACES in 2016, Waxman, who retired from Congress in 2015, stated: "It was a disappointment that we couldn't get a bill all the way through, but we highlighted the issue ... We gave it our best effort. We tried to accomplish that goal. But I know from my own history as a member of Congress, I have to work sometimes decades before some of the proposals I made eventually became law" (Reilly and Bogardus 2016).

The 2010 congressional elections brought a Republican majority to Congress, led by a surge of conservative Tea Party Republicans that grew around opposition to President Obama's efforts to use government to address issues. While other issues such as health-care reform were at the center of the 2010 campaign, the effort to address climate change with the ACES was present as well. Following the 2010 election, the legislative pathway of climate policy narrowed even further. However, an institutional effort in the House developed early in 2016 that may lay the groundwork for a future Congress to pass climate legislation. In the next section, I discuss the Climate Solutions Caucus.

Climate Solutions Caucus in the House

Members of the House are often involved in one or more Congressional Member Organizations (CMO), or caucuses. Caucuses are formed by members that share legislative preferences, and "exist to affect public policy, either directly through policy advocacy for a region or an issue, or indirectly by attracting media attention, or through the socialization and orientation of their Members" (Glassman 2017, i). Currently there are 800 caucuses in the House. It is not clear what measurable policy impact caucuses have, although the Tea Party Caucus of the 112th and 113th Congresses seemed to exert some influence on members of Congress by moving them further right ideologically (Ragusa and Gaspar 2016).

The Climate Solutions Caucus (CSC) was founded in February 2016 by two House members from South Florida, Carlos Curbelo (R–FL) and Ted Deutch (D–FL). The mission of the CSC states that, "The Caucus will serve as an organization to educate members on economically-viable options to reduce climate risk and protect our nation's economy, security, infrastructure, agriculture, water supply and public safety" (Revkin 2016). The CSC brings together members of both parties that are interested in addressing climate change. Indeed, the membership rules of CSC stipulate that for a new member to join, another member of the other party must also join. As of August 2018, the CSC has 86 members in total, with 43 Democrats and 43 Republicans. Using DW-NOMINATE scores from the 115th Congress, Figure 6.4 illustrates the ideological make-up of the current CSC.[6]

DW-NOMINATE scores measure the ideological point of each member of Congress along a single left-right dimension using roll-call votes, and the scores

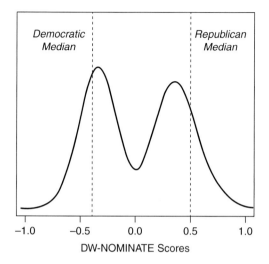

FIGURE 6.4 Ideological distribution of the Climate Solutions Caucus: 115th Congress

range from -1, most liberal, to 1, most conservative (Poole 2005; Poole and Rosenthal 2007). Figure 6.4 displays the ideological distribution of the caucus as well as the median ideological point of each party within the House. As can be seen, the ideological distribution of Republican members tends toward the center, and away from the party median. The Democratic members of the CSC also seem to tend more toward the center, through nearer to the median of their party than Republicans. This is likely because the CSC tends to seek out the centrist members of both parties.

For the most part, members of the caucus are clustered together ideologically, although a few outliers are present including Representatives Jan Schakowsky (D–IL), Nydia Velazquez (D–NY), and Judy Chu (D–CA), who are somewhat more liberal than other members of the CSC. For Republicans, the more conservative members include Representatives Ed Royce (R–CA), Mark Sanford (R–SC), and most notably Matt Gaetz (R–FL). Representative Gaetz is a first-term congressman and introduced a bill in early 2017 to abolish the EPA (Kaufman 2017). Despite his skepticism regarding the effectiveness of the EPA, Gaetz notes that the Earth is warming: "I don't think there's a scientific debate left to be had on if it is happening." He goes to state that, "I also think history is going to judge very harshly climate change deniers, and I don't want to be one of them." Finally, "We should be focused on solutions" (Baucum 2017).

The approach of the CSC is to be bipartisan – as noted, members can only join in pairs with one Democrat and one Republican – and the CSC focuses on market-based solutions to address climate change. In addition, the caucus helps to facilitate coordination on climate among its members. However, critics argue that the CSC has not been particularly effective. For example, shortly after

Representative Gaetz joined the caucus, Melinda Pierce, the legislative director of the Sierra Club, stated:

> The supposed Climate Solutions Caucus is welcome to add any member they'd like – even climate deniers who propose legislation to terminate the EPA … But, until the silent half of the caucus backs up the name of the caucus with actual votes for clean energy solutions and against the fossil fuel industry, being a member will be nothing more than a line on representatives' resumes (Skibell 2017).

In July 2018 the House voted on a resolution that stated a carbon tax, a favored policy among many members of the CSC, would have detrimental impacts on the economy. The resolution passed the House 229–180 and all but four Republican members of the CSC voted in favor of the resolution. However, the following week Carlos Curbelo (R–FL), cofounder of the CSC, introduced carbon tax legislation with a tax that would start at \$24 per ton in 2020 and rise 2 percent a year above inflation until 2030. The bill would also eliminate the gas tax, and the bulk of the revenues from the tax would go toward infrastructure investments.

Despite some concerns, the CSC has been effective in increasing the number of Republicans that are willing to take a public position stating that climate change is happening and solutions are needed. However, the Republican members of the CSC tend to be more moderate than the party as a whole, and as result may be more likely to lose their seat to a Democratic challenger, or even a primary challenge to their right, which happened to caucus member Mark Sanford in his June 2018 primary election. Indeed, in the 2018 midterm elections roughly half of the Republican members of the CSC lost re-election to their Democratic challenger, including cofounder Carlos Curbelo.

The ultimate effectiveness of the CSC is still unknown, although it seems clear that the legislative pathway of climate policy will remain extremely narrow in the near future, even following the 2018 election that gave the Democrats the majority in the House. Next, I turn to the executive branch pathways of environmental policymaking.

The Executive

The executive branch of government consists of the president and the numerous executive agencies. The president is the *unitary* head of the executive branch and is the most public face of American government. Article II of the Constitution lists the powers of the presidency, which include powers to execute the laws, to exercise military authority, issue pardons, engage in diplomacy with foreign nations, veto legislation passed by Congress, and make appointments to executive agencies with the approval of the Senate. The veto power gives the president a direct role in lawmaking, as the veto point is a crucial pivot point in the making of legislation.

Often, presidents use the threat of a veto when negotiating with Congress, which implies that the veto pivot is a bargaining tool rather than a way for the president to achieve his policy preferences. In addition, the president's power to execute the law, embedded in the "take care" clause – "*he shall take Care that the Laws be faithfully executed*" – allows the executive branch to have some power, independent of Congress, to shape and even create policy.

The president often tries to use his public visibility to frame issues to galvanize public opinion and to get environmental issues on to the policymaking agenda of Congress. For example, in his 2015 State of the Union address President Obama stated that, "No challenge – no challenge – poses a greater threat to future generations than climate change." He went on to frame the issue of climate change as one of science and scientific consensus as well as one of national security.

> 2014 was the planet's warmest year on record. Now, one year doesn't make a trend, but this does: 14 of the 15 warmest years on record have all fallen in the first 15 years of this century. I've heard some folks try to dodge the evidence by saying they're not scientists; that we don't have enough information to act. Well, I'm not a scientist, either. But you know what, I know a lot of really good scientists at NASA, and at NOAA, and at our major universities. And the best scientists in the world are all telling us that our activities are changing the climate, and if we don't act forcefully, we'll continue to see rising oceans, longer, hotter heatwaves, dangerous droughts and floods, and massive disruptions that can trigger greater migration and conflict and hunger around the globe. The Pentagon says that climate change poses immediate risks to our national security. We should act like it.
>
> *Obama 2015*

President Obama was using the very public and visible platform of the State of the Union (SOTU) address to try to convince Congress and the public of the need to address climate change. However, similar to the results in Chapter 2 that showed a null effect for presidential mentions of environmental issues in the SOTU, Obama's SOTU mentions of climate change did not seem to be effective at placing the issue on the congressional agenda in 2015.

A few of the direct ways that a president can make policy include the negotiation of international agreements, such as the Paris Agreement, and treaties, such as the Kyoto Protocol. Treaties that are negotiated by the president are required to be ratified by the Senate. The Kyoto Protocol was a treaty, but was never brought to the Senate to be ratified following the Byrd–Hagel resolution, which passed the Senate 95–0. Increasingly, presidents have negotiated executive agreements, such as the Paris Agreement, as a way to assert authority without resistance from Congress (Krutz and Peake 2011; Peake, Krutz, and Hughes 2012).

A second direct form of policymaking for the president is executive orders. Executive orders "instruct government officials and administrative agencies to

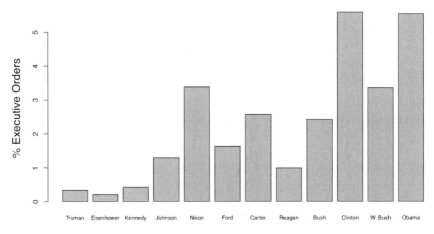

FIGURE 6.5 Environmental executive orders, 1947–2016

take specific actions with regard to both domestic and foreign affairs" (Howell 2003, 16). As a form of policy and an output of the executive branch, executive orders carry the full weight of law and are subject to judicial review. In general, the number of executive orders has been trending downward, although several environmentally relevant executive orders have been issued. Using data from the *Comparative Agendas Project*, Figure 6.5 illustrates the percent of executive orders that dealt with the environment issued by each president from Truman through Obama.

As can be seen, Democratic Presidents Clinton and Obama issued the largest percentage of environmental executive orders with ~6 percent of all of their executive orders dealing with the environment. This was followed by Republican Presidents Nixon and George W. Bush at about ~3 percent. Despite the seemingly partisan differences, the most important executive order in terms of environmental protection was Nixon's Reorganization Plan No. 3 that created the Environmental Protection Agency.

Another executive order important for, though not specific to, environmental policy was issued by President Reagan and dealt with benefit-cost analysis. Benefit-cost analysis estimates in monetary terms the financial costs and benefits of policy alternatives. EO 12291 issued by Reagan stated that, "Regulatory action shall not be undertaken unless the potential benefits to society from the regulation outweigh the potential costs to society" (Reagan 1981). While controversial at the time, subsequent presidents have issued similar executive orders with regard to benefit-cost analysis. President Clinton issued EO 12866 in 1993, which requires the Office of Information and Regulatory Affairs (OIRA), within the Office of Management and Budget, to review "significant" regulations and perform benefit-cost analysis for rules determined to be "economically significant." EO 12866 also states that rules should be adopted only when the benefits justify the costs. President Obama, with EO 13563 issued in 2011, reaffirmed EO 12866 and also required agencies to perform retrospective reviews of their regulations (Sunstein 2013). In addition, the Obama administration in 2009 created the Interagency Working Group on the Social Cost of Carbon (IWG) to develop a *social cost of carbon* to be used to estimate the costs associated with a ton of carbon emissions for the purposes of doing benefit-cost analysis of policies aimed at regulating CO_2.

The social cost of carbon (SCC) monetizes the potential negative impacts of climate change. To estimate the SCC, economists use Integrated Assessment Models (IAMs) that combine climate models with economic models. There are four components that need to be estimated in an IAM including "(1) the future emissions of GHGs, (2) the effects of past and future emissions on the climate system, (3) the impact of changes in climate on the physical and biological environment, and (4) the translation of these environmental impacts into economic damages" (Greenstone, Kopits, and Wolverton 2013, 25). Three IAMs exist in the academic literature that were used by the IWG, including the Dynamic Integrated model of Climate and the Economy (DICE) model (see Nordhaus 2017); the Climate Framework for Uncertainty, Negotiation and Distribution (FUND) model (see Waldhoff et al. 2014); and the Policy Analysis of the Greenhouse Effect (PAGE) model (see Hope 2006). Using those models, the IWG estimated the SCC as $36 per ton of CO_2 emitted, although in 2017 the Trump administration reduced that estimate to between $1 and $6 per ton (Harvey 2017).

President Obama was the first president to use executive orders explicitly aimed at climate change. As the congressional pathway of climate policymaking narrowed, President Obama made use of some of the tools available to him to address climate change. For example, in June 2013 the Executive Office of the President issued *The President's Climate Action Plan*, which laid out ways in which the federal government would work to a) cut carbon pollution, b) prepare for the impacts of climate change, and c) lead global efforts to address climate change (Executive Office of the President 2013). In November of 2013, President Obama issued EO 13653, which directed agencies to pursue strategies to enhance climate change readiness and resilience in the United States, and in September 2014 he issued EO 13677, directing agencies engaged in international development to work on climate resilience. Next, in January 2015, EO 13690 ordered agencies to create a new risk reduction standard for federal projects, noting the expected increase in floods and flood severity as a result of climate change. Finally, EO 13693, issued in March 2015, called for federal agencies to reduce their GHG emissions by 40 percent over the next ten years.

When leaving office, Obama had created a record of achievement on climate change using the presidential power of executive orders. Executive orders do have the force of law and often can live on beyond the particular presidency of whomever issued them, such as the case with the requirement of benefit-cost analysis in rulemaking. However, executive orders can also be revoked by subsequent presidents, and most of the above-listed executive orders were subsequently revoked by the Trump administration. In March 2017, Trump issued EO 13783 that set to undo many of the Obama administration's actions on climate change, including the Clean Power Plan, methane regulations, the social cost of carbon, the Climate Action Plan, and EO 13653 that set out to enhance climate change resilience, among other actions. Next, in May 2017, Trump revoked EO 13693 that called for reducing the GHG emissions of executive agencies, and in August 2017 Trump revoked EO 13690 that aimed to reduce exposure to flood risks that are likely to increase as a result of climate change.

Executive orders are the policymaking pathway most available to the president, although executive orders are easily overturned by subsequent presidents. Other powers of the president that come from the "take care" clause of the US Constitution have evolved such that the president is the chief executive of the administrative state. It is through the role of chief executive that the president can have the most impact on environmental policy (Vig 2019). The administrative presidency developed through a series of efforts by presidents to gain more control over the executive branch in an effort to shape policy (Waterman 2009).

As chief executive of the administrative state, the president oversees all the agencies in the executive branch, including those in the Executive Office of the President, the Cabinet, and several independent agencies. Each of these agencies have separate offices, departments, or bureaus that are part of the green state. The Executive Office of the President includes the Council on Environmental Quality, the Office of Management and Budget, and the Office of Science and Technology Policy. Several cabinet-level departments are active in making environmental policy, including the Department of Agriculture, the Department of Commerce, the Department of Energy, and the Department of the Interior. Finally, several independent agencies impact environmental policy, most importantly the Environmental Protection Agency.

One aspect of the administrative presidency is the use of appointment power to appoint individuals to head the various agencies that share the president's policy preferences. However, presidential appointments require Senate approval, which can work to moderate the ideological tendencies of some appointments (Bertelli and Grose 2011). But, with increasing polarization and under unified government, the potential of the Senate to moderate presidential appointments is weakened, as evidenced by the Senate confirmation of former Oklahoma attorney general Scott Pruitt as Trump's first administrator of the Environmental Protection Agency in February 2017. Pruitt was the most conservative EPA administrator since Anne Gorsuch, and as Oklahoma's attorney-general Pruitt had brought several court actions aimed at limiting the activities of the agency he would now be leading.

A second aspect of the administrative presidency is the involvement of White House staff in the policy activity of executive branch agencies. For example, as a result of executive orders by Presidents Reagan and Clinton, significant rules and regulations promulgated by agencies are subject to review from OIRA. In general, the number of rules that are approved by OIRA without revision has been trending down, indicating a more proactive approach by the Office of the President regarding the rulemaking of the executive branch agencies (Eisner 2007). Finally, the budget process of the executive branch agencies has been centralized such that agency budget requests are scrutinized by OMB.

The powers associated with the administrative presidency create pathways to make lasting policy change, yet they rely on the use of executive branch agencies that are subject to congressional and court oversight. The next section discusses the policymaking pathways of executive agencies.

Executive Branch Agencies

Within the executive branch it is the agencies that have the most information processing and policymaking capabilities. As noted by Workman (2015), "The federal bureaucracy is unique among American political institutions in that it combines all three major functions of government. Bureaucracies perform an array of functions that very closely mirror legislating, executing, and adjudication responsibilities" (86–87). The ways in which federal agencies develop rules and regulations are similar to the legislative process, the implementation of legislation is how agencies execute the law, and finally adjudication is done through administrative courts that review the merits of agency decisions.

To accomplish their myriad goals, executive agencies are organized through a bureaucratic structure. Kettl (2008) delineates the ideas of Max Weber regarding bureaucratic organizational structure into the following elements:

- A mission defined by top officials
- Fixed jurisdictions within the organization, with the scope of work defined by rules
- Authority graded from top to bottom, with higher-level officials having more authority than those at the bottom
- Management by written documents, which creates an institutional record of work
- Management by career experts, who embody the organization's capacity to do work
- Management by rules, which govern the discretion exercised by administrators

The mission of each executive agency is defined by the electoral institutions of Congress and the president, often through authorizing legislation that creates the agency. The bureaucratic form of organizations assists agencies in fulfilling their mission by lowering the transactions costs of coordination through a hierarchical command structure and through the enhanced efficiency that comes from the division of labor and specialization. For example, the mission statement of the Department of the Interior (DOI) states that,

> The Department of the Interior protects and manages the Nation's natural resources and cultural heritage; provides scientific and other information about those resources; and honors its trust responsibilities or special commitments to American Indians, Alaska Natives, and affiliated island communities.[7]

To accomplish this mission the DOI is organized into several specialized bureaus such as the *Bureau of Indian Affairs, Bureau of Land Management, Bureau of Ocean and Energy Management, National Park Service,* and the *US Fish and Wildlife Service.* Each bureau is organized around one, or a few, components of the mission statement and such an organization allows the DOI to work on the various parts of its mission simultaneously.

At the top of the command structure of executive agencies is a politically appointed administrator, although public bureaucracies are staffed largely by civil servants that hold the requisite expertise. Prior to the creation of a federal civil service, jobs within the federal government were political and typically held by supporters of elected officials and political parties. However, the Progressive Era of the late 19th and early 20th centuries pushed for the adoption of a merit-based civil service, where hiring and promotion were on the basis of merit. These reforms were codified in the Pendleton Civil Service Reform Act of 1883.

Coupled with the rise of the federal civil service was the Progressive Era notion of neutral expertise among those in the civil service. At the time it was proposed that the relationship between electoral institutions and agency experts could be explained by the *politics-administration dichotomy* (Goodnow 1900; Wilson 1887). The politics-administration dichotomy describes a relationship of clear division between the electoral institutions that aggregate societal preferences into public policy and the agencies that use their expertise to implement those policies. Under this framework, politics and administration exist in distinct spheres, where political actors exist in one sphere and experts exist in another, and the electoral institutions delegate some authority to the bureaucratic institutions when implementing policy.

Delegation from the electoral institutions to the bureaucracy has been described using a *principal-agent* or *agency theory* framework (see Wood 2010). The logic of the principal-agent framework has its origins in the public-administration dichotomy. Under this framework the electoral institutions are the principals that possess policymaking authority to make policy through the political process (*politics*) and the bureaucracy is the agent that is delegated some authority to implement policies in a value-neutral way based on their expertise (*administration*). Agencies are granted this authority because of their expertise in the relevant areas. The principal-agent dynamic can be problematic if agencies begin to leverage their expertise to move policy in the direction they prefer. This potential is termed *bureaucratic drift*, where policies start to move towards the preferences of the bureaucracy and away from those of the electoral institutions.

To arrest the potential of bureaucratic drift, electoral institutions make use of several levers of political control. Electoral institutions take political control actions that can be seen as proactive or reactive regarding agency decision. Proactive ways of political control include specific legislative language that limits agency discretion, centralized process of review within the executive branch, and political appointments that share the views of elected officials. Reactive measures include executive orders, budget changes, and congressional oversight that can include hearings and investigations. For example, the hearing regarding the Clean Power Plan held by the Environment and Public Works committee discussed in Chapter 5 was an oversight hearing regarding the EPA's proposed greenhouse gas regulations held by a committee chair, James Inhofe (R–OK) that saw the EPA as acting beyond its delegated authority. Each of these control mechanisms can work to undermine the capacity of executive agencies to move beyond the preferences of Congress and the president.

The purpose of congressional delegation to executive branch agencies is to implement the law as prescribed by the "take care" clause. However, effective policy implementation often requires the creation of policy, which occurs largely through regulations promulgated by executive branch agencies. The setting of regulatory standards occurs through the rulemaking process. The rules and regulations put forth by executive agencies have become the major policymaking activity of the executive branch. Executive agency rules provide for policy implementation, meaning that they translate the goals of legislation into routine procedures that the bureaucracy will perform. Often this includes interpreting vague legislative language. For example, the Toxic Substances Control Act of 1976 required the lessening of "an *unreasonable* risk of injury to health or the environment." It is up to the implementing agency or agencies to determine what constitutes an unreasonable risk.

The Administrative Procedure Act of 1946 (APA) provides the steps that agencies must take when making rules, yet the authority of bureaucratic institutions to craft rules and regulations is delegated by Congress, as "no rule is valid unless it is authorized by law and is promoting a statutory purpose of some kind" (Kerwin 2003, 74). Legislation can include requirements and instructions for rules, although legislation varies in the degree to which specific rules are required and this creates some flexibly for policy actors in and outside of the agency to propose rules. Apart from statutory requirements, agency rulemaking can be prompted by leaders within the agency, the president through OMB directives and regulatory reviews, court decisions, other agencies, state and local governments, and interest groups. One study found that discretionary rulemaking made up 60 percent of rulemaking activity and that business and trade associations were the most active in determining what rules reached the agenda of agencies (West and Raso 2013).

The decision agenda-setting process for agency rulemaking is considered the pre-proposal stage. During the pre-proposal stage there are often informal communications between agency personnel and other policy actors, and policy actors, particularly interest groups, attempt to frame the issues for the agency (Rinfret 2011).

Once an agency decides to draft a rule it is placed on the agency's decision agenda and the rulemaking process that was established in the APA begins. The APA requires that agencies first issue a *notice of proposed rulemaking* (NPRM) that is published in the *Federal Register* and alerts the public to the intention of the agency to make a new rule. Next, agencies must allow for a public comment period where other policy actors can provide comments regarding the proposed rule. Finally, after consideration of the public comments, agencies publish a final rule in the *Federal Register*. Final rules have a minimum of 30 days before they become effective.

Apart from the APA, agencies must also follow guidelines provided in several executive orders, most notably EO 12866 issued in October 1993 by President Clinton and discussed above. EO 12866 states that OIRA, located within OMB, will review "significant" rules at both the proposal and final rule stage. Significant rules are those that have an estimated economic impact of $100 million or more, are inconsistent with actions of other agencies, have budgetary impacts, or introduce new legal or policy issues. Additionally, EO 12866 states that "economically significant" rules, defined as those that have an estimated impact of $100 million or more, must be accompanied by a benefit-cost analysis that considers the benefits and costs of the proposed rule as well as those of other alternative approaches. Agencies should only put the rule forward if the benefits justify the costs.

The number of final rules promulgated by executive agencies seems to be trending down since 1976. According to a report by the *Congressional Research Service* (Carey 2016), the number of pages in the "final rules" section of the *Federal Register* went from 7,401 pages in 1976 to 3,410 pages in 2015.

The final rules carry the weight of law just like other forms of policy, and they are subject to judicial review. Indeed, the APA includes a provision that gives the right of judicial review to persons adversely impacted by an agencies action. The APA also specifically noted that the court should compel agency action if action is unreasonably delayed. Additionally, the courts should determine whether the agency actions were an "arbitrary, capricious" use of discretion, unconstitutional, exceeded statutory authority, didn't follow lawful procedures, and were not supported by evidence and facts (Kerwin 2003, 244–245).

In addition to judicial review, the review process of OMB gives the president oversight of agency actions, and the public comment process gives the public and other policy actors ways to inform the rulemaking process. Finally, the Congressional Review Act of 1996 (CRA) gives Congress, in consultation with the president, the ability to repeal an agency rule.

The CRA was part of a package of reforms developed by the 104th Congress, and passed within the Contract with America Advancement Act of 1996. Under the CRA, agencies must report each rule to Congress, then Congress can review and, through a joint resolution passed in the same form by both chambers and signed by the president, can repeal any agency rule within a period of 60 legislative days, or days that Congress is in session. The CRA includes a set of measures to expedite the process of introducing and voting on the resolution of disapproval, particularly for the Senate. Most notably, the CRA limits the amount of time the resolution can be debated to ten hours, which precludes a filibuster, meaning that the resolution can pass the Senate with a simple majority. If an agency rule is repealed by Congress, the agency cannot issue another rule that is substantially similar without new statutory authority granted by Congress (Beth 2001).

To date, the CRA has been used to repeal 15 agency rules. The first instance was in 2001, when a Republican Congress and a Republican president, George W. Bush, repealed a Department of Labor ergonomics rule. The CRA was not used again until 2017 when a Republican Congress and President Trump considered repealing as many as 33 agency rules issued in the last months of the Obama administration, 20 of which dealt with energy and/or environmental issues (Lipton and Lee 2017). Ultimately, 14 rules were repealed, including four dealing with energy and the environment, among them a Security and Exchange Commission rule that required gas, mining, and oil companies to disclose payments made to foreign governments for drilling and mining rights. The remaining three environmental rules were promulgated by the Interior Department, including a rule about federal government land-use planning, a rule meant to restrict hunting in Alaska, and the Stream Protection Rule, which was aimed at the protection of waterways near coal-mining operations.

Notably, however, the Senate fell short on a 49 to 51 vote of repealing the DOI's methane rule, which limits the emission of methane by requiring companies to capture methane that is flared or vented by oil and gas wells (Davenport 2017). The repeal of the methane rule passed the House, but failed in the Senate when three Republicans, Susan Collins (R–ME), Lindsey Graham (R–SC), and John McCain (R–AZ) voted against the repeal resolution. However, in December 2017 the DOI issued a rule delaying the implementation of the methane rule, and in February 2018 it issued a new proposed rule that revises and substantially weakens the 2016 methane rule.

This section discussed some of the dynamics of agency policymaking including the bureaucratic structure of agencies, the inherent tensions involved in delegation, and the rulemaking process that allows agencies to create policy. The next section applies these insights to the Environmental Protection Agency.

The Environmental Protection Agency

The Environmental Protection Agency (EPA) is the key agency for environmental policy, with the stated mission to "protect human health and the environment." Created in 1970, the EPA is an independent regulatory agency with a single chief administrator that reports directly to the president and Congress. The EPA administers several programs largely drawn from legislation developed in the environmentalism era, including the Clean Air Act (CAA), the Clean Water Act (CWA), the Safe Water Drinking Act (SDWA), the Comprehensive Environmental Restoration, Compensation, and Liability Act (CERCLA), the Resource Conservation and Recovery Act (RCRA), the Federal Insecticide, Fungicide, and Rodenticide Act (FIFRA), and the Toxic Substances Control Act (TSCA). As of fiscal year 2017, the EPA has a budget of just over $8 billion and employs around 14,000 workers.

In July 1970, following the recommendation of the President's Advisory Council on Executive Organization, or the Ash Council, Richard Nixon communicated to Congress his desire to establish an independent regulatory agency to oversee and enforce environmental policy. This occurred following the passage of the National Environmental Protection Act (NEPA) and amid growing concern over environmental problems. President Nixon viewed the mission of the agency as being:

- The establishment and enforcement of environmental protection standards consistent with national environmental goals
- The conduct of research on the adverse effects of pollution and on methods and equipment for controlling it; the gathering of information on pollution; and the use of this information in strengthening environmental protection programs and recommending policy changes
- Assisting others, through grants, technical assistance and other means, in arresting pollution of the environment
- Assisting the Council on Environmental Quality in developing and recommending to the President new policies for the protection of the environment (US Environmental Protection Agency 1992)

Along with the statement, Nixon also submitted to Congress the Reorganization Plan No. 3. With the reorganization plan, Nixon sought to combine various activities of several different agencies into one agency (Nixon 1970).

The EPA officially began on December 2, 1970. As with other executive branch agencies, the EPA has a bureaucratic organizational structure. At the top is the Office of the Administrator, which is led by a political appointee. William Ruckelshaus was sworn in as the first EPA administrator on December 4, 1970. In a 1993 interview, Ruckelshaus stated that it was important to show early on that the EPA was responsive to public concerns and capable of addressing environmental issues:

In the first place, given the public concern about the environment that led to the creation of EPA, it seemed to me important to demonstrate to the public that the government was capable of being responsive to their expressed concerns; namely, that we would do something about the environment. Therefore, it was important for us to advocate strong environmental compliance, back it up, and do it; to actually show we were willing to take on the large institutions in the society which hadn't been paying much attention to the environment.

US Environmental Protection Agency 1993

Ruckelshaus was also tasked with creating an organizational structure for the new agency. The initial Ash Council recommendation called for organizing the EPA around functional categories such as monitoring, research, standard-setting, enforcement, and assistance, as opposed to being organized by media such as air, water, and land (Lewis et al. 2006). However, Ruckelshaus ended up creating a hybrid organization that included some elements organized by media and some by function (Marcus 1991).

Currently, the EPA is organized into offices based around the specific media in which it regulates, including an Office of Air and Radiation, Office of Chemical Safety and Pollution Prevention, Office of Land and Emergency Management, and the Office of Water. In addition, the EPA also has several functional offices that help support its mission, such as the Office of Administration and Resources Management, Office of the Chief Financial Officer, Office of Enforcement and Compliance Assurance, Office of Environmental Information, Office of General Counsel, Office of the Inspector General, Office of International and Tribal Affairs, and the Office of Research and Development. Finally, the EPA has ten regional offices based in Boston, New York, Philadelphia, Atlanta, Chicago, Dallas, Kansas City, Denver, San Francisco, and Seattle, and the majority of EPA employees work in these various regional offices.

As a regulatory agency, the EPA focuses on setting national environmental standards and approving standards set by states, oversees the clean-up of contaminated sites, and enforces and monitors regulatory compliance (Powell 1999). The authority for the EPA to set environmental standards comes from statutory provision within legislation, and to set specific regulatory standards the EPA follows the rulemaking process described above. Figure 6.6 shows the number of economically significant rules – those that have an economic impact of $100 million or more – promulgated by the EPA from 1981 to 2016.

As shown in Figure 6.6, the number of economically significant rules generally increased from 1981 to a peak early in the Clinton administration, before generally declining. The decline of rulemaking by the EPA is likely a result of no major environmental legislation since the Clean Air Act Amendments of 1990 as well as a general moving away from command-and-control regulation and towards other approaches such as encouraging voluntary action, collaboration, negotiated rulemaking, and public-private partnerships (Eisner 2007).

The ability of the executive agencies such as the EPA to perform their duties is, in large part, a function of their capacity. Two ways in which an agency's capacity can be measured are its budget authority and its number of workers. Both the monitoring and enforcement activities of the EPA fell after Reagan's first budget (Wood 1988). Figure 6.7 illustrates the budget, in nominal and real inflation-adjusted terms, and the number of workers in the EPA from 1970 to 2016.

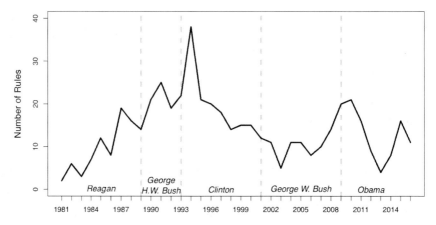

FIGURE 6.6 Economically significant EPA rules, 1981–2016

As Figure 6.7 shows, the inflation-adjusted budget of the EPA saw several fluctuations in the 1970s, as the budget increased in its first few years until the Ford presidency saw drastic cuts, followed by large increases in the late 1970s during the Carter presidency. However, since the early 1980s, the EPA budget has been relatively steady, ranging from ~8 to ~12 billion in 2016 dollars. In terms of workers, the EPA saw steady increases until the first few years of the Reagan administration, which saw a sharp drop-off. The number of workers began to increase again in the mid-1980s and that growth stabilized in the early 1990s before declining again beginning in 2011.

Due to the political control mechanisms discussed above, EPA capacity is largely a function of the electoral institutions. Agency budgets in particular are one way of reducing capacity to prevent bureaucratic drift. The executive branch budget process comes from the Budget and Accounting Act of 1921, where agencies submit their budget requests to the OMB, which then edits and aggregates those requests into the president's budget that is submitted to Congress. The congressional budget process, spelled out in the Congressional Budget and Impoundment Control Act of 1974, states that the budget committees in the House and Senate set an overall budget limit for each budget category and then the appropriation committees, and their 12 subcommittees, evaluate the president's budget request and submit appropriation bills within the limits set by the budget committees. The EPA budget in the House and Senate is produced by the Interior, Environment, and Related Agencies Subcommittee. However, much like the regular-order process with regard to legislation, the regular-order process for appropriation bills has broken down as well. Increasingly, budgets are made through large omnibus spending bills that combine all 12 appropriation bills into one must-pass package (Krutz 2001). As with legislation, this has tended to shift power toward majority party leaders.

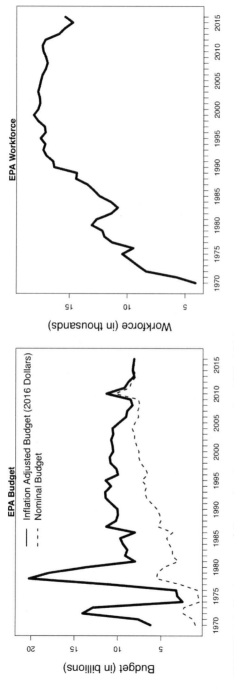

FIGURE 6.7 Environmental Protection Agency capacity, 1970–2016

Given the political nature of the budget process and the polarized nature of environmental policy, I expect EPA capacity to be a function of environmental policymaking system variables such as party control of Congress and the presidency. Specifically, I expect EPA capacity to be higher in terms of budget and workforce during times of unified Democratic governments than during divided or unified Republican control. To test this expectation, I use dummy variables for unified Democratic and Republican control and for a Republican president, which leaves divided government with a Democratic president as the referent group. In addition, the other system variables I expect to influence EPA capacity is congressional attention, measured as appropriation hearings about the environment lagged one year to account for the budget cycle. I also expect EPA capacity to be a function of information signals, so I use the number of *New York Times* articles about the environment to control for information in the problem and policy stream, and I include the public's environmental mood to account for politics stream information. Finally, I control for the previous year's budget and workforce numbers.[8] The results are shown in Table 6.2.

TABLE 6.2 Estimates of EPA Capacity, 1970–2016

	Dependent variable	
	Budget	*Workers*
Unified Democratic control	2,988.194**	375.583
	(1,243.467)	(291.324)
Unified Republican control	1,682.892	126.736
	(1,095.704)	(262.429)
Republican president	−2,075.092	−441.065
	(1,319.270)	(329.237)
Appropriation hearings$_{t-1}$	−22.407	6.143
	(108.951)	(25.301)
New York Times articles$_{t-1}$	91.833	11.617
	(101.204)	(24.218)
Environmental mood of the public$_{t-1}$	243.522**	100.444***
	(90.095)	(22.282)
Budget$_{t-1}$	0.448***	
	(0.131)	
Workers$_{t-1}$		0.846***
		(0.034)
Constant	−13,800.760*	−5,164.256***
	(7,359.716)	(1,632.852)
Observations	44	44
Adjusted R^2	0.417	0.967

Note: *p<0.10; **p<0.05; ***p<0.01

As can be seen in Table 6.2, the capacity of the EPA is a function of unified Democratic control of electoral institutions, public support, and past developments. The budget is in billions, therefore unified Democratic control provides an estimated increase in the budget of $3.05 billion, and an increase of nearly 500 workers, on average. The periods of unified Democratic control include 1977–1980, 1993–1994, and 2009–2010 and, as Figure 6.7 indicates, these periods show increases in the EPA budget.

The environmental mood of the public was also a significant predictor. As public support for the environment increases by 1 on the 0–100 scale, the EPA budget increases by about $250,000 and the number of workers increase by about 110, on average. This illustrates some responsiveness to changes in the politics information stream.

Given the congressional gridlock surrounding environmental issues, policy actors have sought other pathways to achieve policy goals. Some have argued that the use of the executive branch pathways is the result of overreach by active presidents, whereas others argue that, as the electoral institutions became unable to address some issues, action moves to the executive branch out of necessity. The latter view was argued by Meier (1997) who stated that:

> The fundamental problem of governance that has generated the continual state of crisis in political/bureaucratic relationships is that the electoral branches of government have failed as deliberative institutions; they have not resolved conflict in a reasoned manner (196).

The above sentiment is reflected in the statement by President Obama that opened this chapter, as he likely saw the inability of Congress to enact meaningful legislation to address climate change as a failure to resolve conflict in a reasoned manner. In addition, the nature of the environmental policymaking system allows policymaking to be shifted from one pathway to another, particularly by a policy actor with agenda-setting power, like a president. Early in the Obama administration, the EPA began to develop regulations to limit the amount of greenhouse gases that energy producers could emit through the authority granted in the Clean Air Act and the Supreme Court case, *Massachusetts v. the EPA*. The next section discussions the approaches taken by the EPA to address climate change.

The Environmental Protection Agency and Climate Change

Environmental policymaking occurs across several institutional pathways, often simultaneously. Even as the American Clean Energy and Security Act was being considered in Congress, the Obama administration was using the pathways of executive orders and rulemaking to address climate change. The EPA was at the center of rulemaking actions regarding climate change.

During the administration of George W. Bush, it was decided that the EPA did not have the authority to regulate greenhouse gases. As will be discussed below, this finding was challenged in court and it was ultimately decided by the Supreme Court in 2007 that the EPA must regulate greenhouse gases under the Clean Air Act if the EPA determines they pose a risk to human health and safety. In December of 2009 the EPA issued the *endangerment finding* that found that greenhouse gases "endanger both the public health and the public welfare of current and future generations" (US Environmental Protection Agency 2009). The endangerment finding formed the basis of subsequent EPA actions regarding climate change. As noted by Sunstein (2018), when the endangerment finding was finalized, it "was a pivotal moment, in which the United States formally and officially recognized the existence of climate change, and the adverse effects – for the United States and the world – that it was creating and would continue to create" (256).

The endangerment finding was grounded in the science behind the impacts of greenhouse gases, and together with the Clean Air Act and the *Massachusetts v. EPA* decision of the Supreme Court, it provides the legal foundation for the EPA and other agencies to begin to regulate the production of greenhouse gases. One of the limitations of using the CAA to regulate GHG is that it limits the choice of policy instruments available largely to command-and-control type regulations. A command-and-control style regulatory approach to climate change would set either a technology standard or a performance standard on sectors of the economy that produce greenhouse gases.

Figure 6.8 shows the number of rules, notices, and proposed rules undertaken by EPA regarding greenhouse gases from 1994 to 2017.[9]

As shown in Figure 6.8, there was a large spike in EPA activity from 2009 to 2010 in the first years of the Obama administration, which subsequently begin to

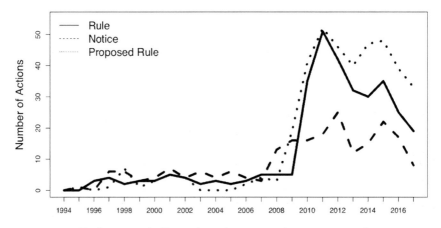

FIGURE 6.8 Environmental Protection Agency actions on greenhouse gases, 1994–2017

decrease. The notices during the Obama administration included such things as the recognition of waivers granted to states, the notification of response to petitions, and the release of draft reports and data. Some of the more important rules and proposed rules include the endangerment finding, as well as several command-and-control regulations including vehicle emission standards, the tailoring rule, and the Clean Power Plan.

With the endangerment finding in place, the EPA was required under the Clean Air Act to develop regulatory standards for greenhouse gas emissions and it began with mobile sources. The EPA worked with the Department of Transportation (DOT) and the state of California in the crafting of GHG emissions standards and fuel economy standards. California is an important stakeholder in mobile emissions standards because the state first developed standards in the mid-1960s and has since produced vehicle emissions standards more stringent than those of the federal government.

The final mobile emissions rule was issued in May 2010 and mandated that light-duty vehicles meet an "estimated combined average emissions level of 250 grams of carbon dioxide (CO_2) per mile in model year 2016, equivalent to 35.5 miles per gallon (mpg) if the automotive industry were to meet this CO_2 level all through fuel economy improvements" (US Environmental Protection Agency 2010, 1). The light-duty vehicle rule was structured to go into effect in two phases, with Phase I covering model years 2012–2016. Phase II was published in October 2012 and called for an average fuel economy level of 54.5 miles per gallon. In addition to standards on light-duty vehicles, the EPA and DOT also issued rules for medium and heavy-duty vehicles that sought to reduce GHG emissions and improve fuel economy.

The Trump administration issued a Notice of Proposed Rulemaking in August 2018 that would reduce the miles-per-gallon requirement from 54.5 to about 37 miles-per-gallon (Davenport 2018). In addition, the proposed rule would end the carve-out in the Clean Air Act of 1970 that allows California to seek a waiver to issue more stringent fuel efficiency standards then the federal government. While it was discussed during the W. Bush administration, no administration has denied California a waiver. As noted in Chapter 3, emissions from transportation are now the leading GHG emissions source in the United States, making the reduction of vehicle emissions increasingly important.

Also in May of 2010, the EPA finalized *the Tailoring Rule* which was meant to tailor the number of greenhouse gas emission sources that were subject to a permit requirement. Stationary sources that are in attainment areas, as defined by the Clean Air Act, may be required to receive a permit under the CAA provision of "Prevention of Significant Deterioration" (PSD). A permit under PSD is required of "major" emitters, which is defined as a source that produces 250 tons or more of "any air pollutant." In addition, Title V of the CAA requires an operating permit for major emitters as well as a demonstration that they are using the "best available control technology" (BACT) to limit emissions. When determining how to regulate GHG, the EPA was concerned that, since GHGs are emitted in larger quantities than other air pollutants, the permitting requirement of 250 tons would mean that up to 6.2 million sources would require an emissions permit (Sunstein 2018). To avoid the large administrative burden of permitting so many facilities, the EPA determined that sources which emit at least 100,000 tons of CO_2 per year would be subject to the permitting requirement. In addition, the Tailoring Rule stated that sources already subject to regulation under the CAA, so-called "anyway" sources, may also be regulated for GHGs. However, the Tailoring Rule was struck down by the Supreme Court in the *Utility Air Regulatory Group v. Environmental Protection Agency* (2014) case.

In October 2015 the EPA issued two rules, based on command-and-control principles, that developed standards of performance to reduce GHG from new and modified stationary sources as well as existing stationary sources. The existing stationary sources rule is better known as the *Clean Power Plan* (CPP). Both rules were issued under the authority of the Clean Air Act (CAA) Section 111, the *Massachusetts v. EPA* Supreme Court decision, and the EPA's endangerment finding of 2009.

The EPA issued regulations regarding the emissions of greenhouse gases for new or modified sources with a rule titled *Standards of Performance for Greenhouse Gas Emissions from New, Modified, and Reconstructed Stationary Sources: Electric Utility Generating Units* (US Environmental Protection Agency 2015b). Section 111(b) of the CAA states that the EPA should establish New Source Performance Standards (NSPS) for any new or modified emissions source. The rule determines the amount of GHG that a new or modified source can emit using "best system of emission reduction" (BSER) as specified in CAA Section 111(a). Under the rule a modified source is defined as a change that increases GHG emissions by 10 percent or more of existing emissions. The rule was challenged in court, although it remains in effect. Despite some controversy, the rule is not expected to have a large economic impact because the decreasing prices of natural gas and renewables have led to a displacement of coal, so it is not likely that new coal plants will be built.

Once the NSPS rule was in effect for GHG emissions, it triggered a requirement that existing sources be regulated as well. Under Section 111(d) of the CAA, the EPA is required to issue regulations providing guidance for states to submit plans for "standards of performance" for pollutants from stationary sources that are not currently covered under the CAA and where NSPS apply (McCarthy et al. 2017). Existing sources were to be regulated under the Clean Power Plan (CPP).

The CPP was a rule titled *Carbon Pollution Emission Guidelines for Existing Stationary Sources: Electric Utility Generating Units*, issued by the EPA in October 2015, that required existing power plants to reduce their emissions of greenhouse gases (US Environmental Protection Agency 2015a). The expected impact, but not a required outcome, of the CPP was to reduce GHG emissions by 32 percent from 2005 levels by 2030. In essence, the CPP is a performance standard for states that sets limits on the amount of GHGs that can be emitted, but allows flexibility in terms of how states reach their established goal. Overall, the CPP set emission limits for 47 states,[10] and required those states to develop their own plan to reduce emissions. If a state doesn't submit its own plan, the EPA would step in with either a statewide cap-and-trade program or a rate-based standard. A rate-based standard is based on emissions produced per unit of some output (e.g., kWh of electricity), and firms can trade emissions if they are above or below the standard (US Environmental Protection Agency 2003).

To determine the performance standard for each state, the EPA developed a formula based on the number of fossil fuel (coal, oil, natural gas) plants in each of the three major electric grids. The three major grids include the Eastern Interconnection, the Texas Interconnection, and the Western Interconnection. Then, the EPA determined the "best system of emissions reductions" (BSER) for reducing GHG emissions at a "reasonable cost" (Plumer 2015). Next, the EPA developed three building blocks that states can use to reduce GHG emissions. The first block is to run coal plants more efficiently so that they produce less CO_2 emissions, the second is to replace coal plants with natural gas, and the third is to increase the use of renewable energy. Then, the EPA determined the expected emission reductions by applying the building blocks to each major grid. Finally, the EPA applied the expected reductions calculations to each state based on their mix of power sources to determine a rate-based and mass-based performance standard for each state.

While the EPA determined the standard for each state using the building blocks, the CPP did not require states to use the blocks to meet their own standard. In addition, states could decide if they wanted to meet the rate-based or mass-based standards. In developing their plans, states could reach the standard through a number of ways, including increased efficiency, increasing their use of natural gas, nuclear, and/or renewable energy, developing their own cap-and-trade program or joining a regional program, and a carbon tax, among others. However, it is not clear if the courts will allow the EPA to set BSER standards for states in the way that it has historically set standards for individual power plants. EPA standards are typically set *within-the-fence-line* of facilities, and courts will likely decide if the EPA can set *beyond-the-fence-line* standards for a state.

Several states and industry groups sued to block implementation of the CPP, and in an unprecedented step the Supreme Court issued a stay on CPP implementation in February 2016, prior to any determination by a lower court. EO 13783 issued by President Trump in March 2017 called on the EPA to revise the CPP to keep it in-line with the deregulatory agenda of the Trump administration. Then, in October 2017, the EPA signaled its intention to end the CPP and asked the courts to stop review of the plan while it developed a replacement.

The Trump administration CPP replacement plan, termed the Affordable Clean Energy (ACE) Rule, was released in August of 2018. The plan seems to accept the requirements of the *Massachusetts* decisions and the Endangerment Finding that the EPA must regulate greenhouse gases, however it rejects the CPP assumption that the EPA can set performance standards beyond-the-fence-line for states as opposed to power plants. The ACE plan states that the best system for emissions reductions (BSER) for GHG is making plants run more efficiently through heat-rate improvements. The heat-rate is the amount of energy used to produce one kilowatt-hour (kWh) of electricity, and such increased efficiency may reduce GHG emissions since power plants would use less energy in producing electricity. However, such efficiency improvements could also create a rebound effect, where plants are used more, thus increasing emissions overall in some states (Keyes et al. 2018). In addition, the ACE rule would allow states to alter New Source Review requirements such that increases in hourly emissions would trigger a review, as opposed to the current standard of a review following any change that may increase a plant's overall emissions.

The Courts

The Supreme Court was established in Article III of the Constitution, while the remainder of the court system was left to Congress to construct. The federal court system was set up by Congress with the Judiciary Act of 1789. The court system in the United States is a dual system, where cases begin in either the state court system or the federal court system. Both the state and federal court systems have multiple tiers, with lower courts, then appellate courts, and finally the state supreme court and the US Supreme Court. Prior to the 1970s, environmental issues were largely considered a state and local concern, therefore most disputes were settled within the state court system. Additionally, prior to the environmentalism era, state environmental cases were often nuisance claims and environmental law was built through common law, where law is developed by decisions made on a case-by-case basis. However, since the beginning of the environmentalism era, environmental cases are often heard in federal courts because they are disputes over actions of the federal government. Courts have been a major policymaking venue for environmentalists seeking to compel actions on the part of governments and business, as well as a venue for business interests to delay policy implementation.

The major source of impact of the courts on environmental policymaking is through judicial review. Judicial review, established in *Marbury v. Madison* (1803), is the authority possessed by the courts to determine the constitutionality of laws and the actions of the legislative and executive branches as well as state and local governments. With the power of judicial review, the courts can significantly impact the development of environmental policy. Indeed, court decisions, particularly appellate courts, create precedents that lower courts are obligated to follow. Court decisions are a form of public policy, making the courts an additional policymaking pathway.

Like the other policymaking institutions, the courts process information relevant for decision-making. Sources of information for judges include the facts of the case they are considering, previous legal decisions, and *amicus curiae* briefs filed by other policy actors. Amicus briefs are directed at appellate courts, including the Supreme Court, and contain arguments that advocates want the justices to consider. As with other information, amicus briefs are signals to decision-makers and the impact of those signals depends on the ability of that information to gain the attention of judges. Box-Steffensmeier, Christenson, and Hitt (2013) find that briefs filed by more connected and collaborative interest groups tend to be more impactful than briefs filed by groups that aren't as well connected. Additionally, as with other policy actors, a judge's ideological beliefs may factor into how they consider evidence and rule on cases (Segal and Cover 1989). The influence of ideology may be particularly true for the Supreme Court because they are less bound by previous decisions (Segal and Spaeth 2002).

The courts provide both opportunities and constraints for policy actors seeking to change policy. Courts are constrained by the nature of the cases they hear as well as by the fact that courts are used to settle disputes between two sides with each side seeking specific remedies (McGuire 2008). However, policy actors often seek judicial remedy as part of a venue-shopping strategy. Courts can shape environmental policy in a number of ways, but the ability to determine standing and the standard of review that the court applies are the most consequential.

Standing involves the requirement that a litigant can show that they have been harmed by the actions (or inactions) of another party. According to Duane (2013),

> The three basic elements of standing today are (1) injury-in-fact (i.e., the party suing must be able to demonstrate injury from the other party's actions), (2) causation (i.e., the party must show that the other party caused the injury, and (3) redressability (i.e., the party must show that the party's injury will be redressed by the court's action in the case (270–271).

Therefore, to achieve standing, a party must demonstrate that they have been harmed as a result of the actions of the other party, and that the court can offer some remedy regarding that harm. Standing has to be established before a case can proceed. Absent the establishment of standing to sue, courts can dismiss cases regardless of their merit. The power to determine standing offers the court a clear mechanism through which to control the judicial agenda.

Two factors from the environmentalism era regarding standing help to make the courts a critical pathway of environmental policymaking (Klyza and Sousa 2013). First, the *Scenic Hudson Preservation Conference v. Federal Power Commission* (1965) case found that a conservation group had standing to sue after the Federal Power Commission approved the construction of a power plant on the scenic Storm King Mountain on the Hudson River. The court found that the group had standing based on injury-in-fact resulting from aesthetic harm. A second factor was that Congress included provisions for citizens to bring suit against agencies and individuals in many of the laws of the environmentalism era (Benzoni 2008).

Another way that courts shape environmental policy is the standard of review that they apply. As a result of *Marbury v. Madison*, all actions of federal and state governments are subject to review by the courts to determine their constitutionality. Courts examine legislation, executive orders, and agency rules. A key part of environmental policymaking involves court review of agency rulemaking. Courts can examine agency actions in terms of how the agency interprets the law, how information is gathered, and how the agency uses its discretion when interpreting the law and applying the information it has gathered (O'Leary 2019).

Historically, courts have given some deference to agencies in how agencies interpret the law. The 1984 case *Chevron U.S.A., Inc. v. Natural Resources Defense Council, Inc.* established the *Chevron doctrine*, where the court codified its practice of deferring to an agency's interpretation of the law. At issue in the *Chevron* case was the EPA's "bubble policy" for stationary sources of air pollution. The bubble policy was an interpretation of the Clean Air Act Amendments of 1977 that allowed a plant with multiple facilities to increase emissions in one facility if those increases were offset by decreases in another facility at the same plant, such that there is no net increase in emissions. The court found that the EPA's bubble policy was a reasonable interpretation of the CAA amendment. Additionally, the court established the Chevron two-step test regarding agency actions. The first step is determining whether or not Congress clearly expressed its intent and, if not, the second step is determining whether or not the agency's reading of the law is permissible or reasonable.

Climate Change in the Courts

Much like the other macro-institutions, the issue of climate change has increasingly reached the agenda of the courts. In general, the growing number of climate change-related cases reflects one of three litigation approaches: a) compel agencies such as the EPA to regulate greenhouse gases using existing regulatory frameworks; b) compel agencies to consider climate impacts in permitting and other decisions; and c) hold emitters liable for climate damages under common law (Engel 2010).

Overall, few Supreme Court cases have dealt specifically with climate change. The most notable climate change case, *Massachusetts v. Environmental Protection Agency* (2007), examined whether or not the EPA can regulate CO_2 and three other greenhouse gases as pollutants under the Clean Air Act. The case arose as a result of two determinations made by the EPA in 2003, after several states, cities, and environmental groups filed a petition to compel EPA to regulate vehicular emissions of greenhouse gases under the Clean Air Act. First, the EPA stated that it did not have the statutory authority to regulate greenhouse gases under the CAA and second, even if such authority was established, the EPA was not willing to set emissions standards for vehicles to address climate change. As a result of that determination, several petitioners sued the EPA, arguing that the CAA broad definition of an air pollutant includes CO_2 and other greenhouse gases. The respondents, including the EPA, several other states, and transportation trade associations, argued that those suing did not have standing to bring a suit.

The first question in the *Massachusetts* case was whether the parties bringing the suit had standing. As noted, standing must be established for a case to proceed and be considered on its merits. Ultimately, the Supreme Court determined that the state of Massachusetts had standing because as a coastal state it had been and will continue to be impacted by sea-level rise caused by climate change, and that risk could be lessened if the suit was successful. Once at least one party was regarded as having standing, the court proceeded to the second question.

The second question was whether carbon dioxide is a pollutant as defined by the Clean Air Act. Section 202(a)(1) of the CAA states that regarding vehicle emissions,

> The Administrator shall by regulation prescribe (and from time to time revise) in accordance with the provisions of this section, standards applicable to the emission of any air pollutant from any class or classes of new motor vehicles or new motor vehicle engines, which in his judgment cause, or contribute to, air pollution which may reasonably be anticipated to endanger public health or welfare.[11]

The court found that CO_2 and the three other greenhouse gases did meet the definition of an air pollutant within the Clean Air Act, and that the EPA must determine whether or not GHGs "endanger public health or welfare." Apart from providing a legal basis for the regulation of GHGs, the *Massachusetts* decision was noteworthy because the court found that an agency's lack of rulemaking was subject to judicial review. In addition, the decision seemed to go against Chevron deference, with the court finding that the EPA's determination that GHGs do not constitute an air pollutant was unreasonable. The scientific evidence makes it clear that the build-up of GHGs in the atmosphere constitutes a danger to public health and welfare, therefore, as noted by Sunstein (2018), "the Court's unusually aggressive decision could be seen as this instruction to the EPA: *Use your knowledge*" (243–244, italics in the original). The decision was 5–4, with Justice Anthony Kennedy providing the crucial swing vote.

In *American Electric Power Company v. Connecticut* (2011) the court reaffirmed the EPA's ability to regulate greenhouse gases under the Clean Air Act. Specifically, the case considered whether or not states could bring common law public nuisance claims against GHG emitters. The court, in an 8–0 decision,[12] found that the federal provisions of the CAA and the EPA's authority to regulate GHGs under the CAA displaces common-law claims regarding GHG emissions.

Both the *Massachusetts* and *American Electric Power Company* cases affirmed the requirement of the EPA to regulate greenhouse gases as an air pollutant under the Clean Air Act. However, a third case, *Utility Air Regulatory Group v. Environmental Protection Agency* (2014), provided some limits on how the EPA can regulate GHG emissions. Specifically, the case examined the EPA's Tailoring Rule, issued in 2010.

In an effort to define the types of stationary sources that the EPA would regulate, the Tailoring Rule called for a permit requirement for sources that emit at least 100,000 tons of CO_2 per year. The permit requirement of the Tailoring Rule would have mostly impacted smaller facilities that may not already be under permit requirement for other types of emissions regulated under the CAA. However, in a highly fractured 5–4 opinion, the Court found that the EPA did not have the authority to "tailor" the rule to facilities not currently regulated for other pollutants. The Tailoring Rule would have applied to roughly 86 percent of the facilities that emit CO_2; under the Court's decision the EPA is able to regulate 83 percent of such facilities.

The most recent major climate case of the Supreme Court involved the Clean Power Plan (CPP). The CPP was challenged in court by 27 states, industry, and labor groups on grounds ranging from: the appropriateness of regulating greenhouse gas emissions under Section 111(d) and Section 112 of CAA; that the CPP required states to shift away from coal; overreach on federalism grounds into determining the state mix of energy sources; and large differences in the proposed and final rules which violated the APA's public comment requirement. The petitioners asked for the CPP to be stayed as the issues were considered in court, but in January 2016 the DC Circuit Court of Appeals denied the stay. However, in February 2016 the Supreme Court in a 5–4 decision granted the stay as the Appeal Court considered the case. It is seemingly the first time the Court has stopped a regulatory action before a lower court had determined the merits of the rule (Heinzerling 2016).

Shortly after the stay of the Clean Power Plan, Justice Antonin Scalia unexpectedly passed away. Then, in an unprecedented move, the Senate refused to consider President Obama's nominee to the high court. Following the election of Trump, the Senate confirmed Justice Neil Gorsuch to the Supreme Court with 55–45 vote in April 2017. Gorsuch, as a conservative, is likely to share Justice Scalia's views on environmental issues broadly, although he appears to be skeptical about Chevron deference in a way that Scalia was not. As a judge on the 10th Circuit Court of Appeals, Justice Gorsuch wrote in an immigration case opinion that,

> Whatever the agency may be doing under Chevron, the problem remains that courts are not fulfilling their duty to interpret the law and declare invalid agency actions inconsistent with those interpretations in the cases and controversies that come before them.
>
> *Quoted in Solomon 2017*

Interestingly, *Chevron* deference arose from the bubbling policy of the EPA that was initiated when Gorsuch's mother, Anne Gorsuch, was EPA administrator. It is likely the Gorsuch's views on *Chevron* deference will play a role in some future climate cases before the court.

In June of 2018, Justice Anthony Kennedy announced his retirement from the Supreme Court. Justice Kennedy had been the swing vote on the *Massachusetts v. EPA* (2007), and with his retirement the EPA's ability to regulate greenhouse gases as a pollutant may be in jeopardy. Generally, the Court is respectful of previous decisions under the doctrine of *stare decisis*, or "let the decision stand." The Court's deference to previous decisions may mean that a narrowing of the EPA's ability to regulate GHG will be the more likely outcome, rather than a complete overturning of the *Massachusetts* decision.

Several climate cases will likely be heard by the Court in the future, including about the Clean Power Plan and/or the Trump administration's American Clean Energy replacement rule. An additional high-profile court case involves investigations by the attorneys-general of New York and Massachusetts into whether or not ExxonMobil committed fraud by not disclosing what it knew about climate change to investors and the public. A second set of cases involves several cities and counties in California, Colorado, and Washington, as well as New York City and the state of Rhode Island, who have all filed civil lawsuits against several fossil fuel companies. The lawsuits are seeking compensation for the mitigation and damage costs as a result of climate change, although two of the California cases and the New York City case were dismissed by federal judges, with both stating that climate change is an issue for the electoral institutions, not the courts. Finally, in *Juliana v. United States of America*, 21 children are suing the federal government for a failure to respond to climate change and thus threatening their futures. Both the Obama and Trump administrations have tried to have the case dismissed, but in July 2018 the Supreme Court refused to issue a stay in the case, meaning that the case can proceed in federal court.

Conclusion

The macro-institutions of the environmental policymaking system provide individualized pathways for environmental policy. However, due to the separation of powers, those pathways are shaped by the critical veto points of the other institutions. Partisan gridlock on environmental issues broadly, and climate change specifically, has made progress on addressing those issues difficult. As a result, there is not yet a comprehensive approach to address climate change on the part of the federal government. With Republican majorities in Congress and the election of Trump, the policy pathways of Congress and the executive branch have been closed. The Supreme Court in the *Massachusetts* decision had helped to open the rulemaking pathway for climate policy, although with recent changes in the Court the future pathways of federal climate policy are very much in doubt. However, the endangerment finding and the *Massachusetts* decision are (as of this writing) still in place, which leaves the rulemaking pathway open for a future administration interested in addressing climate change.

Notes

1 Quote obtained here: http://firstread.nbcnews.com//_news/2014/01/14/22302586-obama-on-exec-action-ive-got-a-pen-and-ive-got-a-phone and here: https://washington.cbslocal.com/2014/01/14/obama-on-executive-actions-ive-got-a-pen-and-ive-got-a-phone/

2 Data comes from a search of congress.gov using the following search terms "climate change" OR "global warming" OR "greenhouse gas" OR "greenhouse effect." The initial search was conducted in February 2017, and a second search was conducted in June 2018. There were discrepancies in the results with regard to the number of bills introduced and the number of bills that received committee consideration. The results from June 2018 are the ones that are shown.

3 The authors made their data available here: https://dataverse.harvard.edu/dataset.xhtml?persistentId=doi:10.7910/DVN/1ELYGA

4 From here: www.congress.gov/congressional-record/2008/6/2/senate-section/article/s4866-3?q=%7B%22search%22%3A%5B%22%5C%22America%27s+Climate+Security+Act+of+2007%5C%22%22%5D%7D&r=8

5 Indeed, Curry (2015) used the ACES process as a case study when discussing the role of party leadership in Congress in shaping the information available to rank-and-file members.

6 Data for the DW-NOMINATE scores are available at https://voteview.com/ and the membership of the CSC is available here: https://citizensclimatelobby.org/climate-solutions-caucus/

7 Obtained here: www.doi.gov/whoweare

8 EPA budget and workforce data comes from www.epa.gov/planandbudget/budget, and the number of *New York Times* articles, the number of congressional hearings, and the environmental mood data come from the *Comparative Agendas Project*.

9 Data comes from a search of using the search term "greenhouse gas" and agency, EPA.

10 Alaska, Hawaii, and Vermont were not included.

11 See here: www.epa.gov/clean-air-act-overview/clean-air-act-title-ii-emission-standards-moving-sources-parts-through-c

12 Justice Sotomayor recused because she had heard the case when she served in a lower court.

References

Baucum, Joseph. 2017. "After Pushing Bill to Abolish EPA, Rep. Matt Gaetz Joins Climate Solutions Caucus." *Pensacola News Journal*. www.pnj.com/story/money/business/2017/11/24/after-pushing-bill-abolish-epa-rep-matt-gaetz-joins-climate-solutions-caucus/893141001/.

Baumgartner, Frank R., Bryan D. Jones, and Michael C. MacLeod. 2000. "The Evolution of Legislative Jurisdictions." *The Journal of Politics* 62(2): 321–349.

Benzoni, Francisco. 2008. "Environmental Standing: Who Determines the Value of Other Life?" *Duke Environmental Law & Policy Forum* 18(Spring): 347–370.

Bertelli, Anthony M., and Christian R. Grose. 2011. "The Lengthened Shadow of Another Institution? Ideal Point Estimates for the Executive Branch and Congress." *American Journal of Political Science* 55(4): 767–781.

Beth, Richard S. 2001. *Disapproval of Regulations by Congress: Procedure Under the Congressional Review Act*. Congressional Research Service.

Bimber, Bruce. 1996. *The Politics of Expertise in Congress: The Rise and Fall of the Office of Technology Assessment.* Albany, NY: State University of New York Press.

Box-Steffensmeier, Janet M., Dino P. Christenson, and Matthew P. Hitt. 2013. "Quality over Quantity: Amici Influence and Judicial Decision Making." *American Political Science Review* 107(03): 446–460.

Broder, John M. 2010. "Tracing the Demise of Cap and Trade." *The New York Times.* www.nytimes.com/2010/03/26/science/earth/26climate.html.

Brulle, Robert J. 2014. "Institutionalizing Delay: Foundation Funding and the Creation of US Climate Change Counter-Movement Organizations." *Climatic Change* 122(4): 681–694.

———. 2018. "The Climate Lobby: A Sectoral Analysis of Lobbying Spending on Climate Change in the USA, 2000 to 2016." *Climatic Change*, forthcoming.

Carey, Maeve P. 2016. *Counting Regulations: An Overview of Rulemaking, Types of Federal Regulations, and Pages in the Federal Register.* Congressional Research Service.

Carter, Jimmy. 1978. "Memorandum from the President on the National Climate Program." *The American Presidency Project.* www.presidency.ucsb.edu/ws/?pid=30082.

Congressional Budget Office. 2008. *S. 2191: America's Climate Security Act of 2007.* www.cbo.gov/sites/default/files/110th-congress-2007–2008/costestimate/s21910.pdf.

———. 2009. *H.R. 2454: American Clean Energy and Security Act of 2009.* Congressional Budget Office. www.cbo.gov/sites/default/files/111th-congress-2009–2010/costestimate/hr24541.pdf.

Cox, Gary W., and Mathew D. McCubbins. 1993. *Legislative Leviathan: Party Government in the House.* Berkeley, CA: University of California Press.

———. 2005. *Setting the Agenda: Responsible Party Government in the US House of Representatives.* Cambridge: Cambridge University Press.

Curry, James M. 2015. *Legislating in the Dark: Information and Power in the House of Representatives.* Chicago, IL: University of Chicago Press.

Davenport, Coral. 2017. "In Win for Environmentalists, Senate Keeps an Obama-Era Climate Change Rule." *The New York Times.* www.nytimes.com/2017/05/10/us/politics/regulations-methane-climate-change.html.

———. 2018. "Trump Administration Unveils Its Plan to Relax Car Pollution Rules." *The New York Times.* www.nytimes.com/2018/08/02/climate/trump-auto-emissions-california.html.

Deering, Christopher J., and Steven S. Smith. 1997. *Committees in Congress.* 3rd ed. Washington, DC: CQ Press.

Duane, Timothy P. 2013. "Courts, Legal Analysis, and Environmental Policy." In *The Oxford Handbook of US Environmental Policy*, eds. Sheldon Kamieniecki and Michael E. Kraft. Oxford: Oxford University Press, 259–279.

Eisner, Marc Allen. 2007. *Governing the Environment: The Transformation of Environmental Regulation.* Boulder, CO: Lynne Rienner.

Engel, Kirsten H. 2010. "Courts and Climate Policy: Now and in the Future." In *Greenhouse Governance: Addressing Climate Change in America*, ed. Barry G. Rabe. Washington, DC: Brookings Institution Press, 229–259.

Executive Office of the President. 2013. *The President's Climate Action Plan.* The White House. https://obamawhitehouse.archives.gov/sites/default/files/image/president27sclimateactionplan.pdf.

Fiorina, Morris P. 1989. *Congress: Keystone of the Washington Establishment.* 2nd ed. New Haven: Yale University Press.

Glassman, Matthew E. 2017. *Congressional Member Organizations: Their Purpose and Activities, History, and Formation.* Congressional Research Service. https://fas.org/sgp/crs/misc/R40683.pdf.

Goodnow, Frank J. 1900. *Politics and Administration: A Study in Government.* New York, NY: Macmillan.

Greenstone, Michael, Elizabeth Kopits, and Ann Wolverton. 2013. "Developing a Social Cost of Carbon for US Regulatory Analysis: A Methodology and Interpretation." *Review of Environmental Economics and Policy* 7(1): 23–46.

Gupta, Kuhika. 2014. "A Comparative Policy Analysis of Coalition Strategies: Case Studies of Nuclear Energy and Forest Management in India." *Journal of Comparative Policy Analysis: Research and Practice* 16(4): 356–372.

Harvey, Chelsea. 2017. "Should the Social Cost of Carbon Be Higher?" *Scientific American.* www.scientificamerican.com/article/should-the-social-cost-of-carbon-be-higher/.

Heinzerling, Lisa. 2016. "The Supreme Court's Clean-Power Grab." *Georgetown Environmental Law Review* 28: 425–441.

Hope, Chris. 2006. "The Marginal Impact of CO2 from PAGE2002: An Integrated Assessment Model Incorporating the IPCC's Five Reasons for Concern." *Integrated Assessment* 6(1): 19–56.

Howell, William G. 2003. *Power Without Persuasion: The Politics of Direct Presidential Action.* Princeton, NJ: Princeton University Press.

Inglis, Bob, and Arthur B. Laffer. 2008. "Opinion: an Emissions Plan Conservatives Could Warm To." *The New York Times.* www.nytimes.com/2008/12/28/opinion/28inglis.html.

Kaufman, Alexander C. 2017. "Florida Congressman Drafts Bill to 'Completely Abolish' the EPA." *Huffington Post.* www.huffingtonpost.com/entry/bill-to-abolish-epa_us_5890e638e4b02772c4e9c552.

Kerwin, Cornelius M. 2003. *Rulemaking: How Government Agencies Write Law and Make Policy.* 3rd ed. Washington, DC: CQ Press.

Kettl, Donald F. 2008. "Public Bureaucracies." In *The Oxford Handbook of Political Institutions,* eds. R.A.W. Rhodes, Sarah A. Binder, and Bert A. Rockman. Oxford: Oxford University Press, 366–384.

Keyes, Amelia, Kathleen F. Lambert, Dallas Burtraw, Jonathan J. Buonocore, Jonathan I. Levy, and Charles T. Driscoll. 2018. *Carbon Standards Examined: A Comparison of At-the-Source and Beyond-the-Source Power Plant Carbon Standards.* www.rff.org/research/publications/carbon-standards-examined-comparison-source-and-beyond-source-power-plant (August 26, 2018).

Kim, Sung Eun, and Johannes Urpelainen. 2017. "The Polarization of American Environmental Policy: A Regression Discontinuity Analysis of Senate and House Votes, 1971–2013." *Review of Policy Research* 34(4): 456–484.

Kim, Sung Eun, Johannes Urpelainen, and Joonseok Yang. 2016. "Electric Utilities and American Climate Policy: Lobbying by Expected Winners and Losers." *Journal of Public Policy* 36(2): 251–275.

King, David C. 1997. *Turf Wars: How Congressional Committees Claim Jurisdiction.* Chicago, IL: University of Chicago Press.

Klyza, Christopher McGrory, and David Sousa. 2013. *American Environmental Policy: Beyond Gridlock.* Cambridge, MA: MIT Press.

Kraft, Michael E. 2019. "Environmental Policy in Congress." In *Environmental Policy: New Directions for the Twenty-First Century,* eds. Norman J. Vig and Michael E. Kraft. Thousand Oaks, CA: CQ Press, 117–143.

Krehbiel, Keith. 1998. *Pivotal Politics: A Theory of US Lawmaking*. Chicago, IL: University of Chicago Press.

Krutz, Glen S. 2001. *Hitching a Ride: Omnibus Legislating in the US Congress*. Columbus, OH: Ohio State University Press.

———. 2005. "Issues and Institutions: "Winnowing" in the US Congress." *American Journal of Political Science* 49(2): 313–326.

Krutz, Glen S., and Paul D. Jorgensen. 2008. "Winnowing in Environmental Policy: Jurisdictional Challenges and Opportunities." *Review of Policy Research* 25(3): 219–232.

Krutz, Glen S., and Jeffrey S. Peake. 2011. *Treaty Politics and the Rise of Executive Agreements: International Commitments in a System of Shared Powers*. Ann Arbor, MI: University of Michigan Press.

Larsen, John, Alexia Kelly, and Robert Heilmayr. 2009. *WRI Summary of H.R. 2454, the American Clean Energy and Security Act (Waxman-Markey)*. World Resources Institute.

Layzer, Judith A. 2012. *Open for Business: Conservatives' Opposition to Environmental Regulation*. Cambridge, MA: The MIT Press.

Lewallen, Jonathan. 2018. "Congressional Attention and Opportunity Structures: The Select Energy Independence and Global Warming Committee." *Review of Policy Research* 35(1): 153–169.

Lewallen, Jonathan, Sean M. Theriault, and Bryan D. Jones. 2016. "Congressional Dysfunction: An Information Processing Perspective." *Regulation & Governance* 10(2): 179–190.

Lewis, Eric, Dwayne Crawford, Bettye Bell-Daniel, Bram Hass, and Rae Donaldson. 2006. *Studies Addressing EPA's Organizational Structure*. US Environmental Protection Agency: Office of Inspector General.

Lipton, Eric, and Jasmine C. Lee. 2017. "Which Obama-Era Rules Are Being Reversed in the Trump Era." *The New York Times*. www.nytimes.com/interactive/2017/05/01/us/politics/trump-obama-regulations-reversed.html,\%0020https://www.nytimes.com/interactive/2017/05/01/us/politics/trump-obama-regulations-reversed.html.

Mann, Thomas E., and Norman J. Ornstein. 2008. *The Broken Branch: How Congress Is Failing America and How to Get It Back on Track*. Oxford: Oxford University Press.

———. 2016. *It's Even Worse Than It Looks: How the American Constitutional System Collided with the New Politics of Extremism*. New York: Basic Books.

Marcus, Alfred A. 1991. "EPA's Organizational Structure." *Law and Contemporary Problems* 54(4): 5.

Mayhew, David R. 2004. *Congress: The Electoral Connection*. 2nd ed. New Haven, CT: Yale University Press.

McCarthy, James E., Jonathan L. Rameseur, Jane A. Leggett, Linda Tsang, and Kate C. Shouse. 2017. *EPA's Clean Power Plan for Existing Power Plants: Frequently Asked Questions*. Congressional Research Service.

McCright, Aaron M., and Riley E. Dunlap. 2003. "Defeating Kyoto: The Conservative Movement's Impact on US Climate Change Policy." *Social Problems* 50(3): 348–373.

McGuire, Kevin T. 2008. "The Judicial Process and Public Policy." In *The Oxford Handbook of Political Institutions*, eds. R.A.W. Rhodes, Sarah A. Binder, and Bert A. Rockman. Oxford: Oxford University Press, 535–554.

Meier, Kenneth J. "Bureaucracy and Democracy: The Case for More Bureaucracy and Less Democracy." *Public Administration Review* 57(3): 193–199.

Moe, Terry M. 1984. "The New Economics of Organization." *American Journal of Political Science* 28(4): 739–777.

Nixon, Richard. 1970. "Reorganization Plan No. 3." US Environmental Protection Agency. https://archive.epa.gov/epa/aboutepa/reorganization-plan-no-3-1970.html.

Nordhaus, William D. 2017. "Revisiting the Social Cost of Carbon." *Proceedings of the National Academy of Sciences* 114(7): 1518–1523.

Obama, Barack. 2015. "Remarks by the President in State of the Union Address." whitehouse.gov. https://obamawhitehouse.archives.gov/the-press-office/2015/01/20/remarks-president-state-union-address-january-20–2015.

O'Leary, Rosemary. 2019. "Environmental Policy in the Courts." In *Environmental Policy: New Directions for the Twenty-First Century*, eds. Norman J. Vig and Michael E. Kraft. Thousand Oaks, CA: CQ Press, 144–167.

Peake, Jeffrey S., Glen S. Krutz, and Tyler Hughes. 2012. "President Obama, the Senate, and the Polarized Politics of Treaty Making." *Social Science Quarterly* 93(5): 1295–1315.

Pew Center on Global Climate Change. 2009. *At a Glance: American Clean Energy and Security Act of 2009*. Pew Center on Global Climate Change.

Pizer, William A., and Raymond J. Kopp. 2003. *Summary and Analysis of McCain-Lieberman "Climate Stewardship Act of 2003" S.139, Introduced 01/09/03*. Resources for the Future.

Plumer, Brad. 2015. "How Obama's Clean Power Plan Actually Works – a Step-by-Step Guide." Vox. https://www.vox.com/2015/8/4/9096903/clean-power-plan-explained.

Poole, Keith T. 2005. *Spatial Models of Parliamentary Voting*. Cambridge: Cambridge University Press.

Poole, Keith T., and Howard L. Rosenthal. 2007. *Ideology and Congress*. 2nd ed. New Brunswick, NJ: Transaction Publishers.

Pooley, Eric. 2008. "Why the Climate Bill Failed." *Time*. http://content.time.com/time/nation/article/0,8599,1812836,00.html.

———. 2010. *The Climate War: True Believers, Power Brokers, and the Fight to Save the Earth*. New York, NY: Hachette Books.

Powell, Mark R. 1999. *Science at EPA: Information in the Regulatory Process*. Washington, DC: Resources for the Future.

Rabe, Barry G. 2010. "Can Congress Govern the Climate?" In *Greenhouse Governance: Addressing Climate Change in America*, ed. Barry G. Rabe. Washington, DC: Brookings Institution Press.

Ragusa, Jordan M., and Nathaniel A. Birkhead. 2015. "Parties, Preferences, and Congressional Organization Explaining Repeals in Congress from 1877 to 2012." *Political Research Quarterly* 68(4): 745–759.

Ragusa, Jordan M., and Anthony Gaspar. 2016. "Where's the Tea Party? An Examination of the Tea Party's Voting Behavior in the House of Representatives." *Political Research Quarterly* 69(2): 361–372.

Reagan, Ronald. 1981. "Executive Order 12291." National Archives. www.archives.gov/federal-register/codification/executive-order/12291.html.

Reilly, Amanda, and Kevin Bogardus. 2016. "7 Years Later, Failed Waxman-Markey Bill Still Makes Waves." *E & E News*. www.eenews.net/stories/1060039422.

Revkin, Andrew C. 2016. "As Rubio Waffles, Two Floridians in the House Seek Bipartisan Climate Solutions." Dot Earth Blog. https://dotearth.blogs.nytimes.com/2016/02/06/as-rubio-waffles-two-floridians-in-the-house-seek-bipartisan-climate-progress/.

Rinfret, Sara R. 2011. "Frames of Influence: US Environmental Rulemaking Case Studies." *Review of Policy Research* 28(3): 231–246.

Segal, Jeffrey A., and Albert D. Cover. 1989. "Ideological Values and the Votes of US Supreme Court Justices." *The American Political Science Review* 83(2): 557–565.

Segal, Jeffrey A., and Harold J. Spaeth. 2002. *The Supreme Court and the Attitudinal Model Revisited*. Cambridge: Cambridge University Press.

Sheingate, Adam D. 2006. "Structure and Opportunity: Committee Jurisdiction and Issue Attention in Congress." *American Journal of Political Science* 50(4): 844–859.

Shepsle, Kenneth A. 2008. "Rational Choice Institutionalism." In *The Oxford Handbook of Political Institutions*, eds. R.A.W. Rhodes, Sarah A. Binder, and Bert A. Rockman. Oxford: Oxford University Press, 23–38.

———. 2010. *Analyzing Politics: Rationality, Behavior and Institutions*. 2nd ed. New York, NY: W.W. Norton & Company.

Shipan, Charles R., and William R. Lowry. 2001. "Environmental Policy and Party Divergence in Congress." *Political Research Quarterly* 54(2): 245–263.

Skibell, Arianna. 2017. "Caucus Boosters Defend Its Embrace of EPA Foe." *E & E News*. www.eenews.net/stories/1060067393.

Solomon, Steven Davidoff. 2017. "Should Agencies Decide Law? Doctrine May Be Tested at Gorsuch Hearing." *The New York Times*. www.nytimes.com/2017/03/14/business/dealbook/neil-gorsuch-chevron-deference.html.

Sousa, David J., and Christopher McGrory Klyza. 2017. "'Whither We Are Tending': Interrogating the Retrenchment Narrative in US Environmental Policy." *Political Science Quarterly* 132(3): 467–494.

Stewart, Charles. 2001. *Analyzing Congress*. New York, NY: W.W. Norton & Company.

Sunstein, Cass R. 2013. *Simpler: The Future of Government*. New York, NY: Simon & Schuster.

———. 2018. "Changing Climate Change, 2009–2016." *Harvard Environmental Law Review* 42: 231–285.

Talbert, Jeffery C., Bryan D. Jones, and Frank R. Baumgartner. 1995. "Nonlegislative Hearings and Policy Change in Congress." *American Journal of Political Science* 39(2): 383–405.

The Center for Responsive Politics. 2018. "Rep. Trey Gowdy – Campaign Finance Summary." OpenSecrets. www.opensecrets.org/members-of-congress/summary?cid=N00030880\&cycle=CAREER\&type=I.

Tsebelis, George. 2002. *Veto Players: How Political Institutions Work*. Princeton, NJ: Princeton University Press.

US Energy Information Administration. 2018. "West Virginia – State Energy Profile Overview – US Energy Information Administration (EIA)." www.eia.gov/state/?sid=WV.

US Environmental Protection Agency. 1992. "The Guardian: Origins of the EPA." https://archive.epa.gov/epa/aboutepa/guardian-origins-epa.html.

———. 1993. "William D. Ruckelshaus: Oral History Interview." william-d-ruckelshaus-oral-history-interview.html (July 4, 2018).

———. 2003. Tools of the Trade: A Guide to Designing and Operating a Cap and Trade Program for Pollution Control. www.epa.gov/sites/production/files/2016-03/documents/tools.pdf.

———. 2009. "Endangerment and Cause or Contribute Findings for Greenhouse Gases Under Section 202(a) of the Clean Air Act." *Federal Register* 74(239): 66496–66546.

———. 2010. "EPA and NHTSA Finalize Historic National Program to Reduce Greenhouse Gases and Improve Fuel Economy for Cars and Trucks." https://nepis.epa.gov/Exe/ZyPDF.cgi/P100AKHW.PDF?Dockey=P100AKHW.PDF.

———. 2015a. "Carbon Pollution Emission Guidelines for Existing Stationary Sources: Electric Utility Generating Units." *Federal Register* 80(205): 64662–64964.

———. 2015b. "Standards of Performance for Greenhouse Gas Emissions from New, Modified, and Reconstructed Stationary Sources: Electric Utility Generating Units." *Federal Register* 80(205): 64510–64660.

US Global Change Research Program. "Legal Mandate." GlobalChange.gov. www.globalchange.gov/about/legal-mandate.

Vandeweerdt, Clara, Bart Kerremans, and Avery Cohn. 2016. "Climate Voting in the US Congress: The Power of Public Concern." *Environmental Politics* 25(2): 268–288.

Vig, Norman J. 2019. "Presidential Powers and Environmental Policy." In *Environmental Policy: New Directions for the Twenty-First Century*, eds. Norman J. Vig and Michael E. Kraft. Thousand Oaks, CA: CQ Press, 88–116.

Waldhoff, Stephanie, David Anthoff, Steven Rose, and Richard S.J. Tol. 2014. "The Marginal Damage Costs of Different Greenhouse Gases: An Application of FUND." *Economics: The Open-Access, Open-Assessment E-Journal* 8(31).

Waterman, Richard W. 2009. "The Administrative Presidency, Unilateral Power, and the Unitary Executive Theory." *Presidential Studies Quarterly* 39(1): 5–9.

West, William F., and Connor Raso. 2013. "Who Shapes the Rulemaking Agenda? Implications for Bureaucratic Responsiveness and Bureaucratic Control." *Journal of Public Administration Research and Theory* 23(3): 495–519.

Wilson, Woodrow. 1887. "The Study of Administration." *Political Science Quarterly* 2(2): 197–222.

Wood, B. Dan. 1988. "Principals, Bureaucrats, and Responsiveness in Clean Air Enforcements." *The American Political Science Review* 82(1): 213–234.

———. 2010. "Agency Theory and the Bureaucracy." In *The Oxford Handbook of American Bureaucracy*, ed. Robert F. Durant. Oxford: Oxford University Press, 181–206.

Workman, Samuel. 2015. *The Dynamics of Bureaucracy in the US Government: How Congress and Federal Agencies Process Information and Solve Problems*. Cambridge: Cambridge University Press.

Workman, Samuel, Bryan D. Jones, and Ashley E. Jochim. 2009. "Information Processing and Policy Dynamics." *Policy Studies Journal* 37(1): 75–92.

7

THE NETWORKED SUBSYSTEMS, INSTITUTIONS, AND ACTORS OF THE CLIMATE CHANGE REGIME

Introduction

In July of 2016, 19 Democratic senators spoke on the Senate floor in support of a resolution warning of the "web of denial" spun by private interests to deny the existence of climate change and to impede any policy response from the federal government. The resolution discussed previous attempts by tobacco companies and lead producers to downplay the risks associated with their products, and accused the fossil-fuel industry of similar tactics. The actors listed as part of the web during the floor speeches included the US Chamber of Commerce, the Heartland Institute, ExxonMobil, Koch Industries, Peabody Energy, and the Competitive Enterprise Institute, among others. Senator Jeff Merkley (D–OR) was one of the first to speak and stated:

> Why, with all of this proof from the scientific community and with all of the proof and facts directly before our eyes, does such strong opposition remain to the effects of climate change? We know the answer. It is because a powerful, moneyed interest has spun a web of deceit, working for years and continuing to work to undermine mainstream, scientific research and deceive the American people about the dangers and causes of climate change.[1]

The Democratic Senators were attempting to shed light on the network of policy actors that constitutes the climate-change counter-movement, which denies the existence of climate change – or at least downplays the risks – and has been active in seeking to delay climate policy (Brulle 2014, 2018). This set of actors points to the important role that *policy networks* play in environmental policymaking. Policy networks refer to the linkages that exist within the environmental policymaking system that connect policymaking venues and policy actors. The networks include linked policy subsystems that constitute policy regimes, linked institutions that constitute subsystems, and linked policy actors that constitute coalitions.

The complex environmental policymaking process involves multiple information signals that come from the social, economic, and natural environment, from the environmental policymaking system that contains the macro-institutions and multiple policy subsystems, and from the system outputs or policies that can take one of multiple forms depending on the institutional pathway through which it developed. At the heart of the environmental policymaking system are multiple semi-autonomous subsystems of actors and institutions organized around particular policy issues that are often far removed from the macro-politics of the major policymaking institutions.

Policy subsystems are the staging areas for policy issues, as much of the processing of information flows occurs within policy subsystems. In essence, policy subsystems are networked institutional components that are connected by a shared jurisdiction over particular policy issues. The networked institutions of subsystems include subunits of the macro-policymaking institutions, such as congressional committees within Congress and bureaus or departments within executive agencies. These subunits shape subsystems and connect them to the larger macro-institutions. In addition, the institutions that structure policy subsystems provide multiple policy venues in which debate and decision-making can occur. Finally, environmental policy subsystems connected to the macro-institutions are also connected to state and local government environmental policymaking.

While policymaking is traditionally understood to occur within semi-autonomous subsystems of actors and institutions, more recent work has begun to move beyond subsystems given that some "wicked" or "super-wicked" policy issues, such as climate change, are boundary-spanning and display trans-subsystem dynamics (Jochim and May 2010; Jones and Jenkins-Smith 2009; May, Jochim, and Sapotichne 2011). Far from being completely autonomous, subsystem jurisdictions often overlap and/or are linked by policy issues (Zafonte and Sabatier 1998). Complex issues such as climate change cut across the traditional bounds of subsystems, with impacts that reach across several seemingly disparate policy domains, creating a *policy regime*. Policy regimes have been defined broadly as "the constellation of ideas, institutional arrangements, and interests that make up the governing arrangements for addressing particular problems" (May and Jochim 2013, 446).

Policy regimes are a part of the environmental policymaking system, and as such they are information-processing entities. Ideas are a key governing arraignment within policy regimes, and the development and spread of ideas depends on the information network that exists within a policy regime. The information network within a policy regime can determine the coherence of the regime as well as the potential for ideas to spread from the bottom up.

Acting within policy regimes and subsystems are strategic *policy actors* that are seeking to have their preferences for policy enacted. Policy actors include those that are *official*, meaning they act within government such as elected officials or bureaucrats, and *unofficial* actors that are acting outside of government such as interest groups, non-government scientists, and other experts. Strategic policy actors pursue multiple strategies to achieve their objectives, including venue-shopping across decision venues and coalition-building by networking with other actors that share policy preferences.

This chapter examines the climate change policy regime in the United States by examining the subsystems, multiple levels of government, actors, and infor-mation network of the regime. First, I discuss the nature of the linked subsystems and subsystem types in environmental policy, including the intergovernmental nature of environmental policy subsystems. Then, I examine important policy actors outside of government, including interest groups and scientists. Finally, using data from congressional hearings about climate change from 1975 to 2016, I examine the nature of the information network that exists within the climate policy regime.

The Climate Change Policy Regime

Climate change is one of the most pressing and complex issues facing governments around the world. As a result of this complexity, multiple interests and institutions are engaged on the issue, which creates a policy regime. The climate policy regime is a network of policy subsystems connected by a shared problem that integrates governing arrangements – ideas, interests, and institutions – that span multiple subsystems. Climate change involves the linkage of subsystems that address energy production, agriculture, and transportation, among others. The existence of policy regimes can provide constraints as well as opportunities to address complex problems.

The constraint imposed by policy regimes is a function of the necessity of a coordinated response by policymakers to address issues in an effective way (May, Sapotichne, and Workman 2006). It may be the case that responding to complex issues requires the development of a strong policy regime, where strong regimes are defined by cohesion and coordination across different subsystems that may each have its own issue focus, actors, and venues. Under this view, a policy regime with the capacity to address complex issues would foster legitimacy, policy coher-ence, and have a high level of durability (May and Jochim 2013). Examining the homeland security regime, May, Jochim, and Sapotichne (2011) found it to be "anemic," with no unifying definition of homeland security, varied involvement of interests, and a lack of clear institutional jurisdiction. A lack of a shared issue defin-ition, disjointed interest mobilization, and fuzzy jurisdictional boundaries serve to limit the legitimacy, coherence, and durability of a policy regime, thereby calling into question its ability to address wicked problems such as climate change.

Yet less coherent policy regimes – what Keohane and Victor (2011) termed a "regime complex" – and the polycentric nature of policymaking authority inherent in them, may provide opportunities for the development of multiple policy approaches across multiple subsystems and levels of government. Under this view, a lack of policy coherence can be a strength, not a weakness, because it allows for policy innovation across subsystems and levels of government. As discussed in Chapter 6, the pathways of climate policy within the macro-institutions are increasingly narrow, although several states and local governments in the United States have put in place policies to mitigate climate change (Karapin 2016, 2018). Polycentricity allows for multiple approaches to address complex problems at multiple levels of government without top-down coordination (Ostrom 2009).

The next section discusses policy subsystems in general, including their intergovernmental component. Then, I examine the subsystems in the climate change policy regime by examining the committees and topics involved in congressional hearings about climate change.

Policy Subsystems

Policy choices are typically made by constellations of actors and institutions that form around specific policy domains. This idea has been assumed by scholars at least as far back as 1939, when Griffith (1939) stated that:

> One cannot live in Washington long without being conscious that it has whirlpools or centers of activity focusing on particular problems... It is my opinion that ordinarily the relationship among these men – legislators, administrators, lobbyists, scholars – who are interested in a common problem is a much more real relationship then the relationships between congressmen generally or between administrators generally. In other words, he would understand the prevailing pattern of our present governmental behavior, instead of studying the formal institutions or even generalizations in the relationships between these institutions or organs, important though all these things are, may possibly obtain a better picture of the way things really happen if he would study these "whirlpools" of special social interests and problems.
>
> *182, as quoted in Anderson 2015, 74*

Since the introduction of the term "whirlpools," multiple other terms have been used to describe this type of arraignment, such as sub-governments, or policy communities (see McCool 1998), but likely the most prominent term is policy subsystem. *Policy subsystems* are defined as semi-autonomous decision arenas consisting of actors and institutions organized around specific policy domains that operate in parallel and exist outside the spotlight of macro-politics (Baumgartner, Jones, and Mortensen 2018; Redford 1969; Thurber 1996). Subsystems are semi-autonomous, meaning that they are often able to make policy choices independently, yet are also subject to external pressures from information signals and the macro-institutions. The actors involved include those from all branches and levels of government, as well as the private sector and interest groups. The institutions include the various policy venues where choices are made, such as congressional committees and executive agencies. As discussed in Chapter 5, policy issues can break out of their confined subsystem arraignments and reach the agenda of the major policymaking institutions, thereby making significant policy change more likely.

The ability of issues to rise to the policymaking agenda depends, in part, on the nature of the relationships within the subsystem and the feedback dynamics that those relationships can create. The nature of policy subsystems can be described as the degree to which the policy subsystem is open and competitive, as well as the relative stability or instability of the subsystem. Openness refers to the ability of policy actors not currently involved or engaged in the subsystem to become active within the subsystem. The environmental policy-making system in the United States has multiple policy venues with overlapping jurisdictions as well as a tradition of a strong civil society, which makes the system as a whole relatively open and accessible to an array of policy actors and stakeholders. However, actors with positions of authority within subsystems, such as congressional committee chairs or political appointees at the upper levels of executive agencies, may act as gatekeepers. Subsystem competitiveness refers to the level of agreement about how the issue is defined. A competitive subsystem is one in which there is disagreement about how an issue should be understood, whereas a less competitive subsystem involves a shared definition of the issue.

A closed and non-competitive subsystem has the features of an *iron triangle*, where the points of the triangle include the relevant congressional committee, bureaucratic agency, and private interest groups. Such subsystem arraignments have also been termed a policy monopoly (Baumgartner and Jones 1993) and a unitary subsystem (Weible 2008). Iron triangle type subsystems contain the *top-down* actors and institutions from the macro-level institutions, such as members of Congress and congressional committees, as well as bureaucratic actors from the various departments within executive agencies. Additionally, iron triangles include interest groups that typically represent private, profit-seeking interests. Stable iron triangle subsystems often exert significant enough negative feedback to limit influences from external actors and institutions. The civilian nuclear energy subsystem of the 1950s and 1960s is an example of an iron triangle, where the major actors involved included the congressional Joint Committee on Atomic Energy, the executive branch Atomic Energy Commission, and the private energy companies interested in developing nuclear technology to produce electricity (Baumgartner and Jones 1991; Nowlin 2016). Each of the actors defined nuclear energy in the same way, as a safe, effective, and reliable way to produce electricity for consumers. Policy decision-making in an iron triangle tends to be incremental, such as modest increases in farm subsidy amounts, with agreement among policy actors.

A subsystem that is open, with multiple actors and institutions involved, coupled with competition over how the issue should be defined, is termed an *issue network* (Heclo 1978). The actors in issue networks include the top-down iron triangle actors, but also include *bottom-up* actors such as public-good interest groups, non-profit agencies, intergovernmental actors, consultants, and academic experts. The air pollution subsystem is an example of an issue network type subsystem, as it includes EPA officials, multiple congressional committees, private sector actors, public interest groups, state agencies, scientists, and others (Anderson 2015).

Policy actors engaged in an open and competitive issue network subsystem tend to align themselves into advocacy coalitions of actors that share a definition of the issue as well as policy preferences. Additionally, policy actors often venue-shop to try and find an alternative policy venue open to their view of the issue, thereby possibly expanding the issue network and creating positive feedback. Figure 7.1 illustrates an iron triangle subsystem as well as a more open, issue network type of subsystem.

As noted, iron triangle type subsystem arraignments typically include only the relevant government agencies, congressional (sub-)committee(s), and private sector interest groups, whereas issue networks include not only those actors but also experts, intergovernmental actors, as well as others. Iron triangle and unitary type subsystems are likely to be less fragmented, share a common issue definition, and have fewer and more highly dense networks than issue network subsystems. Subsystems that are more open tend to have a higher number of actors, more policymaking venues, and sparse, or less dense networks.

Typically, subsystems are not *either* an iron triangle *or* an issue network, rather those subsystems types can be understood as two end-points of a continuum, with closed, uncompetitive iron triangles on one end and open, competitive

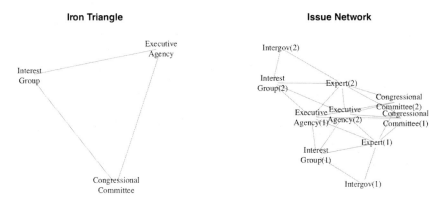

FIGURE 7.1 Policy subsystem types

issue networks on the other (Anderson 2015). Further, the nature of subsystem dynamics creates a process where subsystems are not static but rather dynamic, with a wavering equilibrium that varies from closer to an iron triangle type to closer to an issue network type as the issue evolves and policy develops (Worsham 1998).

Despite their dynamic nature, the foundation of all types of policy subsystems are the iron triangle actors. Indeed, these institutions, particularly congressional committees, structure policy subsystems and tether them to the larger policymaking system. Congressional committees anchor subsystems through the authority granted to them by Congress to consider legislation, collect information, and provide oversight of bureaucracies within the committee's jurisdiction.

The stability of an iron triangle subsystem depends on the ability of the actors and institutions involved to effectively process all relevant information pertaining to the subsystem, thereby allowing them to exert enough negative feedback to keep control of decision-making. If information signals begin to overwhelm the subsystem, perhaps as a result of changed indicators, a focusing event, or an election that shifts the players in the subsystem, then it becomes more likely that the issue will reach the agenda of macro-institutions and/or more policy venues become engaged allowing decision-making authority to shift or diffuse across multiple venues. Often actors that are dissatisfied with the status quo attempt to alter the dynamics of subsystems by attempting to expand conflict by involving actors and venues not currently involved in the issue to become engaged, thereby creating positive feedback by opening and making more competitive the subsystem in an attempt to disrupt decision-making on that issue. The relative openness and plurality of the policymaking in the United States allow strategic policy actors to attempt to expand the conflict beyond the boundaries of current subsystem arraignments and to attempt to engage other actors and policy venues.

Next, I examine the subsystems involved in the climate change policy regime by analyzing the committee and topic network for the 435 congressional hearings about climate change from 1975 to 2016.

Climate Change Regime Subsystems

The climate change regime involves multiple linked subsystems, where subsystems are networked institutional components linked by a shared policy domain. The core subsystems in the climate change regime are those that are organized around the economic sectors that produce greenhouse gases, including land use (agriculture), which produces 9.5 percent of total US GHGs, energy production at 28.6 percent of GHGs, and transportation at 28.7 percent.

Table 7.1 uses hearing topics – land use, energy, and transportation – and congressional committees that held climate change hearings to illustrate some of the various subsystems that are part of the climate change regime. The cells in

TABLE 7.1 Climate Change Regime Subsystems – Topic Percent by Committee

Committee (chamber)	Land use	Energy	Transportation
Agriculture (House)	**100**	40	20
Agriculture, Nutrition, and Forestry (Senate)	**80**	30	10
Commerce, Science, and Transportation (Senate)	14	24	17
Energy and Commerce (House)	8	**55**	18
Energy and Natural Resources (Senate)	16	**57**	9
Environment and Public Works (Senate)	10	**49**	18
Natural Resources (House)	**50**	19	0
Science, Space, and Technology (House)	11	**44**	9
Transportation and Infrastructure (House)	0	25	**100**

Table 7.1 represent the percent of hearings held by that committee that included discussion of each of the three topics. Note that most hearings discussed multiple topics.

As can be seen, the portion of the broader agriculture (land use) subsystem that overlaps with climate is anchored by the Agriculture committee in the House and the Agriculture, Nutrition, and Forestry committee in the Senate. A total of 100 percent of the hearings held by the Agriculture committee addressed land use, as did 80 percent of hearings held by the Agriculture, Nutrition, and Forestry committee. Additionally, 50 percent of the hearings held by the Nature Resources committee in the House were about the land use topic. This indicates that agriculture likely resembles an iron triangle subsystem.

The energy topic was covered by multiple committees, including Energy and Commerce in the House, Energy and Natural Resources in the Senate, Environment and Public Works in the Senate, and Science, Space, and Technology in the House. However, those committees have broad jurisdictions and the energy topic only appeared in 49 to 57 percent of the hearings held by those committees. This indicates that the parts of the broader energy production subsystem that overlap with climate likely have the characteristics of an issue network type subsystem.

Finally, in the context of climate change, the transportation subsystem is defined by the Transportation and Infrastructure committee in the House, where 100 percent of the climate change-related hearings held by that committee included the topic of transportation. The Senate has the Commerce, Science, and Transportation committee, which has a much broader jurisdiction than the House committee and addressed each of the three topics.

Chapter 5 discussed other dimensions of climate change apart from those related to the greenhouse gas-producing economic sectors, and these dimensions – science, international, and climate change impacts – cut across multiple subsystems. Also noted in Chapter 5 is that energy was the most discussed dimension at 47 percent of all hearings, followed by the trans-subsystem dimensions of impacts

(38 percent), international (34 percent), and science (33 percent). Additionally, Chapter 6 showed the number of climate change hearings held by each committee, with the House Energy and Commerce committee, the Senate Environment and Public Works committee, and the House Science, Space, and Technology committee holding the most hearings.

In terms of the connections between committees and topics, the largest cluster of connections involves the Environmental and Public Works, Energy and Commerce, and the Science, Space, and Technology committees, and their connections with the energy, impacts, and science dimensions. The total number of hearings for the cluster include:

Energy and Commerce → Energy (41 hearings)
Environment and Public Works → Energy (35 hearings)
Environment and Public Works → Impacts (33 hearings)
Science, Space, and Technology → Science (30 hearings)

The international dimension was another prominent dimension – it was a topic at 34 percent of hearings – but it was diffused across multiple committees. The committees included the core committees of Energy and Commerce (27 hearings), Environment and Public Works (21 hearings), and Science, Space, and Technology (19 hearings), as well as the Senate Energy and Natural Resources committee (16 hearings), the House Foreign Affairs committee (12 hearings), and the Senate Foreign Relations committee (11 hearings).

The connections between committees and topics show that the core of the climate change policy regime is based on the energy production subsystem and science, including the science associated with the potential impacts. In addition, the transportation dimension is vastly under-represented in proportion to its contribution to climate change. As noted, emissions from the transportation sector have surpassed emissions from the electric power generation sector in the percent of total greenhouse gas emissions in the United States.

Another component of subsystems is that they also connect the federal level of environmental policymaking to state and local policymaking through shared and overlapping jurisdictions across the multiple levels of government. The next section describes the relationship between subsystems and federalism.

Subsystems and Levels of Government

The Tenth Amendment to the Constitution reserves all authority not given to the federal government to the states and to the people. The sharing of policymaking authority creates a system based on federalism, with policymaking authority diffused between the levels of government including federal, state, and local. The diffusion of policymaking authority between the federal government and the states allows the states to act as "laboratories of democracy."

Federalism is defined as a "system of constitutionally derived and apportioned authority where state and national government retain sovereignty yet at the same time are interdependent" (Scheberle 2013, 395). The federalist system creates multiple levels of government that retain some authority, and the allocation of power has varied over the course of the country's development.

During the development era, the United States had a system of *dual federalism*, where states and the federal government had distinct spheres of power over separate policy areas. Under dual federalism, the states largely retained primacy over environmental issues within their borders.

With the conservation era, particularly the overlapping Progressive Era, the balance of power across a host of policy issues began to shift more towards the federal government, creating a system of *cooperative federalism*. Cooperative federalism involves the development of policy at the federal level coupled with shared implementation across levels of government. The policies of the environmentalism era are based in cooperative federalism, which itself is grounded in the national supremacy clause of Article VI, Section 2 of the US Constitution that states that federal laws pre-empt state laws.

The environmentalism era policies, and their model of cooperative federalism, provide a clear connection to the environmental policy subsystems that are tethered to the macro-institutions of the federal government. For example, under the Clean Air Act the EPA sets National Ambient Air Quality Standards (NAAQS) for each criteria pollutant including ozone, carbon monoxide, sulfur dioxide, particulate matter, lead, and nitrogen dioxide. The NAAQS are set at the national level, although the implementation of those standards involves the states setting the means in which they reach those standards. States are required to submit a State Implementation Plan, which can provide flexibility for states, allowing them to account for local conditions. Much like Congress delegated authority to the EPA to develop clean air standards, the EPA delegates authority to the states to put the standards into effect. There are series of sticks such as command-and-control regulations, oversight, technology-based standards, and enforcement, as well as carrots such as education, preventive efforts, technical assistance, and partnerships that the EPA can use to ensure state compliance (Daynes, Sussman, and West 2016).

Cooperative federalism coupled with delegation to states creates a *polycentric* system of policymaking that provide multiple centers of power and policymaking authority. As stated by Ostrom (2010),

> Polycentric systems are characterized by multiple governing authorities at differing scales rather than a monocentric unit (see Ostrom 1999). Each unit within a polycentric system exercises considerable independence to make norms and rules within a specific domain (such as a family, a firm, a local government, a network of local governments, a state or province, a region, a national government, or an international regime).

An advantage of polycentricity is that the autonomy given to states allows them to develop innovative policy solutions. Policy innovation by states creates opportunities for learning by other states and the federal government. For example, California has long been a leader in the development of environmental policy. The geography of California makes it susceptible to smog, particularly in the heavy populated Los Angeles area. In the 1960s, California enacted policies to regulate vehicle emissions, and the California Air Resources Board set the nation's first air quality standards. These actions were a precursor of the federal Clean Air Act, and California received a carve-out in the CAA amendments of 1970 that provided a wavier for the state as long as it continued to require more stringent vehicle emission standards than the federal government. In the area of air quality standards, California's innovation provided a blueprint for federal action.

Federalism and Climate Policy

In July of 2018 the state of California announced that it had hit its greenhouse gas reduction goal four years early. As stated by Governor Jerry Brown, "California set the toughest emissions targets in the nation, tracked progress and delivered results" (Weber 2018).

California has long been a leader on environmental issues, and the passage of AB 32, the California Global Warming Solutions Act, in 2006 set California on track to be a leader on climate policy. AB 32 required California to reduce greenhouse gas emissions to 1990 levels by 2020, and that milestone was reached in 2016 when GHG emissions hit 429.4 million metric tons, down from the 431 million metric tons produced in 1990. In addition, emissions fell even as California's economy continued to expand.

To reach its emission reductions goals set under AB 32, the state of California initiated a host of regulatory and market-based mechanisms, such as a cap-and-trade program, increased energy efficiency, increased use of renewable energy sources, methane capture, and vehicle emission standards, among others. The ability of California to meet its emissions goals early was because of reductions in emissions from electricity production. According to the California Air Resources Board (2018), emissions from the electric power sector declined 18 percent from 2015 to 2016, largely as a result of the state's cap-and-trade program and the state's Renewable Energy Portfolio Standard. In addition, increased rainfall in 2015 boosted hydroelectric power. However, greenhouse gas emissions from the transportation sector – as with the rest of the United States, vehicle emissions are the largest source of emissions in California – declined from 2007 to 2011, but have started to increase since 2013. Overall, the decline in power emissions compensated for the increase in transportation emissions. But for California to hit its next emissions reduction target of 40 percent below 1990 levels by 2030, it is going to need to address transportation emissions.

The experience of California shows that federalism, and polycentricity more broadly, can provide additional pathways for climate policy. Indeed, several states have moved forward on climate policies in the absence of federal action. Currently, climate policy in the United States is in a period of what Derthick (2010) calls *compensatory federalism*. Under compensatory federalism, governments at one level compensate for governments at another level. The environmentalism era can be understood as the federal government compensating for the lack of state approaches to environmental problems, as well as the fact that environmental issues, such as pollution, don't recognize arbitrary political boundaries. However, with climate policy, it is state and local governments that are compensating for the lack of federal government action (Lutsey and Sperling 2008).

Using data from the *Center for Climate and Energy Solutions*, Figure 7.2 shows the growth by number of states from 1996 to 2017 of three policies aimed at climate change, including Climate Action Plans, Greenhouse Gas Emissions Targets, and Carbon Pricing, as well as states with Renewable Energy Portfolio Standards (RPS). RPS are not climate-specific, but they can impact the production of greenhouse gases in a state by encouraging the use of renewable energy.

As can be seen in Figure 7.2, as of 2018 29 states have Renewable Portfolio Standards, 33 states have Climate Action Plans, 20 states have GHG Emissions Targets, and 11 states have Carbon Pricing policies. Additionally, a spike in growth of these policies occurred between 2005 and 2008, which is the same time-period that saw increased attention to climate in Congress. Finally, the number of states adopting climate policies leveled off in 2010.

Renewable Portfolio Standards: Renewable Portfolio Standards are a performance-based requirement that utilities within the state must receive a set percentage, or total megawatts (MW), of energy from renewables or alternative energy sources by a set date. Renewable sources include solar, wind, hydro, geothermal, and biomass. Wind energy has been responsible for 61 percent of renewable energy under RPS, but solar is gaining and in 2016 was 79 percent of RPS builds (Barbose 2017). States vary in their requirements and timetable, with Hawaii being the most aggressive with a 100 percent requirement by 2045. An additional ten states have voluntary goals in place.

Iowa was the first state to initiate an RPS in 1983 with a required 105 MW of renewable generating capacity. Minnesota started an RPS in 1994, but it was substantially reworked in 2007. States began to add RPS more steadily, beginning with Arizona in 1996, but the growth of RPS leveled off around 2010. Only Kansas has repealed an RPS by going from a requirement enacted in 2009 to a voluntary goal in 2015. Additionally, in 2014 Ohio extended its deadline established in 2008 for its 12.5 percent renewable requirement from 2024 to 2026. The adoption of an RPS by a state is largely based on internal factors such as public opinion, rather than the influence of neighboring states (Matisoff 2008). However, the stringency of the requirement does seem to be influenced by the target levels of

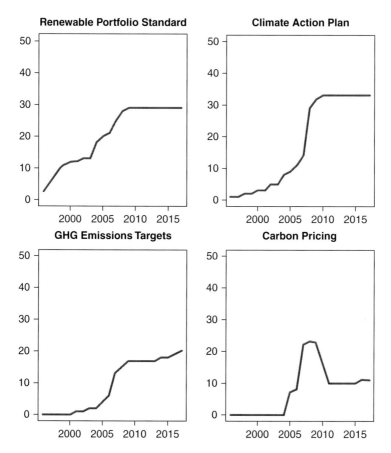

FIGURE 7.2 State climate policies, 1996–2017

neighboring states (Dincer, Payne, and Simkins 2014). Finally, the wind and solar capacity of a state has also been shown to be a factor in RPS adoption (Upton Jr. and Snyder 2015), with increased capacities leading to an increased likelihood to adopt an RPS.

RPS have shown to be effective in increasing the amount of renewable energy used in the United States. According to Barbose (2017), about 50 percent of the growth of renewable energy since 2000 is a result of RPS, although the impact of RPS appears to be diminishing, as 44 percent of new renewable capacity added in 2016 was a result of RPS.

Climate Action Plan: currently, 33 states have a Climate Action Plan (CAP) in place. Generally, a CAP includes steps that states can take to mitigate climate change given the opportunities and constraints provided by the state's economic, political, and natural resources. According to the EPA, a CAP usually includes the following: regional and local climate risks and vulnerabilities; baseline green-house gas emissions; goals and targets; alternative policy options; identification and screening of mitigation actions; forecast impacts of mitigation actions; and recommendations and strategy for implementation.[2]

While CAPs provide recommendations and strategies for stakeholder engage-ment, they do not include required emissions goals, incentives for renewable energy, or other policies that could effectively mitigate greenhouse gas emissions. As a result, CAPs seem to have no effect on reducing a state's GHG emissions (Grant, Bergstrand, and Running 2014). Additionally, the adoption of CAPs tends to be a result of political factors rather than risk factors (Yi and Feiock 2015).

Greenhouse Gas Emissions Targets: greenhouse gas emissions targets (ETs) are reductions in GHG emissions that states set to achieve within a given time. As of 2017, 20 states have emissions targets. Some states have mandatory reduction requirements; for example, California had a mandatory goal of 1990 levels by 2020, which it met by 2016. However, most states have goals that are not mandatory. Even absent a mandatory reduction requirement, ETs have been shown to be effective in reducing emissions after five years (Grant, Bergstrand, and Running 2014).

Carbon Pricing: carbon pricing involves approaches to price the negative external-ities associated with the production of CO_2 and other greenhouse gases. Pricing mechanisms are intended to bring the private marginal cost associated with GHGs in line with the total social cost of their use. The most discussed pricing mechanisms are a carbon tax and a cap-and-trade system. Currently no carbon tax exists in the United States. Washington state had a ballot initiative in the 2016 election to adopt a state-wide carbon tax, although the initiative was defeated by a 59 to 41 percent margin. Yet several states at various times have developed a cap-and-trade program, or began planning for a cap-and-trade system (Rabe 2018).

As with other climate policies, interest in carbon pricing spiked in 2008–2009 when as many as 23 states were developing cap-and-trade programs. California has its own cap-and-trade system that was authorized under AB 32 and began in 2013. In 2016, Washington state's Department of Ecology issued a Clean Air Rule that would have required industries within the state to reduce greenhouse gas emissions by 1.7 percent per year, and those requirements could have met through offsets (Brunner and Bernton 2016). However, in 2017 a state court judged rule the Department of Ecology lacked the authority for the Clean Air Rule absent approval by the legislature. Currently, the Clean Air Rule is suspended.

Apart from California, all other state-based cap-and-trade programs are regional compacts with neighboring states. Currently, the *Regional Greenhouse Gas Initiative* (RGGI) in the Northeast is the only regional cap-and-trade system in the United States.[3] The RGGI began in 2005 when the governors of Connecticut, Delaware, Maine, New Hampshire, New Jersey, New York, and Vermont signed a Memorandum of Understanding to reduce CO_2 emissions in their states through a regional cap-and-trade program. In 2007, Maryland, Massachusetts, and Rhode

Island joined the RGGI, although New Jersey left in 2012, but then rejoined in 2018.

The RGGI places a mandatory cap on the amount of CO_2 emissions from fossil-fuel based electric power facilities that produce at least 25 megawatts (MW) or greater within the ten states. Emission allowances are distributed based on the overall cap. The determination of the cap is made by each state, and allowances are also determined by each state, with 90 percent of allowances sold at a quarterly regional auction. The use of the proceeds from the auction is determined by each state, with the majority being used for energy efficiency, renewable energy programs, and direct bill assistance for homes and businesses (Regional Greenhouse Gas Initiative, Inc. 2017).

Overall, the states in the RGGI have reduced CO_2 emissions from the power sector over 45 percent since 2005. The direct impact of the RGGI in reducing emissions is unclear because the Northeast has traditionally had a lower level of fossil fuel use than other areas of the country, and several of the states in the RGGI had earlier implemented Renewable Portfolio Standards. However, from a political and policy perspective the RGGI is successful in showing that a) states and regions can develop their own programs from the bottom up without federal government guidance, and b) auctioning the allowances and giving states control over the revenue – as opposed to distributing them freely, as was proposed in several congressional cap-and-trade programs – can create a visible, tangible link from the cap-and-trade to a public benefit (Rabe 2018). Additionally, the RGGI has been maintained by governors of both political parties.

While the RGGI can be seen as a success, two other regional cap-and-trade programs were not sustained. *The Western Climate Initiative* (WCI) was launched in February 2007 by the governors of Arizona, California, New Mexico, Oregon, and Washington, with a goal of reducing emissions in the region to 15 percent below 2005 levels by 2020. In 2008, Montana and Utah joined, as well as the Canadian provinces of British Columbia, Manitoba, Ontario, and Quebec. Also, in 2008 the WCI developed design recommendations for a cap-and-trade program that went on to inform California's approach. However, in the 2010 elections the governorships of Arizona and New Mexico switched from Democratic to Republican, and after the failure of cap-and-trade legislation in Congress the other states became less confident in the cap-and-trade approach. All of the US states but California withdrew by 2011, although California and the Canadian providences of British Columbia, Ontario, Quebec, and Manitoba remain in the WCI.[4]

The Midwestern Greenhouse Gas Reduction Accord (MGGRA) was initiated during the Midwestern Governors Association Energy Security and Climate Stewardship Summit held in November 2007. Six US states, including Kansas, Minnesota, Illinois, Iowa, Wisconsin, and Michigan, as well as the Canadian providence of Manitoba signed on to the accord that called for emissions reduction and a regional cap-and-trade program (Walsh 2007). An advisory group report provided recommendations for the cap-and-trade program (see Midwestern Accord

Advisory Group 2009), and presented those recommendations to the Midwestern Governors Association in 2010, yet no action has been taken since 2010.

Given the success of the sulfur dioxide cap-and-trade program, it seemed that cap-and-trade was a panacea for solving a host of pollution problems. However, as Rabe (2016) notes, "The case for cap-and-trade was so path dependent upon the revered sulfur dioxide experience that it was widely assumed that any application to greenhouse gases would self-implement in a cost-effective manner without political challenges" (105). From an efficiency standpoint, pricing the negative externalities associated with CO_2 provides the best option.[5] Yet cap-and-trade at the federal level, as well as two regional programs, were unable to withstand political pressures, which demonstrates that making cap-and-trade politically palatable is a vexing problem.

Broadly speaking, the willingness of states to adopt climate and renewable energy policies is largely a function of internal political considerations such as the ideology of citizens, environmental interest group membership of citizens, and Democratic control of the governor and legislature during the time of adoption (Bromley-Trujillo et al. 2016). Additionally, states tend to not take an either/or approach to mandates versus incentives, but rather states tend to adopt a mix of approaches (Vasseur 2016). However, given the difficulty of navigating the pathways of the macro-institutions, the polycentricity inherent in the nature of policy subsystems and the multiple levels of government provide other opportunities to address climate change.

The environmental policymaking system contains multiple constituent subsystems and multiple levels of government, which provide several venues of decision-making. Most subsystems most of the time exist in equilibrium states that include a stable set of institutions and actors. However, subsystem equilibrium can be disrupted by changes in the information streams as well as by actions of policy actors. Additionally, actors can venue-shop across multiple venues, further destabilizing policy subsystems. The next section discusses important policy actors involved in environmental policymaking.

Policy Actors, Coalitions, and Information Networks

The environmental policymaking system includes the macro-institutions, subsystems, and multiple policy actors within subsystems that are trying to see their preferences for policy enacted. These actors include *official* actors, who are those within government institutions that have constitutionally prescribed roles such as members of Congress, the president, political appointees and civil servants within executive branch agencies, judges, and state and local government officials. Additionally, *unofficial* actors, who are those outside government institutions such as interest groups, also play a major role in environmental policymaking and development.[6] Both official and unofficial actors can act as *policy entrepreneurs* by leveraging changes in the information streams to advocate for policy change (see Mintrom and Norman 2009).

Whether they are official or unofficial, policy actors are motivated by preferences that often are a result of the values discussed in the Chapter 4. Typically, policy actors have preferences over outcomes, although they are usually not able to affect outcomes directly; so policy actors choose behaviors that, in their view, will make it more likely that they will achieve their desired outcome. For example, a member of Congress that is concerned about the problem of increasing greenhouse gases in the atmosphere cannot directly reduce GHG. So, in pursuance of her goal of GHG reduction, she must choose from among a set of alternative strategies that will make achieving her goal more likely. The set of strategies could include introducing legislation, lobbying her colleagues, engaging in coalition-building with both official and unofficial actors, among other strategies.

Examining the role of policy actors in environmental policy involves considering the *mobilization* and *influence* of those actors. Mobilization refers to the degree of involvement in policymaking by various policy actors, and influence refers to the impact policy actors have on policy choices. For official policy actors, degrees of mobilization and influence are largely a function of their institutional role, while questions regarding the mobilization and influence of outside actors are much more open.

With regard to environmental policy, interest groups are a critical set of unofficial actors. Interest groups provide information in the policymaking process and they are active in all three information streams. They provide information about potential problems, they offer ready-made policy solutions favored by their members, and they engage and mobilize the public as well as provide resources for political campaigns.

A second set of critical policy actors in environmental policy are scientists and other technical experts. Science plays a major role in environmental policy including in the identification and defining of problems, the determination of potential solutions, and as a basis for decision-making. Scientists as policy actors are divided between those within government and those outside government, and as a result have a differing degree of mobilization and influence depending on their institutional affiliation.

Finally, official and unofficial policy actors may form *advocacy coalitions* with other actors that share their policy goals. Advocacy coalitions are networks of policy actors that can reduce the transactions costs associated with mobilization and, through coordination, increase the likelihood of being influential. Additionally, advocacy coalitions tend to be relatively stable over time, particularly in contentious policy domains. Policy actors also form other, more temporary, coalitions built from political expediency. The next section first examines interest groups in environmental policy, then science and expertise, and finally coalitions.

Interest Groups

James Madison, in *Federalist #10*, wrote about the nature of factions in any political system. Factions represent the various interests in society that might place demands on government. For Madison, factions were unavoidable and the concern was how to manage factions such that a majority faction was not able to overrun a minority faction. Therefore, a political system should be designed that could check-and-balance the influence of factions, diffuse the influence of any one faction on political decisions, and encourage the development of many factions to provide a counter-balance. As Madison stated in *Federalist #10*, "Take in a greater variety of parties and interests and you make it less probable that a majority of the whole will have a common motive to invade the rights of other citizens." The design of diffuse policymaking authority across the macro-institutions, as well as the First Amendment protections of speech, assembly, and to petition the government, are meant to weaken the power of a majority faction to "invade the rights" of a minority faction.

The notion of competing factions is closely connected to the idea of interest group *pluralism* developed by Truman (1951). In brief, pluralism posits that the various interests in society are free and able to press their demands on government and, as a result, multiple groups form to compete with each other to achieve their policy objectives. Truman-style pluralism assumes that interest groups arise as a result of social disturbances such as "socioeconomic change, often driven by technological development; the behavior of allied groups and opponents; and changes in government institutions or policies" (Grossmann 2012, 36). Therefore, pluralism would predict that interest groups arise and mobilize as a result of changes in one or more of the information streams. Some research exploring the role of interest groups in environmental policy supports the idea of groups forming in response to changes in the problem information stream. For example, Johnson and Frickel (2011) found that environmental organizations arise, in part, as a result of environmental changes such as declining wildlife populations and increased air pollution. In addition, counter-mobilization – where groups on an opposing side in a policy debate mobilize in response to a prior mobilization – may occur as a result of changes in the political information stream. Overall, pluralism would predict a large number of interest groups competing across a wide range of issues such as what exists in an issue network type of policy subsystem.

One prominent criticism of pluralism is *elite theory*, which suggests policy choices are driven by elites rather than the bottom-up mobilization of societal interests that is assumed by pluralism. According to Schattschneider (1960), it is elites that define the policy alternatives that are legitimate, and the defining of alternatives is the "supreme instrument of power" (68). An implication of elite theory is that the public is largely uninformed and disengaged from policy and political choices and therefore relies on cues from elites, such as elected officials or interest group campaigns, in order to shape views on issues. The reliance on elite cues by the public may be, in part, a function of the complexity of the issue and the information costs associated with developing a view on the issue. For example, Rugeley and Gerlach (2012) found that, with more complex environmental issues with higher information costs such as climate change, the public tends to rely more on elite partisan cues, as opposed to less complex issues such as wilderness protection. Under elite theory there is less mobilization and less influence from public interest groups. However, who should be thought of as an "elite" actor varies by ideological attachments, with the left seeing private moneyed interests and the elected officials they contribute to as the elites, whereas the right see academics, Hollywood actors, well-funded environmental interest groups, and civil servants within executive agencies as the elite.

A second criticism of pluralism argues that, since the benefits that could be obtained by interest group activity are diffuse, and the costs, in terms of time, effort, financial, are assumed by the individual, it is likely that individuals will free-ride on the efforts of others (Olson 1965). As a result of this collective-action problem, there will be fewer interest groups present and they will be difficult to maintain over time. In order to overcome collective-action problems, group leaders seek to provide material benefits to members to maintain the existence of the group (Walker 1983). In addition, the need to provide material benefits to members means that when interest groups are engaged in a policy subsystem, they will be likely to pursue their own narrow interest in exchange for relationships with policy-makers. With fewer interests engaged, elites are free to influence policy choices through exchanges of resources. *Exchange theory* posits that,

> interest group origins, growth, death, and associated lobbying activity may all be better explained if we regard them as exchange relationships between entrepreneurs/organizations, who invest capital in a set of benefits, which they offer to prospective members at a price – membership.
>
> *Salisbury 1969, 2*

With exchange theory, the collective-action problem of developing and maintaining group membership is overcome by benefits that are offered to members for joining, and often the benefits include private benefits obtained through the policy process. Along similar lines Godwin, Ainsworth, and Godwin (2013) note that, with exchange theory, "participants in the political process – interest groups, public officials, and citizens – engage in exchanges to improve their economic, social, or political welfare" (17).

Under exchange theory, private interests in the pursuit of *rents* – policy-driven economic advantages such as tax breaks or subsidies – offer resources to elected officials in exchange for their support of the private interest's policy goals. As a result of these exchanges, policymaking is captured by powerful private elite interests, often at the expense of the broader public. Exchange theory would assume an iron triangle type of subsystem arrangement.

In more recent years, pluralism has been modified as *neopluralism* (see Lowery and Gray 2004). The development of neopluralism grew in response to some of the critiques of pluralism in its original form. Neopluralism provides several contextual factors that help to explain the mobilization patterns of various interest groups, such as: a) policymaking involves multiple decisions across multiple venues;

b) the salience of an issue can influence the pattern of mobilization; c) political parties and partisanship play a role in interest mobilization; and d) institutions provide opportunities and constraints on the mobilization and counter-mobilization of interests (Godwin, Ainsworth, and Godwin 2013, 143).

Differences between pluralistic[7] and exchange accounts regarding the nature of interest group mobilization may be resolved, in part, by considering the type of benefit sought and the amount of attention being paid to the issue(s).

Interest groups can be understood to pursue one of two broad types of benefits, either *private* or *collective* benefits. Private benefits – based on private goods that are rivalrous and excludable – include economic advantage for a particular firm or economic sector. Collective benefits refer to benefits associated with public goods, such as the environment and natural resources. Private interests often engage in rent-seeking efforts to gain private benefits and/or to ensure regulatory costs fall on their competitors. Interest groups that pursue public benefits are often looking to place regulatory burdens on private interests to improve overall public welfare, at least in the public interest group's view. The nature of the benefit sought can lead to expectations about the nature of interest mobilization. Groups seeking collective benefits may be more likely to free-ride on the efforts of others given the benefits sought are diffuse across society and subject to what Wilson (1982) called entrepreneurial politics, whereas private benefits are localized to the firm or sector, therefore free-riding may be less likely and interest-group politics arise.

Interest mobilization may also be influenced by the attention being paid to an issue. As issues move from policy subsystems to the agenda of macro-institutions, they become increasingly likely to attract and mobilize diverse interests through positive feedback. When major policy change becomes more likely, the number of groups mobilized tends to increase through mobilization and counter-mobilization. This is part of a larger pattern that suggests interest groups are responsive to government actions (Baumgartner, Gray, and Lowery 2009; Baumgartner et al. 2011; LaPira 2014; Leech et al. 2005).

Overall, the pattern of interest group representation is one of niches, where one (or a few) interest group(s) is engaged in policy subsystems and bandwagons that involve multiple interest groups engaged in a highly salient issue (Baumgartner and Leech 2001).

The growth of environmental interest groups suggests a pattern of pluralism, with a mobilization and maintenance of groups concerned about the environment as a result of social disturbances, or changes in one or more of the information streams (Ingram and Mann 1989). In addition, environmental organizations tend to be among the most numerous public interest groups (Grossmann 2012). Finally, environmental groups have become professionalized and generally well-represented in policy debates (Bosso 2005).

Environmental groups mobilized in waves that corresponded to the type of policies that were occurring within each environmental policy era. The first wave of environmental organization mobilization occurred at the end of the development era and the beginning of the conservation era with the founding of the Sierra Club by preservationist John Muir in 1892. The Sierra Club's initial focus was on the protection and preservation of pristine natural environments. The development of environmental groups with a focus on nature and wildlife continued throughout the conservation era with the National Audubon Society (1905); the National Parks and Conservation Association (1919); the Izaak Walton League (1922); and the National Wildlife Federation (1935).

The second wave of environmental groups occurred during the environmentalism era amid rising concerns about pollution and environmental harm. This period saw the founding of the Environmental Defense Fund (1967); Friends of the Earth (1969); the Natural Resources Defense Council (1970); and Greenpeace (1970).

The third wave began in the 1980s during the reform era that saw efforts to decrease federal government involvement in environmental issue. This period is associated with growth in local, grassroots environmental groups concerned about potential environmental hazards in their own communities (see Freudenberg and Steinsapir 1991).

After having developed in response to changing environmental and political conditions, environmental organizations further divided into three broad categories. As defined by Whitford (2003), these categories include, "the mainstream, the Greens, and the grassroots", where

> Mainstream groups tend to be older, more established groups with significant Washington representation; examples include the Sierra Club, National Audubon Society, Environmental Defense Fund (EDF), and Natural Resources Defense Council (NRDC). The Greens include Greenpeace and Earth First! Grassroots groups, an innovation dating to the 1980s, tend to concentrate on localized or "NIMBY" issues, such as waste facilities (50).

Once formed and mobilized interest groups seek to influence policy choices, and to do so they employ strategies that generally fall into one of two categories; *insider* strategies or *outsider* strategies. Insider strategies include activities that occur within and across the subsystems and institutions of the environmental policymaking system, and usually include efforts to persuade decision makers. Outsider strategies are those activities aimed outside the environmental policymaking system including educating and mobilizing the public, or contributing to political campaigns.

The major strategy that is pursued by interest groups in attempting to influence policy choices is *lobbying*. Lobbying involves any effort on the part of interest groups to persuade decision-makers toward the groups point of view (Baumgartner and Leech 1998). In pursuing insider strategies interest groups and their lobbyists monitor subsystem activity, provide information to policymakers, and establish relationships with other policy actors (Godwin, Ainsworth, and Godwin 2013). Both environmental and private interest groups spend sufficient resources on lobbying.

Figure 7.3 illustrates the mobilization (i.e., the number of environmental and energy groups) as well as the lobbying expenditures of environmental groups and oil, gas, and electric utility interests.[8]

As shown in Figure 7.3, environmental groups have grown steadily since 1970 and outnumber energy interest groups, however, energy groups spend quite a bit more on lobbying efforts. The growth of environmental groups has been nearly linear, whereas, the growth of energy groups leveled off in the mid-1980s. Overall, environmental groups have an advantage with regard to the number of interest groups, and the development of environmental interest groups was influential during the environmentalism era and beyond (Bosso 2005).

Looking to lobbying expenditures, it is clear that private interest groups have a tremendous advantage in spending. As Figure 7.3 shows, lobbying expenditures by the oil and gas, and electric utilities grew during following the 2006 election and peaked at $150–$200 million in 2009 and 2010, during the time that a cap-and-trade bill seemed most likely to pass Congress. One study found that over $2 billion was spent on federal climate lobbying from 2000 to 2016, with renewable energy producers and environmental groups being outspent by fossil fuels interests by a 10:1 ratio (Brulle 2018).

Determining the causal impact of lobbying and spending on policy outcomes is difficult. One large study that examined hundreds of policy issues over time found little evidence that greater resources was decisive in determining success (Baumgartner et al. 2009). Money was less impactful because the various sides of each of the issues tended to be well represented, which points to a pluralistic understanding of interest group representation. In addition, some evidence suggests that interest group lobbyists tend to provide support to allies as opposed to extending resources to convince those on the other side (Hall and Deardorff 2006). This seems to be the case within environmental policy as, according to data available at *OpenSecrets.org*, energy groups contribute overwhelmingly to Republican elected officials and candidates, whereas environmental groups contribute overwhelmingly to Democratic elected officials and candidates.

Despite some evidence demonstrating the limited impacts of money, it is clear that interest groups spend millions and millions of dollars per year on lobbying and campaign contributions. As with mobilization, the lobbying of interest groups may be a result of the type of benefit sought, private vs. public, and the attention, and subsequent competition, the issues garners. One model of lobbying posits that private interests are more likely to lobby when a) the value of the good is high, b) competition is low, c) cost of support for policymakers is low, and d) it is a private benefit (Godwin, Ainsworth, and Godwin 2013, 190–191).

The model of lobbying developed by Godwin, Ainsworth, and Godwin (2013) proposes that lobbying is largely in the service of rent-seeking by private interests.

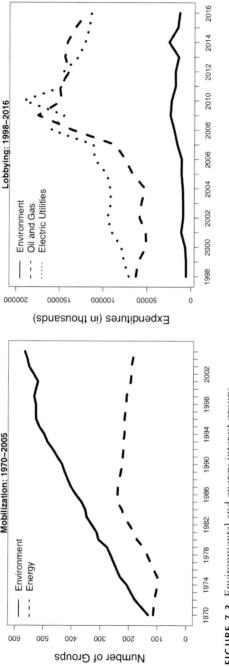

FIGURE 7.3 Environmental and energy interest groups

Rent-seeking includes distributive policies such as tax credits, subsidies, and contracts to provide government-funded services. For example, the Energy Policy Act of 2005 contained over $14.5 billion in tax reductions to energy producers, including coal, oil, gas, and renewable sources, as well as tax credits and loan guarantees for nuclear energy (Holt and Glover 2006). Lobbying as rent-seeking is likely to occur in subsystems that are closer to the iron triangle model, with fewer actors and institutions involved in decision-making as well as less attention from the macro-institutions. In addition, it is also likely that there are exchange relationships between actors in closed, uncompetitive subsystems. Finally, interest groups tend to be more successful when lobbying for private rather than collective benefits (Godwin, Ainsworth, and Godwin 2013).

Issue attention also likely impacts the strategies and influence of interest groups. As issues break out from their subsystems and reach the agenda of the macro-institutions, they are more likely to attract a larger number of groups. When this happens, the subsystem resembles the issue network and pluralism models, with multiple actors and institutions competing over the issue. As a result, policy choices are likely to be based on the equilibrium established by interest groups' competition (Becker 1983). Under these conditions, groups pursuing collective benefits, such as environmental protections, are more likely to be successful (Berry 1999; Smith 2000; Witko 2006). This also follows the observation by Godwin, Ainsworth, and Godwin (2013) that private interests are less likely to lobby as competition increases, perhaps because they are less likely to be successful. However, the effectiveness of collective benefit groups also depends on the counter-mobilization efforts of other interests. For example, Cheon and Urpelainen (2013) found that renewable energy production across several OECD countries is, in part, a function of the amount of high energy-use sectors (e.g., manufacturing) in the country, suggesting that the "stringency" of environmental policy in a country is conditional on the strength of the opposition to environmental policy.

It is important to note that, while there is a debate among scholars about the degree to which money matters in policy outcomes, the advantages in spending that energy groups possess allows them to better perform the various costly tasks associated with lobbying, including monitoring, building relationships, and providing information. In addition, increased spending allows private interest access to more decision points, most notably rulemaking by executive agencies. Business interests tend to be more represented in the rulemaking process than other groups (Furlong and Kerwin 2005; Golden 1998; Yackee and Yackee 2006). The pattern of business being better represented in rulemaking is true in environmental policy as well (Furlong 2007).

The over-representation of business in the rulemaking process raises concerns of *regulatory capture*. Regulatory capture refers to the capture of regulatory agencies such that regulation is in the service of private interest as opposed to the public interest (see Stigler 1971). For example, the Nuclear Regulatory Commission (NRC) has been criticized for not sufficiently regulating nuclear power plants

(Lochbaum 2017), and the Minerals Management Service (MMS) in the Department of the Interior came under fire for poor regulatory practices after the Deepwater Horizon oil spill (Eisner 2017). Regulatory capture is more likely to occur in iron triangle-type subsystems, and may also be driven by information asymmetries between firms and regulators. Firms may be strategic in the type of information they disclose and the transactions costs for agencies such as the EPA to obtain quality information is usually high (Coglianese 2007).

The dynamics of interest group lobbying were on display during the consideration of the American Clean Energy and Security Act of 2009 (ACES). As discussed in Chapters 5 and 6, the ACES was the subject of intense framing debates. The ACES was able to pass the House, although it was never brought to a vote in the Senate, in part because of the blocking power of the filibuster pivot. In addition, the polarization associated with environmental policy in general, and climate change in particular, made passing the ACES difficult. However, the lobbying efforts on the part of interest groups likely played a role as well.

Given the high profile and salience of climate change and the ACES during the 2009–2010 period, it seemed to be ideal circumstances for environmental groups and their allies, including the Democratic majorities in Congress and the Democratic president, to be able to push for policy change on climate. Yet the headwinds faced by those advocating for the ACES included a recession that was proving to be worse than initially estimated, congressional and presidential attention focused on health care reform, and a large counter-mobilization of conservative Tea Party advocates that were a combination of grass-roots and well-funded conservative and libertarian organizations. One study found that the insider strategy pursed by environmental groups and their allies that sought to build a coalition through bargaining with carbon emitters and offering concessions to Republican Senators was doomed to fail because of the doubts that have been manufactured by private interests regarding the seriousness of climate change, which helped to fuel the growth of the Tea Party movement (Skocpol 2013a, 2013b). With the focus on insider strategies, environmental groups were blindsided by the development and power of the Tea Party movement. In her study, Skocpol (2013a) went on to recommend that environmental groups focus more on outsider strategies to build public support for climate policy. However, others disagree with this account and note the role of money in the defeat, as well as the fact that many climate activists were pursuing an outside strategy (Pooley 2013).

Apart from differences in strategy, differences between proponents of the ACES and opponents also included money spent on federal lobbying. As shown in Figure 7.3, in 2009 environmental groups spent $22.4 million on lobbying, which was double the average amount they spent from 2000 to 2008. However, ExxonMobil alone spent $27.4 million in 2009, and the oil and gas industry as a whole spent $175 million. By July of 2010, the oil and gas industry had outspent environmental groups by seven-to-one from 2009 to July 2010.[9] Yet, even with the large spending disadvantage, the ACES was able to pass the House. As Wesley

Warren from the *Natural Resources Defense Council* stated, "It's not only about the money, having money helps, but the other side will always have more and they don't always win" (Mackinder 2010).

The defeat of the ACES in Congress came at a time when another set of important outside actors in environmental policy were noting the growing threat posed by climate change. The next section discusses the importance of science and expertise in environmental policy.

Science, Scientists, and Experts

Scientists, both natural scientists and social scientists, as well as other experts play a vital role in environmental policy. Experts help to identify the nature and extent of problems, develop solutions to problems, and inform regulatory analysis and assessments. In addition, scientific and expert information can also lead to *policy learning* by policy actors, where the beliefs of policy actors shift in response to expert information (Jenkins-Smith 1988; Jenkins-Smith and Sabatier 1993). Finally, science and the scientific method have a place of privilege as a way of gaining knowledge in the United States. The place of privilege for science makes it a potent tool for framing policy debates, as the phrase "sound science" is often used by partisans on both sides of an issue. Despite an overall respect for science and technology, there still exist policy areas, with climate change as the prime example, where the best available scientific knowledge is downplayed or ignored by some policymakers. This section examines ideas about the use of science and expertise in environmental policymaking, and the roles that scientists can assume within that process.

One view of science, or expertise more broadly, holds that the boundaries between science and policy choices is important. Similar to early 20th century ideas of the politics-administration dichotomy, clear boundaries between science and policymaking allow for the development of experts that provide neutral, expertise-based advice to inform and educate policymakers. In addition, clear boundaries prevent both technocracy – rule by experts – and the politicization of science. As noted by Keller (2009),

> Technocratic outcomes arise when scientists dominate decision making to the exclusion of other legitimate participants in democratic processes; politicization occurs when individual or group interests in policy outcomes introduce bias into scientists' actual work or their representation of their work in policy settings (27).

Keller (2009) goes on to state that the idea of clear boundaries between science and policymaking is based in the *rationalist* view of science. Under the rationalist approach, science is independent of politics and is brought to bear on questions of how to implement the decisions or achieve the goals of policymakers that were developed through the political process.

A second view described by Keller (2009), termed *positivist*, holds that science is the only way to truly understand reality and therefore should be the basis of all decision-making. According to proponents of the positivist model, a technocracy would be the preferred form of governance.

Much like the notion of the politics-administration dichotomy, it is generally recognized that a clear boundary between science and policy does not exist in practice, rather that there are multiple roles that science and even individual scientists can play in the environmental policymaking process.

To determine the potential role of science in a democracy, Pielke (2007) builds on questions about science and society as well as expertise in a democracy to develop roles that a scientist may play in policymaking. In examining the role of science in society, Pielke (2007) combines the rationalist and positivist views of science under the rubric of the *linear model* of science. The linear model of science posits that science develops from basic research to applied research and then ultimately results in benefits to society. Similar to the rationalist approach, a boundary should exist between basic research and the political process so that scientists can develop breakthroughs that may (or may not) eventually accrue broader benefits to society. The form of the linear model that is similar to the positivist approach, argues that scientific consensus is a required precursor to policy action, and that science knowledge compels particular policy responses. The other approach to science in society described by Pielke (2007) is the *stakeholder model*, which posits that the boundaries between science and policy are porous such that users can influence the production of science and scientists can influence policy decisions.

In addition to the role of science in society, Pielke (2007) also draws on notions of *pluralism* and *elitism* to examine the role of expertise in a democracy. Based on a pluralist notion of group competition, scientists should align themselves with a particular faction and provide their knowledge and expertise for use in political debates. Under elitism, alternatives are defined and choices are made by the political elite, and therefore scientists, as part of the elite, help define and explain the implications of the problem and proposed alternatives for the public and other elites without siding with a particular faction.

Combining the two approaches to science in society, the linear model and the stakeholder model, with the two approaches to expertise in democracy, pluralism and elitism, produces four possible idealized roles for scientists in policymaking: the Pure Scientist, the Issue Advocate, the Science Arbiter, and the Honest Broker.

Pure Scientist: the Pure Scientist results from the combination of the linear model of science and the pluralist approach to democracy. A Pure Scientist would produce scientific knowledge only for other scientists without regard for its use in policy debates. The knowledge developed by Pure Scientists is available to advocates for use in competitive political debates, yet the scientists themselves that produce the knowledge do not participate. For example, a Pure Scientist would produce climate models that are published in peer-reviewed scientific journals but would not engage in policy debates or advocacy.

Issue Advocate: the Issue Advocate results from the stakeholder model of science and the pluralist approach. A scientist that is an Issue Advocate takes sides in policy debates and leverages their expertise in the pursuit of normative policy goals. Additionally, some scientists may act as stealth advocates by appearing to be Pure Scientists, but in fact are advocating for a particular position.

Within climate science, James Hansen is an example of an Issue Advocate. As noted in Chapter 5, the congressional testimony of Hansen in 1988 when he worked for NASA was an important milestone in getting climate change on the agenda of Congress and the media. At the time, Hansen would have likely considered himself a Pure Scientist (or perhaps a Science Arbiter) who was largely interested in just producing science. However, in recent years Hansen has become an Issue Advocate, even going as far as getting arrested multiple times protesting the development of fossil fuels.

Science Arbiter: the Science Arbiter subscribes to the linear model of science and the elitism theory, therefore they prefer to be separate from the political and policy process, yet they will engage with policymakers to address questions. As noted by Pielke (2007), "A key characteristic of the Science Arbiter is a focus on *positive* questions that can in principle be resolved through scientific inquiry" (16, italics in original). As a rule, a Science Arbiter would avoid normative questions that can't be answered by science. For example, a Science Arbiter, like a Pure Scientist, would produce peer-reviewed scientific work, but they would also appear as expert witnesses at congressional or administrative hearings.

Honest Broker: the Honest Broker combines the stakeholder model of science with the elitism view of expertise. A scientist acting as an Honest Broker would seek to use their expertise to provide multiple alternative courses of action for various advocates. An Honest Broker would not align themselves with a side as an Issue Advocate would, rather they would seek to use their expertise to define scientific knowledge in a way that it could be applied to multiple policy options. With climate policy, an Honest Broker would provide estimates of greenhouse gas reductions under various policy alternatives.

The above understanding of science and scientists can be broadened to provide insights on expertise in general. For example, Jenkins-Smith (1990) noted three roles that policy analysts can play in policymaking, including "objective technicians," "issue advocates," or "client advocates." Objective technicians embody the notion of neutral competence, where an analyst remains separate from the political process and seeks only to use facts and unbiased analysis to determine the best, most efficient, program to implement the goal of the electoral institutions. At the other end of the spectrum are issue advocates, as with the work of Pielke (2007), that are driven by normative beliefs about what policy *should* be and are active participants in the political process. Finally, client advocates are also active in the political process, although they advocate positions that their client prefers.

The role that experts decide to play in environmental policy is likely a function of where they are employed. Scientists and other experts employed in government agencies are likely to be more constrained in their ability to be Issues Advocates than experts employed by interest groups. In addition, the type of role that a scientist or expert can play may be inhibited or encouraged depending on the context of the policy subsystem. For example, objective technicians are more likely to thrive in environments that are high in analytical tractability, where disputes may be resolved through the reduction of uncertainty with data and analyses. Additionally, objective technicians thrive when issues are low in conflict, have closed or professional forums, and have low levels of organizational allegiance. Issue advocates are likely to thrive in subsystems with low analytical tractability, high conflict, open forums, and low organizational allegiance. Finally, client advocates thrive in the same environments as issue advocates, except that client advocates are more likely when organizational allegiance is high (see Jenkins-Smith 1990, 117–118).

Policy Actors and Climate Change

Multiple policy actors are active in the climate change policy regime including those that are official and unofficial. To get a sense of the actors engaged in climate change policy, I use data from witnesses that appeared at hearings addressing climate change. Overall, 3,051 witnesses appeared at the 435 hearings from 1975 to 2016.

Witnesses were coded by their affiliation and aggregated into one of several categories. Categories include *Experts* that are outside government, such as academic or research-oriented institutions, think tanks, and professional associations. *Government* witnesses include official policy actors such as federal agencies, members of Congress, and state and local governments officials. Witnesses from the *Private Sector*, including businesses and trade associations, were coded based on the North American Industry Classification System (NAICS) of economic sectors. The economic sectors include Agriculture, Forestry, Fishing and Hunting (NAICS 11), Manufacturing (NAICS 31–33), Mining, Quarrying, and Oil and Gas Extraction (NAICS 21), Transportation and Warehousing (NAICS 48–49), and Utilities (NAICS 22). Finally, *Interest Groups* include environmental groups (e.g., Sierra Club, NRDC), unions, and the chamber of commerce. Table 7.2 presents the number and percent of total witnesses.[10]

As can be seen, witnesses classified as experts totaled 959 and represented just under a third of all witnesses at 31.43 percent of the 3,051 witnesses. A similar number of government witnesses, 943, appeared, and also represented nearly a third with 30.91 percent of witnesses. Executive agencies alone accounted for 21.30 percent of all witnesses, and representatives from the Environmental Protection Agency (EPA) were the most prominent, with 123 appearances,

TABLE 7.2 Climate Change Hearings Witness Affiliation, 1975–2016

Witness	Number	Percent
Experts		
Academics	387	12.68
National academies	97	3.18
National laboratories	68	2.23
Professional associations	35	1.15
Research institutes	204	6.67
Think tanks	135	4.42
Other experts	33	1.08
Total experts	**959**	**31.43**
Government		
Executive agencies	650	21.30
Members of Congress	81	2.65
State and local	212	6.95
Total government	**943**	**30.91**
Private sector		
Agriculture	66	2.16
Manufacturing	130	4.26
Mining	55	1.80
Transportation	73	2.39
Utilities	285	9.34
Other industries	177	5.80
Total private sector	**786**	**25.76**
Interest groups		
Environmental groups	209	6.85
Other interest groups	87	2.85
Total interest groups	**296**	**9.70**

which represents 4 percent of all witnesses and 18.92 percent of executive agency witnesses. Other agencies with multiple appearances include the Department of Agriculture (21), the Department of Energy (90), the Department of Interior (20), the Department of Transportation (10), the National Aeronautics and Space Administration (60), the National Oceanic and Atmospheric Administration (75), and the State Department (52).

Executive agencies are typically thought to be most engaged in policy implementation, although agencies also have a large role in processing information and alerting electoral institutions, notably Congress, to potential problems. This creates a "dual dynamic" of information-processing and policymaking between electoral and bureaucratic institutions, where executive agencies provide information in the problem and policy streams (Workman 2015). For example, the EPA, the National Oceanic and Atmospheric Administration (NOAA), and the National Aeronautics and Space Administration (NASA) all monitor and provide problem stream information about climate-change indicators.

Witnesses from the private sector represented 25.76 percent of all witnesses, with the utilities sector accounting for 9.34 percent, followed by manufacturing at 4.26, transportation at 2.39, agriculture at 2.16, and mining at 1.80 percent. Finally, interest groups were 9.70 percent of all witnesses, with environmental interest groups at 6.85 percent.

The next section examines the role of coalitions – networks of policy actors – in environmental and climate policy.

Coalitions

Policy actors, both official and unofficial, and their choices are the driving force of the environmental policymaking process. They help to create and shape the information signals in all three information streams; they attempt to define and re-define environmental issues; they work to put issues on and keep issues off the policymaking agenda; and they make strategic use of the policymaking pathways available to them. To achieve these, and other goals, policy actors are also strategic about creating, joining, and maintaining *coalitions*. Coalitions are networks of individuals and groups that share a common policy goal and work to achieve that goal. There are a few different types of coalitions, but in environmental policymaking *advocacy coalitions* are particularly important.

The Advocacy Coalition Framework (ACF), developed by Paul Sabatier and Hank Jenkins-Smith, is a framework for understanding the broader policymaking process (Sabatier and Jenkins-Smith 1993). The ACF proposes that advocacy coalitions, defined as a set of actors that share policy beliefs and preferences and coordinate their actions in a "non-trivial" manner, are central to understanding policy development and change (Jenkins-Smith et al. 2018). In addition, the ACF assumes that the beliefs of policy actors are structured in the hierarchical manner discussed in Chapter 4, where core beliefs and values inform beliefs and values related to specific policy issues, which in turn inform specific attitudes and preferences.

What binds advocacy coalitions together are policy issue beliefs and values, such as those related to the use of natural resources for development versus the importance of environmental protection, rather than the core values associated with ideology or cultural theory. Agreement on policy issue beliefs, what ACF scholars term policy core beliefs, makes it likely that policy actors will be networked in a coalition (Henry 2011; Henry, Lubell, and McCoy 2011; Weible 2005; Weible and Sabatier 2005). In addition, the ACF posits that when policy core beliefs are in dispute, such as the case with environmental policy, the membership of advocacy coalitions will tend toward stability over time.

Apart from advocacy coalitions, other types of coalitions exist in environmental policy. As noted, in polarized and contentious policy subsystems, advocacy coalitions tend to be stable over time, although less permanent coalitions can form to achieve a particular goal. Of note are *bootleggers and Baptists* coalitions that prove the old adage of politics making strange bedfellows (Smith and Yandle 2014). The analogy of bootleggers and Baptists comes from the coalition of actors that support temperance laws, including the bootleggers that support such laws for material reasons and the Baptists that are supportive for moral reasons. Despite not sharing core beliefs and values, bootleggers and Baptists share specific policy preferences regarding the sale of alcohol. However, unlike with advocacy coalitions, bootleggers and Baptists coalitions are less likely to coordinate and less likely to be stable over time. Generally, bootlegger and Baptist coalitions include instances where rent-seeking private interests happen to be on the same side as public good interest groups.

One example of a bootlegger and Baptist coalition in environment policy is the Clean Coal/Dirty Air coalition (Ackerman and Hassler 1981). The Clean Coal/Dirty Air coalition comes from the chemical scrubber requirement to remove some of the sulfur content in coal that was established in the late 1970s. Coal produced in the eastern part of the United States has a higher amount of sulfur than coal produced in the western part of the United States, so one way to reduce the sulfur content of coal is to encourage the use of coal from the western states. However, a coalition of environmental groups, coal producers in eastern states, and elected officials such as Senator Robert Byrd (D–WV) pushed to require all coal producers to use scrubbers. For environmental groups, they were concerned about the harm of coal development for lands in the west, the eastern coal producers were seeking protection from competition from western producers, and the elected officials were protecting their constituents.[11]

Coalitions and Climate Policy

The issue of climate change provides opportunities for multiple types of coalitions. Given the contentious nature of climate change, advocacy coalitions exist that include environmental interest groups, members of Congress, EPA officials, scientists inside and outside of government, state and local government officials, and academics that favor action on climate change, as one advocacy coalition. A second advocacy coalition exists that consists of fossil fuel interest groups, members of Congress, and state and local government officials concerned about the potential climate solutions that have been offered (Knox-Hayes 2012).

Along these lines, Kukkonen, Ylä-Anttila, and Broadbent (2017) found three climate change advocacy coalitions, including an environment coalition, an economy coalition, and a science coalition, that formed networks based on shared climate change-specific beliefs. Their findings came from examining statements about climate change in three leading US newspapers in 2007–2008. The advocacy coalitions were formed based on agreement with three policy issue-based beliefs including: *Climate science is valid*; *Environment is more important than economy*; and *Industry should be regulated*.

Those in the environment coalition – environmental interest groups, Democratic politicians, some industry actors, and some state and local actors – agreed with each statement. However, those in the economy coalition – business and trade associations from energy, manufacturing, and agriculture, Republican politicians, W. Bush administration officials, and conservative think tanks – disagreed with each statement. Finally, those in the science coalition – national and international research organizations such as the IPCC – agreed strongly with the climate science is valid statement, and to a lesser extent with the statement that the environment is more important than the economy. However, no actor in the science coalition took a position on whether or not industry should be regulated. Finally, Kukkonen, Ylä-Anttila, and Broadbent (2017) found no difference with regard to specific policy instruments, with actors from each of the three coalitions supporting cap-and-trade, vehicle efficiency standards, and alternative energy by large margins.

According to a recent analysis, nearly 21 national or regional coalitions exist to address climate change (Brulle 2015). The oldest is the US Climate Action Network (USCAN), which was formed in 1989. The USCAN is a coalition of environmental and progressive organizations with a mission to "build trust and alignments among its members to fight climate change in a just and equitable way."[12] The number of climate change coalitions saw a burst of growth between 2006 to 2009, with a total of 467 environmental organizations belonging to one or more coalitions in 2010.

In January 2007, a coalition of energy, mining, oil, and environmental interest groups, calling themselves the US Climate Action Partnership (USCAP), released a report titled *A Call For Action* that recommended "the prompt enactment of national legislation in the United States to slow, stop and reverse the growth of greenhouse gas (GHG) emissions over the shortest period of time reasonably achievable" (USCAP 2007, 2). The private businesses involved in USCAP in 2007 included General Electric, DuPont, Alcoa, Caterpillar, Duke Energy, PG&E, the FPL Group of Florida, PNM Resources of New Mexico, BP, and Lehman Brothers (Barringer 2007). Then, in 2009 USCAP – having grown to 20 companies – released *A Blueprint for Legislative Action* that called for an economy-wide cap-and-trade program with the following emissions targets: 97–102 percent of 2005 levels by 2012; 80–86 percent of 2005 levels by 2020; 58 percent of 2005 levels by 2030; and 20 percent of 2005 levels by 2050 (USCAP 2009, 5).

In addition to releasing the reports, USCAP was also active in lobbying lawmakers and executive branch agencies. According to data from *OpenSecrets. org*, between 2007 and 2010, USCAP spent $3.5 million in lobbying (The Center for Responsive Politics n.d.). The USCAP coalition was another signal of the momentum for climate policy, and for the American Clean Energy and Security

Act (ACES) in particular. Indeed, the USCAP blueprint became the basis for various aspects of the ACES (Pooley 2010).

Despite the seeming momentum, and as has been discussed, the ACES fell victim to framing, the filibuster pivot, and lobbying, although the nature of coalitions and coalition-building played a role as well. While many of the mainstream environmental groups – the Environmental Defense Fund, the Sierra Club,[13] the Nature Conservancy – favored the ACES, several of the green groups did not. For example, *Greenpeace* came out against the ACES, arguing, among other things, that under the bill,

> The biggest polluters would receive hundreds of billions of dollars in subsidies. This is unacceptable. Taxpayers should not foot the bill for dirty industries hoping to continue business as usual.
>
> Given all of the carbon "offsets" that the bill offers to dirty industries, they could avoid reducing their greenhouse gas emissions for more than a decade. By that time, it could be too late to stop the worst impacts of global warming.
>
> *Gaworecki 2009*

Along similar lines, *Friends of the Earth* stated that,

> the [ACES] would allocate tens of billions of dollars in permits to the industries that contribute greatest to global warming. In fact, the bill allocates pollution permits worth more than $24 billion to oil industry and more than $158 billion to the coal industry over the life-time of the bill.
>
> *Friends of the Earth 2009*

For the green groups, the fact that USCAP included so many energy and manufacturing businesses that in turn supported the ACES only served to undermine the bill in their eyes. The criticism of both *Greenpeace* and *Friends of the Earth* were centered around the ways in which the emissions allowances were distributed. However, it was the distributions of allowances that likely helped to attract the support of several USCAP members, who saw the allowances as a way to protect their consumers from large increases in energy prices (Pooley 2010). Therefore, supporters of the ACES shared aspects of advocacy coalitions with mainstream environmental groups, EPA officials, scientists, Democratic members of Congress, likely in a longer-term advocacy coalition as well as a bootlegger-Baptist coalition that included those actors in the advocacy coalition as well as the energy groups that expected to benefit from the emissions allowances. Indeed, Yandle (1998) made a similar observation, with supporters of the Kyoto Protocol being a bootlegger-Baptist coalition made up of environmentalists and alternative-energy producers. Additionally, conservative groups critical of the ACES made similar arguments as the greens in opposition. For example, opponents used the distribution of allowances to frame the ACES as "cap and tax." As Myron Ebell of the conservative Competitive Enterprise Institute stated, "We turned it into 'cap and tax,' and we turned that into an epithet" (Broder 2010).

More recently, coalitions seem to be forming around the idea of a carbon tax as a mechanism to price carbon. In February of 2017, a group of Republican "elder statesmen" including former Secretary of State James A. Baker III, former Secretary of State George P. Shultz, and former secretary of the Treasury Henry M. Paulson Jr., came out in support of a carbon tax. These supporters argue that a carbon tax, which is a using-markets type of policy instrument, represents "a conservative climate solution" based on its use of markets (Schwartz 2017). Along similar lines, former member of Congress Bob Inglis (R–SC) is involved with the group *RepublicEn* that is aimed at developing support among conservatives and libertarians for market-solutions to climate change, such as a carbon tax. In addition, ExxonMobil has supported a revenue-neutral carbon tax, stating, "revenue-neutral carbon tax would be a more effective policy option than cap-and-trade schemes, regulations, mandates, or standards" (ExxonMobil 2018). Also, several members of the House Climate Solutions Caucus have come out in support of a carbon tax. Finally, the *Citizens Climate Lobby* is working to establish grassroots support for a carbon fee-and-dividend plan that would place a fee on carbon use and then refund the revenue to American households.

The logic of a carbon tax is that a tax on the use of carbon would compensate for the difference between the total social cost of carbon and the private marginal cost. Negative externalities, by definition, mean that the private marginal cost paid by producers and consumers is less than the total social cost that includes the costs of pollution, poor health, and climate change. An ideal carbon tax should be set at the difference in costs between SMC and PMC.

Generally, economists argue that a carbon tax is the most efficient policy for pricing carbon. However, there are several technical and political complexities that make coalition-building around a carbon tax approach to climate change difficult. On a technical basis, it is difficult to know the *true* social cost of carbon, or the true difference between SMC and PMC. On the political side, it is difficult to build support for energy taxes generally – as demonstrated by the failure of the BTU tax in 1993 – and it would be particularly difficult in the politically contentious realm of climate change. As noted by Congressmen Ed Markey (D–MA) during the ACES debate, "I am aware of the economic arguments for a carbon tax, but politics is the art of the possible, and I think cap-and-trade is possible" (Broder 2009). It remains to be seen how successful the movement towards a coalition for a carbon tax in the United States will be.

In the next section, I use the congressional hearings about climate change to explore the information network of the climate change regime. The information network embedded within the climate change regime is based on the policy actors from which the various subsystems draw from to obtain information on climate change.

Policy Actors and the Information Network of the Climate Policy Regime

Climate change is a scientifically and socially complex issue, with a regime that transects multiple subsystems and levels of government within the environmental policymaking system. The environmental policymaking system is an information-processing system, and policy actors within the system create, receive, and shape information in attempts to define the ideas that are part of the foundation of a policy regime. The connection between policy actors and congressional committees constitutes the *information network* that exists within the climate change policy regime.

One of the ways in which Congress receives information about climate change is from witnesses appearing in hearings.[14] When calling witnesses, Congress is able to strategically manipulate the information network by triangulating information from multiple sources, including bureaucrats, private interests, and environmental interest groups, among others (Workman and Shafran 2015). The committees holding hearings and processing information, as well as the policy actors providing that information, constitute the information network within the climate policy regime.

The structure of the information network can vary from a "hollow-core" with multiple actors and committees to a strong core consisting of only a few committees and actors (Grossmann 2013; Heinz et al. 1990). Based on the congressional committees that held hearings and the topics of those hearings, the climate regime seems to have a core that is largely centered in issues of energy and science.

Given the core of energy and science in the climate change regime, the information network is likely to be structured through the energy and science committees in Congress, with experts and agency witnesses. This is evidenced in Table 7.2, which shows nearly 53 percent of witnesses at congressional hearings were either experts or from executive agencies, indicating an interest in expertise with regard to the information gathered at hearings.

As with committees and topics, there is a relatively strong core consisting of a dense cluster of committees and witnesses that includes the Energy and Natural Resources, Energy and Commerce, and the Environmental and Public Works committees, as well as experts, and utility representatives as witnesses. The cluster of committees and witnesses, including the number of appearances made by a witness from a given category include,

Experts → Energy and Natural Resources (105 appearances)
Experts → Energy and Commerce (154 appearances)
Utility Sector → Energy and Commerce (101 appearances)
Experts → Environment and Public Works (143 appearances)

As noted, experts were the most prevalent categories of witnesses, and an expert appeared in a hearing held by every committee that addressed climate change. Experts appeared the most in front of the Science, Space, and Technology Committee in the House with 193 appearances. Utility sector witnesses were not as prevalent overall – they were 9.34 percent of all witnesses – yet they were diffuse and appeared in front of all committees but one. Similarly, intergovernmental actors were only about 7 percent of witnesses, yet they appeared in hearings held by all but two committees.

With regard to executive agencies, Table 7.3 shows the appearances of the most prevalent executive agency witnesses – DOE, EPA, NASA, NOAA, State, and USDA – before the most prevalent committees. The cells represent the percent of executive agency appearances at the particular committees as a percent of all appearances of that agency.

For representatives from the DOE, they appeared the most in front of the Energy and Natural Resources in the Senate, with 27 percent of DOE appearances being before that committee. Following closely are the Science, Space, and Technology Committee at 26 percent, and the Energy and Commerce Committee with 24 percent of DOE appearances.

The EPA appeared at more congressional hearings than any other executive agency, and they appeared the most often at the Energy and Commerce

TABLE 7.3 Climate Change Regime Subsystems – Percent of Executive Agency Appearances by Committee

Committee (Chamber)	DOE	EPA	NASA	NOAA	State	USDA
Agriculture (House)	0	0	2	1	0	**25**
Agriculture, Nutrition, and Forestry (Senate)	0	2	2	1	2	**25**
Commerce, Science, and Transportation (Senate)	2	5	**47**	**29**	4	19
Energy and Commerce (House)	**24**	**29**	7	11	**29**	0
Energy and Natural Resources (Senate)	**27**	6	8	8	12	6
Environment and Public Works (Senate)	7	**24**	5	3	0	0
Foreign Affairs (House)	0	1	0	0	**19**	0
Foreign Relations (Senate)	1	2	0	1	10	0
Natural Resources (House)	1	2	0	8	0	0
Science, Space, and Technology (House)	**26**	13	**23**	**32**	10	19
Transportation and Infrastructure (House)	0	1	0	1	2	0

Committee, with 29 percent of all EPA appearances, followed by the Environment and Public Works committee with 24 percent.

For NASA, nearly half (47 percent) of their appearances were before the Commerce, Science, and Transportation Committee, and another 23 percent before the Science, Space, and Technology Committee. NOAA was most likely to appear before the same committees, with 32 percent of their appearances before the Science, Space, and Technology Committee, and 29 percent before the Commerce, Science, and Transportation Committee.

As discussed above, the international dimension was the most diffuse topic, as it was discussed across several committees. Along similar lines, witnesses representing the State Department were diffused across several committees. The State Department appeared the most in hearings held by the Energy and Commerce Committee with 29 percent, followed by the Foreign Affairs Committees with 19 percent of State Department appearances. Finally, the Energy and Natural Resources accounted for 12 percent of State Department appearances, following by Foreign Relations and Science, Space, and Technology each with 10 percent.

For the Department of Agriculture, they appeared the most at hearings held by the agriculture committees in Congress, including the Agriculture Committee in the House and the Agriculture, Nutrition, and Forestry in the Senate, each with 25 percent of USDA appearances. This was followed by Commerce, Science, and Transportation and Science, Space, and Technology, each with 19 percent.

The appearance of witnesses from executive branch agencies in front of various committees illustrates a similar pattern of subsystems as the topics and committees shown in Table 7.1. The Energy subsystem is anchored by the Energy and Commerce, Energy and Natural Resource, and the Environment and Public Works committees as well as the DOE and the EPA. The Agriculture subsystem includes the Agriculture, the Agriculture, Nutrition, and Forestry, and Natural Resources committees as well as the USDA. The Transportation subsystem is anchored by the Transportation and Infrastructure Committee in the House, but the Department of Transportation only appeared in three hearings about climate change.

In addition to the subsystems connected to greenhouse gases are committees and agencies engaged on the science dimension of climate change. The Commerce, Science, and Transportation, and the Science, Space, and Technology committees, as well as NASA and NOAA, were the most engaged on the science dimension. The international dimension was shaped by the Foreign Affairs and Foreign Relations committees as well as the State Department. However, the State Department appeared in front of several committees.

As noted, Congress can manipulate the information network by "tuning" information signals through the witnesses they call, in order to produce particular types of information. For example, Republicans are more likely to call witnesses that contradict the scientific consensus on climate change, whereas Democrats tend to rely on environmental groups and executive branch agencies (Fisher, Leifeld, and Iwaki 2013; McCright and Dunlap 2003; Park, Liu, and Vedlitz 2014).[15] Next,

I estimate the number of appearances for executive agencies, experts, environmental groups, and the private sector witnesses.

To examine the likelihood of particular witnesses appearing in congressional hearings I use dummy variables based on the Democrats having the majority in the chamber holding the hearings, if the hearing considered one or more specific pieces of legislation, and if the hearing was in the House. In addition, I use dummy variables to control for hearing topic, including Land Use, Energy, Transportation, Science, and Impacts, with the diffuse International dimension being the excluded referent topic. Finally, I used fixed-effects to control for the committee holding the hearing, but those results are not shown. The results are shown in Table 7.4.

As can be seen, executive agencies were more likely to appear when Democrats held the majority in the chamber than when Republicans held the majority. Additionally, executive agencies were more likely to appear at hearings about the science and impacts of climate change than hearings about the international dimension of climate change. Along similar lines, experts were also more likely to appear when Democrats held the majority, at hearings that addressed science and

TABLE 7.4 Estimates of Congressional Witnesses

	Witness categories			
	Federal agencies	Experts	Environmental groups	Private sector
Democratic majority	0.398*	0.601**	0.357***	0.559
	(0.181)	(0.231)	(0.089)	(0.305)
Legislation	-0.008	-0.158	0.121	0.665*
	(0.185)	(0.235)	(0.090)	(0.311)
House	-1.783	-1.541	-1.369	-0.537
	(1.757)	(2.241)	(0.859)	(2.958)
Agriculture	0.349	0.334	0.297*	0.894*
	(0.258)	(0.329)	(0.126)	(0.434)
Energy	-0.284	0.040	0.084	1.132***
	(0.167)	(0.213)	(0.082)	(0.282)
Transportation	0.399	0.726*	0.216	1.421***
	(0.232)	(0.296)	(0.114)	(0.391)
Science	0.564**	1.836***	0.131	-0.473
	(0.182)	(0.232)	(0.089)	(0.306)
Impacts	0.598***	1.556***	0.195*	0.750**
	(0.171)	(0.218)	(0.083)	(0.287)
Constant	1.886	1.358	0.559	-0.691
	(1.595)	(2.034)	(0.779)	(2.685)
Observations	435	435	435	435
Adjusted R²	0.124	0.299	0.126	0.213

Note: Also controlling for congressional committee
* p<0.10; **p<0.05; ***p<0.001

impacts, as well as hearings about transportation. Environmental interest groups were more likely to appear when Democrats held the majority as well as when hearings were regarding agriculture and impacts, as opposed to hearings about the international dimension of climate change. Finally, private sector witnesses are more likely to appear at legislative hearings as well as hearings about energy, transportation, and climate change impacts.

The above analysis illustrated the type of sources from which Congress draws information about climate change. The connections between policy actors and congressional committees form an information network that shapes the nature of the information that Congress receives. The information network is structured with a core of energy and science committees and experts, and representatives of the utility sector. Additionally, the information network is conditioned by party control of Congress, with Democrats more likely than Republicans to draw information from executive agencies, experts, and environmental interest groups.

The US Climate Policy Regime

The climate change policy regime in the United States is based on the network of subsystems and multiple levels of government that process information and produce policy to address climate change. In general, policy subsystems can range from an iron triangle type with a few actors, committees, and executive agencies to an issue network type of subsystem with multiple actors, committees, and agencies.

The main subsystems involved in climate change are energy, agriculture, and transportation, which are some of the leading sources of greenhouse gas emissions. In addition, the climate change policy regime includes multiple levels of government, particularly states, that make their own climate policies. Figure 7.4 illustrates the three major subsystems and the major state level policies discussed earlier.

The portion of the energy subsystem that is engaged on climate issues includes three congressional committees, two executive agencies, and a wide range of policy actors. The nature of the energy subsystem involved in the climate change regime is indicative of climate being largely defined as an energy and environmental issue in the United States.

The agriculture subsystem is also engaged in the climate change regime with three congressional committees, one executive agency, and witnesses largely drawn from the agriculture sector.

The transportation subsystem is involved in climate change but to a degree that is far less than is warranted given that transportation emissions are now the largest sources of greenhouse gas emissions in the United States. The transportation subsystem is represented by one congressional committee, no executive agencies – the Department of Transportation only made three appearances in congressional hearings during this time-period – and witnesses from the transportation sector.

Climate Change Policy Regime

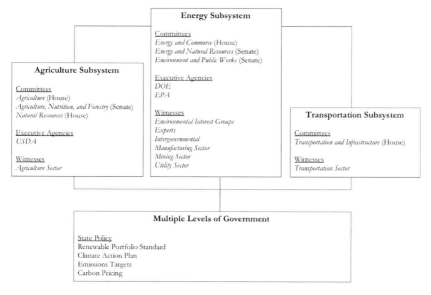

FIGURE 7.4 The climate change regime

Finally, multiple levels of government are engaged in the climate policy regime, with more than half the states having Renewable Energy Portfolio Standards and Climate Actions Plans in place, with fewer having emissions reduction targets and carbon pricing policies. The development of state level climate policy can be understood as compensatory federalism, where the states are compensating for a lack of federal government actions on climate change. While RPS have been effective in encouraging the use of renewable energy, state policy on its own is not likely to be enough to adequately address climate change.

Conclusion

The climate change policy regime involves multiple linked subsystems, institutions, and actors. The linked subsystems include the energy subsystem, the agriculture subsystem, and the transportation subsystem. In addition, the network of issue dimensions and congressional committees included a core consisting of the Environmental and Public Works, Energy and Commerce, and the Science, Space, and Technology committees and their connections with the energy, impacts, and science dimensions. In addition, states are part of the climate regime and are engaged in developing their own approaches to address climate change.

Policy actors including private and environmental interest groups as well as scientists and other experts are also a key part of the climate policy regime. Various policy actors provide information to Congress by appearing in hearings held by various congressional committees. The committees and actors testifying constitute the information network of the climate change, which has a core that includes the Energy and Natural Resources, Energy and Commerce, and the Environmental and Public Works committees as well as experts, and utility representatives as witnesses. However, the shape of the information network can vary by the party in control of the chamber holding hearings, if the hearing considers legislation, and the topic that the hearing is about.

Notes

1 From here: www.congress.gov/congressional-record/2016/7/11/senate-section/article/s4948-4q=%7B%22search%22%3A%5B%22%5C%22web+of+denial%5C%22%22%5D%7D&r=1
2 Archived site here: https://archive.epa.gov/epa/statelocalclimate/developing-state-climate-change-action-plan.html
3 For more see: www.rggi.org/
4 See here: www.wci-inc.org/
5 However, in one study command-and-control instruments were found to be the most effective in increasing renewable energy use (Park 2015).
6 The terms *official* and *unofficial* actors comes from Birkland (2016).
7 I will use the term pluralism to refer to both traditional Truman-style pluralism as well as neopluralism.
8 Data on mobilization comes from the *Encyclopedia of Associations*, available from the *Comparative Agendas Project*, and the lobbying data comes from *OpenSecrets.org*.
9 The numbers used here come from Mackinder (2010).
10 Of the 3,051 witnesses, 2,984 fit into one of the categories. The remaining 67 witnesses are excluded from the table but are included in the percent calculations.
11 Despite the scrubber requirement, a 2011 Government Accountability Office (GAO) report found that 56 percent of tall smokestacks – 500 ft or higher – used at coal plants are not using scrubbers for SO_2 and 63 percent lack control tools for NO_x (US Government Accountability Office 2011).
12 See here: www.usclimatenetwork.org/
13 However, Sierra Club support was tepid.
14 An additional source of information for Congress are reports from its agencies such as the Congressional Budget Office, the Government Accountability Office, and the Congressional Research Service (see Auer and Cox 2010).
15 Although Republicans tend to call witnesses that question the science of climate change, overall at least up until 2005, the scientific consensus has been well represented in congressional hearings (Liu et al. 2015).

References

Ackerman, Bruce, and William T. Hassler. 1981. *Clean Coal/Dirty Air: Or How the Clean Air Act Became a Multibillion-Dollar Bail-Out for High-Sulfur Coal Producers*. New Haven, CT: Yale University Press.
Anderson, James E. 2015. *Public Policymaking*. 8th ed. Stamford, CT: Cengage Learning.

Auer, Matthew R., and Michael Cox. 2010. "Appraising Climate Change Information Reported to Congress." *International Journal of Climate Change Strategies and Management* 2(2): 118–133.

Barbose, Galen. 2017. *US Renewables Portfolio Standards: 2017 Annual Status Report.* Lawrence Berkeley National Laboratory.

Barringer, Felicity. 2007. "A Coalition for Firm Limit on Emissions." *The New York Times.* www.nytimes.com/2007/01/19/business/19carbon.html.

Baumgartner, Frank R., Jeffrey M. Berry, Marie Hojnacki, David C. Kimball, and Beth L. Leech. 2009. *Lobbying and Policy Change: Who Wins, Who Loses, and Why.* Chicago, IL: University of Chicago Press.

Baumgartner, Frank R., Virginia Gray, and David Lowery. 2009. "Federal Policy Activity and the Mobilization of State Lobbying Organizations." *Political Research Quarterly* 62(3): 552–567.

Baumgartner, Frank R., and Bryan D. Jones. 1991. "Agenda Dynamics and Policy Subsystems." *The Journal of Politics* 53(4): 1044–1074.

———. 1993. *Agendas and Instability in American Politics.* Chicago, IL: University of Chicago Press.

Baumgartner, Frank R., Bryan D. Jones, and Peter B. Mortensen. 2018. "Punctuated Equilibrium Theory: Explaining Stability and Change in Public Policymaking." In *Theories of the Policy Process*, eds. Christopher M. Weible and Paul A. Sabatier. New York, NY: Westview Press, 55–102.

Baumgartner, Frank R., Heather A. Larsen-Price, Beth L. Leech, and Paul Rutledge. 2011. "Congressional and Presidential Effects on the Demand for Lobbying." *Political Research Quarterly* 64(1): 3–16.

Baumgartner, Frank R., and Beth L. Leech. 1998. *Basic Interests: The Importance of Groups in Politics and Political Science.* Princeton, NJ: Princeton University Press.

———. 2001. "Interest Niches and Policy Bandwagons: Patterns of Interest Group Involvement in National Politics." *The Journal of Politics* 63(04): 1191–1213.

Becker, Gary S. 1983. "A Theory of Competition Among Pressure Groups for Political Influence." *The Quarterly Journal of Economics* 98(3): 371–400.

Berry, Jeffrey M. 1999. *The New Liberalism: The Rising Power of Citizen Groups.* Washington, DC: Brookings Institution Press.

Birkland, Thomas A. 2016. *An Introduction to the Policy Process: Theories, Concepts, and Models of Public Policy Making.* 4th ed. New York, NY: Routledge.

Bosso, Christopher J. 2005. *Environment, Inc.: from Grassroots to Beltway.* Lawrence, KS: University Press of Kansas.

Broder, John M. 2009. "House Bill for a Carbon Tax to Cut Emissions Faces a Steep Climb." *The New York Times.* www.nytimes.com/2009/03/07/us/politics/07carbon.html.

———. 2010. "Tracing the Demise of Cap and Trade." *The New York Times.* www.nytimes.com/2010/03/26/science/earth/26climate.html.

Bromley-Trujillo, Rebecca, J.S. Butler, John Poe, and Whitney Davis. 2016. "The Spreading of Innovation: State Adoptions of Energy and Climate Change Policy." *Review of Policy Research* 33(5): 544–565.

Brulle, Robert J. 2014. "Institutionalizing Delay: Foundation Funding and the Creation of US Climate Change Counter-Movement Organizations." *Climatic Change* 122(4): 681–694.

———. 2015. "The US National Climate Change Movement." In *Changing Climate Politics: US Policies and Civic Action*, ed. Yael Wolinsky-Nahmias. Thousand Oaks, CA: CQ Press, 146–170.

————. 2018. "The Climate Lobby: A Sectoral Analysis of Lobbying Spending on Climate Change in the USA, 2000 to 2016." *Climatic Change*, forthcoming.

Brunner, Jim, and Hal Bernton. 2016. "Washington to Force State's Biggest Carbon Polluters to Cut Emissions." *The Seattle Times*. www.seattletimes.com/seattle-news/environment/washington-to-force-states-biggest-carbon-polluters-to-cut-emissions/.

California Air Resources Board. 2018. California Greenhouse Gas Emissions for 2000 to 2016: Trends of Emissions and Other Indicators.

Cheon, Andrew, and Johannes Urpelainen. 2013. "How Do Competing Interest Groups Influence Environmental Policy? The Case of Renewable Electricity in Industrialized Democracies, 1989–2007." *Political Studies* 61(4): 874–897.

Coglianese, Cary. 2007. "Business Interests and Information in Environmental Rulemaking." In *Business and Environmental Policy: Corporate Interests in the American Political System*, eds. Michael E. Kraft and Sheldon Kamieniecki. Cambridge, MA: The MIT Press, 185–210.

Daynes, Byron W., Glen Sussman, and Jonathan P. West. 2016. *American Politics and the Environment*. 2nd ed. Albany, NY: State University of New York Press.

Derthick, Martha. 2010. "Compensatory Federalism." In *Greenhouse Governance: Addressing Climate Change in America*, ed. Barry G. Rabe. Washington, DC: Brookings Institution Press, 58–72.

Dincer, Oguzhan, James E. Payne, and Kristi Simkins. 2014. "Are State Renewable Portfolio Standards Contagious?" *American Journal of Economics and Sociology* 73(2): 325–340.

Eisner, Marc Allen. 2017. *Regulatory Politics in an Age of Polarization and Drift: Beyond Deregulation*. New York, NY: Routledge.

ExxonMobil. 2018. "Learn About How ExxonMobil Works to Meet Energy Supplies in a Way That Is Environmentally Responsible." *ExxonMobil*. http://corporate.exxonmobil.comhttps://corporate.exxonmobil.com/en/current-issues/climate-policy/climate-perspectives/engagement-to-address-climate-change.

Fisher, Dana, Philip Leifeld, and Yoko Iwaki. 2013. "Mapping the Ideological Networks of American Climate Politics." *Climatic Change* 116(3): 523–545.

Freudenberg, Nicholas, and Carol Steinsapir. 1991. "Not in Our Backyards: The Grassroots Environmental Movement." *Society & Natural Resources* 4(3): 235–245.

Friends of the Earth. 2009. "Waxman-Markey Gives Big Bucks to Polluters." *Friends of the Earth*. https://foe.org/2009-06-waxman-markey-gives-big-bucks-to-polluters/.

Furlong, Scott R. 2007. "Businesses and the Environment: Influencing Agency Policymaking." In *Business and Environmental Policy: Corporate Interests in the American Political System*, eds. Michael E. Kraft and Sheldon Kamieniecki. Cambridge, MA: The MIT Press, 155–184.

Furlong, Scott R., and Cornelius M. Kerwin. 2005. "Interest Group Participation in Rule Making: A Decade of Change." *Journal of Public Administration Research Theory* 15(3): 353–370.

Gaworecki, Mike. 2009. "Why Greenpeace Can't Support Waxman-Markey." Greenpeace USA. www.greenpeace.org/usa/why-greenpeace-cant-support-waxman-markey/.

Godwin, R. Kenneth, Scott Ainsworth, and Erik K. Godwin. 2013. *Lobbying and Policymaking: The Public Pursuit of Private Interests*. Thousand Oaks, CA: CQ Press.

Golden, Marissa Martino. 1998. "Interest Groups in the Rule-Making Process: Who Participates? Whose Voices Get Heard?" *Journal of Public Administration Research and Theory* 8(2): 245–270.

Grant, Don, Kelly Bergstrand, and Katrina Running. 2014. "Effectiveness of US State Policies in Reducing CO2 Emissions from Power Plants." *Nature Climate Change* 4(11): 977–982.

Griffith, Ernest S. 1939. *The Impasse of Democracy: A Study of the Modern Government in Action*. New York, NY: Harrison Hilton Books.

Grossmann, Matt. 2012. *The Not-So-Special Interests: Interest Groups, Public Representation, and American Governance*. Stanford, California: Stanford University Press.

———. 2013. "The Variable Politics of the Policy Process: Issue-Area Differences and Comparative Networks." *The Journal of Politics* 75(01): 65–79.

Hall, Richard L., and Alan V. Deardorff. 2006. "Lobbying as Legislative Subsidy." *American Political Science Review* 100(01): 69–84.

Heclo, Hugh. 1978. "Issue Networks and the Executive Establishment." In *The New American Political System*, ed. Anthony King. Washington DC: American Enterprise Institute, 87–107.

Heinz, John P., Edward O. Laumann, Robert H. Salisbury, and Robert L. Nelson. 1990. "Inner Circles or Hollow Cores? Elite Networks in National Policy Systems." *The Journal of Politics* 52(2): 356–390.

Henry, Adam Douglas. 2011. "Ideology, Power, and the Structure of Policy Networks." *Policy Studies Journal* 39(3): 361–383.

Henry, Adam Douglas, Mark Lubell, and Michael McCoy. 2011. "Belief Systems and Social Capital as Drivers of Policy Network Structure: The Case of California Regional Planning." *Journal of Public Administration Research and Theory* 21(3): 419–444.

Holt, Mark, and Carol Glover. 2006. *Energy Policy Act of 2005: Summary and Analysis of Enacted Provisions*. Congressional Research Service.

Ingram, Helen M., and Dean E. Mann. 1989. "Interest Groups and Environmental Policy." In *Environmental Politics and Policy: Theories and Evidence*, ed. James P. Lester. Durham, NC: Duke University Press, 135–157.

Jenkins-Smith, Hank C. 1988. "Analytical Debates and Policy Learning: Analysis and Change in the Federal Bureaucracy." *Policy Sciences* 21(2): 169–211.

———. 1990. *Democratic Politics and Policy Analysis*. Pacific Grove, CA: Brooks/Cole Publishing Company.

Jenkins-Smith, Hank C., Daniel Nohrstedt, Christopher M. Weible, and Karin Ingold. 2018. "The Advocacy Coalition Framework: An Overview of the Research Program." In *Theories of the Policy Process*, eds. Christopher M. Weible and Paul A. Sabatier. New York, NY: Westview Press, 135–172.

Jenkins-Smith, Hank C., and Paul A. Sabatier. 1993. "The Dynamics of Policy-Oriented Learning." In *Policy Change and Learning: An Advocacy Coalition Approach*, eds. Paul A. Sabatier and Hank C. Jenkins-Smith. Boulder, CO: Westview Press, 41–56.

Jochim, Ashley E., and Peter J. May. 2010. "Beyond Subsystems: Policy Regimes and Governance." *Policy Studies Journal* 38(2): 303–327.

Johnson, Erik W., and Scott Frickel. 2011. "Ecological Threat and the Founding of US National Environmental Movement Organizations, 1962–1998." *Social Problems* 58(3): 305–329.

Jones, Michael D., and Hank C. Jenkins-Smith. 2009. "Trans-Subsystem Dynamics: Policy Topography, Mass Opinion, and Policy Change." *Policy Studies Journal* 37(1): 37–58.

Karapin, Roger. 2016. *Political Opportunities for Climate Policy: California, New York, and the Federal Government*. Cambridge: Cambridge University Press.

———. 2018. "Not Waiting for Washington: Climate Policy Adoption in California and New York." *Political Science Quarterly* 133(2): 317–353.

Keller, Ann Campbell. 2009. *Science in Environmental Policy: The Politics of Objective Advice*. Cambridge, MA: The MIT Press.

Keohane, Robert O., and David G. Victor. 2011. "The Regime Complex for Climate Change." *Perspectives on Politics* 9(1): 7–23.

Knox-Hayes, Janelle. 2012. "Negotiating Climate Legislation: Policy Path Dependence and Coalition Stabilization." *Regulation & Governance* 6(4): 545–567.

Kukkonen, Anna, Tuomas Ylä-Anttila, and Jeffrey Broadbent. 2017. "Advocacy Coalitions, Beliefs and Climate Change Policy in the United States." *Public Administration* 95(3): 713–729.

LaPira, Timothy M. 2014. "Lobbying After 9/11: Policy Regime Emergence and Interest Group Mobilization." *Policy Studies Journal* 42(2): 226–251.

Leech, Beth L., Frank R. Baumgartner, Timothy M. LaPira, and Nicholas A. Semanko. 2005. "Drawing Lobbyists to Washington: Government Activity and the Demand for Advocacy." *Political Research Quarterly* 58(1): 19–30.

Liu, Xinsheng, Arnold Vedlitz, James W. Stoutenborough, and Scott Robinson. 2015. "Scientists' Views and Positions on Global Warming and Climate Change: A Content Analysis of Congressional Testimonies." *Climatic Change* 131(4): 487–503.

Lochbaum, Dave. 2017. *The Nuclear Regulatory Commission and Safety Culture: Do as I Say, Not as I Do.* Union of Concerned Scientists. www.ucsusa.org/sites/default/files/attach/2017/02/NRC-Safety-Culture.pdf.

Lowery, David, and Virginia Gray. 2004. "A Neopluralist Perspective on Research on Organized Interests." *Political Research Quarterly* 57(1): 163–175.

Lutsey, Nicholas, and Daniel Sperling. 2008. "America's Bottom-up Climate Change Mitigation Policy." *Energy Policy* 36(2): 673–685.

Mackinder, Evan. 2010. "Pro-Environment Groups Outmatched, Outspent in Battle over Climate Change Legislation." OpenSecrets Blog. www.opensecrets.org/news/2010/08/pro-environment-groups-were-outmatc/.

Matisoff, Daniel C. 2008. "The Adoption of State Climate Change Policies and Renewable Portfolio Standards: Regional Diffusion or Internal Determinants?" *Review of Policy Research* 25(6): 527–546.

May, Peter J., and Ashley E. Jochim. 2013. "Policy Regime Perspectives: Policies, Politics, and Governing." *Policy Studies Journal* 41(3): 426–452.

May, Peter J., Ashley E. Jochim, and Joshua Sapotichne. 2011. "Constructing Homeland Security: An Anemic Policy Regime." *Policy Studies Journal* 39(2): 285–307.

May, Peter J., Joshua Sapotichne, and Samuel Workman. 2006. "Policy Coherence and Policy Domains." *Policy Studies Journal* 34(3): 381–403.

McCool, Daniel. 1998. "The Subsystem Family of Concepts: A Critique and a Proposal." *Political Research Quarterly* 51(2): 551–570.

McCright, Aaron M., and Riley E. Dunlap. 2003. "Defeating Kyoto: The Conservative Movement's Impact on US Climate Change Policy." *Social Problems* 50(3): 348–373.

Midwestern Accord Advisory Group. 2009. *Midwestern Energy Security and Climate Stewardship Roadmap: 2009.* Midwestern Governors Association. http://climatechange.lta.org/wp-content/uploads/cct/2018/03/MidwesternRoadmap.pdf.

Mintrom, Michael, and Phillipa Norman. 2009. "Policy Entrepreneurship and Policy Change." *Policy Studies Journal* 37(4): 649–667.

Nowlin, Matthew C. 2016. "Policy Change, Policy Feedback, and Interest Mobilization: The Politics of Nuclear Waste Management." *Review of Policy Research* 33(1): 51–70.

Olson, Mancur. 1965. *The Logic of Collective Action: Public Goods and the Theory of Groups.* Cambridge, MA: Harvard University Press.

Ostrom, Elinor. 2009. "Polycentric Systems as One Approach to Solving Collective-Action Problems." In *Climate Change and Sustainable Development: New Challenges for Poverty Reduction*, ed. M.A. Mohamed Salih. Edward Elgar Publishing, 17–35.

———. 2010. "Polycentric Systems for Coping with Collective Action and Global Environmental Change." *Global Environmental Change* 20(4): 550–557.

Ostrom, Vincent. 1999. "Polycentricity (Parts 1 and 2)." In *Polycentricity and Local Public Economies: Readings from the Workshop in Political Theory and Policy Analysis*, Ann Arbor, MI: University of Michigan Press, 52–74; 119–138.

Park, Hyung Sam, Xinsheng Liu, and Arnold Vedlitz. 2014. "Analyzing Climate Change Debates in the US Congress: Party Control and Mobilizing Networks." *Risk, Hazards & Crisis in Public Policy* 5(3): 239–258.

Park, Sunjoo. 2015. "State Renewable Energy Governance: Policy Instruments, Markets, or Citizens." *Review of Policy Research* 32(3): 273–296.

Pielke, Roger A. 2007. *The Honest Broker: Making Sense of Science in Policy and Politics*. Cambridge: Cambridge University Press.

Pooley, Eric. 2010. *The Climate War: True Believers, Power Brokers, and the Fight to Save the Earth*. New York, NY: Hachette Books.

———. 2013. "Why the Climate Bill Failed: It's Not That Simple." Grist. https://grist.org/climate-energy/why-the-climate-bill-failed-its-not-that-simple/.

Rabe, Barry G. 2016. "The Durability of Carbon Cap-and-Trade Policy." *Governance* 29(1): 103–119.

———. 2018. *Can We Price Carbon?* Cambridge, MA: The MIT Press.

Redford, Emmette S. 1969. *Democracy in the Administrative State*. Oxford: Oxford University Press.

Regional Greenhouse Gas Initiative, Inc. 2017. The Investment of RGGI Proceeds in 2015. www.rggi.org/sites/default/files/Uploads/Proceeds/RGGI_Proceeds_Report_2015.pdf.

Rugeley, Cynthia R., and John David Gerlach. 2012. "Understanding Environmental Public Opinion by Dimension: How Heuristic Processing Mitigates High Information Costs on Complex Issues." *Politics & Policy* 40(3): 444–470.

Sabatier, Paul A., and Hank C. Jenkins-Smith. 1993. *Policy Change and Learning: An Advocacy Coalition Approach*. Boulder, CO: Westview Press.

Salisbury, Robert H. 1969. "An Exchange Theory of Interest Groups." *Midwest Journal of Political Science* 13(1): 1–32.

Schattschneider, E.E. 1960. *The Semi-Sovereign People: A Realist's View of Democracy in America*. New York, NY: Holt, Rinehart and Winston.

Scheberle, Denise. 2013. "Environmental Federalism and the Role of State and Local Governments." In *The Oxford Handbook of US Environmental Policy*, eds. Sheldon Kamieniecki and Michael E. Kraft. Oxford: Oxford University Press, 394–412.

Schwartz, John. 2017. "'A Conservative Climate Solution': Republican Group Calls for Carbon Tax." *The New York Times*. www.nytimes.com/2017/02/07/science/a-conservative-climate-solution-republican-group-calls-for-carbon-tax.html.

Skocpol, Theda. 2013a. "Naming the Problem: What It Will Take to Counter Extremism and Engage Americans in the Fight Against Global Warming." ClimateAccess.org.

———. 2013b. "You Can't Change the Climate from Inside Washington." Foreign Policy. https://foreignpolicy.com/2013/01/24/you-cant-change-the-climate-from-inside-washington/ (September 25, 2017).

Smith, Adam, and Bruce Yandle. 2014. *Bootleggers and Baptists: How Economic Forces and Moral Persuasion Interact to Shape Regulatory Politics*. Washington, DC: Cato Institute.

Smith, Mark A. 2000. *American Business and Political Power*. Chicago, IL: University of Chicago Press.

Stigler, George J. 1971. "The Theory of Economic Regulation." *The Bell Journal of Economics and Management Science* 2(1): 3–21.

The Center for Responsive Politics. "Lobbying Spending Database – US Climate Action Partnership, 2010." OpenSecrets. www.opensecrets.org/lobby/clientsum.php?id=D000058047\&year=2010.

Thurber, James A. 1996. "Political Power and Policy Subsystems in American Politics." In *Agenda for Excellence: Administering the State*, eds. B. Guy Peters and Bert A. Rockman. Chatham, NJ: Chatham House, 76–104.

Truman, David B. 1951. *The Governmental Process: Political Interests and Public Opinion.* New York, NY: Knopf.

Upton Jr., Gregory B., and Brian F. Snyder. 2015. "Renewable Energy Potential and Adoption of Renewable Portfolio Standards." *Utilities Policy* 36: 67–70.

USCAP. 2007. *A Call for Action.* United States Climate Action Partnership. www.merid. org/~/media/Files/Projects/USCAP/USCAP-A-Call-for-Action.

———. 2009. *A Blueprint for Legislative Action.* United States Climate Action Partnership. www.merid.org/~/media/Files/Projects/USCAP/USCAP-A-Blueprint-for-Legislative-Action.

US Government Accountability Office. 2011. *Air Quality: Information on Tall Smokestacks and Their Contribution to Interstate Transport of Air Pollution.* www.gao.gov/products/GAO-11–473.

Vasseur, Michael. 2016. "Incentives or Mandates? Determinants of the Renewable Energy Policies of US States, 1970–2012." *Social Problems* 63(2): 284–301.

Walker, Jack L. 1983. "The Origins and Maintenance of Interest Groups in America." *The American Political Science Review* 77(2): 390–406.

Walsh, Bryan. 2007. "US States Sign Global Warming Pact." *Time.* http://content.time.com/time/health/article/0,8599,1684745,00.html.

Weber, Christopher. 2018. "California Meets Greenhouse Gas Reduction Goal Years Early." AP News. www.apnews.com/942b5a251fac413a84fc4eb93a67c46c.

Weible, Christopher M. 2005. "Beliefs and Perceived Influence in a Natural Resource Conflict: An Advocacy Coalition Approach to Policy Networks." *Political Research Quarterly* 58(3): 461–475.

———. 2008. "Expert-Based Information and Policy Subsystems: A Review and Synthesis." *Policy Studies Journal* 36(4): 615–635.

Weible, Christopher M., and Paul A. Sabatier. 2005. "Comparing Policy Networks: Marine Protected Areas in California." *Policy Studies Journal* 33(2): 181–201.

Whitford, Andrew B. 2003. "The Structures of Interest Coalitions: Evidence from Environmental Litigation." *Business and Politics* 5(1): 45.

Wilson, James Q. 1982. "The Politics of Regulation." In *The Politics of Regulation*, Basic Books, 357–394.

Witko, Christopher. 2006. "PACs, Issue Context, and Congressional Decisionmaking." *Political Research Quarterly* 59(2): 283–295.

Workman, Samuel. 2015. *The Dynamics of Bureaucracy in the US Government: How Congress and Federal Agencies Process Information and Solve Problems.* Cambridge: Cambridge University Press.

Workman, Samuel, and JoBeth S. Shafran. 2015. "Communications Frameworks and the Supply of Information in Policy Subsystems." In *Policy Paradigms in Theory and Practice, Studies in the Political Economy of Public Policy*, eds. John Hogan and Michael Howlett. Palgrave Macmillan UK, 239–267.

Worsham, Jeff. 1998. "Wavering Equilibriums: Subsystem Dynamics and Agenda Control." *American Politics Research* 26(4): 485–512.

Yackee, Jason Webb, and Susan Webb Yackee. 2006. "A Bias Towards Business? Assessing Interest Group Influence on the US Bureaucracy." *The Journal of Politics* 68(01): 128–139.

Yandle, Bruce. 1998. Bootleggers, Baptists, and Global Warming. https://www.researchgate. net/profile/William_Sutherland/publication/32022720_Global_warming/links/ 02e7e53496db2607c2000000.pdf.

Yi, Hongtao, and Richard C. Feiock. 2015. "Climate Action Plan Adoptions in the US States." *International Journal of Climate Change Strategies and Management* 7(3): 375–393.

Zafonte, Matthew, and Paul A. Sabatier. 1998. "Shared Beliefs and Imposed Interdependencies as Determinants of Ally Networks in Overlapping Subsystems." *Journal of Theoretical Politics* 10(4): 473–505.

8

CONCLUSION

How should the environment and natural resources be managed? That is the central question of environmental policy and governance. The United States has a market-based economy and a political culture built on personal liberty and the free market, and therefore the default position is a reliance on market forces to address the proper distribution and management of resources, including natural resources. However, in some circumstances and with some types of goods, markets on their own fail to achieve optimal results. Given the nature of environmental issues that involve externalities, common-pool goods, and public goods, markets often produce sub-optimal outcomes. When this occurs, the public sector, which includes governments at all levels, is brought in to achieve the results that society prefers.

Once the public sector is engaged, environmental policy choices are made through a complex environmental policymaking process that takes inputs in the form of information signals from the social, economic, and natural environment and, through the environmental policymaking system, transforms those inputs into policy outputs. The environmental policymaking system includes the macro-institutions of Congress, the executive branch, and the judiciary, as well as the various policy subsystems that are structured by subunits of the macro-institutions around specific policy issues. Environmental policy change and development happens as a result of changes in one or more of the information streams, coupled with factors operating within the environmental policymaking system that can hamper or expedite policy change. Often the system either over- or under-reacts to information signals, which creates system outputs that produce no change, incremental change, or large, punctuated change that shifts subsystem dynamics into a new equilibrium.

The development of the modern green state largely occurred during the environmentalism era, which lasted from 1962 to 1980. The environmentalism era developed, in part, as a result of changes in the problem information stream, such as the publication of *Silent Spring*, visible smog in several major cities, the Santa Barbara oil spill, the Cuyahoga River fire, and the *Earthrise* photograph, as well as changes in the politics information stream, including the first Earth Day and strong public support for environmental protection. Within the environmental policymaking system at the time, the overwhelming strength of the information signals, coupled with bipartisan support for addressing environmental problems and an overall confidence in the ability of government to address problems, led to a shift in the equilibrium of several environmental policy-related subsystems and the creation of the green state. The thickening of the green state occurred as legislation passed, executive agency rules went into force, and judicial decisions were made that all worked to codify and define the contours of the green state. The major policy instruments employed as part of the green state are command-and-control instruments such as performance or technology standards. However, as the environmentalism era gave way to the reform era, the use of market-based instruments – using markets and creating markets – became more prevalent.

The reform era arose at a time that skepticism about the ability of governments to address societal problems generally, as well as skepticism about the efficacy of the command-and-control instruments of the green state more specifically, became conventional wisdom. In addition, by the mid-1990s partisan polarization on environmental issues begin to solidify. Together these two trends combine to create additional friction within the environmental policy system, which makes addressing pressing environmental problems such as climate change more difficult.

The skepticism that brought about the reform era and the subsequent rise in polarization added further friction to the already contentious nature of environmental policy and politics. Environmental policy conflicts have traditionally been shaped by values, issue definitions, property-rights, and the politics associated with regulatory policies. In addition, the diffuse nature of the macro-institutions policymaking creates a status-quo bias, which makes policy change difficult. Finally, environmental issues include a host of collective-action problems such as shirking and free-riding. All of these factors combine to make all environmental issues particularly challenging for societies to address, although climate change has several challenges of its own in addition to those listed above. Next, I conclude the book with some thoughts on the important factors that will shape the future of climate governance.

The Future of Climate Change Governance in the United States

At the end of 2015 a clear path was set for the world to begin to address climate change. Virtually every country in the world agreed in Paris that climate change was occurring and changes were necessary in order to mitigate some of its potential impacts. In the United States, greenhouse gas emissions from the utility sector were trending downward, and with the Clean Power Plan the United States had developed a framework for continuing to ratchet down emissions from the electric power sector. In addition, the Obama administration had put a series of actions in place that could potentially reduce GHG emissions, including developing a social cost of carbon measure to use in benefit-cost analysis, reducing emissions from federal agencies, protecting large swaths of land and ocean areas from coal, oil, and gas extraction, and developed fuel efficiency standards that would reduce transportation-related emissions, the current leader in US emissions. It appeared that the story of environmental policy in the United States was going to continue as it had already done, with slow and halting yet steady progress – a green drift – in the face of a still-present desire among some for retrenchment on environmental issues. It even appeared that slow and steady progress was being made on addressing climate change, although likely not to the degree that is required and likely not without further challenges.

The election of Donald Trump in 2016 has halted much of the climate policy progress in the executive branch that the United States seemed to be making. Almost immediately, the Trump administration began to undo many of the executive actions on climate change initiated during the Obama administration, as well as removing the United States from its emission-reduction pledge under the Paris Agreement. In addition, the EPA, first under the leadership of Scott Pruitt and then Andrew Wheeler, has sought to alter regulations such as the Clean Power Plan and the vehicle emissions standards to make them less stringent. Despite the lack of policy progress, the emissions of greenhouse gases in the United States has been trending down, largely because of increased use of natural gas and renewable sources of electricity. Figure 8.1 shows the emissions of GHGs in CO_2e in the United States from 1990 to 2016 by sector.[1]

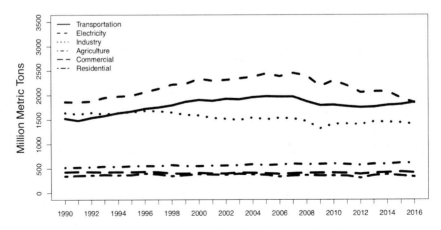

FIGURE 8.1 US emissions of CO_2 equivalents by sector, 1990–2016

As can be seen, emissions from the electricity generating sector – the leading sector in emissions from 1990 to 2015 – peaked in 2007 and have been trending downward since. The transportation sector, the third highest emitter in 1990, is now the leading producer of GHG emissions and is trending upward. Industry emissions are the third most prevalent source of emissions, but have been trending downward since 1997. The remaining sectors of agriculture and commercial and residential real-estate have been trending down as well. Even with the progress of emission reductions from the power sector, the United States will need some policies in place to further reduce emissions. Next, I discuss several important factors that are likely to influence the potential for climate policy development over the next several years.

Polarization: any discussion of climate change policy and governance would have to begin with polarization. Polarization involves the value-based differences in opinion regarding policy issues among both elites and the public. These values can include core values such as political ideology and culture as well as environmental values, yet polarization is largely recognized as being between the two major political parties because of the importance of political parties in public opinion formation and political organizing. With regard to environmental issues, polarization has increased markedly in the two last decades and, as discussed in Chapter 4, this increase is likely due, in part, to a value-based aversion to the command-and-control type policy instruments that are the hallmark of the green state. As the dominant frame for environmental issues became the trade-off between economic growth and the environment, polarization increased. For climate change, that frame seemingly worked to solidify polarization between the parties, beginning during the debate over the Kyoto Protocol, and polarization has continued to harden over time, particularly among political elites.

Typically, the focus of discussions of polarization impacts are on the outputs, or lack thereof, of the environmental policymaking system, although, as shown in Chapter 5, polarization has also impacted the likelihood that the system responds to significant changes in the problem stream. Previous research had shown that, up until 2005, climate change was likely to reach the congressional agenda in response to changes in information related to problems such as focusing events, scientific publications, and net increases in atmospheric CO_2 (Liu, Lindquist, and Vedlitz 2011). However, extending this analysis to 2016 showed that the only factor related to climate change being on the congressional agenda was the party that held the majority in Congress. As a result of polarization, the environmental policymaking system is becoming increasingly less responsive, not only with regard to addressing problems through policy but also with regard to issues even reaching the agenda.

An additional impact of polarization is the lessening of the capacity of executive branch agencies such as the EPA to carry out their duties as prescribed by law. As shown in Chapter 6, the budget of the EPA is a function of party control of Congress and the presidency. On average, the budget of the EPA increases during periods of unified Democratic control of the electoral institutions as well as in response to public support for increased environmental protections. With the increasing polarization of Congress and the subsequent lack of legislation to address many pressing problems, policy development is likely to move more to the executive branch pathway. However, even as that happens, polarization may undermine the capacity of executive branch agencies to develop and implement policy.

As noted, the growth of polarization is likely a result of solution-aversion to standard environmental policy instruments, although, and somewhat paradoxically, polarization and the resulting gridlock have led to less new policy ideas being developed or tried at the federal level. The reform era brought an increased interest in the use of market-based policy instruments to address environmental issues as opposed to command-and-control instruments. However, polarization was a large part of the reason for the failure of cap-and-trade legislation – a creating markets type of policy instrument that has historically been supported by conservatives – being successful in Congress, despite multiple attempts between 2003 and 2010.

The American Clean Energy and Security Act (ACES) was the major legislative vehicle for a federal cap-and-trade program. The ACES passed the House, although companion legislation was not successful in the Senate. As shown in Chapters 5, 6, and 7, the failure to address climate change through policy action generally is a result of framing, institutional veto points, interest group activities, and the difficulties of coalition-building. Each of these factors creates friction in the environmental policymaking system, and each contributed to the inability of Congress to pass the ACES. In addition, the impact of each is exacerbated by polarization. As examples, the impacts of framing are amplified in their ability to mobilize when actors are polarized; institutional veto points when controlled by the opposite party become more difficult to navigate; interest group lobbying and campaign contributions become more one-sided as environmental issues become increasingly polarized; and coalition-building across parties or across interest groups that align with a particular party becomes much less likely.

The clearest and most often discussed impact of polarization is an increased likelihood of gridlock, or an inability of the environmental policymaking system to address important problems through policy initiatives. However, polarization has also increased the already-present friction that exists in the system. Polarization makes it less likely that the system responds to changes in strong information signals, it undermines the capacity of executive branch agencies, and amplifies the effects of framing, veto points, interest groups, and coalitions.

Polarization on climate and other environmental issues shows no sign of lessening. Therefore, moving forward on climate policy at the federal level is likely only to occur during periods of unified Democratic control or a Democratic president that uses executive branch policy pathways in ways that are allowed by the courts. However, policies that would have climate benefits but are not as polarized, such as supports for expanding renewable energy, may be possible regardless of the partisan make-up of the electoral institutions.

Mobilization: the mobilization of policy actors, including both elite actors and the public, is a major element of the feedback process in environmental policy-making. Mobilization of new actors seeking policy change can create positive feedback that can then cascade and create instability within a policy subsystem or regime. A counter-mobilization of policy actors may occur in response, which can produce negative feedback that works to provide system stability. One factor of a stable equilibrium in a policy subsystem is a balance between mobilization and counter-mobilization. In addition, the thermostatic nature of public opinion that shifts as a result of government actions is another example of the mobilization and counter-mobilization dynamic. The thermostatic dynamic of public opinion was evidenced by increased support for environmental spending in response to attempts at retrenchment in the early 1980s, as shown in Chapter 4.

The environmental movement of the 1960s and 1970s was a major mobilization of actors both inside and outside the environmental policymaking system that made the creation of the green state possible. Since then, activists and other policy entrepreneurs have been trying to recreate a similar public mobilization around environmental issues generally, and climate change in particular. Mobilizing the public around environmental issues is a difficult task because, as shown in Chapter 5, a majority of the public is generally concerned about environmental issues and climate change, but they are much more concerned about other issues. Therefore, mobilizing the public to vote or contact their elected representatives about climate change is difficult. This dynamic is compounded by the fact that, for most people, the expected negative impacts of climate change appear distant in terms of both time and space, whereas other concerns such as healthcare, education, the economy, and the price of energy are present now.

As concern about climate change has risen in the last couple of decades, one of the major vehicles of mobilization has been communicating the scientific consensus regarding the causes and potential consequences of climate change to both elite policy actors and the public. However, the evidence is mixed regarding the effectiveness of the climate consensus message on mobilization. As discussed in Chapter 4, value-based cognition influences the ways in which both public and elite actors view contentious issues, and higher levels of sophistication can serve to further polarize. As a result, knowledgeable (in terms of political knowledge or scientific knowledge) conservatives become generally less likely to accept climate change than less sophisticated conservatives. In addition, a counter-mobilization of interests has worked to create doubt regarding the scientific consensus, and those efforts have been reasonably successful, particularly among those ideologically predisposed to reject government regulatory efforts. Despite the questions surrounding the effectiveness of the consensus message to mobilize actors to address climate change on its own, it has to be part of the overall message that is meant to communicate the seriousness of climate change. The scientific consensus is strong and is indicating increasing urgency.

A large part of attempts to mobilize are connected to framing issues in a way to motivate action. Recently, advocates are discussing natural hazards and events in the context of climate change. Framing a potential focusing event as a result of climate change can be an effective way to draw attention to and motivate action on climate change. This is likely to become increasingly potent as the science of attribution improves such that scientists are better able to link the probabilities associated with events and/or their severity to climate change, and as such events become more common in the future. Droughts, floods, heatwaves, and wildfires are all expected to become more common and more severe as a result of climate change, and hurricanes are likely to be stronger and the impacts of storm surge due to sea-level rise are likely to become more devastating as a result of climate change. Changes in weather patterns such as increased temperatures have been shown to impact the public's view on climate change (Egan and Mullin 2012) as have floods (Demski et al. 2017), and superstorm Sandy (Rudman, McLean, and Bunzl 2013). Therefore, connecting the probability of these events to climate change may increase the likelihood of public mobilization. However, the effects of weather events on public views about climate change seem to be relatively short-lived (Konisky, Hughes, and Kaylor 2016), and therefore might not alone be sufficient grounds for extended public mobilization.

The election of Trump has seen a movement away from addressing climate change, such as the stated intention to withdraw from the Paris Agreement; however, the election and the subsequent actions of the Trump administration have mobilized other actors to engage on climate. The group *We Are Still In* – made up of mayors, governors, and business leaders that remain committed to the US goals in the Paris Agreement – grew in response to Trump's announced intention to withdraw the United States from the climate agreement (see We Are Still In 2018). Additionally, other groups, such as the *Citizens Climate Lobby*, are working to organize efforts around building political support for market-based instruments.

Effective mobilization on climate change would likely need to balance an emphasis on the scientific consensus, the evidence that suggests some impacts of climate change are already occurring, and a set of policy solutions that appeal to multiple actors.

The Endangerment Finding: the EPA's 2009 endangerment finding states that CO_2 and other greenhouse gases were a pollutant under the Clean Air Act. The endangerment finding followed from the *Massachusetts v. EPA* case that was brought against the W. Bush-era EPA. The endangerment finding creates a legal obligation for the federal government to regulate GHG. The Clean Power Plan was developed to address that requirement, and the replacement American Clean Energy (ACE) rule is as well. However, the ACE proposes to reduce emissions only through efficiency improvements.

Because of the requirement to regulate that it entails, the endangerment finding has been criticized by conservatives and others less concerned about climate change. For example, Senator Inhofe (R–OK) in an August 2018 press release praising the ACE rule stated, "I maintain that the best course of action remains to completely overturn the endangerment finding so that there is neither statutory nor legal need for any greenhouse gas regulations. I will continue to work with President Trump and Acting Administrator Wheeler toward this goal" (Inhofe 2018). However, the EPA under the Trump administration has yet to attempt to undo the endangerment finding despite the urging of some conservative advocates. The endangerment finding is a critical component for the future of climate policy, particularly for the executive agencies' policymaking pathways.

The Courts: the courts have played a key role in environmental policymaking, and this is in part by design, as several of the major pieces of legislation that formed the green state (e.g., the Clean Air Act and the Clean Water Act) included provisions that gave individuals power to sue industries and governments for pollution. With regard to climate policy, the courts have been the only macro-institution to address climate policy in a lasting way, given that the executive branch efforts developed by the Obama administration have been repealed or undermined by the Trump administration. Of note is the *Massachusetts* Supreme Court decision that compelled action by the EPA on greenhouse gas regulation.

While the Supreme Court determined that greenhouse gases can be regulated under the Clean Air Act, the court has yet to rule on the Clean Power Plan and the fate of the CPP in the courts is unclear. The *Massachusetts* decision was a 5–4 split with Justice Anthony Kennedy providing the key swing vote. The retirement of Justice Kennedy will likely lead to a shift on the court in a more conservative direction, particularly with regard to regulatory questions. One potential outcome of the rightward shift of the court is a reversal of *Massachusetts*, where the court rules that greenhouse gases are not a pollutant under the Clean Air Act. A more likely outcome is that a conservative court limits the Clean Power Plan, or a similar future plan, with regard to the beyond-the-fenceline approach of developing standards for states as opposed to facilities. Additionally, courts are likely to decide the adequacy of the Trump administration's American Clean Energy rule with regard to the regulation of greenhouse gases. Other issues that the courts may consider include several lawsuits brought by states, cities, and children that are aimed at the fossil-fuel industry as well as governments. With the growth of climate litigation and the polarized nature of the electoral institutions, the courts are the most likely macro-institution climate pathway of the near future.

Polycentricity: polycentricity – multiple centers of decision-making authority across various levels of government – is a key feature of international, national, and sub-national climate governance. The essence of polycentricity is an absence of a central regulatory body that governs in a top-down fashion. As defined by Ostrom (2012), "A polycentric system exists when multiple public and private organizations at multiple scales jointly affect collective benefits and costs" (355). Given the scientific and political complexities of climate change, as well as the associated collective-action problems, a polycentric approach to climate governance at both the international level and in the United States may be the most likely path of greenhouse gas emission reductions (see Ostrom 2009; Cole 2011, 2015).

At the international level, the Paris Agreement represented a polycentric, bottom-up approach, with each country determining its own emission reduction targets as opposed to emissions targets being developed by an international body and then imposed on a country. The bottom-up approach of the Paris Agreement seemed to help overcome some of the sticking points of previous international climate agreements, thereby allowing nearly every country to sign up to the agreement and commit to a pledge-and-review process every five years. The pledge-and-review process creates a "transparency framework," where the implementation of each country's reduction targets is monitored and adjustments are encouraged (Jacoby, Chen, and Flannery 2017). However, even if each country meets its current obligations, we are still not likely to reach the goal of keeping temperature increases below 2°C, and it's not clear yet how successful the pledge-and-review process will be in encouraging countries to reduce emissions further. In addition, the withdrawal and lack of leadership by the United States is also likely to hamper progress, particularly with regard to climate-financing meant to assist countries with developing economies (Urpelainen and Graaf 2017).

In the United States, the various subsystems and levels of government within the environmental policymaking system create multiple points where climate change may be addressed, absent a top-down federal policy. With regard to the United States, a polycentric approach may be advantageous, given that the macro-institutions, and the general green state, may not be able to adequately address climate change (see Rosenbaum 2010; Rabe 2010). In addition, the current political environment and the potential shift in the Supreme Court likely present the greatest opportunity for retrenchment on environmental issues since the environmentalism era began, making the likelihood of a concerted effort by the macro-institutions to address climate change highly unlikely in the near future.

As shown in Chapter 7, the climate policy regime in the United States is largely centered around the energy, environment, and science dimensions, with those dimensions being the most discussed at the federal level and the most addressed by policies at the state level. Some of those state policies, particularly the Renewable Portfolio Standards (RPS), played a role in the reduction of emissions from the electricity-producing sector shown in Figure 8.1, in the absence of any federal policy. The effectiveness of RPS, coupled with the mobilization of state and local governments in response to Trump's threat to withdraw the United States from the Paris Agreement, point to the need to understand climate governance in the United States in the context of polycentricity.

While policy played some role in emission reductions, market forces, such as the falling price of natural gas due to hydraulic fracturing and the falling prices of renewable energy sources, likely played a larger role. In addition, several large private corporations such as Walmart, Apple, Microsoft, and Google, among others, have all committed to reducing their greenhouse gas emissions (Vandenbergh and Gilligan 2017). Indeed, private sector innovation and technological development will likely be needed to remove some of the CO_2 and other greenhouse gases that have already been emitted if we are going to be successful in avoiding the worst-case scenarios of climate change. A polycentric approach encourages all levels of government and the private sector to be engaged.

One concern about polycentricity is that some states or cities will not take any steps to reduce their emissions absent some federally mandated requirement. This is a valid concern, as states whose economies depend on the production and/or use of fossil fuels will not be likely to act to reduce emissions. However, polycentricity differs from compensatory federalism, where state and local actions are needed to compensate for the lack of federal action. For a polycentric approach to be fully effective, some federal policy will need to be in place to avoid a race to the bottom in emissions standards. However, any federal approach should retain maximum flexibility to allow regions, states, and cities to adopt policies specific to their needs and preferences. Using markets approaches such as tax incentives and subsidies are one way to incentivize behavior change in a flexible way, and such approaches may create positive feedbacks, where private sector actors become more supportive of policies aimed at further emissions reductions (see Meckling et al. 2015). In addition, performance standards such as those developed under the Clean Power Plan – which would have required states to meet specific carbon reduction targets, although states were able to develop their own emission reductions plans that met the specified target – are also a way for the federal government to encourage emission reductions without command-and-control technology standards. With the Endangerment Finding in place, the legal framework exists to structure a Clean Power Plan-style performance standard to encourage states to meet emission reduction goals. However, such an approach is only likely to occur under a Democratic president and it will likely need to survive scrutiny from a more conservative Supreme Court.

A final advantage to polycentricity is that is allows learning to take place across actors and the various levels of government. As noted by Ostrom (2010),

> Each unit within a polycentric system exercises considerable independence to make norms and rules within a specific domain (such as a family, a firm, a local government, a network of local governments, a state or province, a region, a national government, or an international regime). Participants in a polycentric system have the advantage of using local knowledge and learning from others who are also engaged in trial-and-error learning processes. As larger units get involved, problems associated with non-contributors, local tyrants, and inappropriate discrimination can be addressed and major investments made in new scientific information and

innovations. No governance system is perfect, but polycentric systems have considerable advantages given their mechanisms for mutual monitoring, learning, and adaptation of better strategies over time (552).

The challenge of climate change is one of staggering complexity with incredibly high stakes. Mitigating and adapting to the changes we are likely to see will require some actions on the part of all parts of society, including all levels of government, private actors, and individuals. The potential for action is there, the tools of the green state are there, and a seemingly growing willingness of actors at multiple levels of government as well as the private sector to act is there as well. The longer we wait, the more drastic action will be needed, and the more costs will be incurred.

Speaking at the 15th Conference of the Parties in Copenhagen in 2009, President Obama stated that,

> Unchecked, climate change will pose unacceptable risks to our security, our economies, and our planet. This much we know. So the question before us is no longer the nature of the challenge. The question is our capacity to meet it. For while the reality of climate change is not in doubt, I have to be honest. I think our ability to take collective action is in doubt right now.
>
> *Pooley 2010, 430*

That doubt remains ever-present.

Note

1 Data is from the EPA US Greenhouse Gas Inventory. $CO_2e = CO_2$ equivalent, which is a measure that standardizes all greenhouse gas emissions in terms of the equivalent amount of CO_2 that would have the same impact on climate change.

References

Cole, Daniel H. 2011. "From Global to Polycentric Climate Governance." *Climate Law* 2(3): 395–413.

———. 2015. "Advantages of a Polycentric Approach to Climate Change Policy." *Nature Climate Change* 5(2): 114–118.

Demski, Christina, Stuart Capstick, Nick Pidgeon, Robert Gennaro Sposato, and Alexa Spence. 2017. "Experience of Extreme Weather Affects Climate Change Mitigation and Adaptation Responses." *Climatic Change* 140(2): 149–164.

Egan, Patrick J., and Megan Mullin. 2012. "Turning Personal Experience into Political Attitudes: The Effect of Local Weather on Americans' Perceptions About Global Warming." *The Journal of Politics* 74(03): 796–809.

Inhofe, James. 2018. "Inhofe Statement on Trump Administration Rollback of Obama Climate Rule: US Senator for Oklahoma." The official US Senate website of

Senator James M. Inhofe of Oklahoma. www.inhofe.senate.gov/newsroom/press-releases/inhofe-statement-on-trump-administration-rollback-of-obama-climate-rule?wpisrc=nl_energy202\&wpmm=1.

Jacoby, Henry D., Y.-H. Henry Chen, and Brian P. Flannery. 2017. "Informing Transparency in the Paris Agreement: The Role of Economic Models." *Climate Policy* 17(7): 873–890.

Konisky, David M., Llewelyn Hughes, and Charles H. Kaylor. 2016. "Extreme Weather Events and Climate Change Concern." *Climatic Change* 134(4): 533–547.

Liu, Xinsheng, Eric Lindquist, and Arnold Vedlitz. 2011. "Explaining Media and Congressional Attention to Global Climate Change, 1969–2005: An Empirical Test of Agenda-Setting Theory." *Political Research Quarterly* 64(2): 405–419.

Meckling, Jonas, Nina Kelsey, Eric Biber, and John Zysman. 2015. "Winning Coalitions for Climate Policy." *Science* 349(6253): 1170–1171.

Ostrom, Elinor. 2009. "A Polycentric Approach for Coping with Climate Change." The World Bank. Policy Research Working Paper 5095. http://aeconf.com/articles/may2014/aef150103.pdf.

———. 2010. "Polycentric Systems for Coping with Collective Action and Global Environmental Change." *Global Environmental Change* 20(4): 550–557.

———. 2012. "Nested Externalities and Polycentric Institutions: Must We Wait for Global Solutions to Climate Change Before Taking Actions at Other Scales?" *Economic Theory* 49(2): 353–369.

Pooley, Eric. 2010. *The Climate War: True Believers, Power Brokers, and the Fight to Save the Earth.* New York, NY: Hachette Books.

Rabe, Barry G. 2010. "Can Congress Govern the Climate?" In *Greenhouse Governance: Addressing Climate Change in America*, ed. Barry G. Rabe. Washington, DC: Brookings Institution Press.

Rosenbaum, Walter. 2010. "Greenhouse Regulation: How Capable Is EPA?" In *Greenhouse Governance: Addressing Climate Change in America*, ed. Barry G. Rabe. Washington DC: Brookings Institution Press, 286–312.

Rudman, Laurie A., Meghan C. McLean, and Martin Bunzl. 2013. "When Truth Is Personally Inconvenient, Attitudes Change: The Impact of Extreme Weather on Implicit Support for Green Politicians and Explicit Climate-Change Beliefs." *Psychological Science* 24(11): 2290–2296.

Urpelainen, Johannes, and Thijs Van de Graaf. 2017. "United States Non-Cooperation and the Paris Agreement." *Climate Policy*.

Vandenbergh, Michael P., and Jonathan M. Gilligan. 2017. *Beyond Politics: The Private Governance Response to Climate Change.* Cambridge: Cambridge University Press.

We Are Still In. 2018. "We Are Still In." www.wearestillin.com/.

INDEX

Made in United States
North Haven, CT
24 April 2024

51711950R00163